From 9/11 to Terror War

The Dangers of the Bush Legacy

Douglas Kellner

ROWMAN & LITTLEFIELD PUBLISHERS, INC.
Lanham • Boulder • New York • Oxford

ROWMAN & LITTLEFIELD PUBLISHERS, INC.

Published in the United States of America
by Rowman & Littlefield Publishers, Inc.
A Member of the Rowman & Littlefield Publishing Group
4501 Forbes Boulevard, Suite 200, Lanham, Maryland 20706
www.rowmanlittlefield.com

P.O. Box 317, Oxford OX2 9RU, United Kingdom

British Library Cataloguing in Publication Information Available

Library of Congress Cataloging-in-Publication Data

Kellner, Douglas, 1943–
    From 9/11 to terror war : the dangers of the Bush legacy / Douglas Kellner.
        p.   cm.
    Includes bibliographical references and index.
    ISBN 0-7425-2637-2 (alk. paper)—ISBN 0-7425-2638-0 (pbk. : alk. paper)
        1. United States—Foreign relations—2001–   2. United States—Military policy.   3. United States—Politics and government—2001–   4. Bush, George W. (George Walker), 1946–   5. September 11 Terrorist Attacks, 2001—Causes.   6. War on Terrorism, 2001——Causes.   7. Terrorism—Political aspects.   8. Globalization—Political aspects.   I. Title: From nine eleven to terror war.   II. Title.
E902 .K45   2003
973.931—dc21   2002151738

Printed in the United States of America

⊗™ The paper used in this publication meets the minimum requirements of American National Standard for Information Sciences—Permanence of Paper for Printed Library Materials, ANSI/NISO Z39.48-1992.

Contents

Acknowledgments

S everal pieces of this text were published earlier and I am grateful to Norm Denzin for useful editorial comments on pieces published in *Cultural Studies<>Critical Methodologies,* to Toby Miller for an article published in *Television and New Media,* and to the editors of *Theory, Culture, and Society* for comments on a study published in that journal.[1] For help in producing this text, I am especially grateful to Richard Kahn who edited the text in its entirety, provided many useful comments, and disseminated various parts of the text on the Internet via my homepage, which he has faithfully administered over the past year. I am also appreciative to Kahn for helping develop a BlogLeft, on which I have posted parts of this text and material used in research for this since the spring of 2002.[2] Thanks also to Rhonda Hammer, who made many critical comments on the manuscript and put up with yet another obsessive research project, and to Carl Boggs who made many helpful comments on the text. I would also like to acknowledge the support of Dean Birkenkamp, who has constructively commented on several drafts of the manuscript, encouraged its publication, and help shepherd it through the Rowman & Littlefield production process. For copyediting, cheers to Cheryl Adam and to Jehanne Schweitzer for helping to bring the manuscript into print. And finally, I would like to thank those who daily assembled articles and commentary on the events of September 11 and their aftermath that were collected at www.bushwatch.com, www.buzzflash.com, Phil Agre's *Red Rock Eater* at dlis.gseis.ucla.edu/people/pagre/rre.html, Bill Weinberg's *World War 3 Report,* and a variety of other Internet sources that I draw upon in this study.

Introduction: The Bush Administration and the September 11 Attacks

O n September 11, 2001, there were alarming reports that an airplane had crashed into one of the towers of the World Trade Center (WTC) in New York City. Shortly thereafter, another plane plowed into the second WTC tower, and television images captured its impact and explosion. During the same hour, a third jetliner hit the Pentagon, while a fourth plane, possibly destined for a White House collision, went down in Pennsylvania. The latter was reportedly crash-landed by passengers who had learned of the earlier hijackings and struggled to prevent another calamity.

The world stood transfixed with the graphic videos of the World Trade Center buildings exploding and discharging a great cloud of rubble. Subsequent images depicted heroic workers struggling to save bodies and then themselves becoming victims of the unpredictable collapse of the towers or shifts in the debris. The World Trade Center towers, the largest buildings in New York City and a potent symbol of global capitalism, were down, and the mighty behemoth of American military power, the mythically shaped Pentagon, was penetrated and on fire. Terrorists celebrated their victory over the American colossus, and the world remained transfixed for days by the media spectacle of "America under attack" and reeling from the now highly feared effects of terrorism.

TERRORISM AND THE RISKS OF UNILATERALISM

For some weeks after the September 11 attacks, there was intense debate and speculation concerning the U.S. response (see chapter 2). On October 7, 2001, George

1

W. Bush announced the beginning of a military campaign in Afghanistan to destroy the Al Qaeda network and the Taliban regime that was hosting them. Within two months, the Taliban was in retreat and Afghanistan entered a highly uncertain stage. Although the media and public have generally accepted the Bush administration's policy as a success, its primarily unilateral and military response to terrorism is highly flawed and potentially disastrous in its short- and long-term effects.

The Bush administration and Pentagon policies in the Afghanistan war were poorly conceived, badly executed, and are likely to sow the seeds of future blowback and reprisal. Hence, although the overthrow of the Taliban regime and the assault on the Al Qaeda infrastructure were arguably justifiable and a salutary blow against global terrorism, the Bush administration and Pentagon's campaign in Afghanistan was arguably misconceived and, in many ways, unsuccessful. Terrorism is a global problem that requires a global solution. The Bush administration's policy, however, is largely unilateral; its military response is flawed and has hindered more intelligent and potentially successful efforts against terror networks, while quite possibly creating more terrorists and enemies of the United States.

A global campaign against worldwide terror networks will require multilateral and coordinated efforts across many fronts: financial, legal-judiciary, political, and military. On the financial front, the Bush administration has failed to adequately coordinate large-scale efforts to fight terror networks, and reports indicate that Al Qaeda has continued to be able to raise and distribute significant funds and the global effort to shut down their financial network has not been a success.[1] Domestically, critics argue that conflicts between the Treasury Department, Commerce Department, and Justice Department have hampered coordination even in the United States. The Bush administration had systematically pursued a deregulatory policy toward financial markets and has not been able to successfully regulate the flow of funds supporting either the terror networks or the other global criminals and corporate allies of the Bush administration that prefer to secure and launder their funds in offshore banks.

On the legal and judicial front, the Bush administration has also failed to construct a lasting and active international alliance against terror. Whereas many foreign countries have arrested and broken up terror networks in Britain, France, Spain, Italy, Singapore, and elsewhere, the U.S. Justice Department has not been so successful and the Bush administration has failed to adequately coordinate global anti-terrorist activity with other countries.[2] On the whole, the U.S. has alienated itself from many of its allies in the war against terror by its aggressive unilateralism and efforts to affirm and assert U.S. military hegemony. Moreover, it has alarmed and offended many in the global community by its arrest of suspects that have been held in detention camps without legal rights and forced to face military tribunals and death penalties. In particular, the detention center in Guantanamo Bay, Cuba, has generated worldwide controversy and driven many European allies to question cooperation with the U.S. because of the conditions of the incarceration of suspects, the proposed military trials, and threatened use of death penalties.

Politically and militarily, the Bush administration has failed to develop a global coalition against terrorism because of its largely unilateral and military-centric approach. Rather than engage the UN and NATO on the political and military fronts, the Bush administration largely chose to go it alone, turning Afghanistan into a battlefield with the U.S. military alone leading the fight to destroy Al Qaeda and overthrow the Taliban—a policy with at best mixed results. The Bush administration chose not to criminalize bin Laden and his Al Qaeda network, preferring a largely military solution and thus shunting aside development of a worldwide political and judicial campaign to shut down the terrorists. Many countries are reluctant to send terrorist suspects to the United States because of the secret military courts, lack of standard legal procedures, and dangers of capital punishment that are banned in much of the world. Moreover, the Bush doctrine that maintains "you are with us or against us," and that constantly expands its "axis of evil," has positioned the U.S. as a strictly unilateralist force carrying out *its* war against terror, and has thus undermined developing a more global and multilateral campaign against terrorism. In particular, threatening war against Iraq has alienated the U.S. from both its European and moderate Arab allies, while the Bush administration's escalating threats against other countries is isolating the U.S. and making multilateral coalitions against terrorism extremely difficult.

There is also a sense that the U.S. is losing the struggle for the hearts and minds of Arabs and Muslims because of its bellicose nationalism, aggressive militarism, often uncritical support of Israel, and failure to improve relations with Muslim nations and peoples. As I will show in my analysis of the Afghanistan war, the excessive bombing of civilians, the lack of a decent U.S. humanitarian program or plan to rebuild Afghanistan, and Bush's unsuccessful propaganda efforts have perhaps produced more enemies than friends in the Arab and Muslim world, and thus have increased the potential for the rise of future terrorist Islamist cadres against the U.S.[3]

This situation was especially aggravated as hostilities exploded between the Israelis and Palestinians in 2002. In much of the Arab world, the United States is seen as the major supporter of Israel and the inability of the Bush administration to mediate growing conflicts between Israel and the Palestinians, combined with the Bush administration's neglect of the problem during its first fifteen months, has helped create an explosive situation in the Middle East with no solution in sight. In addition, the lack of ability and will of the Bush administration to moderate the aggressive Israeli responses to suicide bombings and terror acts against Israel in 2002 have created more hatred of the U.S. in the Arab world and a growing tendency to equate Israelis and Americans, Jews and Christians, as the main enemies of Islam.

Thus, the goals of creating better images of the United States in the eyes of the Arab, Islamic, and global world, and improving relations between the U.S. and Arab world, have failed miserably. The incapacity to enhance U.S. and Western relations with the Islamic world is largely the result of the botched military campaign, an inept political strategy, and the failure to engage in a fruitful dialogue with Arabs and Muslims. Consequently, Bush administration policy is inhibiting the creation of coalitions for peace and the rebuilding of devastated parts of the Arab world like Afghanistan. Part of the justification for the Afghan war was to not only eliminate Al Qaeda terrorist forces, but to forge more creative relationships with Arab and Islamic countries, and this goal remains unrealized and unrealizable under the Bush administration's unilateralist policy.

A successful campaign, then, would communicate the message that the United States respects the Islamic world; wants to carry out more productive activities with it; and desires dialogue, peace, and better relations. But this project has not succeeded, in part, because of the violent and destructive military campaign of the Bush administration and Pentagon, which put military priorities over beginning the reconstruction of Afghanistan well into 2002 (see chapter 11). In addition, the propaganda efforts undertaken by the Bush administration have been extremely crude and have mostly backfired, losing more hearts and minds than were gained, as I will document in the chapters that follow (see especially chapters 4 and 11). Later historians of the Afghanistan war and its propaganda campaign will find Bush administration policy in the war of ideas embarrassingly inept, pointing to another serious deficiency in its handling of its war against terrorism.

From a strictly military standpoint, the major goals for the Afghanistan war were not achieved and the deeply flawed campaign will be costly and consequential in its later effects. In particular, the Afghanistan campaign is at best a partial military success because of the failure to capture or destroy key Al Qaeda and Taliban leadership and cadres. This was largely due to a refusal to effectively use ground troops to deal with the Al Qaeda and Taliban leadership and their major fighting forces. The Afghanistan campaign, like the Gulf War, Kosovo War, and other U.S. military interventions in the past decade, relied largely on bombing at a distance and the refusal to use U.S. ground troops, following the "zero casualty tolerance" policy of the past years. The result was that in the decisive battles of Kandahar and Tora Bora, significant numbers of Al Qaeda and Taliban forces escaped, including their leadership and perhaps Osama bin Laden himself (see chapter 7).

Moreover, the military component of the Afghanistan campaign was excessively privileged to the detriment of dealing with humanitarian problems in Afghanistan and helping to reconstruct the country. For months, the United States refused to allow humanitarian aid groups in the country and opposed British and European Union (EU) proposals and efforts to solve the human crisis and to begin the reconstruction of Afghanistan. Instead, the Bush administration insisted through the last months of 2001 (after the fall of the Taliban) and into 2002 that its military forces must finish its mission of destroying the Al Qaeda and Taliban and that "humanitarian" efforts must be considered a distraction. Since the fall of Kandahar in December 2001, however, U.S. military efforts have been highly problematic due to an unfortunate reliance on local intelligence and Afghan forces that used the U.S. to gain revenge against old opponents. This "proxy war" has resulted in a long string of U.S. military actions against noncombatants, with a large number of civilian deaths, ambushes of American troops, and the continued escape of key terrorist forces that were the intended targets of the Bush administration war against terrorism.[4]

What is needed, then, is an international and multilateral mission in Afghanistan and elsewhere that combines political, military, police, humanitarian, and reconstruction efforts. The United States initially said it will train an Afghanistan army but not use U.S. forces for police or security action. In fact, given the chaos in Afghanistan, it is unwise to separate military and police forces. Likewise, a multilateral force of European Union countries, the United States, and Arab and other countries should train an Afghanistan military as they police and patrol the country, fight remnants of Al Qaeda and the Taliban, and rebuild the country. The Bush administration policy, by contrast, has not adequately dealt with humanitarian, security, or the sociopolitical needs of the country, preferring to focus primarily on military action against Al Qaeda and Taliban forces.

In 1989–1990, the first Bush administration pulled out of Afghanistan after the U.S. had supported Islamic forces against the Soviet Union occupation, thereby helping to create the vacuum and chaos that produced later terrorism. There were charges, justified in retrospect, that the United States had abandoned Afghanistan in the 1990s after using it as a Cold War battlefield, choosing not to help rebuild and stabilize the country. The result was civil war in Afghanistan, the takeover by the Taliban, their fateful alliance with Al Qaeda, and another war in Afghanistan that is not yet over (see chapter 1).

Moreover, there are worries that once again the U.S. and the West will abandon Afghanistan amidst signs that the U.S. is currently not adequately involved in securing and rebuilding Afghanistan and that, once again, the country will be a harbor of terror that will threaten U.S. and other lives and interests. The current Bush administration seems to have no end strategy for their intervention in Afghanistan and no vision for the region beyond securing the interests of the oil companies to which they are allied and getting military contracts and construction jobs for their supporters.

The primarily military and unilateral strategy of the Bush administration in their response to terrorism constitutes the major Achilles' heel of its policy, with its decision not to engage in a multilateral approach to international terrorism. The unilateral U.S. policy has produced an excessive militarizing and inadequate criminalizing of the problem of dealing with terrorism, and Bush administration policies are increasingly isolating the U.S. from potential allies in a global campaign against terrorism. Moreover, the Bush administration's unilateral policies will more than likely position the U.S. and its citizens as the targets of future terror attacks. Increasingly, the Bush administration's foreign policy is being resisted by much of the world and is encountering mounting hostility from allies and enemies alike. This is especially so since Bush's "axis of evil" speech and since the intensification of the Israel and Palestine conflict, generated in part by the Bush administration's failure to successfully mediate it.

By contrast, a multilateral campaign would make it clear that in a worldwide struggle against terror, it is the combined forces of civilization that are allied against international terror networks. Such a campaign would rely on global forces on political, judicial, economic, and military fronts, rather than privileging the militarist solution of war. Indeed, since December 2001, the Bush administration has expanded the front of its "war against terrorism," sending U.S. troops to the Philippines, Pakistan, and a whole ring of Central Asian countries, while threatening military action in Somalia, Indonesia, Yemen, and the infamous "axis of evil": Iraq, Iran, and North Korea. The list was expanded in May 2002 to include Syria, Libya, and Cuba. George W. Bush has declared that unrelenting Terror War is the major focus of his administration and the Pentagon has discussed developing smaller nuclear weapons to be used against terrorist forces, as well as other hi-tech weapons, ruthless bombing, and covert assassination.

In addition, the Bush administration manipulated the September 11 terror attacks to push through a hard-right domestic agenda that constitutes a clear and present danger to U.S. democracy. As governor of Texas, George W. Bush consistently performed favors for his largest contributors, like the Enron Corporation and oil and energy companies, and as president he has done the same (Kellner 2001). Since September 11, the Bush administration has exploited the fear of terrorism to push through further bailouts of corporations that contributed to his campaign, and the center of its economic program has been to create tax breaks for the most wealthy while cutting back on liberal social programs and environmental legislation and while carrying out the most right-wing law-and-order domestic policy in U.S. history.

On the foreign policy front, the Bush administration made use of the September 11 tragedy to renounce arms treaties it had already opposed and thus jettisoned the idea of arms control on a worldwide scale. It also used the September 11 attacks to legitimate an increased military budget and series of military interventions, to test and build new nuclear weapons, to threaten countries like Iraq and Iran with military attacks, and to abandon multilateralism for an unilateralist "America First" approach to foreign affairs. In June 2002, the Bush administration proclaimed a dangerous "first strike" policy, saying that henceforth it would engage in "preemptive strikes," abandoning the containment policy and diplomatic strategy for dealing with crises and adversaries in the post–Second World War era.

Consequently, the Bush administration claimed repeatedly that "World War III" had started and that the Cold War was being succeeded by a dangerous and long-term period of Terror War. In the following studies, I am using the term "Terror War" to describe the Bush administration's "war against terrorism" and its use of aggressive military force and terror as the privileged vehicles of constructing a U.S. hegemony in the current world (dis)order. The Bush administration has expanded its combat against Islamic terrorism into a policy of Terror War by which they have declared the right of the U.S. to strike any enemy state or organization presumed to harbor or support terrorism, or to eliminate "weapons of mass destruction" that could be used against the U.S. The right wing of the Bush administration seeks to promote Terror War as the defining struggle of the era, coded as an apocalyptic battle between good and evil. My studies will disclose the dangers of such policies and worldviews and will depict how Bush administration Terror War played out in the Afghanistan war and subsequent military adventures, as well as domestically.

THE FAILURE TO DETECT AND STOP THE
SEPTEMBER 11 ATTACKS

The likely result of the Bush administration's Terror War is that, in a global world, the United States will become ever more isolated and will continue to be the major source of international anger and terrorist attacks. Not only is the Bush administration's foreign policy dangerous and reckless, but it has also demonstrated stunning incompetence on the domestic front in the so-called war against terror and was highly negligent in making the U.S. vulnerable to the September 11 terrorist attacks in the first place. In mid-May 2002, a political uproar erupted when CBS News broadcast a report on May 15 that the CIA briefed George W. Bush on August 6, 2001 (when he was vacationing at his ranch in Texas) about the bin Laden network's plans to hijack airplanes. There was immediately a firestorm of controversy, raising questions for the first time in a public debate about what the Bush administration knew about possible terrorist attacks pre–September 11 and what they had done to prevent them. Also, during May 2002, a Phoenix, Arizona, FBI memo from summer 2001 was released that warned of the dangers of Middle Eastern men going to flight school in order to gain the skills necessary to hijack planes and of the dangers of the Al Qaeda network carrying out such hijackings. Moreover, the arrest of Zacarias Moussaouri, the alleged twentieth Al Qaeda hijacker who had also been taking flying lessons and acting suspiciously, in Minnesota in late August 2001 should have raised warning signals.

Over the summer of 2001, there had been reports that there were dangers of an airplane terrorist attack on the G8 economic summit in Genoa, Italy, that George W. Bush attended. There were purportedly so many intelligence reports circulating of the dangers of imminent terrorist attacks on the U.S. that a government official Richard Clarke, the National Security Council's counter-terrorism coordinator, warned FBI, Federal Aviation Administration (FAA), Immigration and Naturalization Service (INS), and other crucial government agencies to be on the highest alert and not to take vacations during a six-week period over the summer. U.S. Attorney General John Ashcroft was ordered to take government jets instead of commercial airlines and the FAA passed down several alerts to the commercial airlines.

It was also well-known in political circles that in 1994 the French had foiled a terrorist airplane attack on the Eiffel Tower, and in 1995 arrests were made of terrorists who allegedly planned to use an airplane to attack the CIA headquarters. Philippine police subsequently warned the United States that Ramzi Yousef, who had helped plan the 1993 World Trade Center bombing, had schemes to hijack and blow up a dozen U.S. airliners and was contemplating taking over and crashing a plane into the CIA headquarters himself. Thus, in the light of all of this information, it is scandalous that the Bush administration did not take stronger antiterrorist actions. Senate Intelligence Committee Vice Chair Richard Shelby (R-Ala.) stated: "There was a lot of information. . . . I believe, and others believe, that if it had been acted on properly, we may have had a different situation on September 11."

Furthermore, there had been a whole series of U.S. government reports on the dangers of terrorism and need for a coordinated response. A 1996 report by the White House Commission on Aviation Safety and Security, headed by then–Vice President Al Gore, developed a report on the dangers of airplane hijacking that was never acted on. A 1999 National Intelligence Council report on Terrorism specifically warned that bin Laden's Al Qaeda network might undertake suicide plane hijackings against U.S. targets; the report noted that members of the Al Qaeda network had threatened to do this before and that the U.S. should be alert to such strikes. Perhaps most significantly, blue-ribbon commission reports by former U.S. Senators Gary Hart and Howard Rudman and by the Bremer National Commission highlighted the dangers of a domestic terrorist attack against the U.S. and the need to develop appropriate protective measures. The Hart-Rudman report recommended consolidating U.S. intelligence on terrorism and organizing federal responses to prevent and fight domestic terrorist attacks on the U.S.[5]

Despite all this, the Bush administration failed to act on warnings of imminent terrorist attacks and the need to provide systematic government responses to coordinate information and attempt to prevent and aggressively fight terrorism. Moreover, it halted a series of attempts to fight the bin Laden network that had been undertaken by the Clinton administration. Just after the September 11 attacks, a wave of revelations came out, which were generally ignored in the U.S. media, concerning how high-ranking officials in the Bush administration had neglected threats of terrorist attacks by the bin Laden network and even curtailed efforts to shut down the terrorist organization that had been initiated by the Clinton administration.

A controversial book published in France in mid-November 2001 and translated into English in 2002, *Bin Laden, la verite interdite (Forbidden Truth)* by Jean-Charles Brisard and Guillaume Dasquie, claimed that under the influence of oil companies, the Bush administration initially blocked ongoing U.S. government investigations of terrorism while it bargained with the Taliban over oil rights, pipeline deals, and handing over bin Laden. This evidently led to the resignation of an FBI deputy director, John O'Neill, who was one of the sources of the story. In protest against curtailment of the efforts to shut down Al Qaeda, Brisard and Guillaume contend that the Bush administration had been a major supporter of the Taliban until the September 11 events and had blocked investigations of the bin Laden terror network. Pursuing these leads, the British *Independent* reported on October 30: "Secret satellite phone calls between the State Department and Mullah Mohammed Omar and the presentation of an Afghan carpet to President George Bush were just part of the diplomatic contacts between Washington and the Taliban that continued until just days before the attacks of 11 September."[6] Furthermore, Greg Palast had published an FBI memo that confirmed that the FBI was given orders to lay off the bin Laden family during the early months of George W. Bush's rule.[7]

The U.S. media completely ignored these and other reports concerning how the Bush administration had shut down or undermined operations against the bin Laden network that were initiated by the Clinton administration. An explosive article by Michael Hirsch and Michael Isikoff, "What Went Wrong?" published in the May 28, 2002, *Newsweek,* however, contained disturbing revelations of how the Bush administration had missed signals of an impending attack and systematically weakened U.S. defenses against terrorism and the bin Laden network. According to the *Newsweek* story, the Clinton administration's National Security Advisor Sandy Berger had become "'totally preoccupied' with fears of a domestic terror attack and tried to warn Bush's new National Security Advisor Condoleezza Rice of the dangers of a bin Laden attack." But although Rice ordered a security review, "The effort was marginalized and scarcely mentioned in ensuing months as the administration committed itself to other priorities, like National Missile Defense (NMD) and Iraq."

Moreover, *Newsweek* reported that U.S. Attorney General John Ashcroft was eager to set a new right-wing law-and-order agenda and was not focused on the dangers of terrorism, while other Bush administration high officials also had their ideological agendas to pursue at the expense of protecting the country against terrorist attacks. Ashcroft reportedly shut down wiretaps of Al Qaeda–related suspects connected to the 1998 bombing of African embassies and cut $58 million from an FBI request for an increase in its antiterrorism budget (while at the same time switching from commercial to government jets for his own personal flight). On September 10, when Ashcroft sent a request for budget increases to the White House, it covered sixty-eight programs, none of them related to counter-terrorism—nor was counter-terrorism in a memorandum he sent to his heads of departments stating his seven priorities. According to *Newsweek,* in a meeting with FBI Chief Louis Freeh, Ashcroft rebuffed Freeh's warnings to take terrorism seriously and turned down an FBI request for hundreds of additional agents to be assigned to tracking terrorists.[8] In the *Newsweek* summary:

> It wasn't that Ashcroft and others were unconcerned about these problems, or about terrorism. But the Bushies had an ideological agenda of their own. At the Treasury Department, Secretary Paul O'Neill's team wanted to roll back almost all forms of government intervention, including laws against money laundering and tax havens of the kind used by terror groups. At the Pentagon, Donald Rumsfeld wanted to revamp the military and push his pet project, NMD [National Missile Defense]. Rumsfeld vetoed a request to divert $800 million from missile defense into counterterrorism. The Pentagon chief also seemed uninterested in a tactic for observing bin Laden left over from the Clinton administration: the CIA's Predator surveillance plane. Upon leaving office, the Clintonites left open the possibility of sending the Predator back up armed with Hellfire missiles, which were tested in February 2001. But through the spring and summer of

2001, when valuable intelligence could have been gathered, the Bush administration never launched even an unarmed Predator. Hill sources say DOD [Department of Defense] didn't want the CIA treading on its turf.

A *Time* magazine cover story later in the summer by Michael Elliot, "The Secret History," provides more detail concerning how the Clinton administration had a program to attack Al Qaeda in November 2001 when the contested election battle in Florida was raging. The Clinton administration was not able to implement the plan, however, because, "With less than a month left in office, they did not think it appropriate to launch a major initiative against Osama bin Laden." Clinton administration officials claim that Bush's National Security Advisor Condoleezza Rice was fully informed of this plan and that Clinton National Security Advisor Sandy Berger stressed the need for a major initiative against bin Laden and Al Qaeda, but nothing was done. Moreover, the head of antiterrorist operations in the Clinton administration, Richard Clarke, who stayed on for the Bush administration, had himself drawn up the plan and urged its implementation when the Bush team took office. According to Elliot:

> Clarke's proposals called for the "breakup" of Al Qaeda cells and the arrest of their personnel. The financial support for its terrorist activities would be systematically attacked, its assets frozen, its funding from fake charities stopped. Nations where Al Qaeda was causing trouble—Uzbekistan, the Philippines, Yemen—would be given aid to fight the terrorists. Most important, Clarke wanted to see a dramatic increase in covert action in Afghanistan to "eliminate the sanctuary" where Al Qaeda had its terrorist training camps and bin Laden was being protected by the radical Islamic Taliban regime. . . . In the words of a senior Bush administration official, the proposals amounted to "everything we've done since 9/11."

Unfortunately, fighting terrorism was not a priority in the Bush administration that was hell-bent on pushing through its right-wing and pro-corporate agenda, and so the plan for attacks on Al Qaeda went through the usual layers of bureaucracy, finally reaching Bush and his inner circle in early September, too late to prevent the September 11 attacks. As these revelations unfolded in summer 2002, Democrats and others called for blue-ribbon commissions to study intelligence and policy failures that made possible the September 11 terrorist attacks. Republicans, led by Vice President Dick Cheney, predictably attacked the patriotism of anyone who ascribed blame to the U.S. government concerning the September 11 attacks. Moreover, according to Democratic Senate Majority Leader Tom Daschle, Cheney had repeatedly urged him not to hold hearings on U.S. policies or failures that led to the September 11 attacks. Bush administration spokespeople also attacked California Senator Dianne Feinstein, who retorted in a memo:

> I was deeply concerned as to whether our house was in order to prevent a terrorist attack. My work on the Intelligence Committee and as chair of the Technology and

Terrorism Subcommittee had given me a sense of foreboding for some time. I had no specific data leading to a possible attack.

In fact, I was so concerned that I contacted Vice President Cheney's office that same month [July 2001] to urge that he restructure our counter-terrorism and homeland defense programs to ensure better accountability and prevent important intelligence information from slipping through the cracks.

Despite repeated efforts by myself and staff, the White House did not address my request. I followed this up last September 2001 before the attacks and was told by "Scooter" Libby [Cheney's assistant] that it might be another six months before he would be able to review the material. I told him I did not believe we had six months to wait.[9]

This is highly shocking and calls attention to the key responsibility of Vice President Dick Cheney in failing to produce an adequate response to the dangers of terrorism. A year previous, in May 2001, the Bush administration announced that "Vice President Dick Cheney is point man for [the Bush] administration . . . on three major issues: energy, global warming, and domestic terrorism." On a May 19, 2002, interview with *Meet the Press,* Cheney acknowledged that he had been appointed head of a Bush administration task force on terrorism before September 11 and claimed that he had some meetings on the topic. Yet Cheney and others in the Bush administration seemed to disregard several major reports that cited the dangers of terrorist attacks, including congressional reports by former Senators Gary Hart and Howard Rudman in early 2001 that had called for a centralization of information on terrorism, but it appeared that the Bush administration failed to act on these recommendations. Obviously, Cheney concentrated on energy issues to the detriment of paying attention to terrorism and should thus be held in part responsible for Bush administration ignoring of pre–September 11 terrorist threats.[10]

Crucially, plans to use airplanes as vehicles of terrorist attack should have been familiar to the intelligence agencies and to Cheney and the Bush administration. Furthermore, there were many other reports disseminated from foreign and domestic intelligence services that the U.S. had reason to fear terrorist attacks from the bin Laden network provided just before the September 11 terror attacks.[11] Thus, there should have been attempts to coordinate intelligence between the various agencies, warnings to the airlines industry regarding potential hijacking, and security alerts to the public to be on the lookout for terrorist attacks.

Consequently, serious questions should be raised to the Bush administration, and to the head of their antiterrorism task force Dick Cheney, concerning what they knew and did not know and what they did and did not do in response to the reports from domestic and foreign intelligence concerning the likelihood of Al Qaeda airplane hijackings and terrorist attacks on the U.S. As head of the Bush administration's task force on terrorism, Dick Cheney should be held especially accountable, but so far the media and Democrats have not raised this issue and Cheney himself is aggressively attacking anyone who raises such issues as "unpatriotic." Obviously, there was no apparent coordination of information on terrorist threats in the Bush administration and if Cheney was head of the task force that was supposed to deal with terrorism, it is disgraceful that he did not establish a group to centralize information, focus more on the dangers of terrorism, and do more to prevent the September 11 attacks.

It therefore appears that top officials of the Bush administration did little or nothing to protect the U.S. against domestic terror attacks. When confronted with reports that Bush had been advised of impending terrorist threats and had not acted on them, Bush was highly indignant, attacking those who criticized him for "second guessing" and engaging in "partisan politics." He shrilly retorted that had he known exactly what was to happen, he would have prevented it. This was not, of course, the issue. Rather, at stake was the failure of the Bush administration to take seriously the threats of terrorism and to develop an antiterror policy. In fact, Bush was on an unprecedentedly long one-month summer vacation at his ranch in Crawford, Texas, when he was briefed on the dangers of looming Al Qaeda attacks, and no one could expect the highly unqualified president-select to "connect the dots" and see the need to organize the country against domestic terrorist attacks. But his administration as a whole is responsible for neglecting a wide series of reports and warnings and for engaging in a series of actions that made the attacks more likely.

Yet various pundits and critics blame different factions of the U.S. government for failing to prevent the September 11 attacks, with some going after the FBI, others the CIA, and others either the Clinton or Bush administration—or a combination thereof.[12] Republicans and right-wingers from the start blamed the Clinton administration (see chapter 2), while serious questions have been raised concerning Bush administration policy failures that made possible the September 11 terror attacks. I maintain that the collective failure is that of both the Bush administration as a whole and the national security apparatus, in particular the FBI and CIA. The Bush administration is responsible for failing to organize an antiterrorist task force to coordinate information and action, cutting back on efforts that the Clinton administration had made in this direction, ignoring government reports that highlighted the need to organize the government to better deal with terrorism, and also failing to respond to a large number of specific warnings about forthcoming Al Qaeda attacks from a wealth of sources.

Of course, the breakdown of specific intelligence agencies is also in question, as well as the issue of coordinating information between the CIA, FBI, and other agencies. Responding to what now appears as the greatest U.S. intelligence fiasco in history, Congress began hearings into FBI malfunctioning in May 2002 after revelations of the failure of the agency to respond to the Phoenix, Arizona, FBI memos concerning potential Al Qaeda terrorists taking flight lessons and the arrest in Minnesota of a potential hijacker, Zacarias Moussaouri, who had alleged Al Qaeda connections. The result of investigating these intelligence malfunctions was scandalous revelations of FBI bureaucratic inertia and failure to respond to local intelligence reports, to coordinate information with the CIA and Bush administration, and in general to provide adequate analysis and actions. Serious debates over the FBI, CIA, and other agencies' intelligence lapses were being aired in the media in summer 2002 and it appeared that the Bush administration was content to let them take the heat for the failures that had helped facilitate the September 11 terror attacks.

One shocking revelation disclosed that Coleen Rowley, an FBI operative in its Minnesota office, sent a 13-page letter to the congressional committee that is investigating the government's lack of preparedness for the September 11 attacks. Rowley's memo documented frustration with the FBI bureaucracy's inability to respond to serious concerns about an imminent terrorist attack and to get the agency to investigate potential Al Qaeda terrorists more seriously. Published in the May 21, 2002, issue of *Time* magazine, the memo provides a sharp critique of FBI bureaucratic inertia and incompetence.

Indeed, it is appalling to read media reports or congressional testimony of FBI and CIA bureaucratic inability to properly interpret intelligence reports from the field concerning dangers of a pending Al Qaeda terrorist attack; the lack of information sharing between the FBI, CIA, and other intelligence agencies; and the Bush administration's disinterest in addressing these problems pre–September 11.[13] It is clear that the FBI, CIA, and the rest of the U.S. government are mired in bureaucracy and that the national security apparatus needs to be completely reorganized. Obviously, there should be blue-ribbon investigations of exactly what went wrong and why. But it is the responsibility of the sitting political administration to protect the country and, in the case of September 11, the Bush administration failed in multiple ways.

Yet Congress and the media are also to blame for not focusing more intently on problems of terrorism over the previous decade. During the 1980s, terrorism emerged as a major problem and there were frequently news reports, specials, documentaries, and media discussion of the problem. Yet in the 1990s, the corporate media became increasingly tabloidized, focusing on the O. J. Simpson trials, the Clinton sex scandals, and the other journalistic obsessions of the moment.[14] As noted, major reports on dangers of terrorism were released without media scrutiny. The Hart-Rudman report, "Road Map for National Security: Imperative for Change," warning of dangers of a terrorist attack on the U.S., had been released in January 2001 and was ignored by much of the mainstream media as well as by Congress and the Bush administration.[15] Instead, there was an obsessive focus on tabloid stories pre–September 11 in the mainstream media, such as the disappearance of intern Chandra Levy and her affair with Congressman Gary Condit.

Not surprisingly, many elaborate conspiracy theories emerged alleging U.S. government complicity in the September 11 terror attacks, since there were many unexplained strange elements of the attacks on the New York World Trade Center and Pentagon—and because the Bush administration and military establishment were the main beneficiaries of the terror attacks. Additionally, the shocking history of the Bush family to engage in daring and major conspiracies may have contributed to the widespread circulation of allegations concerning U.S. government involvement in the September 11 terror attacks. There are, in fact, three major possibilities to explain the Bush administration's responsibility or complicity in the September 11 terror attacks: 1) The Bush administration was completely incompetent and too focused on pushing through its right-wing agenda to detect the obvious signs of impending Al Qaeda terror attacks that I have just outlined; 2) key members of the Bush administration may have known that attacks were indeed coming but welcomed them as a chance to push through its stalled right-wing and militarist agenda; or 3) the Bush administration, or rogue sectors of the U.S. government, were actively involved in the conspiracy.[16] As of now, it is impossible to confidently affirm the precise responsibility of the Bush administration for the September 11 attacks, but obviously this is a matter of grave concern and should be thoroughly investigated.

The Bush administration's surprise call on June 6, 2002, for a new cabinet-level Homeland Defense Agency, however, was seen by critics as an attempt to deflect attention from investigations of Bush administration and intelligence failures. As I discuss later in the book, there have been widespread fears that the Bush-Cheney gang would increase bureaucracy and even provide the apparatus for a Gestapo-type police state. Indeed, the USA Patriot Act pushed through following September 11 already was erecting the powerful trappings of a police state. It included allowing the government the right to eavesdrop on all electronic and wireless communication, to arrest individuals without specific charges and hold them indefinitely, to monitor conversations between lawyer and client, and to carry out secret military trials of suspected terrorists (see chapter 4).

Moreover, domestically since September 11, the Bush administration's actions against terrorists in the U.S. have been strikingly inept. Although terrorist cells have been broken up all over the world, so far U.S. government agencies have arrested few, if any, major members of the Al Qaeda network post–September 11. Nor have they caught the perpetrators of the anthrax attacks, although evidence exists that members of the national security state itself may have produced the high-grade military anthrax used in the attacks on the media and government.[17] The Bush administration has repeatedly made warnings of imminent terror attacks, keeping the country jittery in order to "justify" their unjustifiable foreign and domestic policies, but they have done little to make the country safer and have instead exploited the crisis to push through their hard-right agenda.

In addition, the Bush administration's assault on civil liberties has weakened constitutional democracy and the rule of law in the United States. On August 15, 2002, Human Rights Watch released a report that claimed: "The U.S. government's investigation of the September 11 attacks has been marred by arbitrary detentions, due process violations, and secret arrests." Human Rights Watch discovered that over 1,200 noncitizens were secretly arrested and incarcerated and that "the U.S. government has held some detainees for prolonged periods without charges; impeded their access to counsel; subjected them to coercive interrogations; and overridden judicial orders to release them on bond during immigration proceedings. In some cases, the government has incarcerated detainees for months under restrictive conditions, including solitary confinement. Some detainees were physically and verbally abused because of their national origin or religion. The vast majority are from Middle Eastern, South Asian, and North African countries. The report describes cases in which random encounters with law enforcement or neighbors' suspicions based on no more than national origin and religion led to interrogation about possible links to terrorism."[18] Yet not only has the Bush administration dangerously undermined the U.S. constitutional order, but their economic policies have produced endemic economic crisis, scandal, and corruption.

BUSHONOMICS: ECONOMIC CRISIS, SCANDAL, AND CORRUPTION

In one of the most stunning economic reversals in U.S. history, the Bush administration gave away record budget surpluses in taxes to the rich and returned to the dangerous levels of budget deficits brought about by the Reagan and first Bush administrations. During the Reagan presidency, the national deficit was doubled to $2 trillion dollars while in the four years of the first Bush administration, the deficit doubled again to an almost inconceivable record $4 trillion debt, flipping the U.S. from the position of the first major creditor nation to the number-one debtor nation. George W. Bush is well on the way to matching his father's disastrous economic performance as he piles up skyrocketing deficits, gives away profuse tax cuts to the rich, and provides corporate favors to his allies in the business and military-industrial complex.[19]

Although both George W. Bush and Dick Cheney have been largely immune from personal criticism for their responsibilities concerning the September 11 terror attacks, beginning in July 2002 their business records were sharply scrutinized and discussed in a media blitz of investigative and critical reporting. During July, the stock market underwent one of its major declines in recent history, thereby wiping out the savings of millions. Moreover, the Bush administration announced that the national deficit for the next year would be over $165 billion, corporate scandals continued to multiply, and it was becoming clear that the Bush administration was completely mismanaging the economy. ABC News reported on July 15 that since March 2001, the stock market had lost an unparalleled $7.7 trillion dollars and the news was full of stories of working- and middle-class families who had lost much of their life savings and who had their retirement funds devastated. Heartwrenching tales multiplied through the media of many average families who saw their dreams of a better future shattered under Bush Junior's tenure.

Further, there was a perhaps unprecedented contemporary media focus upon the corruption of corporate capitalism in the light of the Enron, Arthur Andersen, WorldCom, and related corporate scandals. Moreover, burgeoning reports indicated that Bush and Cheney were allegedly guilty of the same sort of corporate corruption that was daily being vilified in the press. Investor confidence was shaken by reports of foreign investor disgust with U.S. corporate management and growing anger at Bush administration policies, leading to escalating amounts of foreign investment taken out of the U.S. economy.[20] As the economic situations of many worsened, growing attention was focused upon the Bush administration's responsibility for people's economic woes and upon Bush and Cheney's participation in corporate corruption and fraud.

A July 2, 2002, op-ed piece in the *New York Times* by Paul Krugman, "Everyone Is Outraged," criticized Bush administration officials for being guilty of the same crimes that they were admonishing. A July 7 follow-up piece by Krugman, "The Insider Game," raised the question concerning the longtime allegations that Bush had engaged in insider trading with Harken Energy stocks when he was on the company's board of directors.[21] The country was outraged when it was revealed that Enron executives had unloaded their stock when they discerned that the company's financial mess was going to lead to a collapse of the stock's worth; as further corporate scandals unfolded, there was an uproar that other executives had unloaded their stocks in insider trading before their companies' woes were announced to the public.

There had long been allegations that George W. Bush had used insider information of declining profits to unload his Harken Energy stocks in 1991 and there had been an inconclusive Securities and Exchange Commission (SEC) investigation. Bush's accounts of this event over the years were always contradictory and unconvincing, and amidst the focus on insider trading scandals in July 2002 new material was released that indicated that Bush had received accounts of Harken's declining profit situation just before he sold his stocks. This constituted insider trading and appeared as the very type of unethical corporate behavior that Bush's own rhetoric claimed to denounce. As a result, major media outlets began looking into the story and new twists and nuances emerged almost daily, keeping the story in media focus.[22]

In addition, the revelations of Cheney's checkered career as CEO of Halliburton were much more current and even more shocking. During his last year as CEO before becoming Vice President, Cheney was paid $36 million by the Halliburton Corporation in salary, stock options, and bonuses, providing another striking example of CEO overcompensation and excessive corporate greed. There were allegations that Halliburton had engaged in the same sort of profit frauds that Enron and others had been using, with reports that Halliburton had set up a fake company within the corporation so that assets sold from one branch to another could be accounted as profits to cover over losses.

Moreover, a video of Cheney endorsing the same Arthur Andersen accounting company that had been involved in so many corporate frauds showed that Cheney was deeply complicit in the most corrupt and failed sectors of corporate capital. Stories circulated concerning illegal sales by Halliburton under Cheney's leadership to Iraq and Libya, states that had been on terrorist lists prohibiting direct U.S. corporate involvement. Moreover, Halliburton's stock had fallen sharply since Cheney's tenure and many analysts ascribed the failure of the company to Cheney's merger with Dresser Industries as CEO, a company long connected with the Bush family. Adding to his headaches, Cheney and Halliburton were sued by the conservative group Judicial Watch, a nemesis of Bill Clinton, which filed a lawsuit alleging account fraud that led to shareholder losses.[23]

While the Bush administration had proudly touted Bush and Cheney's supposed business success and the virtues of having corporate CEOs running the country, these alleged assets turned into liabilities as the country focused on the scandals involving major corporations and found that Bush and Cheney had similar shady business records. There are two sides to the economic and political scandals that permeate the Bush administration: ideological and practical. The ideology of market neoliberalism, which attacks all regulation and believes in an unregulated market as the royal road to freedom and prosperity, helped deregulate the economy and block the sort of meaningful regulation that would have at least mitigated the corporate scandals that erupted during the Bush era. The other aspect of Bush administration corruption revealed by the scandals is the obvious tendency of the Bush-Cheney clique to abuse power to enrich their contributors and associates, accompanied by an atmosphere of permissiveness and greed. The result was growing revelations concerning how key players in the Bush administration and their closest corporate allies had enriched themselves through shady business and political practices, using the state to gain wealth and power in often audacious crony capitalism scams with attendant risks of criminal prosecution.

Many were coming to perceive the Bush administration as one of the most corrupt political cabals in U.S. history and George W. Bush and Dick Cheney were emerging as poster boys for greed, sleaze, and corruption. Bush's entire business career was predicted on exploiting family friends and connections for his personal gain, and in using those who wanted to buy influence from various Bush administrations to invest in his usually failed business ventures. Bush's first profitable venture in Harken Energy involved getting questionable loans from the company to buy stock, and then unloading it when he learned that profits would be down and the future of the company was in question. Likewise, Cheney was finally being accurately vilified as the type of corporate CEO who had engaged in exactly the forms of unethical business practices being attacked in the press, and as a man who had enriched himself at the cost of the shareholders and corporation.

Moreover, Bush and Cheney had long used the institutions of government to enrich themselves and their corporate allies and contributors. As governor of Texas, Bush gave Enron and other favored corporations every tax break, state contract, handout, and regulatory largess that they requested and was doing the same in Washington both before and after September 11. Cheney's Halliburton firm had received over $2.3 billion in government contracts during his tenure as CEO and was awarded billions in key contracts while Cheney was vice president, despite many examples of Halliburton subsidiaries overcharging the government and the obvious impropriety of a former CEO using his influence to enrich his former company.

Indeed, Halliburton's stock was in such serious crisis, because in part of Cheney's poor management, that the company would probably collapse without its pipeline of lucrative government contracts. Furthermore, while Cheney was CEO, Halliburton escaped paying taxes for five of the six years in which Cheney headed the company through setting up offshore subsidiaries to launder profits in order to avoid paying taxes in the United States.[24]

The Bush administration's economic policy can be accurately described as a pro-corporate one that lets the oil and energy companies write oil and energy policy; allows Wall Street and big banks to formulate banking and investment laws; permits the credit card companies who had contributed to Bush's campaign to write credit laws; and provides other major contributors to Bush campaigns with the laws, regu-lations, tax breaks, or other federal giveaways that they requested (Kellner 2001). In sum, the Bush-Cheney gang has primarily represented permissibility and a hard-right deregulatory market ideology, promoting a wheeling and dealing crony capital-ism. They have used government to enrich themselves and their corporate allies and have engaged in practices that were destroying investor confidence and greatly harm-ing the U.S. and global economy. As part and parcel of the corruption involving corporate America and its political sector now coming to light, both Bush and Cheney have long engaged in unsavory and failed business and political practices. So far, the consequences of business-as-usual politics have been the freefall of the U.S. economy and the creation of escalating antipathy toward the United States throughout the globe.

As the reports of Bush and Cheney's corruption multiplied in July and August 2002, the Bush administration continued to leak rumors concerning an impending war against Iraq and speculation mounted that the Bush administration would wage war in Iraq to distract attention from its mounting scandals and the worsening eco-nomic situation. It appeared likely that the Bush administration would attack Iraq to boost its sagging ratings and to distract attention from its growing scandals and the increasingly critical press coverage, especially of Bush and Cheney, who were emerging as symbols of the corporate corruption and deregulatory and permissive politics that had caused current escalating U.S. and global economic and political woes. The fruits of the theft of election 2000 were ever more poisonous, and whether U.S. democracy would survive was at stake.

THE BUSH REICH

The consequences of the Bush administration's failed Terror War policies and domestic policy outrages are frightening. The Bush Reich seems to be erecting an Orwellian totalitarian state apparatus and plunging the world into ongoing war that could generate a military and police state both domestically and abroad. In his pro-phetic novel *1984*, George Orwell envisaged a grim condition of total warfare in which his fictional state Oceania ruled its fearful and intimidated citizens through war, police state terror, surveillance, and the suppression of civil liberties. This constant warfare kept Oceania's citizens in a perpetual situation of mobilization and submission. Furthermore, the Orwellian state controlled language, thought, and behavior through domination of the media, and was thereby able to change the very meaning of language ("war is peace") and to constantly rewrite history itself.[25]

Orwell's futuristic novel was, of course, an attack on the Soviet Union and therefore a favorite of conservatives over the years, but it uncannily describes the horrors and dangers of the regime of George W. Bush. Orwell's totalitarian state had a two-way television screen that monitored its citizens' behavior and a system of spies and informers that would report on politically incorrect thought and activity. Bush's police state has its USA Patriot Act that enables the state to monitor the communications of e-mail, wireless, telephones, and other media, while allowing government to arrest citizens without warrants, to hold them indefinitely, to monitor their conversations, and to submit them to military tribunals, all of which would be governed by the dictates of the supreme leader (in this case, a dangerously demagogic figurehead ruled by right-wing extremists).

The Bush administration also proposed a Terrorist Information and Prevention System (TIPS) program, which would turn citizens into spies who would report suspicious activities to the government and encourages truck drivers, mail carriers, meter readers, and others to "report what they see in public areas and along transportation routes," thus turning workers into informants. In addition, U.S. Attorney General John Ashcroft has proposed concentration camps in the United States for citizens that he considers "enemy combatants."[26] Sign me up, because I'm an enemy of Bush-style Orwellian fascism and it is clear that the United States needs a regime change if its democracy is to be preserved.

With their Orwellian-sounding Office of Homeland Security, the short-lived Office of Strategic Influence, shadow government, and the USA Patriot Act, the Bush administration has in place the institutions and apparatus of a totalitarian government. Since Election 2000, the Bush clique has practiced a form of Orwellian "Bushspeak" that endlessly repeats the Big Lie of the moment. Bush and his propaganda ministry engage in daily propagandistic spin to push its policies and slime their opponents while showing little regard for the canons of truth and rights that conservatives have traditionally defended.[27]

To keep the public in a state of fear, Bush and his administration have repeatedly evoked the specter of renewed terrorist attacks and promised an all-out war against an "axis of evil." This threatening "axis," to be redefined periodically by the Bush administration, allegedly possesses "weapons of mass destruction" that could be used against the U.S. Almost without exception, the mainstream media have been a propaganda conduit for the Bush administration's Terror War and have helped generate fear and even mass hysteria. But the mainstream corporate media have largely failed to advance an understanding of the serious threats to the U.S. and to the global economy and polity, and have failed to debate the range of possible responses to the September 11 attacks, their respective merits, and their possible consequences.

In a speech to West Point cadets on June 1, 2002, George W. Bush proclaimed a new "doctrine" that the U.S. would strike first against enemies. It was soon apparent that this was a major shift in U.S. military policy, replacing the Cold War doctrine of containment and deterrence with a new policy of preemptive strikes—one that could be tried out in Iraq. U.S. allies were extremely upset with this shift in U.S. policy toward an aggressive U.S. unilateralism. In an article, "Bush to Formalize a Defense Policy of Hitting First," David E. Sanger wrote in the *New York Times* (June 17, 2002), "The process of including America's allies has only just begun, and administration officials concede that it will be difficult at best. Leaders in Berlin, Paris and Beijing, in particular, have often warned against unilateralism. But Mr. Bush's new policy could amount to ultimate unilateralism, because it reserves the right to determine what constitutes a threat to American security and to act even if that threat is not judged imminent."[28]

After a summer of debate on the prospects of the U.S. going to war against Iraq to destroy its weapons of mass destruction, on August 26 U.S. Vice President Dick Cheney applied the new preemptive strike and unilateralist doctrine to Iraq, arguing: "What we must not do in the face of a mortal threat is to give in to wishful thinking or willful blindness. . . . Deliverable weapons of mass destruction in the hands of a terror network or murderous dictator or the two working together constitutes as grave a threat as can be imagined. The risks of inaction are far greater than the risks of action." Cheney was responding to many former generals and high-level members of the first Bush administration who had reservations about the sort of unilateralist U.S. attack against Iraq that hawks in the Bush administration were urging.[29]

Bush and others in his circle regularly described Terror War as World War Three, Rumsfeld said that it could last as long as the Cold War, and Cheney, speaking like a true militarist, said it could go on for a "long, long time, perhaps indefinitely." Such an Orwellian nightmare could plunge the world into a new millennium of escalating war with unintended consequences and embroil the U.S. in endless wars, normalizing war as conflict resolution and creating countless new enemies for the would-be American Hegemon. Indeed, as Chalmers Johnson writes in *Blowback* (2000), empire has hidden costs. Becoming a hegemon breeds resentment and hostility, and when the empire carries out aggression it elicits anger and creates enemies, intensifying the dangers of perpetual war.

On September 20, 2002, it was apparent that the hawks' position in the Bush administration had triumphed, at least on the level of official military doctrine, when the Bush administration released a document signaling some of the most important and far-ranging shifts in U.S. foreign and military policy since the end of the Cold War. Titled, "The National Security Strategy of the United States," the 33-page report outlined a new doctrine of U.S. military supremacy, providing justifications for the U.S. to wage unilateral and preemptive strikes in the name of "counterproliferation." This clumsy Orwellian concept was offered as a replacement for the concept of nonproliferation and would legitimate unilateral destruction of a country's presumed weapons of mass destruction. The document, in effect, renounced the global security, multilateralism, and rule by international law that to some degree had informed U.S. thinking since World War Two and that appeared to be an emerging consensus among Western nations during the era of globalization.

The Bush administration's language of "preemptive strikes," "regime change," and "anticipatory self-defense" is purely Orwellian, presenting euphemisms for raw military aggression. Critics assailed the new "Strike first, ask questions later" policy, the belligerent unilateralism, and the dangerous legitimization of preemptive strikes.[30] Israel, Pakistan, Russia, China, and lesser powers had already used the so-called Bush doctrine and war against terrorism to legitimate attacks on domestic and external foes, and there were looming dangers that it could legitimate a proliferation of war and make the world more unstable and violent. As William Galston states:

> A global strategy based on the new Bush doctrine of preemption means the end of the system of international institutions, laws and norms that we have worked to build for more than half a century. What is at stake is nothing less than a fundamental shift in America's place in the world. Rather than continuing to serve as first among equals in the postwar international system, the United States would act as a law unto itself, creating new rules of international engagement without the consent of other nations. In my judgment, this new stance would ill serve the long-term interests of the United States.[31]

The Bush doctrine of preemptive strikes could indeed unleash a series of wars that would plunge the world into the sort of nightmare militarism and totalitarianism as sketched out in George Orwell's *1984*. The Bush policy is highly barbaric, taking the global community to a social Darwinist battleground where decades of international law and military prudence will be put aside in perhaps the most dangerous foreign policy doctrine in U.S. history. It portends a militarist future and an era of perpetual war in which a new militarism could generate a cycle of unending violence and retribution, of the sort evident in the Israel and Palestine conflict.

Around the time that the Bush administration was pushing its new strategic doctrine and seeking to apply it in a war against Iraq, a 2000 report circulated titled "Rebuilding American Defense: Strategies, Forces and Resources for A New American Century." Drawn up by the neoconservative think tank Project for a New American Century (PNAC) for a group that now comprises the right-wing of the Bush administration, including Cheney, Rumsfeld, and Paul Wolfowitz, the document spelled out a plan for U.S. world hegemony grounded in U.S. military dominance of the world and control of the Persian Gulf region with its oil supplies.[32] Its upfront goals were a "Pax Americana" and U.S. domination of the world during the new millennium. The document shows that core members of the Bush administration had longed envisaged taking military control of the Gulf region, with the PNAC text stating: "The United States has for decades sought to play a more permanent role in Gulf regional security. While the unresolved conflict with Iraq provides the immediate justification, the need for a substantial American force presence in the Gulf transcends the issue of the regime of Saddam Hussein."

   The PNAC document argues for "maintaining global U.S. preeminence, precluding the rise of any great power rival, while shaping the international security order in accordance with American principles and interests." The vision is long-range, urging U.S. domination of the Gulf "as far into the future as possible." It is also highly militarist, calling for the U.S. to "fight and decisively win multiple, simultaneous major theatre wars" as a "core mission." American armed forces would serve as "the cavalry on the new American frontier," with U.S. military power blocking the emergence of other countries challenging U.S. domination. It would enlist key allies such as Britain as "the most effective and efficient means of exercising American global leadership," and would place the U.S., and not the UN, as leader of military interventions and peacekeeping missions. It envisions taking on Iran after Iraq, spotlights China for "regime change," calls for the creation of "U.S. Space Forces" to dominate outer space, positions the U.S. to totally control cyberspace and prevent "enemies" from "using the Internet against the U.S."

   The Bush administration Terror War thus raises the possibility that Orwell's *1984* might provide the template for the new millennium, as the world is plunged into endless wars, as freedom and democracy are being snuffed out in the name of Bush-defined "freedom," as language loses meaning, and as history is constantly revised (just as with Bush and his scribes, who constantly rewrote his own personal history). There is thus the danger that Orwell's dark grim dystopia may replace the (ideological) utopia of the "information society," the "new economy," and a prosperous and democratic globalization that had been the dominant ideology and vision of the past decade. Questions arise: Will the Bush administration's Terror War lead the world to apocalypse and ruin through constant war and the erection of totalitarian police states over the façade of fragile democracy? Or can more multilateral and global solutions be found to the dangers of terrorism that will strengthen democracy and increase the chances for peace and security?

   There is indeed a danger that Terror War will be a force of historical regression and the motor of destruction of the global economy, liberal polity, and democracy itself, all to be replaced by an aggressive militarism and totalitarian police state. It could well be that Orwell will be the prophet of a coming New Barbarism with endless war, state repression, and enforced control of thought and discourse, and that George W. Bush and his minions are the architects of an Orwellian future.

   It could also be the case, however, that the Taliban, bin Laden, Al Qaeda, and the Bush administration represent obsolete and reactionary forces that will be swept away by the inexorable forces of globalization and liberal democracy. The opposing sides in the current Terror War between the Bush administration reactionaries and Al Qaeda could be perceived as representing complementary poles of a reactionary right-wing conservatism and militarism confronted by an atavistic and premodern version of Islam and nihilistic terrorism.[33] In this scenario, both poles can be perceived as disruptive and regressive forces in a global world that need to be overcome to create genuine historical progress. If this is the case, Terror War would be a momentary interlude in which two obsolete historical forces battle it out, ultimately to be replaced by more sane and democratic globalizing forces.

This is, of course, an optimistic scenario and probably, for the foreseeable future, progressive forces will be locked into intense battles against the opposing forces of Islamic terrorism and right-wing militarism. Yet if democracy and the human species are to survive, global movements against militarism and for social justice, ecology, and peace must emerge to combat and replace the atavistic forces of the present. As a new millennium unfolds, the human race has regressed into a New Barbarism unforeseeable prior to September 11 (see chapter 8). If civilization is to survive, individuals must organize to fight for a better future, an argument I lay out in the conclusion to this book.

Consequently, I argue that the Bush administration's militarism is not the way to fight international terrorism, but is rather the road to an Orwellian future in which democracy and freedom will be in dire peril and the future of the human species will be in question. These are frightening times and it is essential that all citizens become informed about the fateful conflicts of the present, gain clear understanding of what is at stake, and realize that they must oppose international terrorism, Bushian militarism, and an Orwellian police state.

September 11, the subsequent Terror War, the Enron scandals, other often Bush-Cheney related corporate scandals that emerged during these events, and the ongoing misadventures of the Bush administration constitute what I am calling "the New Barbarism." It was scandalous that civilized countries tolerated the Taliban and allowed the bin Laden–Al Qaeda network to develop, while the Bush Terror War unleashed new forces of barbarism now evident in Afghanistan, the Middle East, and elsewhere in the world. The term "New Barbarism" denotes frightening regression to an era of highly uncivilized and violent behavior. Although one would hope that the new millennium would signal a chance for progress and historical optimism, instead the human species is moving into a situation in which the universal values of the Enlightenment, the institutions of democracy, the global economy, and the earth and human species itself are faced with challenges of survival.

As a response to the September 11 terror attacks, the Bush administration has answered with an intensified militarism that threatens to generate an era of Terror War, a new arms race, accelerated military violence, U.S. support of authoritarian regimes, an assault on human rights, constant threats to democracy, and destabilizing of the world economy. The New Barbarism also includes Bush administration practices of providing political favors to its largest corporate and other supporters, unleashing unrestrained Wild West capitalism as exemplified in the Enron scandals, and a form of capitalist cronyism whereby Bush administration family and friends are provided with government favors while social welfare programs, environmental legislation, and protections of rights and freedoms are curtailed.

The corporate media, especially television, are part and parcel of the New Barbarism, spewing forth almost unopposed propaganda for the Bush administration and fanning war fever and terrorist hysteria, while cutting back on vigorous political

debate and varied sources of information as it produces waves of ideologically conservative talk shows and mindless entertainment. I have been closely tracking the
media and the crisis of democracy for over a decade now (see Kellner 1990, 1992,
1995, and 2001) and the current crisis marks the low point of U.S. media performance. The U.S. corporate media at first fanned the flames of war and hysteria (see
chapter 2), and then became a conduit for Bush administration and Pentagon propaganda during the subsequent Terror War rather than a forum of reasoned debate,
serious discussion, exposure of the dangers and failures of Bush administration
responses to terrorism, and exploration of saner alternatives.

In view of the enormity of the events of September 11 and their frightening aftermath and consequences, it is now appropriate to reflect on what happened, why it
happened, and what lessons we can learn as we seek to apply such insights to the
crisis that we now find ourselves in. It's a time for honing our wits, not losing our
wits. A time for intelligence, not kneejerk reaction, a time for thought and not for
hysteria. It's a time for reflection, figuring out what went wrong, and taking
informed and intelligent action that will get at the source of our problems. It's also
a time for stocktaking, taking account individually and collectively of our views of
the world, everyday behavior, and democratic institutions. A situation of crisis provides an opportunity for positive change and reconstruction as well as for barbaric
regression. Thus, now is the time for reflection on such things as democracy; globalization; and the flaws, limitations, and fallacies in our individual thought and action,
as well as problems with U.S. institutions and leadership.

Momentous historical events, like the 9/11 terrorist attacks and the subsequent
Terror War, test social theories and provide a challenge to give a convincing account
of the event and its consequences. They also provide cultural studies an opportunity
to trace how political and ideological discourses, propaganda, and mythologies play
themselves out in media discourse and representations. Major historical events and
media spectacles also provide an opportunity to examine how the broadcast media
and other dominant media of communication perform or fail to perform their democratic role of providing accurate information and discussion.

In the following analysis, I will first try to make sense of the 9/11 events, theorizing what happened, how and why it happened, and what novelties and shifts in the
current sociopolitical situation emerged out of the terror attacks on the United
States (see chapter 1). Drawing upon key contextual accounts of earlier U.S. intervention in Afghanistan and the Middle East to provide historical background for
the terrorist attacks, I attempt to help explain why the U.S. was subject to such
violent assaults and what specific policies and forces in the recent past supported,
armed, and trained the terrorist groups. I suggest how certain dominant social theories were put in question during the momentous and world-shaking events of fall
2001. In chapter 2, I examine how highly problematic discourses circulated through
the media, and how the media on the whole performed disastrously and dangerously, whipping up war hysteria while failing to provide a coherent account of what

happened, why it happened, and what would count as responsible and intelligent U.S. responses to the terrorist attacks.

Subsequent chapters describe U.S. military intervention in Afghanistan; the ways that dominant corporate media in the U.S. legitimated military action; and the critical discourses and accounts left out of the U.S. corporate media, especially television (chapters 3–10). These chapters unfold the narrative of the vicissitudes of the Afghanistan Terror War and will systematically compare the accounts of this spectacle presented by the Bush administration, the Pentagon, and U.S. corporate broadcast media with those presented by more critical media accounts from U.S., British, and other sources. A concluding chapter sketches out the need for a global social movement against terrorism and militarism and for peace, democracy, social justice, and responsible environmentalism.

Quite possibly, we will never know exactly what happened in the Afghanistan war. I published one of the first books on the Gulf War (Kellner 1992), largely based on Internet sources, the newspapers of record, government press conferences, and other material available on the Internet. I followed closely subsequent memoirs of military participants in the war, journalists providing first-person accounts, and other studies. But no definitive history of the Gulf War has yet emerged, and we still do not know all of the shadowy details of relations between George H. W. Bush and Saddam Hussein, why Iraq invaded Kuwait, what knowledge the United States did or did not have of Iraqi plans, how the United States orchestrated the Gulf War, or what actually happened. Yet it is always possible to expose the fallacies and holes in official accounts, to expose lies and misinformation, and to provide contextualization and interpretations of major historical events like the Gulf War, the September 11 terror attacks, and the Afghanistan war.

In any case, I draw upon the best sources available to me in order to provide an account of what happened in the September 11 terror attacks and the succeeding Terror War. I have closely chronicled the actions of the Reagan and Bush administrations that provide many of the same personnel in Bush Junior's administration. In this study, I draw on daily readings of several major newspapers; regular viewing of the British and Canadian Broadcasting Corporation; ABC and other U.S. television networks; and articles collected at www.bushwatch.com, www.buzzflash.com, Phil Agre's *Red Rock Eater,* and a variety of Internet sources as well as popular and scholarly texts that contextualize and interpret the September 11 terror attacks and subsequent Terror War.

I argue that a combination of critical social theory and cultural studies can help illuminate the 9/11 events, their causes, effects, and importance in shaping the contemporary moment. Continuing my analysis of the vicissitudes of media and politics in the United States over the past decades, I provide a direct follow-up to my book *Grand Theft 2000* (Kellner 2001), which tells the story of how the Bush team stole the election in 2000 with the support of major corporations and the complicity of the corporate media. The problematic in this book is also closely related to my book, *Media Spectacle* (Kellner 2003), which analyzes how contemporary politics and culture are organized into media events in which primary conflicts of the era are played out, as in the Gulf War of 1991, the O. J. Simpson trial of the mid-1990s, or the Clinton sex and impeachment scandals of the late 1990s.

Certainly, the terror spectacle of September 11 is one of the major media and political events of our day, and interpreting the affair and its aftermath provides crucial insight into the dynamics and conflicts of the present era. The subsequent Terror War appears to be the major ongoing spectacle of the new millennium that the Bush administration is using to promote its agenda and to build up the U.S. military as a hegemonic force, generating the "new world order" that Bush Senior had wanted to create at the end of the Gulf War. As envisaged by the second Bush administration, Terror War is projected as the defining feature of the new millennium for the foreseeable future.

It is time, however, to critically engage what actually happened in the Bush administration and Pentagon's Terror War in Afghanistan and to seriously debate future options and policies. As I bring this text to a close in December 2002, it appears that the Afghanistan war is winding down. Accordingly, I try to present an overview of this event and a critique of Bush administration and Pentagon policy. The extent to which there is intelligent debate on Terror War and how to engage terrorism will determine the quality of the future and whether what I call the New Barbarism is the defining feature of the millennium or a passing phase in a troubled age. This story is embedded in the broader story of the consequences of the Bush gang's theft of the election in 2000 and the consequences of having a Bush-Cheney presidency, a fateful event whose baleful effects are becoming all too obvious and that will accordingly be a major theme of this book.

1

Theorizing 9/11

The historic events of September 11 and their aftermath have, in the view of some, opened up a new historical epoch. Certainly, they have produced a frightening start for a new millennium and require fresh thinking and historical contextualization to make sense of the events. In the following analyses, I want first to suggest how certain dominant social theories were put in question during the world-shaking events of 9/11, and then offer an analysis of the historical background necessary to understand and contextualize the terror attacks. I take up the claim that "everything has changed" in the wake of 9/11 and attempt to indicate both changes and continuities to avoid one-sided exaggerations and ideological simplifications. I argue for the need for historical contextual understanding to grasp the origins and nature of the terrorist attacks, and that the events of September 11 show contradictions in the nature of globalization and information technologies that require dialectical analysis of these phenomena. In these ways, I develop a historical and theoretical framework, which I will flesh out in the following chapters to interpret the atrocities of 9/11 and their aftermath.

SOCIAL THEORY, FALSIFICATION, AND THE EVENTS OF HISTORY

Social theories generalize from past experience and provide accounts of historical events or periods that attempt to map, illuminate, and perhaps criticize the dominant social relations, institutions, forms, trends, and events of a given epoch. In turn, they can be judged by the extent to which they account for, interpret, and critically assess contemporary conditions or predict future events and developments. One dominant social theory of the past two decades, Francis Fukuyama's *The End of History* (1992), was strongly put into question by the events of September 11 and their aftermath.[1] For Fukuyama, the collapse of Soviet communism and the triumph of Western capitalism and democracy in the early 1990s constituted "the end of history." This signified for him "the end point of mankind's ideological evolution and the universalization of Western liberal democracy as the final form of human government." Although there may be conflicts in places like the Third World, over-all for Fukuyama liberal democracy and market capitalism have prevailed, subsequent politics will devolve around resolving routine economic and technical problems, and the future will accordingly be rather mundane and boring.

Samuel Huntington polemicizes against Fukuyama's "one world: euphoria and harmony" model in his *The Clash of Civilizations and the Remaking of World Order* (1996). For Huntington, the future holds a series of clashes between "the West and the Rest." Huntington rejects a number of models of contemporary history, including a "realist" model that nation-states are primary players on the world scene who will continue to form alliances and coalitions that will play themselves out in various conflicts. He also rejects a "chaos" model that detects no discernible order or structure.

Instead, Huntington asserts that the contemporary world is articulated into competing civilizations that are based on irreconcilably different cultures and religions. For Huntington, culture provides unifying and integrating principles of order and cohesion, and from within dominant cultural formations emerge a number of different civilizations that are likely to come into conflict with each other, including Islam, China, Russia, and the West. For Huntington, religion is "perhaps *the* central force that motivates and mobilizes people" and is thus the core of civilization.

Although Huntington's model seems to have some purchase in the currently emerging global encounter with terrorism and is becoming a new major conservative ideology, it tends to overly homogenize both Islam and the West, as well as the other civilizations he depicts. As Tariq Ali argues (2002), Huntington exaggerates the role of religion while downplaying the importance of economics and politics.[2] Moreover, Huntington's model lends itself to pernicious misuse and has been deployed to call for and legitimate military retribution against implacable adversarial civilizations by conservative intellectuals like Jeane Kirkpatrick, Henry Kissinger, and members of the Bush administration.

Huntington's work provides too essentialist a model that covers over contradictions and conflicts both within the West and within Islam. Both worlds have been divided for centuries into dueling countries, ethnic groups, religious factions, and complex alliances that have fought fierce wars against each other and that continue to be divided geographically, politically, ideologically, and culturally (see Ali 2002). Islam itself is a contested terrain and in the current situation there are important attempts to mobilize more moderate forms of Islam and Islamic countries against Osama bin Laden's Al Qaeda terror network and Islamic extremism.

Hence, Huntington's binary model of inexorable conflict between the West and Islam is not only analytically problematic, but it also covers over the crucial battle within Islam itself to define the role and nature of the religion in the contemporary world. It also decenters the important challenge for the West to engage the Islamic world in a productive dialogue about religion and modernity and to bring about more peaceful, informed, and mutually beneficial relations between the West and the Islamic world. Positing inexorable conflicts between civilizations may well describe past history and present challenges, but it does not help produce a better future and is thus normatively and politically defective and dangerous.

Globalization includes a homogenizing neoliberal market logic and commodification, cultural interaction, and hybridization, as well as conflict between corporations, nations, blocs, and cultures. Benjamin Barber's book *McWorld vs. Jihad* (1996) captures both the homogenizing and conflicting elements of globalization. Barber divides the world into the modernizing, homogenizing, Westernizing, and secular forces of globalization, dominated by multinational corporations, opposed to the premodern, fundamentalist, and tribalizing forces at war with the West and modernity. The provocative "Jihad" in the title seems to grasp precisely the animus against the West in Islamic extremism. But Jihad scholars argue that the term has a complex history in Islam and often privilege the more spiritual definitions of "jihad," such as a struggle for religion and spiritualization or a struggle within oneself for spiritual mastery. From this view, bin Laden's militarization of Jihad is itself a distortion of Islam that is contested by its mainstream.[3]

Barber's model also oversimplifies present world divisions and conflicts and does not adequately present the contradictions within the West or the "Jihad" world, although he postulates a dialectical interpenetrating of both forces and sees both as opposed to democracy. His book does, however, point to problems and limitations of globalization, noting serious conflicts and opponents, unlike Thomas Friedman's harmonizing duality of *The Lexus and the Olive* (1999), which suggests that both poles of capitalist luxury and premodern roots are parts of the globalization process. In an ode to globalization, Friedman assumes the dual victory of capitalism and democracy, à la Fukuyama, while Barber demonstrates contradictions and tensions between capitalism and democracy within the New World (Dis)Order, as well as the antidemocratic animus of Jihad.

Dominant dualistic theories that posit a fundamental bifurcation between the West and Islam are thus analytically suspicious in that they homogenize complex civilizations and cover over differences, hybridizations, contradictions, and conflicts within these cultures. Positing inexorable clashes between bifurcated blocs à la Huntington and Barber fails to illuminate specific discord within the opposing spheres and the complex relations between them. These analyses do not grasp the complexity in the current geopolitical situation, which involves highly multifaceted and intricate interests, coalitions, and conflicts that shift and evolve in response to changing situations within an overdetermined and constantly evolving historical context. As Tariq Ali points out (2002), dualistic clashes of civilization also occlude the historical forces that clashed in the 9/11 attacks and the subsequent Terror War.

Consequently, the events of September 11 and their aftermath suggest that critical social theory needs models that account for complexity and the historical roots and vicissitudes of contemporary problems like terrorism rather than abstract theoretical generalizations. Critical social theory also needs to articulate how events like September 11 produce novel historical configurations while articulating both changes and continuities in the present situation.[4] It requires historical accounts of the surprising origins of current Islamic radicalism and its complicity with U.S. imperialism, as I recount in the next section. I suggest that Chalmers Johnson's concept of "blowback" (2000) provides a more convincing account than dualizing civilizational discourses of the September 11 terrorist attacks; that it better contextualizes, explains, and even predicts such events; and that it also provides cogent suggestions concerning viable and inappropriate responses to global terrorism.

The causes of the September 11 events and their aftermath are highly complex and involve, for starters, the failure of U.S. intelligence; the destructive consequences of U.S. interventionist foreign policy since the late 1970s; and the policies of the Carter, Reagan, Clinton, and both Bush administrations. In other words, there is no one cause or faction responsible for the catastrophe but a wide range of responsibility to be ascribed. Taking account of the history and complexity of the issues involved, Johnson's model of blowback arguably provides the most convincing account of how U.S. policy and institutions contributed to producing the worst terrorist crime in U.S. history with fateful consequences still threatening.[5]

THE BUSH ADMINISTRATIONS,
THE CIA, AND BLOWBACK

In retrospect, the events of September 11 can be seen as a textbook example of blowback, a concept developed in a book with this title by Chalmers Johnson (2000), who uses it to describe the unintended consequences of unwise policies; it is a shorthand term for describing that a nation reaps what it sows. As Johnson notes: "The term 'blowback,' which officials of the Central Intelligence Agency first invented for their own internal use, is starting to circulate among students of international relations. It refers to the unintended consequences of policies that were kept secret from the American people. What the daily press reports as the malign acts of 'terrorists' or 'drug lords' or 'rogue states' or 'illegal arms merchants' often turn out to be blowback from earlier operations" (2000, 8).

The concept of blowback, as I attempt to show, can be applied to the September 11 events since bin Laden and the radical Islamic forces associated with the Al Qaeda network were supported, funded, trained, and armed by the CIA and several U.S. administrations. In this reading, the United States' catastrophic failure was not only to have not detected the danger of a terrorist attack on the U.S. and taken action to prevent it, but to have actively contributed to producing the groups who are implicated in the 9/11 attacks and other terrorist assaults on the U.S.

Johnson provides a wealth of examples of blowback from problematic U.S. foreign policy maneuvers and covert actions that had unintended consequences, as when the U.S. became associated with the support of terrorist groups or authoritarian regimes in Asia, Latin America, or the Middle East and its clients turned on their sponsors. For instance, the U.S. helped overthrow a democratically elected government in Iran in the 1950s and install the autocratic Shah. When the Shah was overthrown in 1979, Iranian militants seized the U.S. embassy and took its inhabitants hostage; since then, Iran has maintained hostile, although complex, relationships with the U.S.

In Johnson's sense, 9/11 is a classic example of blowback, in which U.S. policies generated unintended consequences that had catastrophic effects on U.S. citizens and on the American (and, indeed, global) economy. U.S. policy in Afghanistan from the end of the Cold War to the present contributed to the heinous events of September 11. A useful summary by Alexander Cockburn and Jeffrey St. Clair describes U.S. covert operations in Afghanistan in the late 1970s that had momentous consequences:

> In April of 1978 an indigenous populist coup overthrew the government of Mohammed Daoud, who had formed an alliance with the man the United States had installed in Iran, Reza Pahlevi, a.k.a. the Shah. The new Afghan government was led by Noor Mohammed Taraki, and the Taraki administration embarked, albeit with a good deal of urban intellectual arrogance on land reform, hence an attack on the opium-growing feudal estates. Taraki went to the UN where he managed to raise loans for crop substitution for the poppy fields.
>
> Taraki also tried to bear down on opium production in the border areas held by fundamentalists, since the latter were using opium revenues to finance attacks on Afghanistan's central government, which they regarded as an unwholesome incarnation of modernity that allowed women to go to school and outlawed arranged marriages and the bride price. Accounts began to appear in the western press along the lines of this from the *Washington Post,* to the effect that the *mujahedeen* liked to "torture their victims by first cutting off their noses, ears and genitals, then removing one slice of skin after another."
>
> At that time the *mujahedeen* was not only getting money from the CIA but from Libya's Moammar Q'addaffi who sent them $250,000. In the summer of 1979 the U.S. State Department produced a memo making it clear how the U.S. government saw the stakes, no matter how modern minded Taraki might be or how feudal the Muj. It's another passage Nat might read to the grandkids: "The United States' larger interest would be served by the demise of the Taraki-Amin regime, despite whatever setbacks this might mean for future social and economic reforms in Afghanistan. The overthrow of the DRA [Democratic Republic of Afghanistan] would show the rest of the world, particularly the Third World, that the Soviets' view of the socialist course of history being inevitable is not accurate."[6]

In a 1998 *Le Monde* interview, President Jimmy Carter's National Security Advisor Zbignew Brzezinski had bragged about how he conceived of arming extremist Islamic militants against the Afghan government as a ploy to draw in the Soviet Union more deeply and thus help destroy their system.[7] What Brzezinski proudly proclaimed as his contribution to defeat the Soviet Union in the Cold War appears

in retrospect as a highly problematic U.S. intervention in the late 1970s that intensified civil war in Afghanistan. Overthrow of the secular and modernizing regime in
Afghanistan by Islamic fundamentalists helped mobilize and empower the forces
that would turn on the U.S. and institute a reign of global terrorism in the current
situation.

U.S. intervention in the Afghan conflict, which now appears as the last great clash
of the Cold War, helped create the context for the current crisis. As a response to
U.S. intervention, the Soviet Union sent increased aid and personnel to prop up the
moderate modernizing Taraki regime that was opposed by Islamic fundamentalists
in Afghanistan. When Afghan army officers killed Taraki in September 1979, the
Soviets invaded in force in December 1979 and set up a government to avoid a
fundamentalist Islamic and U.S.-backed takeover.

In the 1980s, the U.S. began more aggressively supporting Islamic fundamentalist
Jihad groups and the Afghan project was a major covert foreign policy project of
the Reagan-Bush administration. During this period, the CIA trained, armed, and
financed precisely those Islamic fundamentalist groups who later became part of the
Al Qaeda terror network that is now the nemesis of the West, the new "evil empire."
In the battle to defeat Soviet Communism in the Cold War, the U.S. poured billions
of dollars into Afghanistan to train "freedom fighters" that would overthrow the
purportedly communist regime. This was a major project with overt and covert aid
from the U.S., Pakistan, China, Saudi Arabia, and other countries. The military aid
went into training and arming radical Islamic groups who would emerge with a
desire to fight other wars for Islam in the countries that had earlier supported them
in their Jihad against the Soviet-backed regime in Afghanistan administrations. Bin
Laden and his Al Qaeda network thus emerge as a Frankenstein of U.S. policy.

Indeed, the blowback from the Reagan-Bush-CIA Afghanistan intervention was
astonishing. John K. Cooley in his important study *Unholy Wars: Afghanistan,
America and International Terrorism* (2000) documents the momentous consequences of the U.S. and its allies sustaining the Islamists who fought to overthrow
the Soviet-backed government in Afghanistan. Egypt's Anwar Sadat was an early ally
of the support for the Islamists against the Soviets and was repaid with assassination
by fanatic Islamics in 1981. Pakistan's president, Zia al-Haq, whose secret services
played a major role in arming and organizing the Islamic fighters in Afghanistan,
was killed in a mysterious plane crash in 1988 and more radical Islamic forces have
threatened to take over in Pakistan ever since. The Pakistani secret services helped
organize the group that became the Taliban in the mid-1990s and the Taliban eventually took over control of most of Afghanistan. The Taliban formed an alliance with
bin Laden and his Al Qaeda group, which used Afghanistan to form networks that
engaged in terrorism throughout the world. These Islamic fundamentalists eventually turned on the U.S., one of the countries that had helped to fund, train, and arm
them.

Not only did the U.S. secret war in Afghanistan to organize Islamic militia against
the Soviets help create the Islamic terror network that is now the scourge of the

West, but the same Islamic radical forces, with the complicity of the CIA and other foreign intelligence services, produced one the most stupendous proliferations of drugs in history. As Cooley summarizes: "Never has so much South Asian marijuana, opium, and semiprocessed opium products and heroin, reached the drug pushers, the adult addicts, the children, and the general populations of the West, as in the late 1990s. Much of this was another direct consequence of the CIA's holy war of 1979–89" (Cooley 2000, 5). It is, of course, impossible to document how much tonnage of drug products were exported, but although Afghanistan produced mostly for local consumption before 1979, according to UN figures production in 1995–1996 had risen to 2,600 tons of raw opium, increasing to 2,800 tons in 1997 (Cooley 2000, 150). The results were skyrocketing drug addiction in neighboring countries and massive exporting of drugs to the West.

In 1989, Soviet troops left Afghanistan in defeat and a civil war continued for the next several years. The first Bush administration, in one of its most cynical and fateful decisions, decided to completely pull out of Afghanistan rather than work to build democracy and a viable government in that country. In retrospect, this was both inhumane and catastrophic. Over 2 million people had died in the ten years of the Afghan war, and the U.S. had invested billions of dollars in overthrowing the Russian-sponsored regime and in arming, training, and financing the Islamic fundamentalists. But rather than help the Afghan people produce a viable government, the first Bush administration turned away, and the most radical extremist Islamic fundamentalist groups that the U.S. and Pakistan had organized took over the country after some years more of civil war, setting up the present conflict (see Cooley 2000; Rashid 2001; and Ali 2002).

Although later in the 1990s, certain U.S. interests would be attracted to the oil and gas possibilities in Afghanistan and would cozy up to and support the Taliban, in the early 1990s, the first Bush administration had other fish to fry, in particular Iraq—another Bush I intervention that had momentous consequences. For after arousing the Arab ire and opposition to the U.S. military intervention against Iraq, at the end of the Gulf war in 1991, the Bush administration persuaded the Saudi government to allow the U.S. to continue to maintain military forces in their country, the Holy Land of Islam. This auspicious event has yet to be fully perceived in its blowback effects, for it was the permanent positioning of U.S. troops in what was perceived as the Islamic Holy Land that especially angered bin Laden and more radical Islamic groups. When Saudi Arabia continued to allow the presence of U.S. troops after the Gulf War, bin Laden broke with his country and was declared persona non grata by the Saudis for his provocative statements and behavior. It was also reported at this time that the Saudis put out a contract on bin Laden's life, supposedly with the assent of the first Bush Administration (Weaver 1996) and later with the assent of the Clinton administration, although assassination attempts obviously failed and may not have been seriously attempted at all.

After civil war in Afghanistan in the mid-1990s, the Taliban eventually took over control of much of the country (see Rashid 2001). The Taliban were recognized by the Saudis and Pakistanis as the legitimate government of Afghanistan, but not by the UN or by much of the rest of the world, which recognized the Northern Alliance groups fighting the Taliban as the legitimate representative of Afghanistan. When bin Laden and his associates were expelled from Sudan in 1996, they entered into a fateful association with the Taliban and went to Afghanistan where they solidified their network, developed training camps, and solicited recruits and financing.

The Clinton administration at first engaged the Taliban government in dialogue, but soon broke off relations and failed to deal with the bin Laden problem. In the 1980s and 1990s, bin Laden established an organization of former Afghanistan holy war veterans, called Al Qaeda, "the base."[8] In February 1998, Al Qaeda issued a statement, endorsed by several extreme Islamic groups, declaring it the duty of all Muslims to kill U.S. citizens—civilian or military—and their allies everywhere. The bombing of U.S. embassies in Africa later in 1998 was ascribed to the bin Laden–Al Qaeda network, and the Clinton administration responded by shooting seventy Cruise missiles at a factory supposedly owned by bin Laden in Sudan that produced chemical weapons and at camps in Afghanistan that supposedly were populated by bin Laden and his group. The factory in Sudan turned out to be a pharmaceutical company and the camps in Afghanistan were largely deserted, producing another embarrassment for U.S. policy in the Middle East. Clinton later claimed that his administration also was plotting to assassinate bin Laden, but that a change of Pakistani government disrupted the plot.[9]

Although this is rarely mentioned in the mainstream media, the George W. Bush administration became one of the largest financial supporters of the Taliban, providing over $100 million in early 2001 in what they described as "humanitarian aid," as well as a supplemental grant of $43 million in May of 2001 for the Taliban's promise to declare opium production "unIslamic" and thus to cut back on a potent source of the world's drug trade. Critics have suggested that the Bush administration was acting in the interests of the Unocal oil consortium to build an oil pipeline across Afghanistan, and of the Enron corporation, a major contributor to the Bush administration, which had done a feasibility study for the project. Enron and Unocal had lavishly courted the Taliban and encouraged U.S. support of the regime since they were deemed the group most likely to stabilize Afghanistan and allow the pipeline to be built.[10]

In *Forbidden Truth,* Brisard and Dasquie (2002) claim that under the influence of oil companies, the Bush administration initially blocked ongoing U.S. government investigations of Al Qaeda terrorism while it bargained with the Taliban over oil rights, pipeline deals, and handing over bin Laden. This evidently led to the resignation of an FBI deputy director, John O'Neill, who was one of the sources of the story. Brisard and Dasquie contend that the Bush administration had been a major supporter of the Taliban until the September 11 events and had blocked investigations in the bin Laden terror network. Pursuing these leads, the British *Independent* reported on October 30: "Secret satellite phone calls between the State Department and Mullah Mohammed Omar and the presentation of an Afghan carpet to President George Bush were just part of the diplomatic contacts between Washington and the Taliban that continued until just days before the attacks of 11 September."

Thus, just as Bush Senior turned on Saddam Hussein whom he supported in the 1990s, so too did Bush Junior turn on the Taliban whom he had been generously supporting, supposedly with the hopes that his friends could do energy deals with them. The Taliban, of course, were a highly theocratic and repressive fundamentalist regime that some have described as "clerical fascism" (Chip Berlet), or "reactionary tribalism" (Robert Antonio). Their treatment of women was notorious, as was their cultural totalitarianism that led to banning of books and media, destruction of Buddhist statues, and other outrages (see Rashid 2001).

The Taliban practice a form of Islam called Deobandism, influenced by a nineteenth-century sect that tried to purify Islam of its modern aspects (see Rashid 2000, 88–90), much as the Saudis' version of "Wahabbism" follows strict Islamic law while rejecting much of the modern world. The Taliban went further than the Saudis in trying to purify Islam in a particular antimodern version by following an especially reactionary strain of Muslim fundamentalism that is rejected by the more mainstream Sunni and Shiite Islamic schools. The Taliban have also been the host of Osama bin Laden and the Al Qaeda network since they were expelled from Sudan in 1996 due to U.S. pressure and insistence. Although bin Laden and Al Qaeda were designated enemies of the U.S. since their evident involvement in a series of terrorist crimes, the Bush administration continued to provide support to the Taliban group that hosted and protected them until the 9/11 terror attacks.

Moreover, there has been a close relationship between the Bush and bin Laden families for years. Salem bin Laden, head of the family empire and Osama's eldest brother, reportedly invested in George W. Bush's first business venture, Arbusto Energy. According to several sources, the deal was brokered by Bush's friend James Bath, who was also involved in the infamous BCCI bank scandals, was allegedly a CIA agent recruited by W's father, and was a business agent for the bin Laden family.[11] The bin Laden family has also been involved in other ventures with the Bush family. Internet commentator Sally Slate cited an interesting passage from a PBS *Frontline* website on the bin Laden and Bush connection:

> Like his father in 1968, Salem [bin Laden] died in a 1988 air crash . . . in Texas. He was flying a BAC 1–11 which had been bought in July 1977 by Prince Mohammed Ben Fahd. The plane's flight plans had long been at the center of a number of investigations. According to one of the plane's American pilots, it had been used in October 1980 during secret Paris meetings between U.S. and Iranian emissaries. Nothing was ever proven, but Salem bin Laden's accidental death revived some speculation that he might have been "eliminated" as an embarrassing witness. In fact, an inquiry was held to determine the exact circumstances of the accident. The conclusions were never divulged.[12]

This shocking report indicates that the Bush and bin Laden families might have been involved in covert political activities as well as business deals, including the

"October Surprise," one of the most controversial stories of the Reagan-Bush years. There have long been claims that representatives from the Reagan-Bush election team in 1980 negotiated with Iranians to hold Americans hostage until after the 1980 election, depriving then–President Carter of an "October Surprise" from release of the long-held U.S. hostages in Iran that might give Carter the election.[13] The PBS *Frontline* story suggests the longtime, secretive, and highly complex relations between the Bush and the bin Laden families. It is highly suspicious that bin Laden's father and Salem bin Laden, who had inherited control of the family's empire of business and political interests after his father's death, both died in Texas airplane crashes. As I note later, the Bush and bin Laden families were involved in many enterprises. Unraveling these threads will no doubt be an important and revealing task for future historians.

Whatever the bizarre and shady past relations between the Bush and bin Laden family, it is striking that relations between the families continued up until September 11. It has been widely reported that the bin Laden family had been an investor in the Carlyle investment group, in which James Baker and George H. W. Bush are major partners.[14] Moreover, Bush Senior and the bin Ladens were allegedly involved in the earlier major global scandal of its era, the Bank of Credit and Commerce International (BCCI) that funneled the money of spies, criminals, shady businesses, and the CIA during the Reagan-Bush era (see Brewton 1992; Brisard and Dasquie 2002; and Cooley 2000).

The official spin line of Bush and bin Laden family spokespeople is that the family has long expelled and condemned their wayward son Osama and cannot be held responsible for Al Qaeda crimes. But as Sally Slate notes: "Last Thursday on ABC's *Primetime,* Carmen bin Laden, the estranged wife of Osama's brother Yeslam, told Diane Sawyer, in regard to Osama's standing in Saudi Arabia, 'What I have heard is he has the backing of some of the royal family. They think the same way. Not all of them, but some of them. You have to understand, I think in Saudi Arabia Osama bin Laden has a little following. And in my opinion, this is what makes him dangerous. . . . Because he has, I think, he has the backing of a lot of people there.'"[15]

Other commentators have claimed that the bin Laden–Al Qaeda network has been supported by wealthy Saudis, including members of bin Laden's family, and that up until the September 11 terror attacks there were close connections between the Bush administration, the Saudis, and the Taliban. A November 2001 PBS *Frontline* report, "The Saudi Time Bomb," made clear the support of bin Laden, the Taliban, and the Al Qaeda network by Saudi Arabian groups. It also revealed that many in the bin Laden–Al Qaeda network and the Saudis shared a similar Wahabbi interpretation of Islam that is rooted in an eighteenth-century attempt to return to the early version of Islam, is highly puritanical and repressive of women, and is exceptionally hostile to the West. The Saudis helped fund the Taliban and set up throughout the world fundamentalist Wahabbi Islamic schools that became recruiting grounds for bin Laden and the Al Qaeda network. Other Saudis directly contributed to Al Qaeda through "charitable" foundations or other means.

Not only did the Bush family have a long and mysterious history of dealings with the bin Ladens and with other dubious Saudi families who funded the Al Qaeda network, but, as noted, Bush Senior and friends would strongly benefit from the war through their connections with the Carlyle group, which heavily invests in the military-defense sector and include as investors the bin Laden family, election thief and Bush family friend James Baker, and George H. W. Bush, leading the conservative group Judicial Watch to insist that Bush Senior resign from the group because of conflict of interests. An FBI memo later revealed that the agency was ordered by the Bush administration to stop investigating connections between the Al Qaeda network and bin Laden family and to "lay off the bin Ladens," perhaps because of the longtime Bush–bin Laden family connections.[16]

The Bush-Baker-Cheney-Saudi band have, of course, long been involved in Mideast oil wheeling and dealing and assorted sordid business deals and political intrigue in the region. Many believe that the U.S. intervention in Afghanistan was at least partly motivated by an interest in controlling the flow of Mideast oil and enhancing these business interests—as was the last Bush-Cheney operation, the Gulf War.[17] Reports abound of the tremendous oil and gas reserves in Central Asia and the need to build pipelines across Afghanistan that would secure their passage. Using U.S. government sources, Michael Klare writes that the Caspian Sea basin "harbors as much as 270 billion barrels of oil, or about one-fifth of the world's total proven reserves of petroleum. Only the Persian Gulf, with 675 billion barrels in proven reserves, holds a larger supply. The Department of Energy also estimates that the Caspian Sea region houses some 665 trillion cubic feet of natural gas, representing one-eight of the world's gas reserves." Moreover, "the untapped oil of the Caspian Sea basin . . . was estimated by the Department of State in 1997 to be worth some $4 trillion" (Klare 2001, 15).

The energy industry–oriented machinators in the Bush administration were considering different ways to control the flow of Caspian Sea basin oil and gas, including pipelines that would be built across Afghanistan. The desirability of secure terrain around the pipeline led, according to some, to Bush administration support of the Taliban, who had promised to build the pipeline and create internal security to protect it. But when it was obvious that the Taliban could not be trusted and were involved with the bin Laden network and terrorism, Bush-Cheney turned on their former allies, as did Bush Senior, Cheney, and Powell against Saddam Hussein, who had been a U.S. ally throughout the 1980s (see Kellner 1992).[18]

Of course, it would be a mistake to reduce events like the Gulf War or the Afghanistan Terror War to oil and one needs to factor in the military interests, geopolitical goals, and specific agendas of the Bush administrations. Rather than providing causal analyses that reduce complex events to one factor or dimension, issues like the Gulf War (see Kellner 1992) or Afghan war require multifactored analyses that include economic, political, military, cultural, and other relevant aspects.

In any case, the events of the September 11 terrorist attacks should be seen in the context of several U.S. administrations and the CIA providing support from the late

1970s, through the Reagan-Bush years, to the present for the perpetrators of the monstrous assaults on the United States. This is not to simply blame U.S. policy in Afghanistan for the terrorist assault of September 11, but it is to provide some of the context in which the events can be interpreted. During the hysterical fear of terrorism in the aftermath of the September 11 and anthrax attacks, there was a surge of patriotism whereby many argued that anyone who mentions political causes of Arab hostility toward the U.S. is part of the "blame America" crowd. Indeed, even liberals resisted the "blowback" thesis as illicitly blaming the victim. It is rather a question, first, of gaining historical understanding of the context and situation concerning those radical Islamic sectors of the Arab and Islamic world who have declared Jihad against the U.S. Second, it is a question of ascribing responsibility for those in the U.S. foreign policy establishment who helped organize, fund, train, and arm the terrorists now plaguing the U.S. and other parts of the world. If we do not understand the past, not only are we condemned to repeat it, but we also have no chance of constructing an intelligent, enlightened, and peaceful future.

There are, of course, other flaws of U.S. foreign policy over the past decades that have helped generate enemies of the United States in the Middle East and elsewhere, such as excessive U.S. support for Israel and inadequate aid for the Palestinians; U.S. backing of authoritarian regimes; and innumerable misdeeds of the U.S. empire over the past decades that have been documented by Chomsky, Herman, Johnson, and other critics of U.S. foreign policy. Thus, although there were no doubt a multiplicity of contributing factors, the 9/11 events can be read as a blowback of major policies of successive U.S. administrations and the CIA who trained, funded, supported, and armed the cadres alleged to have carried out the terrorist attacks on the United States. The obvious lesson is that it is highly dangerous and potentially costly to align one's country with terrorist cadres, that support of groups or individuals who promote terrorism is likely to come back to haunt you, and that it is hazardous to make Machiavellian pacts with obviously brutal and treacherous forces in violent parts of the world.

Consequently, the conjuncture of Islamic radicalism with the failure of subsequent U.S. administrations to take seriously the threats that terrorist groups posed helped to make possible the 9/11 terrorist attacks on the United States, as did the failure of U.S. intelligence agencies. Before engaging the responses of the Bush administration, Pentagon, and media to these attacks in chapters 2–11, I will raise the question of how the events of 9/11 changed U.S. politics and society.

9/11 AND TERROR WAR:
HAS EVERYTHING CHANGED?

In the aftermath of 9/11, there was a wealth of commentary arguing that "everything has changed," that the post–September 11 world is a different one, less innocent, more serious, and significantly altered, with momentous modifications in the economy, polity, culture, and everyday life. There were some doubters such as historian Alan Brinkley, who stated in a *New York Times* interview (September 14, 2002): "I'm skeptical that this is a great rupture in the fabric of history."[19] Time alone will tell the depth of the magnitude of change, but there are enough significant shifts that have occurred already to see 9/11 as a *transformational event* that has created some dramatic alterations in both U.S. and global society, signaling reconfigurations and novelties in the current world.

In the context of U.S. politics, 9/11 was so far-reaching and catastrophic that it flipped the political world upside down; put new issues on the agenda; and changed the political, cultural, and economic climate almost completely overnight. To begin, there was a dramatic reversal of the fortunes of George W. Bush and the Bush administration. Before September 11, Bush's popularity was rapidly declining. After several months of the most breathtaking hard-right turn perhaps ever seen in U.S. politics, Bush seemed to lose control of the agenda with the defection of Vermont Republican Senator Jim Jeffords in May 2001. Jeffords's defection gave the Democrats a razor-thin control of Congress, the ability to block Bush's programs, and the ability to advance their own (see Kellner 2001, chapter 11). Bush seemed disengaged after this setback, spending more and more time at his Texas ranch. He was widely perceived as incompetent and unqualified, and his public support was seriously eroding.

With the terror attacks of September 11, however, the bitter partisanship of the previous months disappeared and Bush was the beneficiary of a extraordinary outburst of patriotism. Support for the Bush administration was strongly fueled by the media that provided 24/7 coverage of the heroism of the fire, police, and rescue workers at the World Trade Center. The response of ordinary citizens to the tragedy showed American courage, skill, and dedication at its best, as rescue workers heroically struggled to save lives and deal with the immense problems of removing the Trade Center ruins. New York City and the country pulled together in a remarkable display of community, heroism, and resolve, evident in the ongoing media coverage of the tragedy. There was an explosion of flags and patriotism and a widespread desire for military retaliation, which was fanned by the media.

There was also demonizing coverage of bin Laden and his Al Qaeda network of terrorists and a demand for strong military retaliation. The anthrax attacks, still unsolved as I write this at the end of 2002, fueled media hysteria and mass panic that terrorism could strike anyone, at any time, and at any place. Bush articulated the escalating patriotism, vilification of the terrorists, and the demand for stern military retaliation, and a frightened nation supported his policies, often without seeing their broader implications and threat to democracy and world peace.

There was a brief and ironic ideological flip-flop of Bush administration policy, in which it temporarily put aside the unilateralism that had distinguished its first months in office in favor of a multilateral approach. As the Bush administration scrambled to assemble a global coalition against terrorism with partners such as Pakistan, China, and Russia, which it had previously ignored (or, in the case of China, even provoked), illusions circulated that the U.S. would pursue a more multilateral global politics. With the collapse of the Taliban and the de facto conclusion of the intense military phase of the Afghanistan Terror War by December 2001, however, the Bush administration has arguably reverted to its old unilateralism. Thus, the Bush doctrine articulated in his January 2002 State of the Union address projected an "axis of evil" threatened by U.S. military action, called for unprecedented military action and buildup, and evoked an image of an era of war via U.S. military intervention throughout the world for the foreseeable future. The threat of a new militarism as the defining feature of the Bush era was intensified as his administration came to formulate his doctrine of "preemptive strikes" during the summer of 2002.

Previous to September 11, the Bush administration had been rabidly pro–"free markets" and antigovernment, but it was forced by the September 11 events to recognize the need for stronger government programs. There was widespread consensus that federal funds and programs were necessary to help rebuild New York, provide increased domestic security, and regulate industries like the airplane business, which showed itself to be woefully lacking in security measures. Yet it should be noted that the main government interventions undertaken by the Bush administration were in the areas of "homeland security" and a gigantic military build-up. These included a highly illiberal right-wing law-and-order program of unleashing government agencies to surveil, arrest, and detain those suspected of being terrorists in what many see as the most outrageous assault on civil liberties and the open society in U.S. history. There have been no serious initiatives in the area of investing to rebuild infrastructure of cities, highways, or the public health system. Moreover, Bush's proposed "economic stimulus" package largely consisted of tax breaks for the wealthy rather than new government programs to help the poor and those losing their jobs during a severe economic downturn.

In addition, government bailouts went mainly to Bush administration allies such as the airlines and insurance industries, with no funds for job retraining and support for laid-off workers. Hence, although the September 11 tragedy created an amazing reversal of fortune for George W. Bush, it has so far not produced any fundamental restructuring of the U.S. economy or polity, outside of right-wing law-and-order programs and tightened airport and domestic security. The 9/11 terror attacks and subsequent anthrax attacks did, however, point to a vulnerability to terrorism and danger not previously experienced on U.S. soil.

The new vulnerability caused a reversal of priorities, both national and personal, for many people, and made it clear that the U.S. had to address problems of globalization and terrorism—issues that were far from the hearts and minds of the average U.S. citizen. For a while, irony was out and seriousness was in, and a new sobriety replaced the usual American concern with triviality and diversion. Americans, like people in most of the world, had to learn to live with finitude, contingency, risk, and other concepts that were previously philosophical categories and were now realities of everyday life. There was a sudden sense that everything could change within days or weeks, and that technologies that were part and parcel of everyday life, such as airplanes or mail delivery, could be weapons of destruction. Furthermore, fears proliferated that terrorism threatened Americans anywhere and anytime, creating new forms of insecurity and anxiety that the media fueled with hysterical coverage of the anthrax attacks, endless accounts of terrorist networks, and highly dramatized reports of the Afghanistan Terror War.

Crucially, the 9/11 events dramatized that globalization is a defining reality of our time and that the much-celebrated flow of people, ideas, technology, media, and goods could have a downside as well as an upside and expensive costs as well as benefits. The 9/11 terror attacks also call attention to the complex and unpredictable nature of a globally connected networked society and the paradoxes, surprises, and unintended consequences that flow from globalization. Al Qaeda is at once a product of globalization and a response to it. It presents an example of a hidden and secretive decentered network dedicated to attacking the U.S., while their Afghanistan base represented what theorists called "wild zones" or "zones of turmoil" that exist out of the boundaries of "safe zones" of globalized metropoles like Wall Street and northern Virginia (see Mann 2001 and Urry 2002).

Globalization thus generates its Other, its opponents, just as it destroys tradition and incorporates otherness into its modernizing and neoliberal market. For the first time, the American people were obliged to perceive that it had serious enemies throughout the globe and that global problems had to be addressed. No longer could the U.S. enjoy the luxury of isolationism, but was forced to actively define its role within a dangerous and complex global environment. Moreover, the terror attacks of 9/11 put in question much conventional wisdom and forced U.S. citizens and others to reflect upon the continued viability of key values, practices, and institutions of a democratic society. In particular, the events of September 11 force the rethinking of globalization, new technology, democracy, and national and global security. 9/11 and its aftermath demonstrate the significance of globalization and the ways that global, national, and local scenes and events intersect in the contemporary world. The terror spectacle also pointed to the fundamental contradictions and ambiguities of globalization, undermining one-sided pro- or anti-globalization positions.

9/11 was obviously a *global event* that dramatized an interconnected and conflicted networked society in which there is a constant worldwide flow of people, products, technologies, ideas, and the like. 9/11 could only be a mega-event in a *global media world,* a society of the spectacle, in which the whole world is watching and participates in what Marshall McLuhan (1964) called a global village. The 9/11 terror spectacle was obviously constructed as a media event to circulate terror and to demonstrate to the world the vulnerability of the epicenter of global capitalism and American power.

Thus, 9/11 dramatized the interconnected networked globe and the important role of the media in which individuals everywhere can simultaneously watch events of worldwide significance unfold and participate in the dramas of globalization.

Already, Bill Clinton had said before September 11 that terrorism is the downside, the dark side, of globalization, and after 9/11 Colin Powell interpreted the terrorist attacks in similar fashion. Worldwide terrorism is threatening in part because globalization relentlessly divides the world into haves and have-nots, promotes conflicts and competition, and fuels long-simmering hatreds and grievances—as well as bringing people together, creating new relations, interactions, and hybrids. This is the objective ambiguity of globalization that both brings people together and brings them into conflict, that creates social interaction and inclusion as well as hostilities and exclusions, and that potentially tears regions and the world apart while attempting to pull things together. Moreover, as different groups gain access to technologies of destruction and devise plans to make conventional technologies, like the airplane, instruments of destruction, then dangers of *unexpected terror events* at any place and any time proliferate and become part of the frightening mediascape of the new millennium.

Globalization is thus messier and more dangerous than previous theories had indicated. Moreover, global terrorism and megaspectacle terror events are possible because of the lethality and power of new technology and its availability to groups and individuals that previously had restricted access. In a perverted distortion of Andrew Feenberg's theory of the reconstruction and democratization of technology (1999, 2001), terrorist groups seek technologies of mass destruction that in the past were monopolized by the state, and they take instruments of mass transportation and communication run by corporations and the state, like airlines and mail delivery, and reconvert these instruments into weapons of mass destruction and terror. I might parenthetically note here the etymology of the term "terrorism," which derives from the Latin verb *terrere,* "to cause to tremble or quiver." It began to be used during the French Revolution, and especially after the fall of Robespierre and the "reign of terror," or simply "the Terror," in which enemies of the revolution were subjected to imprisonment, torture, and beheading—the first of many modern examples of state terrorism.

Hence, 9/11 exhibited a technological terror that converts benign instruments like airlines and buildings into instruments of mass destruction. Within a short time after the 9/11 terror attacks, in early October, the U.S. mail system was polluted by anthrax. Since infected letters were sent to politicians and corporate media, there was maximum public attention on the dangers of a lethal anthrax attack, making postal work, mail delivery, and the opening of mail a traumatic event infused with fear. This is exactly the goal of terrorism, and media hysteria over anthrax attacks went far in promoting fear and war fever that led the public to unquestionably support whatever military retaliation or domestic politics the Bush administration choose to exert. Curiously, although the Bush administration seemed at first to blame the Al Qaeda network and then Iraq for the anthrax attacks, it appears that the military high grade of anthrax has the genetic footprint of U.S. laboratories in Fort Detrick, Maryland. Eventually the FBI and academic experts believed that the source of the attacks was an individual working for the U.S. defense and biological weapons establishment.[20]

It is clear from 9/11 that the new technologies disperse power, empowering angry disempowered people, leveling the playing field, and distributing the use and application of information technology and some technologies of mass destruction. Many military technologies can be obtained by individuals and groups to use against the superpowers and the access to such technology produces a situation of asymmetrical war in which weaker individuals and groups can go after superpowers. The possibility of new forms of cyberwar and terrorist threats from chemical, biological, or nuclear weapons creates new vulnerabilities in the national defense of the overdeveloped countries and provides opportunities for weaker nations or groups to attack stronger ones. Journalist William Greider, for instance, author of *Fortress America: The American Military and the Consequences of Peace,* claims, "A deadly irony is embedded in the potential of these new technologies. Smaller, poorer nations may be able to defend themselves on the cheap against the intrusion of America's overwhelming military strength"[21]—or exercise deadly terrorism against civilian populations.

Hence, the United States discovered that it is vulnerable domestically to terrorist attack. Likewise, it is becoming clear that the more technologically advanced a society is, the more susceptible it is to cyberwar. There are now, of course, serious worries about the Internet and cyberterrorism disrupting the global economy and networked society. It is somewhat surprising that terrorist groups have not, in fact, gone after the Internet and attempted to shut it down since they were obviously attempting to disrupt global business by attacking the World Trade Center and airlines industry. Already Paul Virilio evoked the frightening possibility of the collapse of the Internet through a major technological "event" that would cause its shutdown—disruptions previewed by hacker attacks, worms, and viruses over the past years.[22]

Rather, the Al Qaeda terror network used the Internet, as it used globalization, to move its communication, money, people, propaganda, and terror. 9/11 thus dramatizes that all of the most positive aspects of globalization and new technology can be turned against the U.S., or, in general, positive aspects of globalization can turn into their opposite, as in Adorno and Horkheimer's "dialectic of Enlightenment" in which reason, science, technology, and other instruments of Enlightenment turned into their opposites in the hands of German fascism and other oppressive social groups (1972 [1946]). Globalization makes possible global terror networks as well as networks of commerce and communication. The circulation of commodities, technologies, ideas, money, and people can facilitate networks of terror, as well as trade and travel. The Internet makes possible the spreading of hate and fear, as well as knowledge and culture. Computers can be an integral part of a terror network just as they are part of businesses everywhere and many of our own everyday lives. And biotechnology, which promises such extravagant medical advances and miracles, can provide weapons of mass destruction as well.

Thus, 9/11 and its aftermath exhibit the contradictions and ambiguities of globalization, the Internet, biotechnology, and technology in general in the contemporary age. Globalization has upsides and downsides, costs and benefits, which are often interconnected and are consequently intrinsically ambiguous. New technologies can be used positively or negatively and in fact are at once potentially empowering and productive *and* disempowering and destructive, and are thus fraught with contradictions. Often, the positives and negatives of globalization and new technology are intertwined, as when the free and open society enabled the deadly movement of terrorists; the open architecture of the Internet enabled terrorists to communicate, circulate money, and organize their terror attacks; and the networked society of globalization, with its dark sides, enabled terrorists to attack the very symbols of American global wealth and power.

Certainly bin Laden's Al Qaeda network represents bad globalization, most would agree, and the perverted use of technology. But in a sense the Al Qaeda Jihad is the reverse image of McWorld, which imposes its Jihad on tradition and local culture, wanting to create the world in its image. Just as Al Qaeda dreams of imposing a radical premodern Islam on the world, taking over and destroying Western infidel culture and replacing it with a homogenized Islamic fundamentalism, so too does McDonald's want to destroy local and traditional eating habits and cuisine and replace them with a globalized and universalized menu, a potent symbol of modernization and Westernization eradicating its other. And just as the Taliban can blithely destroy Buddhist statues that represent sacred traditions and history, so too can neoliberal globalization destroy centuries of tradition and community in the name of modernization and "progress."

Hence, whereas theories of globalization, the Internet, and cyberculture tended to be on the whole one-sided, either pro or con, 9/11 and its aftermath showed the objective ambiguity and contradictions of these phenomena and need for a more dialectical and contextualizing optic. On one hand, the events showed the fundamental interdependence of the world, dramatizing how activities in one part of the world affected others and the need for more global consciousness and politics. 9/11 exposed the dangers and weaknesses inherent in constructions of Fortress America, and the untenability of isolationism and unilateralist policies. It made evident that we are in a global world with global problems, which require global solutions. On the other hand, as the Bush administration pursued increasingly unilateralist policies after seeming to make gestures toward a multilateralist response, the aftermath of 9/11 shows the limited possibilities for a single nation to impose its will on the world and to dominate the complex environment of the world economy and politics.

9/11 also revealed the failures of the laissez-faire conservative economics, which claimed that there was a market solution to every problem. Just as *Grand Theft 2000* revealed the failure of voting technology, the electoral registration process, and the very system of voting, as well as the malfunctioning of the media and judicial system (see Kellner 2001), so too did 9/11 reveal the massive breakdown of U.S. intelligence agencies, the National Security State, and the U.S. government to protect the people in the country, as well as cities and monuments, against terrorist attack. The privatization undergone by the airlines industry left travelers vulnerable to the hijacking of airplanes and the confused and ineffectual response by the federal government to the anthrax attacks uncovered the necessity of a better public health system, as well as more protection and security against bioterrorist attacks. Going after the terror networks disclosed the need for tighter financial regulation, better legal and police coordination, and an improved intelligence and national security apparatus. Rebuilding New York City and the lives of those affected by the terror attacks showed the need for a beneficent welfare state that would provide for its citizens in their time of need.

Thus, 9/11 ends the fantasies of Reagan-Bush conservative economics that the market alone can solve all social problems and provide the best mechanism for every industry and sector of life. The Bush-Enron and other corporate scandals also reveal the utter failures of neoliberalism and the need for a stronger and more effective polity for the United States to compete and survive in a highly complex world economy and polity (see chapter 9).

On the whole, 9/11 and its aftermath have made the world a much more dangerous place. Regional conflicts from the Israel-Palestine hostilities in the Middle East to the India-Pakistan conflict to discord in Africa, the Philippines, Colombia, and elsewhere have used the Bush administration's discourse against terrorism to suppress human rights, to legitimate government oppression, and to kill political opponents throughout the world. The Bush administration's unilateralism in pursuing the war against terror throughout the world, including against an imagined "axis of evil" not directly related to the Al Qaeda terror network, has weakened multilateral agreements and forces from NATO to the UN and has increased collective insecurity immensely. The Bush administration polarizing policy of "you are with us or against us" has divided alliances, is ever more isolating the U.S., and is producing a more polarized and conflicted world. The alarming buildup of U.S. military power is escalating a new militarism and proliferating enemies and resentment against the United States, now being increasingly seen as a rogue superpower. Finally, aggressive U.S. threats and military action throughout the world, failed propaganda in the Arab world, and what is perceived as growing U.S. arrogance and belligerence is producing more enemies in the Arab world and elsewhere that will no doubt create dangerous blowback effects in the future.

Not only has the Bush administration's unilateralist foreign policy exposed the U.S. to new attacks and enemies, but its domestic policy has also weakened democracy, civil liberties, and the very concept of a free and open society. Draconian anti-terror laws embodied in the so-called USA Patriot Act have frighteningly increased government powers of surveillance, arrest, and detention. The erection of military prison camps for suspected terrorists, the abrogation of basic civil liberties, and the call for military trials undermine decades of progress in developing a democratic policy and have produced the most regressive U.S. domestic policies in history.

The Bush administration's economic policy has also done little to strengthen the "new economy," largely giving favors to its major contributors in the oil, energy, and military industries. Bush administration censorship of websites, e-mail, and wireless communication; its refusal to release government documents; and its curtailment of the freedom of information act signals the decline of the information society and perhaps of a free and open democratic society. Traditional Bush family secrecy explains part of the extreme assaults on the open society, but there are also signs that key members of the Bush administration are contemptuous of democracy itself and threaten to drastically cut back democratic rights and freedoms.

Thus, Bush administration policy has arguably exploited the tragedy of September 11 for promoting its own political agenda and interests, while threatening to undermine the U.S. and world economy and American democracy in the process. 9/11 thus represents a clear and present danger to the U.S. economy and democracy as well as to the threat of terror attacks. Of course, many people lost loved ones in the September 11 terror attacks and their lives will never be the same. Other individuals have returned to the routines and patterns of their pre–September 11 life, and there are thus continuities in culture and everyday life as well as differences and changes. It is not clear if there will be a significant and lasting resurgence of civic reengagement, but it is clear that global politics are now perceived as highly significant and there should be more focus and debates on this terrain than previously.

Still, many corporate and political interests and individual citizens pursue business as usual at the same time that important differences are enforced in the economy and politics. There are, however, intelligent and destructive ways to fight global terrorism and such a virulent global problem obviously requires a multilateral solution, demanding alliances of a complex array of countries on the legal, police, economic, and military fronts. In this global context, there are serious dangers that the Bush administration will make the problem of terrorism worse and will immeasurably harm the U.S. and the global economy and polity in the process.

Indeed, my narrative of the September 11 terror attacks and their aftermath in this book documents stunning economic crisis and the failures of Bushonomics to deal with a complex economic situation; the decline of civil liberties and attacks on democracy in Bush administration policy; a failed policy of unilateralism that is arguably not the appropriate response to terrorism; a flawed military and political policy in the Afghan war; and the dangers of intensified war, militarism, and historical regression in the years to come.

In the next chapter, I analyze the complicity of the mainstream media, especially television, in giving the Bush administration a free hand to pursue its own domestic and foreign policy agenda, often at the expense of the people of the U.S. and the world. I will argue that serious debate concerning the proper response to global terrorism and the September 11 attacks never took place in the mainstream media and throughout this book will argue that the very survival of U.S. democracy requires a many-sided dialogue over the problems of terrorism and the failures of the Bush administration to properly address it. In the chapter that follows, I discuss how certain social discourses were deployed within the media and public policy debates and served to inform or legitimate policies advanced by the Bush administration that privileged a U.S. military response to the problem of terrorism. In a study of the dominant discourses, frames, and representations that informed the media and public debate after the September 11 terrorist attacks, I show how the Bush administration and mainstream media in the United States privileged the "clash of civilizations" model, established a binary dualism between Islamic terrorism and civilization, and largely generated war fever and retaliatory feelings and discourses that called for and supported a form of military intervention. I argue that such one-dimensional militarism could arguably make the current crisis worse, rather than advance more intelligent responses to the problem of global terrorism. Thus, while the media in a democracy should critically debate urgent questions facing the nation, in the terror crisis the mainstream U.S. corporate media, especially television, promoted war fever and military solutions to the problem of global terrorism.

2

❖

9/11, the Media, and War Fever

September 11 began in the East Coast of the United States as an ordinary fall day, with fair weather and no dramatic headlines in the daily papers. My hometown *Los Angeles Times* featured a story, "Stock Markets around the World Take a Beating," discussing the collapse of European stock markets to "their lowest values in recent years," the continued slumping in the U.S. market, and the "atmosphere of gloom darkening the world economic outlook." An accompanying story headlined, "GOP's Latest Tax Plan Hints at Scramble to Fix Economy," describing Bush's planned new tax break for the rich and the Democratic Party's opposition to the cuts. On page 11, a headline read, "Economists Warn against New Tax Cuts," with a subheading reading: "Analysts once hailed such stimulus packages as potent tools. They now label the latest ideas as unworkable."

Meanwhile, President Bush's approval rating was rapidly declining and he appeared to be blocked in carrying through his domestic agenda of giving more tax breaks to the rich, doling out favors to his corporate contributors, and pushing through a hard-right agenda. On September 10, *Newsweek*'s September 17 edition was released on the newsstands and contained articles such as "The Accidental President" and "How History Will Judge the Court," raising questions concerning Bush's legitimacy in regard to the Florida recount wars and the highly controversial U.S. Supreme Court decision to stop the counting of votes and declare Bush president.[1] Hence, on the day of the September 11 terror attacks, the economy was declining, Bush had lost control of the Congress and the political agenda, and questions were beginning to be raised about his legitimacy and competency to be president.

On September 11 Bush was in Florida scheduled for a photo-op reading session with schoolchildren and arriving around 9:00 A.M., just after the first bomb hit the New York World Trade Center. Bush spontaneously remarked to the press that there must have been "one awfully bad pilot" and went on with the event. Shortly after the second World Trade Center tower was hit at 9:03 A.M., Bush's Chief of Staff

Andrew Card whispered in his ear the news and Bush nodded slightly and kept listening to the children read, commenting: "Really good readers, whew. This must be the sixth grade." But as he got up some minutes later to be briefed by his staff, Bush appeared agitated, his eyes swiftly darted from left to right, and a strange nervous look shot across his face. Some minutes later, he returned to read a hastily written statement stating the obvious: "Today we've had a national tragedy," he said, as if announcing a weather report. But then he got more than just the delivery wrong. "I have spoken to the vice president, to the governor of New York, to the director of the FBI and have ordered . . . a full-scale investigation to hunt down and to find those folks who committed this act." Critics found Bush's announcement "jarring" and the reference to the terrorists as "folks" extremely weird.

Throughout the day of September 11, one of the most dramatic media spectacles in history was unfolding as TV cameras and commentators throughout the world focused on downtown New York. Shocking footage showed the second tower being hit by a plane that appeared to penetrate right through the building, exploding into a ball of flames. Subsequent images displayed wounded and dazed people fleeing from the tower, ashes and debris flying through the air, reams of sooty office paper littering the streets, and a panic scene that would intensify as the towers continued to burn and eventually collapse, creating another great spectacle and heartwrenching disaster.

Pictures of a third airplane hitting the Pentagon at 9:45 A.M. brought the spectacle to a new level of seriousness and danger. If the World Trade Center represented global capital, the Pentagon symbolized U.S. imperial military power. It seemed impossible that the U.S.'s military fortress could be penetrated and hit, and now viewers all over the world wondered what would be next. Apparently the United States, the world's major superpower, was vulnerable to domestic attacks on a scale previously unimagined. The spectacle of terror dominated world media and traumatized U.S. citizens more than any previous media spectacle in recent memory.[2]

Shortly afterward, reports appeared that a fourth plane had been hijacked and around 10:10 A.M. officials confirmed that a United Airlines flight from Newark to San Francisco had crashed in Shanksville, Pennsylvania. Speculation proliferated that the flight may have been headed toward Washington, D.C., with the White House as its target. Relatives of passengers on the flight, who had cell-phoned passengers on the fourth flight and told of the other hijackings, indicated that a group of passengers was planning to attack the hijackers after they were informed of the previous assaults on buildings. One doomed passenger's phrase, "Let's roll!" became an anthem of U.S. resistance to terrorism.

After his strange performance in Florida, Bush hurried off to his Air Force One plane that flew his entourage to a military base in Louisiana, where he arrived around 11:45 A.M. When Bush entered the base commander's office, reporters described him as looking "grim" with "red-rimmed eyes." After a telephone call to Cheney, Bush briefly appeared before reporters, declaring, "Freedom itself was attacked this morning by a faceless coward," replicating a term Ronald Reagan frequently used to describe terrorism and thus inaugurating a debate over who was and wasn't a coward. Shortly thereafter, Bush again briefly appeared on television and for one eyewitness, "It was not a reassuring picture. He spoke haltingly, mispronouncing several words as he looked down at his notes." Another wrote, "He looked nervous, and the tape of the appearance was jumpy and grainy. 'It was not our best moment,' one administration official conceded."[3]

Shortly after 1:30 P.M., Bush took off again for the U.S. Strategic Command headquarters at the Offutt Air Force Base outside Omaha, Nebraska. Meanwhile, as Bush flew around the U.S., there was chaos in Washington with rumors of attacks on the White House, Congress, and additional government buildings. Cheney, Laura Bush, and others were taken out of the White House, and panicked government employees and citizens created traffic gridlock in the nation's capital. No official spokesperson appeared to calm the nation or explain what was happening. When Karen Hughes, Bush's "communications director," appeared mid-afternoon at the FBI building to say that everything was under control and that the government was "functioning," the absence of higher Bush administration officials speaking to the public belied the spinmistress's declaration, leading to criticism that the Bush administration was not effectively communicating to the public.

Bush's behavior so far had been unsettling, giving rise to questions concerning his competency and ability to govern. Why hadn't Bush or his security team immediately perceived the dangers of a terrorist attack and ordered airplanes into the sky to deal with the emergency? Why, if Bush had been informed of an attack on the World Trade Center before his Florida school-reading photo opportunity, did he decide to go along with the exercise? Even stranger, why, after being informed of the second attack, did Bush continue to sit for at least six minutes listening to the schoolchildren reading and making small talk before conferring with his staff concerning what had been happening? And why weren't airplanes ordered in the sky to patrol Washington after the first or at least the second World Trade Center attack, an obvious protective measure that could have protected the Pentagon and would have been the obvious response?[4]

There is no doubt that Bush's behavior was extremely weird during September 11. But it could be explained by the notion that he is primarily a puppet who just performs what his handlers script him to say, and that he was not involved in initial U.S. government discussions and responses to the terror attacks because he is out of the circuit anyway in key discussions of policy. Moreover, sitting in front of schoolchildren and listening is Bush's usual role, and flawed memory of past events is typical of Bush in general. It is harder to explain, however, why the U.S. military did not send up planes earlier and defend the Pentagon, since the FAA reportedly received information around 8:20 A.M. that a plane had been hijacked and there was an hour between the hit on the first World Trade Center tower and the Pentagon, surely enough time to get planes in the air over Washington. It was also odd that the first planes scrambled were from Otis Air National Guard Base in Cape Cod and Langley Air Force Base, which is over 120 miles from Washington, whereas the planes at

Andrews Air Force Base, the center of Washington air defense and a mere ten miles from the Pentagon, did not go up until after the Pentagon was hit. If this was negligence, it is criminal, but so far there has been no investigation of U.S. military failures on September 11 or disciplining of those responsible for allowing an attack on the Pentagon and failing to deploy U.S. air defenses in a timely fashion.

In any case, the U.S. government and Bush administration seemed to have lost control on September 11. While New York Mayor Rudy Giuliani was visible the entire day grappling with the September 11 attack, key figures in the Bush administration were not visible. How, indeed, could the U.S. government allow such a dastardly attack to take place on U.S. soil? While the Bush administration maintained a very low profile on September 11, it was television that reigned during the day of September 11, unfolding an increasingly bizarre and disturbing spectacle of terror, of a magnitude never seen before, unfolding live to a global audience.

THE TERROR SPECTACLE

Over the past decades, terrorists have constructed spectacles of terror to promote their causes, attack their adversaries, and gain worldwide publicity and attention. There had been many major terror spectacles before, both in the U.S. and elsewhere. Hijacking of airplanes had been a standard terrorist activity, but the ante was significantly upped when in 1970 the Popular Front for the Liberation of Palestine hijacked three Western jetliners. The group forced the jets to land in the Jordanian desert and then blew up the planes in an incident known as "Black September," which was the topic of a Hollywood film. In 1972, Palestinian gunmen from the same movement stunned the world when they took Israeli athletes hostage at the Munich Olympic Games, producing another media spectacle turned into an Academy Award–winning documentary film.

In 1975, an Organization for Petroleum Exporting Countries (OPEC) meeting was disrupted in Vienna, Austria, when a terrorist group led by the notorious Carlos the Jackal entered, killing three people and wounding several others in a chaotic shootout. Americans were targeted in a 1983 attack in Beirut, Lebanon, in which 243 U.S. servicemen were killed in a truck bombing orchestrated by Shiite Muslim suicide bombers, leading the U.S. to withdraw its troops from Lebanon. In 1985 U.S. tourists were victims of Palestinians who seized the cruise ship *Achille Lauro,* when sixty-nine-year-old Leon Klinghoffer, a crippled Jewish American, was killed and his body and wheelchair were thrown overboard.

In 1993, the World Trade Center was bombed in New York by Islamist terrorists linked to Osama bin Laden, providing a preview of the more spectacular September 11 aggression. An American-born terrorist, Timothy McVeigh, bombed the Alfred P. Murrah Federal Building in Oklahoma City, killing 168 and wounding more than 500. And the bin Laden group had assaulted U.S. embassies in Africa in 1998 and a U.S. destroyer harbored in Yemen in 2000. Terror spectacle is thus part of the game of terrorism, and the bin Laden group had systematically used the spectacle of terror to promote its agenda. But the September 11 assaults were the most deadly strike on U.S. targets in its history and the first foreign attack on its mainland territory since the war of 1812.

Extravagant terrorist acts are thus orchestrated in part as media spectacles to gain worldwide attention, dramatize the issues of the terrorist groups involved, and achieve specific political objectives. Previous Al Qaeda strikes against the U.S. hit a range of targets to try to demonstrate that the U.S. was weak and vulnerable to terrorism. The earlier 1993 World Trade Center bombing in New York, the embassy assaults in Kenya and Tanzania in 1998, and the attack on the *USS Cole* in 2000 combined surprise with detailed planning and coordination in well-orchestrated, high-concept terror spectacles.

Terrorism thus works by using dramatic media spectacle to catch attention, hoping thereby to spread further terror and anxiety. The September 11 terror spectacle looked like a disaster film, leading Hollywood director Robert Altman to chide his industry for producing cinematic extravaganzas that could provide models of attack. Was *Independence Day* (1996) the template for 9/11 in which Los Angeles and New York were attacked by aliens and the White House was destroyed? September 11 indeed had resonances of *The Towering Inferno* (1975), which depicted a high-rise building catching on fire, burning, and collapsing, or even *Earthquake* (1975), which depicted the collapse of entire urban environments. For these two Hollywood disaster films, however, the calamity emerged from within the system in the case of the first, and from nature itself in the second. In the September 11 terror spectacle, by contrast, the villains were foreign terrorists obviously committed to wreaking maximum destruction on the United States and it was not certain how the drama would end or if order would be restored in a "happy ending."

The novelty of the September 11 terror acts resulted from the combination of airplane hijacking and the use of airplanes to crash into buildings in order to disrupt and wound urban and economic life. The targets were partly symbolic, representing global capital and American military power, and partly material, intending to disrupt the airline industry, the businesses centered in downtown New York, and perhaps the global economy itself through potentially dramatic downturns of the world's largest stock market and primary financial center. Indeed, as a response to the drama of the terror spectacle, an unparalleled shutdown occurred in New York, Washington, and other major cities throughout the United States, with government and businesses closing up for the day and the airline system canceling all flights. Wall Street and the stock market were shut down for days, baseball and entertainment events were postponed, Disneyland and Disney World were closed, McDonald's locked up its regional offices, and most major U.S. cities became eerily quiet.[5]

Thus, the September 11 terror spectacle was partly a symbolic event, traumatizing many who experienced it live, or on television, and sending out a message that the U.S. was vulnerable to terror attack. The terror spectacle made clear that terrorists could create great harm and that anyone at anytime could be subject to a violent terror attack. The suffering, fear, and death that many people endure on a daily basis in violent and insecure situations in other parts of the world was brought home to U.S. citizens. Suddenly, the vulnerability and anxiety suffered by many people throughout the world were also deeply experienced by U.S. citizens, in some cases for the first time. The terror attacks thus had material effects, attempting to harm the U.S. and global economy, and psychic effects, traumatizing a nation with fear. The spectacle of terror was broadcast throughout the global village, with the whole world watching the terror assault and New York's attempts to cope with the attacks.[6]

The live television broadcasting brought a "you are there" drama to the September 11 spectacle. The images of the planes striking the World Trade Center, the buildings bursting into flames, individuals jumping out of the window in a desperate attempt to survive the inferno, and the collapse of the towers and subsequent chaos provided unforgettable images that viewers would not soon forget. The drama continued throughout the day with survivors being pulled from the rubble, and the poignant search for bodies and attempts to deal with the attack produced resonant iconic images seared deeply into spectators' memories. Many people who witnessed the event suffered nightmares and psychological trauma. For those who viewed it intensely, the spectacle provided a powerful set of images that would continue to resonate for years to come, much as the footage of the Kennedy assassination, iconic photographs of Vietnam, the 1986 explosion of the space shuttle *Challenger,* or the death of Princess Diana and young JFK Jr. in the 1990s provided unforgettable imagery.

The September 11 terror attacks in New York were claimed to be "the most documented event in history" in a May 2002 HBO film *In Memoriam,* which itself provided a collage of images assembled from professional news crews, documentary filmmakers, and amateur videographers and photographers who in some cases risked their lives to document the event. As with other major media spectacles, the September 11 events took over TV programming for the next three days without commercial break as the major television networks focused on the attack and its aftermath.[7]

For some years, a growing number of "expert consultants" have been hired by television networks to explain complex events to the public. Hence, on September 11 political and military experts began appearing to try to clarify the event and delineate appropriate U.S. responses. The military consultants hired by the networks had close connections to the Pentagon and usually would express the Pentagon's point of view and spin of the day, making them more propaganda conduits for the military than independent analysts. Political commentators and U.S. government representatives, like Senator John McCain (R-Az.), Henry Kissinger, Lawrence Eagleburger, James Baker, Jeane Kirkpatrick, and other longtime advocates of the military-industrial complex who were trotted out before the cameras on September 11, immediately described the attacks as an "act of war" and called for military retaliation, a line that would continue to be dominant for days to come.

For instance, Senator McCain denounced the attacks as "an act of war" and demanded direct military retaliation. Senator John Kerry (D-Mass.) claimed that he knew instantly it was Osama bin Laden and his group and that they should be punished. Former Secretary of State Lawrence Eagleburger, a longtime Kissinger associate who exemplified the "iron triangle" of officials going from government to the military and private sector to enrich themselves, came blustering onto CNN with a demand that the United States immediately go after "terrorists and the governments that support them," starting with bin Laden and Afghanistan. He startled CNN anchor Judy Woodruff when he huffed that there was no need for evidence because "we know who these people are" and we should just go "and kill some of them," eventually suggesting the use of nuclear weapons.

For hawkish pundits, the terror attacks thus required an instant military response and dramatic expansion of the U.S. military. Many of these hawks were former government officials, like Kissinger, Eagleburger, and Baker, who were currently tied into the defense industries, guaranteeing that their punditry would be paid for by large profits for the military-industrial complex that they were part of. Indeed, the Bush family, James Baker, and other advocates of large-scale military retribution were connected with the Carlyle Fund, one of the largest investors in military industries in the world. Consequently, these advocates of war stood to profit immensely from sustained military activity, an embarrassment rarely mentioned on television or the mainstream press but widely discussed in alternative media and the Internet.[8]

The network anchors as well framed the event as a military attack, with Peter Jennings of ABC stating, "The response is going to have to be massive if it is to be effective." Yet, on the whole, Jennings, like Dan Rather at CBS, cautioned that until there was firm evidence concerning who was responsible for the attack, there should be no calls for specific retaliation. NBC, which is owned by General Electric, the largest U.S. military corporation, as usual promoted military action and its talk shows were populated by commentators who invariably urged immediate military retribution.

Late in the afternoon of September 11, Bush administration officials leaked to the TV networks that they had evidence that the Osama bin Laden group was responsible, and many heard for the first time of his Al Qaeda organization and its previous attacks on the United States. Senator Orin Hatch (R-Utah) stated that he had been informed that U.S. intelligence had intercepted communication of members of the bin Laden group indicating that they had hit their target. By evening, there were leaks that suspected hijackers who were on the airplanes had connections with the bin Laden group.

CNN's reporting of the U.S. terror attacks was interrupted about 6:00 P.M. EST with live images via a video telephone with correspondent Nik Robertson in Kabul. Robertson reported that Kabul was under attack and the CNN pictures showed bombs exploding, traces of antiaircraft fire, and an apparent attack on the Afghan capital. The images of Kabul being bombed with artillery and missiles, its fuel depot ablaze, explosions erupting, and the traces of munitions and antiaircraft defenses shooting through the air added a level of intense drama and transformed the events of the day into a global spectacle. The night-camera images of war in a distant Middle Eastern country were eerily reminiscent of the Gulf War and it appeared that a global war was yet again erupting live on television.

The world appeared to be cascading into a state of chaos as sudden events brought the possibility of global war into everyday life. In fact, the CNN drama in Afghanistan was merely a bombardment of Kabul by Northern Alliance troops who were enraged that their leader Ahmad Masoud had been assassinated the previous day, and so they hit a Taliban arms depot with missiles shot from helicopters. Yet the CNN montage provided an uncanny anticipation of the Terror War that was soon to explode in Afghanistan and that will be the subject of coming chapters.

Indeed, it was through these very broadcasts that many heard for the first time of the Taliban regime that was hosting bin Laden and Al Qaeda. The Taliban held a news conference, broadcast throughout the global village, claiming that they were "peaceful," that bin Laden was not responsible for the terror acts, and that he was a respected guest in their country who was doing no harm to anyone. This, of course, would turn out to be seriously false and the Taliban would pay heavily for their lies and connections to bin Laden.

As the day went on, TV "experts" began delineating connections between the Taliban and bin Laden. Major political figures, such as former UN diplomats, cabinet members of the Clinton administration like Bill Richardson and Richard Holbrooke, and conservatives, were holding the Taliban responsible for hosting bin Laden and enabling him to organize his terrorist networks and carry out attacks. Thus, when George W. Bush finally made an address to the country at 8:30 P.M., he said that both the terrorists and any country that supported them would be held responsible, setting up the war against the Taliban in Afghanistan that would unfold some weeks later.

Whereas Bush would be praised for his handling of the crisis after the terror spectacle, in fact his performance was hardly reassuring on September 11. After being informed of the second terror attack while reading with schoolchildren in Florida after 9:00 A.M., he continued his activity as if nothing untoward were happening. But soon after, he looked frightened and unsure as his aides informed him of the magnitude of the event, and then after reading a short statement, he disappeared, flying from one military base to another before returning to Washington. As he began his speech, Bush appeared nervous, opening with an abrupt "Good evening" and jerking his hands in an inappropriate gesture until he began reading his speech. The speech set up the dichotomy between good and evil that would dominate Bush's discourse, as I examine in detail in the next section. Bush claimed that the U.S. was attacked "because we are a beacon of freedom and opportunity," establishing a highly unconvincing causal chain. He repeated the term "evil" five times, obviously attempting to fix the concept as the defining trope for terrorism, a discourse that he would continue to exploit in the months to come. Repeating his father's phrase after the Iraqi invasion of Kuwait in 1990, he stated: "Terrorism against our nation will not stand," signaling a military response and a coming epoch of Terror War.

CONCEPTUALIZING THE EVENT: SEPTEMBER 11 AND THE DOMINANT MEDIA FRAMES

To help generate and sustain widespread public desire for military intervention, over the next few days the networks played segment after segment detailing the harm done to victims of the bombing. They kept their cameras aimed at "Ground Zero" to document the damage, destruction, and drama of discovery of dead bodies. Moreover, they constructed report after report on the evil of bin Laden and the Al Qaeda terrorists who had allegedly committed the atrocities. To continue the sense of drama and urgency, and to ensure that viewers kept tuned into the story and their channels, the television cable news networks all added "crawlers" to the bottom of their screens, providing endlessly repeating bulletins of the latest news highlighting the terrorist attack and its consequences. It was amazing, in fact, how quickly the media corporations produced frames for the event, constructed it as it was going on, and generated innovative and striking visuals and graphics to capture viewer attention. Already on September 11, CNN constructed a four-tier graphic presentation with a capitalized and blazing "Breaking News" title on the top of their screen, followed by a graphic describing the "Attack on America," or whatever slogan was being used to construct the event. Next, a title described what was being currently portrayed in the visuals flashed across the screen, with the crawlers scrolling the headlines along the bottom of the screen.

In a remarkable presentation of the statement by Israeli Prime Minister Ariel Sharon on September 11, for instance, the visuals were split between Sharon's picture in Tel Aviv, images of the World Trade Center bomb site, and the graphics summarizing Sharon's talk, with headlines crawling along the bottom of the screen. While the public obviously had no idea what was happening to the U.S., and as Bush's presidential plane frantically flew around the country and Vice President Dick Cheney was carried off to an "undisclosed location" to hide, the TV networks were fully in control with frames, discourses, and explanations of the momentous events. It was a tremendous formal accomplishment for the hi-tech, flashy visual production capabilities of the networks, although one could question the intelligence of the interpretations or the calls for military retribution being fervently espoused without contradiction.

September 11 was thus a genuine world historical event, a media spectacle that "turned the world upside down," dominating the global media for days on end. Such events demand conceptualization and interpretation. Therefore, concurrent with the media construction of the event, there was also the attempt to find language with which to present and describe the terror attacks, analysis to make sense of what had happened, and, in this case, an articulation and defense of a political response to retaliate against the perpetrators.

The dominant response on U.S. television was to interpret the terror attacks as an "act of war" and a "second Pearl Harbor," requiring military retaliation. On the day of the terrorist attacks upon the World Trade Center and Pentagon, the U.S. TV networks brought out an array of national security intellectuals, usually ranging from the right to the far right, to conceptualize and explain the horrific events of September 11. The Fox network presented former UN Ambassador and Reagan administration apologist Jeane Kirkpatrick, who rolled out a simplified version of Huntington's clash of civilizations, arguing that we were at war with Islam and should defend the West. Kirkpatrick was the most discredited intellectual of her generation, legitimizing the Reagan administration's alliances with unsavory fascists and terrorists as necessary to beat Soviet totalitarianism. Her 1980s propaganda line was premised on a distinction between fascism and communist totalitarianism. Kirkpatrick argued that alliances with authoritarian or right-wing terrorist organizations or states were defensible since these regimes were either open to reform efforts or historically undermined themselves and so disappeared. Soviet totalitarianism, by contrast, Kirkpatrick thought should be resolutely opposed since a communist regime had never collapsed or been overthrown, and thus communism was to be taken as an intractable and dangerous foe that had to be fought to the death with any means necessary. Of course, the Soviet Union collapsed in the early 1990s, along with its empire, and although Kirkpatrick was totally discredited, she was awarded a professorship at Georgetown and allowed to continue to reproduce her crackpot views.

On the afternoon of September 11, Ariel Sharon, leader of Israel and himself implicated in war crimes in Sabra and Shatila in Lebanon in 1982, came on television to convey his regret, condolences, and assurance of Israel's support in the war on terror. Sharon called for a coalition against terrorist networks, which would contrast the civilized world with terrorism, representing the Good versus Evil, "humanity" versus "the bloodthirsty," and "the free world" against "the forces of darkness," who he saw as trying to destroy "freedom" and our "way of life."

Curiously, the Bush administration would take up the same tropes with Bush attacking the "evil" of the terrorists, using the word repeatedly in his televised response to terror assaults. Bush continued to portray the conflict as a war between good and evil in which the U.S. was going to "eradicate evil from the world," "to smoke out and pursue . . . evil doers, those barbaric people." The semantically insensitive and dyslexic Bush administration also used cowboy metaphors, calling for bin Laden "dead or alive," and he described the campaign as a "crusade" until he was advised that this term carried offensive historical baggage of earlier wars between Christians and Muslims. Similarly, the Pentagon at first named the war against terror "Operation Infinite Justice," until they were advised that only God could dispense "infinite justice" and that Americans and others might be troubled about a war expanding to infinity.

Disturbingly, in mentioning the goals of the impending war, Bush never used the term "democracy," and the new name for the campaign became "Operation Endur-ing Freedom." The Bush administration's mantra was that the war against terrorism is being fought for "freedom." But we know from the history of political theory and history that freedom must be paired with equality or things like justice, rights, or democracy to provide adequate political theory and legitimization for political action. Indeed, it has arguably been the contempt for democracy and self-autonomy that has characterized U.S. foreign policy in the Middle East for the past decades, which is a prime reason why groups and individuals in the area passionately hate the United States (see Ali 2001; Chomsky 2001; and Vidal 2002).

In the days following September 11, the Bush administration promised a "white paper" by September 18 outlining the evidence that it was indeed the Osama bin Laden group that had committed the terror attacks, and Britain did in fact release such a paper. The U.S., however, never distributed its own evidence, leading many in the Muslim world and beyond to doubt whether it was certain that bin Laden was actually responsible for the crimes. Since the Bush administration was releasing information on a daily basis that links existed between the hijackers and bin Laden, there was no need for a formal demonstration of evidence of bin Laden's guilt, as the public was ready to believe that Al Qaeda was the perpetrator and was demand-ing revenge in passionate tones.[9]

Warmongering and pressures for immediate retaliation were fanned by the TV networks, especially the Fox and the NBC cable networks, on talk radio, and in right-wing Internet sites. On September 13, Fox television presented a symptomatic segment of *The O'Reilly Factor,* featuring the ignorantly demagogic Bill O'Reilly, who provides an appropriate media mouthpiece for the arrogance and demagoguery of the Bush administration. O'Reilly had as his guests the discredited Jeane Kirkpat-rick and Newt Gingrich, the disgraced leader of the ultraright takeover of Congress who had been forced to resign for never-specified reasons. O'Reilly bragged how he had been "forced" to earlier throw off an Arab-American guest from his show because the guest was failing to exhibit "rationality," a trait in fact lacking in O'Reilly himself. The major thrust of the discourse, which characterized both the Fox position and the right-wing take on the terror attacks, was to blame Bill Clinton for the lapses in security that had led to the attacks.

Later, it would come out that the Clinton administration had focused major efforts of the intelligence establishment, U.S. Justice Department, and military on bin Laden and made fighting terrorism a national security priority. The Bush administration, by contrast, allegedly told the FBI to lay off the bin Ladens and Saudis and cut back budgets for antiterrorism units while decentering focus to other issues.[10] Nonetheless, caller after caller to the O'Reilly show was trashing Clinton, and O'Reilly himself pushed this line. Moreover, he was arguing that Saddam Hus-sein and Iraq were heavily involved in the attack, a point with which both Gingrich and Kirkpatrick agreed, adding that it was a mistake to leave Hussein in power after the Gulf War and that he needed to be taken out immediately. Kirkpatrick insisted that Iraq had "a major role" in the attack and Gingrich in turn also urged an attack on Iraq.

O'Reilly also shot from the hip and proffered vicious comments about guests or targets of his vitriol, such as his attack against an Arab American professor who he accused of supporting Palestinian terrorist organizations and whom he insulted with a chilling parting shot that if he were in the CIA, "I'd follow you wherever you went."[11] There was probably no one on television as ignorant, demagogic, bombastic, aggressive, and arrogant as Bill O'Reilly, unless it was *The O'Reilly Factor*'s viewers, who called in with their "opinions," which were often stunningly uninformed, belligerent, and sometimes bloodthirsty. The Fox Network reveled in this pseudo-populism. Fox News was run for Australian right-wing media baron Rupert Murdoch by Roger Ailes, a former Nixon administration official known for his dirty tricks, ultraright political views, and crude demeanor and behavior. Grossly overweight, ill-mannered, and highly antagonistic, Ailes was becoming infamous for the nasty e-mails he would send out to critics. Fox, under his "leadership," had become a propaganda ministry for the Bush administration, the right wing, and militarism. For years, it had spearheaded the most vicious attacks against a sitting president in history, continued to blame Bill Clinton for every problem in the world, and was a willing conduit and defender for whatever policies and lines of the day the Bush administration was pushing.

Meanwhile, on September 13, Bush administration handlers allowed Bush to face the press for the first time and the result was not encouraging. After soundbiting the line of the day, Bush blubbered, tears welling in his eyes: "I'm a loving guy, but I'm also a guy who has a job to do and I'm going to do it." This, of course, was blood-curdling because it signaled that major mayhem was going to be unleashed and Bush was going to front for the warmongers.

The next few days, Bush went to carefully staged events, visiting victims of the Pentagon bombing and then going to a memorial service in the Washington Cathedral attended by all the living presidents (with the exception of Ronald Reagan, who was in poor health). In a visit to New York's "Ground Zero" at the World Trade Center site on September 14, Bush got off to a slow start saying that "the nation was on bended knee" in honor of the tragedy of September 11. This was a rather inappropriate metaphor for the ultramasculine hardhats working ferociously to save lives (Bush was referring to church services all around the country, but the term "on bended knee" has other, less religious, connotations). After this gaffe, Bush then connected with the crowd when, after shouts that they couldn't hear his precanned speech, he upped his volume and shouted out determination to get the rats who caused the carnage all around him. The crowd erupted with chants of "USA! USA!" and Bush managed to look good on television.

After resting up for a few days, in his speech to Congress on September 20 declaring his war against terrorism, Bush described the conflict as a war between freedom and fear. The coming Terror War was, he explained, a conflict between "those governed by fear" who "want to destroy our wealth and freedoms" and those on the side of freedom. Bush insisted that "you're either with us, or you're with the terrorists," and laid down a series of non-negotiable demands to the Taliban while Congress wildly applauded. Bush's popularity soared with a country craving blood revenge and the head of Osama bin Laden. Moreover, proclaiming what his administration and commentators would describe as "the Bush doctrine," Bush also asserted that his administration held accountable those nations who supported terrorism—a position that could nurture and legitimate military interventions for years to come.

What was not noted was that the dominant right-wing and Bush administration discourses, like those of bin Laden and radical Islamists, are fundamentally Manichean, positing a binary opposition between Good and Evil, Us and Them, civilization and barbarism. It is assumed by both sides that "we" are the good, and "they" are the wicked, an assertion that Bush made in his incessant assurance that the "evildoers" of the "evil deeds" will be punished, and that the "Evil One" will be brought to justice, implicitly equating bin Laden with Satan himself.

Such hyperbolic rhetoric is a salient example of Bushspeak that communicates through codes to specific audiences, in this case domestic Christian right-wing groups that are the preferred subjects of Bush's discourse. But demonizing terms for bin Laden both elevate his status in the Arab world as a superhero who stands up to the West, and anger those who feel such discourse is insulting. Moreover, the trouble with the discourse of "evil" is that it is polarizing, totalizing, and absolutistic, allowing no ambiguities or contradictions. It assumes a binary logic in which "we" are the forces of goodness and "they" are the forces of darkness. The discourse of evil is also cosmological and apocalyptic, evoking a cataclysmic war with cosmic stakes. On this perspective, evil cannot be just attacked and eliminated one piece at a time, through incremental steps, but it must be totally defeated and eradicated from the earth if good is to reign. This discourse of evil raises the stakes of violence and conflict, and it nurtures more apocalyptic and catastrophic politics, fueling future cycles of hatred, violence, and wars.

The very term "evil" is highly archaic and has a mystifying, supernatural quality that exaggerates the power of the perpetrator so designated. "Good" and "evil" are not properly political categories, but are moral ones. The "political" in a democratic context involves the negotiation of difference, complexity, and multiplicity, requiring debate, mutual understanding, and consensus. Moral categories of good and evil are more absolutistic and binary, reducing politics to simple oppositions between Us and Them and moral crusades against "the other."

Deploying the discourse of evil also makes bin Laden and Al Qaeda much more irrational than they in fact are and makes it harder to understand and to defeat them. The bin Laden network is not just a group of fanatic terrorists, but a well-financed and organized network including many mosques, madrassas and religious schools, and organizations throughout the world. It has its financial institutions, business fronts, charity and religious institutions, and tacit and operative supporters. To defeat the bin Laden network thus requires cultivating an entire global network in a multilateral coalition and activity across the legal, judicial, political, military, ideological, and pedagogical fronts, a task not aided by extreme moral rhetoric and the discourse of "evil."

Personalizing the problem as bin Laden and demonizing him as evil thus deflects attention from the global network of Jihadism and the many dimensions of the struggle. It exaggerates the importance of military action as a violent and retaliatory tool of the destruction of evil and decenters the importance of dialogue with allies and the Muslim world, coalition-building, and using the instruments of global finance, law, and politics to isolate and overcome the forces of global terrorism.

It is especially offensive and hypocritical that George W. Bush deploys "evil" as his favorite word for terrorism as it implies that he himself is "good," whereas scrutiny of his biography indicates that Bush Junior is hardly a paragon of virtue. After years of frat boy ribaldry at Yale, Bush got his father to pull strings so he would not have to go to Vietnam and he got into the Texas National Guard Air Reserves. During his lost years in the 1970s, he reportedly went AWOL for a year from National Guard duty, was a heavy alcohol and drug abuser, and a ne'er-do-well failure who finally decided to put together an oil company when he was already well into his thirties. Investors reportedly included the bin Laden family and other unsavory types, and his initial company, Arbusto, went bust and was taken over by Harken Energy, with family friends again jumping in to bail young Bush out. Harken received a lucrative Bahrain oil contract in part as a result of Bush family connections, and the Harken stock went up. But as a member of the board of directors, Bush Junior knew that declining profit figures for the previous quarter, about to be released, would depress the value of the stock, so George W. unloaded his stock in what some see as an illegal insider trading dump. Moreover, Bush failed to register his questionable sale with the SEC, although later a paper was produced indicating that he had eventually recorded the sale some eight months after he dumped his stock (it helped that his father was president when the favored son should have been investigated for his questionable business dealings).[12]

With the money made from his Harken disinvestiture, George W. invested in the Texas Rangers baseball team and was made general manager when some other Texas good old boys put up the money. Using a public bond issue that he pushed upon voters to finance construction of a new Rangers stadium, the stock value of the baseball team went up. Once again, Bush sold out for a hefty profit and then ran as governor of Texas, despite no political experience and a shaky business history. His two terms in office wrecked the state economy as it went from surplus to deficit thanks to a tax bill that gave favors to the wealthiest and sweetheart deals and deregulation bonanzas to his biggest campaign contributors, which helped make Texas the site of the most toxic environmental pollution and outrageous corporate skullduggery in the country. Bush provided questionable favors to a nursing home corporation that faced state investigation and strong support for the wheelin' and dealin' Enron Company, one of the biggest financial contributors to Bush's campaigns and, as we shall see, a corporation that underwent the biggest collapse of any U.S. company in history under highly questionable circumstances.

Promising to do for the United States and global economy and polity what he did for Texas, Bush had the gall to run for president, stealing the 2000 election with the help of the Bush family gang in Florida and its consigliere James Baker (Kellner 2001), as well as the treason of Supreme Court "justices," whom fabled prosecutor Vincent Bugliosi (2000) dubbed the "felonious five." During his first 100 days in office, Bush gave his biggest corporate contributors unparalleled tax and regulatory breaks, which threaten to push through the most scandalous transfer of wealth from poor to rich since the Reagan-Bush regimes and to seriously weaken the U.S. and global economy. Bush also tried to push through a hard-right social agenda. After the Democrats seized control of the domestic agenda in late May 2001 with the defection of Republican Senator Jim Jeffords, Bush's hard-right agenda seemed sidetracked. But the September 11 attacks strengthened his hand and enabled his cronies to carry through even more radical assaults on civil liberties and on the free and open society, as well as to attempt more federal theft through the mechanism of an economic "stimulus" package. Such stimulus, as proposed by the Bush administration, would constitute even greater corporate giveaways and tax breaks to the rich and his biggest contributors.[13]

George W. Bush was thus hardly someone who could use the discourse of "evil" with impunity, and all the denial in the world and bombing of Afghanistan cannot purge him of a lifetime of sleaze, corruption, and hypocrisy. Every time Bush or a member of the Bush administration uses the term "evil," one should put out the crap detector and challenge the speaker to defend what is good about George W. Bush's entire life and political record and the domestic and foreign policies of the Bush administration.

Bush continued for months to insist that the bin Laden terrorists "fear" Western freedom and democracy, as if their hatred were motivated by rejection of positive Western values. No doubt some of the terrorists were motivated by anti-Western hatred of U.S. culture, but it was simply a Big Lie to claim that it was Western values and "our way of life" that were the target of the terror attack. Rather, Arab anger concerning the U.S. and the West was primarily a result of U.S. policies, such as excessive support for Israel and reactionary forces like the Saudi monarchy and U.S. interventions in the Middle East.

Not only has Bush made the discourse of "good" and "evil" impossible to use by honorable people, but the Bushspeak dualisms between fear and freedom, barbarism and civilization, and the like can hardly be sustained in empirical and theoretical analysis of the contemporary moment. In fact, there is much fear and poverty in "our" world, just as there is wealth, freedom, and security in the Arab and Islamic worlds—at least for privileged elites. No doubt, freedom, fear, and wealth are distributed in both worlds, so to polarize these categories and to make them the legitimating principles of war is highly irresponsible. And associating oneself with "good" while making one's enemy "evil" is another exercise in binary reductionism, involving the projection of all traits of aggression and wickedness onto the "other" while constituting oneself as good and pure.

It is, of course, theocratic Islamic fundamentalists who themselves engage in similar simplistic binary discourse that they use to legitimate acts of terrorism. For certain Manichean Islamic fundamentalists, the United States is "evil," is the source of all the world's problems, and deserves to be destroyed. Such one-dimensional thought does not distinguish between U.S. policies, people, or institutions while advocating a Jihad, or holy war, to eradicate the American infidel. The terrorist crimes of September 11 appeared to be part of this Jihad and the monstrousness of the actions of killing innocent civilians shows the horrific consequences of totally dehumanizing an "enemy" deemed so "evil" that even innocent members of the group in question deserve to be exterminated.

Many commentators on U.S. television offered similarly one-sided and Manichean accounts of the cause of the September 11 events, blaming their favorite opponents in the current U.S. political spectrum as the source of the terror assaults. For fundamentalist Christian ideologue Jerry Falwell, and with the verbal agreement of Christian Broadcast Network President Pat Robertson, the culpability for this "horror beyond words" fell on liberals, feminists, gays, and the ACLU. Jerry Falwell said, and Pat Robertson agreed, "The abortionists have got to bear some burden for this because God will not be mocked. And when we destroy 40 million little innocent babies, we make God mad. I really believe that the pagans, and the abortionists, and the feminists, and the gays and the lesbians who are actively trying to make that an alternative lifestyle, the ACLU, People for the American Way—all of them who have tried to secularize America—I point the finger in their face and say, 'You helped this happen.'" In fact, this argument is similar to a right-wing Islamic claim that the U.S. is fundamentally corrupt and evil and thus deserves God's wrath, an argument made against Falwell by his critics that forced the fundamentalist fanatic to apologize.[14]

For right-wingers like Gary Aldrich, the "president and founder" of the Patrick Henry Center, it was the liberals who were at fault: "Excuse me if I absent myself from the national political group-hug that's going on. You see, I believe the Liberals are largely responsible for much of what happened Tuesday, and may God forgive them. These people exist in a world that lies beyond the normal standards of decency and civility." Other rightists, like Rush Limbaugh, argued incessantly that it was all Bill Clinton's fault, and election thief manager James Baker (see Kellner 2001) blamed the catastrophe on the 1976 Church report that put limits on the CIA.[15]

On the issue of "what to do," right-wing columnist Ann Coulter declaimed: "We know who the homicidal maniacs are. They are the ones cheering and dancing right now. We should invade their countries, kill their leaders and convert them to Christianity."[16] While Bush was declaring a "crusade" against terrorism and the Pentagon was organizing "Operation Infinite Justice," Bush Administration Deputy Defense Secretary Paul Wolfowitz said the administration's retaliation would be "sustained and broad and effective" and that the United States "will use all our resources. It's not just simply a matter of capturing people and holding them accountable, but removing the sanctuaries, removing the support systems, ending states who sponsor terrorism."

Such all-out war hysteria was the order of the day, and throughout September 11 and its aftermath ideological warhorses like William Bennett came out and urged that the U.S. declare war on Iraq, Iran, Syria, Libya, and whoever else harbored terrorists. On the Canadian Broadcasting Network, former Reagan administration Deputy Secretary of Defense and military commentator Frank Gaffney suggested that the U.S. needed to go after the sponsors of these states as well, such as China and Russia, to the astonishment and derision of the Canadian audience.[17] And right-wing talk radio and the Internet buzzed with talk of dropping nuclear bombs on Afghanistan, exterminating all Muslims, and whatever other fantasy popped into their unhinged heads.

My point is that broadcast television allowed dangerous and arguably deranged zealots to vent and circulate the most aggressive, fanatic, and downright lunatic views, creating a consensus around the need for immediate military action and all-out war. The television networks themselves featured logos such as "War on America," "America's New War," and other inflammatory slogans that assumed that the U.S. was at war and that only a military response was appropriate. I saw few cooler heads on any of the major television networks that repeatedly beat the war drums day after day, without even the relief of commercials for three days straight, driving the country into hysteria and making it certain that there would be a military response and war.

Radio was even more frightening. Not surprisingly, talk radio oozed hatred and hysteria, calling for violence against Arabs and Muslims, demanding nuclear retaliation and global war. As the days went by, even mainstream radio news became hyperdramatic, replete with music, patriotic gore, and wall-to-wall terror hysteria and war propaganda. National Public Radio, Pacifica, and some discussion programs attempted rational discussion and debate, but on the whole radio was all propaganda, all the time.

There is no question concerning the depth of emotion and horror with which the nation experienced the first serious assault on U.S. mainland territory by its enemies. The constant invocation of analogies to "Pearl Harbor" inevitably elicited a need to strike back and prepare for war. The attack on the World Trade Center and New York City evoked images of assault on the very body of the country, whereas the attack on the Pentagon represented an assault on the country's defense system, showing the vulnerability, previously unperceived, of the U.S. to external attack and terror. It is not surprising that the country should pull together in the face of such a horrific terrorist assault, but the media in a democracy should provide more clarification of the historical background of the event, intelligent discussion of rational and effective responses, and debate what responses would be most appropriate and successful in dealing with the problem of global terrorism.

The media thus served as what Gore Vidal (2002) ironically referred to as "weapons of mass distraction," focusing audiences on the minutiae of the human tragedy involved; the evil of bin Laden, al Qaeda, and terrorism; and the virtues of the U.S., exactly the line that the Bush administration itself was promoting. There was little debate, no investigative reporting or even speculation on the U.S. government's failure to prevent the attacks, and a wave of patriotism and flag-waving in which it would be difficult to raise critical issues. The attacks on New York and Washington were a gaping sore and wound, a lesion in the body politic visible in the around-the-clock focus on "Ground Zero," as the World Trade Center site was referred to, appropriating the term for the epicenter of U.S. nuclear bombing and testing to the New York site. The sensationalistic and melodramatic coverage created fear and hysteria, helping prepare a country to accept whatever the government did in response. Consequently, the constant beating of the war drums on the broadcast media and the unending demands for military retaliation made war inevitable.

A stunning excerpt from Bob Woodward's book *Bush at War* contains the report that Fox News President and former Nixon, Reagan, and Bush advisor Roger Ailes sent the White House a confidential memo urging Bush to act fast and harshly following 9/11. According to a summary by Mike Allen, "CIA's Cash Toppled Taliban," in the November 16 *Washington Post*:

> Roger E. Ailes, a media coach for Bush's father and now chairman of the Fox News Channel, sent a confidential communication to the White House in the weeks after the terrorist attacks. Rove took the Ailes communication to the president.
>
> His back-channel message: "The American public would tolerate waiting and would be patient, but only as long as they were convinced that Bush was using the harshest measures possible," Woodward wrote. He added that Ailes, who has angrily challenged reports that his news channel has a conservative bias, added a warning: "Support would dissipate if the public did not see Bush acting harshly."

Thus not only did Fox News and other media beat the war drums, but in the case of Fox they militated for war! In the case of CNN, when the U.S. began its military intervention in Afghanistan, its President Walter Isaacson stated, "It seems perverse to focus too much on the casualties or hardship in Afghanistan," and sent out a memo telling CNN commentators that when they mention casualties they should also remind the viewers of the horrors of the 9/11 attacks.[18]

WARMONGERING, PATRIOTISM, AND MEDIA PROPAGANDA

The U.S. corporate media continued to fan the war fever and there was an orgy of patriotism such as the country had not seen since World War II. Media frames shifted from "America under Attack" to "America Arising," "America Strikes Back," and "America's New War"—even before any military action was undertaken, as if the media frames were to conjure the military response that eventually followed.

As indicated, during the initial day of attack on September 11 and for the next few weeks, the networks continued to beat the war drums and the mouthpieces of the military-industrial complex continued to shout for military action, with little serious reflection on its consequences visible on the television networks. There was, by contrast, much intelligent discussion on the Internet, showing the dangers of the takeover of broadcasting by corporations who would profit by war and upheaval.

The flag became a dominant icon for television news logos and graphics, as well as a potent advertising device for a wealth of products. TV entertainment shows peppered its programs with flags, as regular series like *The West Wing* and *Law and Order* used computer-generated flags inserted into their dramas to help capture viewer attention and spread the new patriotism. Flags in ads for automobiles, soft drinks, and other products multiplied endlessly. As patriotism swept across the country, advertisers picked up on the vibe with General Motors broadcastings ads to "Keep America Rolling," while Ford Motors insisted that "Ford drives America." The flag and the traditional red, white, and blue provided a bonanza for web designers, as major corporations immediately redesigned their websites to reflect the new patriotism with major U.S. corporations ranging from PepsiCo to Proctor & Gamble, Microsoft, Dell, the Gap, and Ask Jeeves, redesigning their websites in flashy red, white, and blue.

A return to normal was signaled by the comeback of TV entertainment, advertising, and the evening late-night talk shows, after a few days of all-news-all-the-time. But it was not an especially proud moment for American television. CBS anchor Dan Rather, in one of the most embarrassing media performances of his life, blubbered on the *David Letterman Show* that "George W. Bush is my president" and that he would do whatever told—a pathetic collapse of a once-critical and respected journalist. Fox TV and the NBC networks continued to be wall-to-wall propaganda for whatever line the Bush administration was putting out, and CNN became almost totally propagandistic, in a stunning collapse of a respectable news organization into a vehicle of conservative ideology.

The elevation of George W. Bush from intellectually challenged dunce and right-wing stooge to Maximum Leader was stunning. As noted, Bush's popularity had been rapidly declining before September 11 and he had been blocked from pushing through a rightist economic and political agenda that most of the country opposed. Suddenly, however, the media was full of praise for his "decisiveness," resolute leadership, and determination to extract retribution. There was deafening silence on the failure of his administration to prevent the terrorist attacks, the connection of his family to the networks that organized and financed terrorism, and the policies that had enabled the terrorist attacks to take place.

Instead, the networks provided legitimacy for a president that many considered illegitimate, given that he had lost the popular vote in election 2000 by over 500,000 votes and had won Florida and the election primarily because the U.S. Supreme Court stepped in and stopped the recount (see Kellner 2001). The TV network White House correspondents were especially obsequious in commending how Bush was handling the crisis. From the beginning, despite some poor initial Bush performances that I noted, CNN White House correspondent Major Garrett and others had nothing but praise for the president, comparing him to Roosevelt and Churchill and pouring effusive compliments on his every utterance and appearance.

To assure immunity from criticism, the White House made sure that they went after anyone who criticized Bush, the Pentagon, and the Bush administration. After Bill Maher, host of the late-night TV show *Politically Incorrect*, questioned the Bush administration's characterization of the terrorists as "cowards" and suggested that the U.S. military policy of using cruise missiles rather than ground troops was really cowardly, there was a campaign to get Maher fired. White House Press Secretary Ari Fleischer attacked Maher and sent out a chilling warning to the press that they had better "watch what they say, watch what they do."

Indeed, there was fierce retribution against anyone who dared speak out against Bush and his administration. When Peter Jennings of ABC criticized Bush's September 11 erratic flying around the country and clumsy statements, there was a barrage of attacks on him. A columnist for the *Oregon Daily Courier*, Dan Gutherie, claimed that he was fired for criticizing Bush in a column for "hiding in a Nebraska hole" instead of demonstrating leadership on September 11. Likewise, Tom Gutting, editor of the *Texas City Sun*, was fired for criticizing Bush's behavior on the day of the terror attacks. Progressive radio host Peter Werbe also lost his show for criticizing the Bush administration's failure to protect the country against terrorism; the cartoon *Boondocks* was removed from several papers after depicting earlier Republican administrations as allied with bin Laden; and the Clear Channel radio consortium put out a list of 150 songs that it suggested that its over 1000 station radio network not play, including Simon and Garfunkel's "Bridge over Troubled Water." On the academic front, the University of Texas President Larry Faulkner attacked journalism professor and activist Bob Jensen for his criticism of the Bush administration, and Lynne Cheney, cultural warrior and wife of the U.S. vice president, arranged a series of interventions attacking U.S. intellectuals and teachers who criticized the Bush/Pentagon Afghan war policy.[19] Moreover, instead of engaging in serious debate concerning the appropriate response to terrorism, the U.S. broadcasting networks engaged in unrelenting focus on the tragedy of the World Trade Center victims, the evil of the bin Laden network, and the need for military retribution. Criticizing the Bush administration was taboo and would continue to be throughout the Afghanistan Terror War.

The result was an appalling performance by the mainstream U.S. media during a time that should have been marked by a profound national debate over the proper response to the terrorist threat, as was being conducted daily on the Internet and in some of the foreign press and media. The unrelenting war hysteria on the television networks, and their utter failure to produce anything near a coherent analysis of what happened on September 11 and what would constitute a reasonable response to the terrorist attacks, put on display the frightening consequences of allowing corporate media institutions to hire ideologically compliant news teams who have no competency to deal with complex political events and who allow the most irresponsible views to circulate. I saw few, if any, intelligent presentations of the complexity of U.S. history in the Middle East on television, or accounts of the origins of bin Laden and his network that discussed the complicity of the United States in training, funding, arming, and supporting the groups that became Islamic fundamentalist terrorists. Nor did I see any accounts that went into the U.S. relations between the Taliban, the multifaceted U.S. role in Afghanistan, or the complications of Middle Eastern politics that would make continuous retaliatory military action extremely dangerous and potentially catastrophic. Such alternative information spread through the media, including major newspapers, but rarely found its way into American television, which emerges at this point in the current crisis as a thoroughly irresponsible source of information and understanding.

Many U.S. citizens were genuinely perplexed at the amount of hatred in the Arab world for America and the print media predictably featured articles, symposia, and discussions of "Why do they hate us?" The Bush administration's answer was that it was precisely because of what was best about the United States that produced fear and hatred: our freedoms, wealth, and open society. Critics of U.S. foreign policy, who rarely were allowed on television, argued that it was what was worst about the U.S. that incurred hatred: its aggressive foreign policy, support of corrupt dictators in the Arab world as well as Israel, and its general superpower status. In fact, although one never heard such complex analyses in the broadcasting world, it was a contradictory mixture of both what is best and worst about the U.S. that generated hatred of it in the Arab world. Bin Laden and his operatives regularly repeated the litany of Arab grievances of U.S. policy. But it is also true that radical Islamists seriously hated U.S. culture and modernity, in particular those features that attracted fascination throughout the world, such as U.S. consumer culture, fashion and style, media and communications, technology, multiculturalism, and open lifestyles and sexuality. Likewise, the tremendous differences between the haves and have nots, between American wealth and global poverty, generated resentment. Probably superpowers will always be partially admired and partially resented, but in an era of globalization, U.S. supremacy in the world economy, polity, culture, media, and technology generated a potent mixture of attraction and repulsion, love and hatred, expressing itself in a variety of ways.

U.S. broadcasting thus provided exceptionally impoverished understanding of the historical context of terrorism and war, constantly promoted war fever, generated untold hysteria, and thus carried out generally anti-Enlightenment functions. Yet one could get a wealth of information, cogent analyses, historical contextualizations, and intelligent diversity of opinion and debate on the Internet. Surveys indicated that during this period of intense crisis and terror, audiences in the United States tended to turn to television for clarification and this was arguably a disastrous mistake. Rarely has television functioned so poorly in an era of crisis, generating more heat than light; more sound, fury, and spectacle than understanding; and more blatantly grotesque partisanship for the Bush administration than genuinely democratic debate over what options the country and the world faced in the confrontation with terrorism.

This situation calls attention once again to the major contradiction of the present age in regard to information and knowledge. On one hand, the United States has available the most striking array of information, opinions, debate, and sources of knowledge of any society in history with its profusion of print journalism, books, articles, and Internet sources in contrast to the poverty of information and opinion on television. This is truly a scandal and a contradiction in the construction of contemporary consciousness and political culture. Thus, whereas television functioned largely as propaganda, spectacle, and the producer of mass hysteria close to brainwashing, fortunately there is a wealth of informed analysis and interpretation available in print media and on the Internet, as well as a respectable archive of books and articles on the complexity of U.S. foreign policy and Middle East history. I draw on this literature in the following chapters as I dissect the U.S. mainstream media, Bush administration, and Pentagon versions of Afghanistan Terror War and provide alternative accounts based on critical journalism from throughout the world and scholarly reports beginning to emerge.

3

❖

Operation Enduring Freedom and the Proliferation of Terror War

For several weeks following 9/11, the global community appeared to be building an effective strategy to fight terrorism by arresting suspected members of the Al Qaeda network, tracking and blocking their financial support, and developing internal and global mechanisms and policies to fight terrorism. Suddenly, however, the campaign against terrorism turned to war. On Sunday, October 7, just short of one month after the September 11 attacks, the Bush administration unleashed a full-scale military assault on Afghanistan. The stated goal was purportedly to annihilate the bin Laden network and to destroy the Taliban regime in Afghanistan that had allowed the Al Qaeda network to operate in their country. The unilateralism of the U.S. response was striking, and leading American newspapers provided a rationale for U.S. rejection of a multilateral UN or NATO military coalition against international terrorism:

> In the leadup to a possible military strike, senior administration and allied officials said Mr. Rumsfeld's approach this week made clear that the United States intends to make it as much as possible an all-American campaign.
>
> One reason, they said, is that the United States is determined to avoid the limitations on its targets that were imposed by NATO allies during the 1999 war in Kosovo, or the hesitance to topple a leader that members of the gulf war coalition felt in 1991.
>
> "Coalition is a bad word, because it makes people think of alliances," said Robert Oakley, former head of the State Department's counter-terrorism office and former ambassador to Pakistan.
>
> A senior administration official put it more bluntly: "The fewer people you have to rely on, the fewer permissions you have to get." (*New York Times,* October 7, 2001)

And so, on October 7, the U.S. unleashed a largely unilateral military assault on Afghanistan, with minimal British military support, assuring that the U.S. and Britain would eventually pay for the intervention with the lives of their citizens in later Islamic terrorist retribution.[1] Announcing the attack in a speech from the Oval Office, George W. Bush proclaimed that the U.S. was carrying out military action in Afghanistan because the Taliban had refused to hand over bin Laden; thus, "the Taliban will pay a price. By destroying camps and disrupting communications we will make it more difficult for the terror network to train new recruits and coordinate their evil plans." And so, following the "Bush doctrine," the United States was not only going after bin Laden and his Al Qaeda network, but also the Taliban that hosted them.

OSAMA BIN LADEN'S MEDIA WAR

Within the hour, in a startling interruption of the mainstream media's pro-U.S. military intervention in Afghanistan, the world television networks released a video feed of a speech from bin Laden and his chief partners-in-crime, which had been fed to the Qatar-based Al Jazeera network in advance. Playing to an Arab audience, Ayman al-Zawahri, the Egyptian doctor who many believed to be a major political and strategic force in the Al Qaeda terrorist network, assailed the U.S. support of Israel, the U.S. failure to help produce a Palestinian state, the U.S.-led assault against Iraq in the Gulf War, and the subsequent stationing of U.S. troops in Saudi Arabia, the Arab Holy Land, and other Arab grievances.

Then bin Laden himself came on in his turban and camouflage jacket, an assault rifle by his side, with desert landscape and a cave behind him. Commentators noted that bin Laden's camouflage jacket signified that he's at war, while the white turban replicated the Muslim's traditional color of martyrdom. In ornate Arabic, rendered erratically by the network translators who were trying to put his speech into English, bin Laden praised the September 11 strike on America that "destroyed its buildings" and created "fear from North to South," praising Allah for this attack. Calling for a Jihad to "destroy America," bin Laden attacked the "debauched," "oppressive" Americans who have "followed injustice," and exhorted every Muslim to join the Jihad. The world was now divided, bin Laden insisted, into two sides, "the side of believers and the side of infidels," and everyone who stands with America is a "coward" and an "infidel."

Remarkably, bin Laden's Manichean dualism mirrored the discourse of Sharon, Bush, and those in the West who proclaimed the war against terrorism as a Holy War between Good and Evil, Civilization and Barbarism. Both dichotomized their Other as dominated by fear, Bush claiming that his Holy War marked freedom versus fear, evoking Arab animosity against Western values and prosperity. Bin Laden's Jihad, in turn, poised fearful America against his brave warriors, characterizing as well his battle as that of justice versus injustice. Both appealed to God, revealing a similar fundamentalist absolutism and Manicheanism, with both characterizing their

Other as "evil." And both sides described their opponents as "terrorists," convinced that they were right and virtuous while the other side were villains.

Yet it should be made clear that the interpretation of Islam by the Al Qaeda network goes against a reading of the Koran that prohibits suicide and violence against children and innocents, and that in no way promises sainthood or eternal happiness to terrorists. Islam, like Christianity, is complex and contested with various schools, branches, and sects (Ali 2002). To homogenize Islam is precisely to play the game of bin Laden and his associates who want to construct a Manichean dualism of Islam versus the West. In fact, just as the West is divided into highly complex blocs of competing ideologies, interests, states, regions, and groups, so too are Islam and the Arab world. Only by grasping the complexity of the contemporary world can one begin to solve intractable problems like international terrorism.

Bin Laden was quickly elevated into an international media superstar, reviled in the West and deified in parts of the Islamic and Arab world. Books, artifacts, and products bearing his name and image sold around the world. For his fans, he personified resistance to the West and fidelity to Islam, while to his enemies he was the personification of Evil, the antichrist. Needless to say, entrepreneurs everywhere exploited his image to sell products. On the Internet, one could purchase toilet paper with bin Laden's visage and choose from three slogans: "Wipe out bin Laden," "If he wants to attack he can start with my crack," or "If your butt gets to cloddin' just wipe with bin Laden." In addition, condoms, shooting targets, dartboards, golf balls, voodoo dolls, and violent video games featured bin Laden's now iconic image. Websites presented bin Laden porn, tasteless cartoons, and computer games in which the player could dismember the Al Qaeda terrorist.

Documentaries and news reports circulated endlessly every extant image and footage of bin Laden, shown in either negative or positive contexts, depending on the media venue. Viewing the countless video and images of Osama bin Laden, one is struck by his eyes. He never seems to look into the eyes of others or the camera when he speaks. Bin Laden seems to be in another sphere, above and beyond mundane social interaction. His communiqués are thus ethereal and bloodless in their presentation, even if their content is highly bloodthirsty, as his eyes look up and away into a transcendent horizon. The Iranian revolutionary, the Ayatollah Khomeini, by contrast, had contempt, mixed with slight fear, in his eyes that always turned down and away from Westerners who looked at him. Khomeini's look-away was usually dour and rejecting, while occasionally one sees a twinkle in bin Laden's eye, betraying a telltale worldliness, before it darts into a beyond that guides and bedevils him.

George W. Bush, by contrast, is known for his propensity to stare directly into other people's eyes and famously claimed he could eye the Russian president's soul by looking into his eyes. Bush is good at eye contact with the camera, providing the illusion that he is speaking directly to the people, face-to-face, while bin Laden is staring out in space and speaking to eternity. To be sure, sometimes the camera catches the vacant and blank Bush whose small eyes point to the littleness within.

At other times, the camera catches Bush's infamous smirk, which reveals his arrogance and contempt, or shows Bush's eyes darting erratically from one side to the other, acknowledging insecurity and anxiety.

As the U.S. military campaign unfolded, the Bush administration backed away from personalizing the conflict as one between Bush and bin Laden. Perhaps members of the Bush administration recalled how the first Bush's presidency collapsed in part because he was not able to remove the personification of evil in the Gulf War, Saddam Hussein, who continued to taunt the U.S. and who some Bushites believed supported the Al Qaeda terrorist network. In fact, while I have used the term "bin Laden" throughout my analysis, I think that it is a mistake to personalize the September 11 events or to contribute to the demonization of bin Laden, the flip side of which is deification. This, of course, is precisely what Al Qaeda wants, and Bush was playing into its hands by personalizing Osama's role in the September 11 attacks. In fact, "bin Laden" is better interpreted as what Sorel called a "revolutionary myth," a figurehead for a network and movement to which his opponents ascribe great power and evil while his followers ascribe wondrous effectiveness and good.

Indeed, there appears to be a worldwide radical Islamic theocratic network that has taken up terrorism and "propaganda of the deed" to help produce a Holy War between the East and West. Given the extent of this network and its fanaticism, it appears certain that the problems of terrorism will not be solved by the arrest or elimination of bin Laden and other top leaders of his Al Qaeda network who Bush put on his "Most Wanted" list on October 10. This inventory suggests that the war against terrorism will be a long one and raises questions of whether the U.S. military strategy is the most effective way to stop global terrorism. Questions should also be asked concerning whether terrorism can ever be eliminated in the modern world, and what are the most viable conditions for a world without terror—questions not raised in the U.S. as military fever engulfed the nation in a vise of patriotism in which critical thinking and dissent were seen as treason.

BUSH'S OPERATION INFINITE WAR

Yet as the U.S. continued its bombing campaign in October and threatened to expand its war against terrorism to states like Iraq, worries began to circulate that the U.S. military intervention might create more problems than it would solve. When U.S. Secretary of Defense Donald Rumsfeld likened the war on terror to the Cold War, which lasted more than fifty years, the specter of endless war was invoked, which is perhaps what the Pentagon had in mind when they first named their military intervention "Operation Infinite Justice." Jokes spread through the Pentagon that an endless war on terrorism would drag them into "Operation Infinite War." President Bush regularly referred to World War III in speeches and pledged that he would dedicate his administration to the cause of defeating terrorism (later it was claimed by a Pakistani journalist who had interviewed bin Laden that the Al Qaeda head also frequently spoke of World War III).

Endless war would no doubt be a hard project to sell the public for the long term, and one wondered how long it would take for the costs to overwhelm the benefits. Although war throughout the new millennium would keep America's troops fully employed and the Pentagon budget ever escalating, it would keep U.S. citizens in a state of fear from terrorist retaliation, for unending war would no doubt generate endless terror. Moreover, it was not clear how the U.S. could afford to finance an open-ended war against terrorism, nor how the global economy could function in a situation of fear and war.

Indeed, hysteria and panic reigned throughout the U.S. after it was reported on October 8 that the Bush administration believed that a significant terrorist response to their military intervention was certain. Reports of an isolated anthrax case in Florida mushroomed on October 9 when it was reported that a second episode had appeared in the same place. Media focus on the anthrax threat intensified when it was revealed that the site of the infection was a building that housed the *National Enquirer* and other tabloids, which had relentlessly demonized bin Laden, his network, and the Taliban. Reports spread that a Middle Eastern intern who had worked in the building left a threatening e-mail. Another account indicated that the *Sun* tabloid had received a "weird love letter to Jennifer Lopez" with a "soapy, powdery substance" and a Star of David charm in the letter, evoking the specter of an anthrax-infected postal system that could attack anyone.

Throughout the day of October 9, hysteria in the United States escalated. People were calling the police in when powdery substance appeared in letters and offices, while frantic tabloid representatives tried to assure the public that buying their papers would not expose them to anthrax. There was a run on anthrax antibiotics in Florida and elsewhere, and bioterrorism threats closed an IRS Center in Kentucky and a subway in Washington, D.C.[2] And the Internet buzzed with rumors of cyberterror disrupting the great global commerce, culture, and communications network.

Meanwhile, it was appearing that things were initially not going well on the war front. Although the U.S. could claim to control Afghanistan's airspace after several days of bombing, this did not amount to much since the Taliban had no real air force or even air defense. Furthermore, reports of "collateral damage" were beginning to appear, including the death of four UN workers purportedly killed by the U.S. assault and subsequent accounts of U.S. bombing of Afghan civilian neighborhoods. Most ominously, throughout the world there were regional reports of potential worrisome responses to the U.S. military adventure. Pakistan was scarred by riots and there were fears of upheaval and perhaps a long-simmering explosion of tensions with neighboring India; indeed, within days fighting broke out between Indian and Pakistani forces over their long dispute over Kashmir. Moreover, anti-American demonstrations erupted in Pakistan, Egypt, Nigeria, Indonesia, and other countries throughout the Islamic world, causing hundreds of deaths and nurturing hatred of the U.S. that could last for decades. There would be hell to pay, and many worried that the Al Qaeda threats that Americans would henceforth live in fear were being realized.

While British and U.S. TV networks had been engaging in relentless war propaganda for the first several days of the bombing, on October 9 both BBC TV in Britain and ABC TV in the U.S. were remarkably critical. The network reports cited civilian damage and the killing of UN workers in Afghanistan via U.S. bombing, the anthrax scare and hysteria in the U.S., refugee problems in Afghanistan, and protests in the Arab world. They also noted problems with the food deliveries that were supposed to legitimate the intervention and construct it as a humanitarian operation that would benefit the Afghan people. UN and other aid workers in Afghanistan appeared on television, indicating that the U.S. military intervention had made it impossible for aid agencies to continue their food delivery, that the food delivered by the United States was totally inadequate, and that dropping food in mine-laden Afghanistan was highly dangerous to the people.

After the live television broadcast on October 9 of yet another Al Qaeda radical threatening more terrorist strikes against the U.S. and asserting that Jihad against America was now "the duty of every Muslim," Condoleezza Rice, Bush's National Security Advisor and a rabid unilateralist, had a conference call with top television executives. She implored them to no longer broadcast live bin Laden tapes since they could send "secret messages" to "sleeper" agents and unleash new terror. Even more chilling, Ari Fleischer, head Bushspeak flak, called Howell Raines, executive editor of the *New York Times,* to ask him to refrain from publishing transcripts of statements released by bin Laden and his gang, although Raines' response was reportedly chilly to the request to freeze information.[3] The previous week, Colin Powell had urged the Emir of Qatar, leader of the country that houses the Arab Al Jazeera network that had been releasing Al Qaeda tapes, to restrict broadcast of these tapes and the views of bin Laden spokespeople, leading Al Jazeera broadcast executives to wonder why the country that invented "freedom of the press" and extolled its "free press" was telling other countries not to exert this right.

On October 10, Bush testily attacked Congress for releasing classified national security information by informing the country that a retaliatory terrorist strike on the U.S. after the beginning of Afghanistan bombing was "100 percent certain." By the next day, he relented, promising to share security information with Congress and declaring that "our calling" is the eradication of terrorism around the world. Taking a page from his father's Gulf War book, Bush affirmed, "Now is the time to draw the line in the sand against the evil doers."

The same day, Islamic leaders meeting in Qatar questioned the U.S. intervention and called for the U.S. to only attack those it could prove were involved in the terrorist strikes. They also called for a dialogue of civilizations and not extending the war any further. On the previous day, however, U.S. Ambassador to the UN John Negroponte, who had been involved himself in funding and arming terrorists in the Iran-Contra scandal of the 1980s, delivered a message to Iraq, threatening them with military action and defeat and causing suspicions that the war would be extended, long, and dangerous.

Moreover, concerns were circulating about how the U.S. could afford to pay for its intervention and the impact of its military intervention on the U.S. and global economy. In mid-October it was reported that there would be no surplus for 2001, that the U.S. would once again plunge into deficit spending as it had during the earlier Reagan-Bush years, and that the entire global economy was in peril because of the turmoil. In response to calls for government spending to help avoid deep recession, the Bush administration responded with a call for $70 billion in additional tax cuts, most of which would be capital gains tax cuts for the rich, suggesting again that the Bush administration was largely a criminal enterprise organized to rob the federal treasury of money for its most wealthy contributors and supporters (see Kellner 2001). Their partners in crime, the House Ways and Means Committee, approved a $90 billion stimulus package on October 13, although some Democrats vowed to fight the corporate giveaway.[4]

Although the mainstream media constantly praised the "confident" and "effective" President Bush, claiming that he had risen to the occasion and was like a new person, others wondered if he was really up to the job and knew what he was doing. During the morning of the September 11 terror attacks, Bush was reading to schoolchildren in Florida. The Bush administration privileged sending the not-too-educated or articulate president to schools where he would give speeches to children that were soundbited for the evening news, providing clear presentations of whatever message of the day the Bush administration was attempting to send out. Evidently, the Bush administration felt that U.S. citizens were like children and needed to have simple explanations and well packaged sound bites for every issue.

As noted, on the day of the September 11 bombing, Bush continued his photo opportunity with Florida schoolchildren after being informed of the first World Trade Center attack, and after being informed of the second attack, he first continued to listen to children reading, and then hurriedly read a statement and ran off to his Air Force One plane that flew him to military bases in Louisiana and Nebraska. While New York Mayor Rudy Giuliani and other top New York officials were shown all day at Ground Zero, providing leadership and actively participating in the response to the terror attack, Bush was shown fleeing across the country and out of the circuit.

Eventually, Bush flew back to Washington on the night of September 11 to address the nation, but there was criticism that he had gone AWOL at a crucial time, just as he had disappeared for a year when he was supposed to be doing National Guard Reserves duty.[5] To cut off criticism, a White House official and spinmeister, Karl Rove, called conservative *New York Times* columnist William Safire and fed him the line that the reason Bush had not immediately returned to Washington was that U.S. intelligence had intercepted a message that Air Force One codes were compromised and the plane was under threat of attack. This story was an outright fabrication, consistent with the Rove-Hughes-Bushspeak tendency to use the Big

Lie when necessary, but it provided a temporary cover to put aside the question of why Bush had not provided better leadership on September 11.[6]

For the next weeks, Bush's handlers carefully programmed him and he performed relatively well. After his effectively read speech to Congress on September 20, Bush returned, however, to his bland teleprompter mode and erratic form of spontaneous, albeit scripted, public communication. In a verbal slip not generally noted in the media, on October 4, Bush wound up a speech on the rough and long road ahead needed to defeat terrorism by proclaiming: "And there is no doubt in my mind, not one doubt in my mind, that we will fail" (*Los Angeles Times,* October 5, 2001). In several mid-October speeches that had obviously been written that morning by his speechwriters and that Bush did not have sufficient time to fully understand, he returned to his reading-a-speech-that-may-be-beyond-me mode, nose buried in text and then furtively darting his eyes around the audience as if to say, "Do they know that I don't understand what I'm reading?" while seeking approval. When the audience claps or responds appropriately, Bush smirks, knowing that he'd pulled off his performance.

As the second week of bombing of Afghanistan continued, reports began surfacing that all was not going well and that the Bush administration was not sure how to proceed. U.S. generals were frustrated that their bombing had not flushed out more Taliban–Al Qaeda forces, although Seymour Hersh reported that CIA sources indicated that U.S. forces had missed an opportunity to get Taliban leader Omar's caravan the first night of the bombing, but were unable to decide if they should target him. Other reports through the weekend of October 13–14 documented U.S. bombing of a village that killed scores, with pictures of dead Afghan children and women travelling through the global media.[7]

In particular, there were disturbing reports and images of devastation of a small town of Khorum (also spelled as Kadam) in eastern Afghanistan. The *Sydney Morning Herald* reported on October 15 that:

> One week after United States–led forces began bombarding Afghanistan, disturbing evidence is emerging of unacceptably high civilian casualties and ill-defined military and political objectives. Afghans reaching the Pakistani city of Peshawar 60 kilometres from the border said the bombing on Friday of Kadam, a small rural community in Surkh Rud district near the eastern city of Jalalabad, had killed scores, possibly hundreds of civilians.[8]

British newspapers reported that eyewitnesses described a devastating firestorm over the village, that U.S. jets circulated back twice to unload additional ordnance on the site, and that there were many civilian casualties. The U.S. dismissed the charges as Taliban propaganda, but when reporters entered the scene they were appalled by the sight of dying victims in a hospital, descriptions of heavy U.S. bombing of civilians, and obvious images of devastation, including body parts, dead animals, and bomb craters that were telecast around the world. Rumsfeld insisted that the U.S. had bombed ammunition dumps in tunnels and had not hit the village at all, although reporters on the scene saw copious evidence of destruction and it appeared to many that once again the Pentagon was dissembling and lying—and getting caught in its prevarications.[9]

Diplomats realized that the U.S. was losing the propaganda war, and belatedly the military started dropping leaflets explaining the reasons they were attacking the Taliban and explaining the benefits for Afghanistan if the Taliban were overthrown. But bombs had been dropping on Afghanistan for over a week and the U.S. propagandists had generally failed to grasp that every time a picture of a dead Muslim was shown in the global media, the entire Muslim world feels violated, and that every bombing of civilians exponentially increased hatred of Americans in the world and furthered the possibilities of terrorist retaliation in the future. There were also reports spreading that Afghanistan faced a starvation problem of an immense magnitude, that as many as 7.5 million people could waste away as the relentless Afghan winter approached and the bombing and flow of refugees continued unabated. Thus, although the U.S. had started off with a propaganda offensive that they were dropping bread and bombs, that their military intervention was humanitarian and that they would feed the Afghan people, so far only the results of bombing were visible to the world and images of murdered, mutilated, and starving people were circulating through the global media.

As Colin Powell traveled to Pakistan for a meeting to reassure the country's ruling generals who had allowed the U.S. to use its landing facilities and airspace in the Afghanistan bombing campaign, merchants in Pakistan went on strike to protest U.S. military support in the country. An Islamic group had been brutally turned away from attacking a U.S. airbase in Pakistan over the weekend and violent demonstrations continued against the U.S. intervention throughout the Muslim world, with scores dying in a demonstration in Nigeria. Bombings of civilian targets continued: On October 16 the U.S. hit a Red Cross depot, with a Bush administration spokesman first denying that the U.S. had hit the installation and then the Pentagon admitting to it. Civilian neighborhoods continued to be "collateral damage," and the Taliban claimed that the U.S. bombed a caravan of civilians fleeing the war on October 17.

Al Jazeera television reported on October 18 that several buildings were destroyed with civilian residents inside in Kabul. According to one summary:

At least four bombs hit an apartment complex in [a] Makrurian neighborhood. Footage showed huge craters and piles of rubble amid the apartment blocks, and what appeared to be a dead child covered in dust. Some of the standing buildings had broken windows and other damage. Families were shown distraught and crying, and digging through rubble for survivors. One man covered in dust pointed at a pile of rubble, saying his mother and several relatives were inside the destroyed building. In one building, residents said an 18-year-old man and his new bride were killed along with their entire family. Al-Allouni said residents were angered by US claims to not target civilians, and

that the strike on Makrurian caused more people to flee, with footage of residents load-
ing up old cars. Al-Jazira also quoted claims by Taliban officials that a refugee convoy
had been bombed near Jalalabad, killing 12.[10]

Meanwhile, Afghanistan appeared to be in chaos. Taliban gangs robbed UN food
depots and supplies of medicine, international aid agencies begged for a halt in the
bombing to feed the famished people, refugees fled to neighboring countries, and
internally the civil war intensified with advances by the Northern Alliance countered
by what was claimed to be fierce Taliban resistance. There were also stories of thousands of young Islamic militants flooding into Afghanistan from neighboring countries to fight Americans in a Jihad, and demonstrations intensified throughout the
Muslim world. Surveys revealed that alarming numbers of individuals in the Islamic
world believed that Israel or the U.S. itself was responsible for the September 11
terrorist attacks, viewed bin Laden as a hero, and declared themselves passionately
against the U.S. military intervention. Critics worried about the stability of the
region, anticipating possible Islamic upheavals in Pakistan, Egypt, Saudi Arabia, and
other states in the region that had large and angry Islamic populations.[11]

ALL ANTHRAX, ALL THE TIME

The worldwide turbulence from the U.S. military intervention in Afghanistan was
largely unnoticed by the U.S. public as its media became obsessed with the anthrax
attacks that were apparently intensifying. Reports multiplied of individuals being
exposed to anthrax powder through the mail, and false alarms or hoaxes reaped hysteria in homes and offices everywhere, as well as in airplanes or public spaces where
panic erupted when suspicious white powder was found. More anthrax was discovered at NBC, ABC, and then CBS, forcing the shutdown of offices in these media
institutions for health inspections and guaranteeing that anthrax would be the story
of the week. NBC's Tom Brokaw dramatized his own participation in the anthrax
drama, closing a broadcast with a grim smile and declaration that "In Cipro we
trust," holding a bottle of the antibacterial drug that was being prescribed for those
exposed to anthrax. It appears that in the home of the free and the brave, trust in
drugs had replaced trust in the Big Guy, while some public health experts argued
that the current craze for Cipro could be highly harmful to individuals and that the
more modest drug penicillin might be more effective.[12]

The U.S. Congress as well was exposed to anthrax and shut down. On October
15, it was discovered that a package of anthrax with a threatening letter was sent to
the office of Senate Majority Leader Tom Daschle (D-S.D.), and his aide was
exposed and tested positive. On October 17, it was claimed that this form of anthrax
was extremely sophisticated and lethal and that over thirty other Senate aides had
been exposed and tested positive. The House majority leader announced that
anthrax was found "in the ventilation system" of the Senate building as well. Later

in the day, government officials claimed that the anthrax was a "garden-variety" grade and that the Senate ventilation system had not been infected. But when the House and Senate announced that both were being closed for the rest of the week to allow full-scale inspection, obviously something serious was happening.

Indeed, this was the first time that Congress had ever been closed down during a scheduled session. Bizarrely, House leaders disparaged grandstanding senators for remaining open for their afternoon session, while members of the Senate denigrated the House for prematurely closing down, and the right-wing New York Post featured a boldfaced "WIMPS" on their headline with pictures of the House leaders. Hence, a war broke out between the House and Senate over how to deal with the anthrax exposures and scares, with the Bush administration still failing to adequately inform even elected U.S. representatives.

The following Monday, anthrax was found in both the House and Senate buildings and the House of Representatives' caution was no longer questioned. Indeed, throughout the world, anthrax scares and hoaxes multiplied at an astonishing rate. Over 100 letters claiming to contain anthrax were sent to family planning and abortion clinics across the U.S., replaying a 1998 and 1999 campaign when similar tactics were used by anti-abortion extremists, leading to speculation that some of the actual anthrax attacks might have been carried out by U.S. right-wing domestic groups or deranged psychotics, and not Islamic terrorists. From Hong Kong to Italy, from Kenya to Sydney, there were announcements that anthrax powder had been found; jets all around the globe landed prematurely when suspicious substances were found on planes, and hoaxes, panic, and hysteria proliferated, globalization at work in its more sinister and bizarre forms.

By October 18, it was clear that the Bush administration was as inept at handling the domestic anthrax war as it was the terrorist war abroad. There seemed to be no coordination among federal and local agencies on the anthrax attacks, no national policies, and a highly hamfisted response. The Secretary of Health and Human Services, Tommy Thompson, first dismissed the discovery of the Florida anthrax case at the tabloid media center as the result of a "natural" spore, perhaps encountered while fishing, and nothing to be alarmed at. Later, of course, it was revealed that this was a severe problem and Thompson was seriously discredited. Thompson, who was caught up in misstatements and confusion during the summer stem cell debate,[13] appeared to be more interested in protecting the patent rights of the anthrax vaccine company that had failed to provide adequate supply and the company that made the antidote Cipro than in protecting U.S. citizens threatened by the attack. He obviously did not have the scientific qualifications for the job and was not effective in communicating with the public during the initial phase of the anthrax scare. In one amusing episode, one of Thompson's Department of Health and Human Service spokespersons, Campbell Garrett, provided a thoroughly Orwellian response to one of Thompson's earlier statements: "Something's that's factual at this moment proves not to be factual in retrospect. That doesn't mean it wasn't factual at the time." One needed to go back to the Nixon administration when officials would declare yesterday's lies or misstatements "inoperative" to find such gems of Doublespeak.

The bumbling Thompson was quickly taken out of the public spotlight, acknowledging that the Bush administration had appointed a conservative corporate flunkey as head of the Department of Health and Human Services when someone more competent was required. Moreover, days went by before there was a thorough investigation of the Florida site where the anthrax was first found and where it turned out that many employees were exposed. The same pattern evolved at NBC, where at first federal authorities failed to thoroughly investigate the incident and allowed days to go by before closing offices for a methodical investigation. New York Mayor Rudy Giuliani was so outraged by the FBI that he ordered them out of the investigation of the New York anthrax attacks and made it a New York Police affair.

The head of the Federal Emergency Management Agency (FEMA), Joe Albrow, an incompetent and awkward member of Bush's Texas "Iron Triangle" who had proven himself an able political hatchet man for Bush over the years, was not visible to the public during the anthrax crisis. Nor, for some time, was Bush's new Head of Homeland Security, Tom Ridge, another Bush political crony whose competence was in doubt. Dick Cheney, previously the head of the Bush administration group on antiterrorism but obviously more interested in collecting tax breaks and government favors for his oil industry buddies, was almost invisible. Cheney's few public comments on anthrax were contradictory and muddled, as were the daily comments of the ultraright and not-too-bright Attorney General John Ashcroft. Ashcroft had lost a senate election to a dead man in 2000, was generally considered the most right-wing extremist of a hard-right Bush administration, and was carring out the most radical assault on civil liberties and rights in U.S. history. Ashcroft's response to the terrorist attacks was to push through the most repressive law-and-order legislation imaginable, an extreme right-wing dream of government surveillance, arrest, and seizure that had moderate conservatives as well as liberals worried.[14]

Bush administration officials tried to assure the public regarding the anthrax attacks on October 19, but the media kept hyping and dramatizing public hysteria, providing all-anthrax-all-day coverage just as with media spectacles like the O. J. Simpson trial and Clinton and Condit sex scandals. Tom Ridge and John Ashcroft tried to reassure the public, but they were highly ineffectual, merely noting that the U.S. was offering a million-dollar award for information concerning who sent out the anthrax in the mail. They at first tried to assure the public that there were plenty of drugs on hand to treat the disease and other potential plagues. But soon, the Bush administration was forced to admit that drugs dealing with lethal biochemical diseases were in short supply and the public health system could not cope with widespread crisis. While some senators tried to calm the public by indicating that there was little chance they would be exposed to anthrax, that the spores were hard to spread through large areas, and that the symptoms could be treated, the media created immense hysteria with hypes of every account, many rumors, and repeated warnings about the disease and what to do.

Put in perspective, everyday Americans and others are exposed to thousands of toxic organisms and diseases, many die daily from such often-mysterious causes, and rarely is attention focused on the deadly byproducts of everyday life in the modern world. But the anthrax scare had created a nation of hypochondriacs and the media were producing a great panic scare, one that was paralyzing the economy and polity. There was an investigation with media hype every time white powder was found in office buildings, public spaces, transportation vehicles, or homes. Police and public health officials were being heavily overburdened with white powder chases, much of which turned out to be talcum powder or doughnut sugar.

Yet more and more anthrax traces were found in U.S. government buildings ranging from the Supreme Court, to the Justice Department, to the White House mail room, and everyday exposures and deaths from anthrax increased. Meanwhile, Bush himself veered from the Andover cheerleader mode where one day he told people to go on with their lives, that everything would be OK, and that the government was in control. Then he or others in his administration would give out warnings that there were serious threats to the public that required alertness and that the war against terrorism would go on for years. One day the president would assert that although "our nation is still in danger," "the government is doing everything in our power to protect our citizenry." Bush told the country that Americans could help fight back by "going to work, going to ball games, getting on airplanes, singing with joy and strength, like you all did today. They will not take this country down!" he proclaimed as his audience cheered (*Newsweek,* October 22, 2001).

Most bizarrely, when asked in a White House briefing if he had been tested for anthrax, Bush curtly answered, "I don't have anthrax," repeating the answer twice when reporters queried him about dangers of anthrax in the White House. But when questioned as to whether the bin Laden network was behind the anthrax attacks, Bush would respond, "I wouldn't put it past him," and then lashed out against "the evildoers," the "new dangers" facing Americans, and the need for vigilance and patience. The FBI had labeled the threatened anticipated major terrorist attacks "Skyfall," which elicited hundreds of frightened calls that forced the FBI to pull the warning from its website and rethink its linguistic politics. And the fact that Vice President Dick Cheney was kept secured in "an undisclosed secure location," rumored to be a mountain hideaway outside of Washington, did not help to breed confidence.

Wildly conflicting stories as to the source of the anthrax attacks spread through the media. Certain members of the Bush administration, eager to attack Iraq, continued to leak to the media that Iraq was behind the attacks, and these rumors were reproduced through the media from the *National Enquirer* to ABC News. The British *Guardian* reported on October 24 that the U.S. was closer to blaming anthrax on Al Qaeda, "the operating suspicion on the White House for a considerable period of time" and sometimes insinuated by Bush. But in an October 27 *Washington Post* article, Bob Woodward and Dan Eggen reported, "FBI and CIA Suspect Domestic Extremists: Officials Doubt Any Links to Bin Laden"—a report that was instantly questioned by many in the Bush administration and media. Speculation continued to multiply concerning the possibility of a home-grown right-wing source, with domestic terrorism expert David Neiwert publishing a history of U.S. right-wing fascination with the drug, attempted use of it, and motives and inclinations to attack the U.S. government and the media sources that had been most exposed to it.[15] Indeed, no conservative politicians or right-wing media like Fox had been exposed to anthrax during the opening weeks of the anthrax exposures, and eventually the FBI would attribute the anthrax mailings to a domestic disgruntled loner or unhinged member of the National Security State itself.

U.S. government sources also admitted that Cipro was not the only drug useful to fight anthrax, and was also not necessarily the most efficient. Cheaper drugs, such as penicillin and doxycycline, were considered to be as effective as the more expensive and harder to get Cipro, and perhaps had less noxious side effects. In fact, the only testing on Cipro had been on monkeys and it wasn't clear what strains the drug would treat, the side effects, or if it would make individuals resistant. Earlier, during the Gulf War, troops had been given anthrax vaccines that had not been adequately tested, so in effect Gulf troops were guinea pigs with disquieting results. Many feared that the anthrax vaccines had contributed to the "Gulf War syndrome," which adversely affected thousands of Gulf War veterans with symptoms ranging from tumors to mysterious flulike illness (see Kellner 1992 and Hersh 1998). Now there was a rush to approve a range of anthrax drugs by the FDA so that U.S. citizens could serve as a round of guinea pigs for the anthrax exposures proliferating in the country.

The great anthrax mystery grew as different experts and intelligence personnel weighed in on one of the most remarkable terrorist attacks in history. The viability of the U.S. postal service was in question and the Bush administration continued to suffer a credibility deficit. The hapless Tommy Thompson was kept out of the public after his stumbling performance, and the Bush administration officials put out daily to explain the anthrax attacks to the public, including Attorney General John Ashcroft, Homeland Defense Secretary Tom Ridge and Postmaster General John Potter, were hardly reassuring. Ashcroft especially gave the nation the willies with his constant warnings of impending doom and his inability to provide a coherent explanation of possible and actual terrorist attacks and the U.S. response. The most right-wing member of the government, the dour Ashcroft's voice trembled as he moralistically condemned the terrorists but failed to reassure that anything was being done to protect the public. Some speculated that Ashcroft's own ultraright history made him singularly unable to go after potential domestic terrorists, whom many speculated were behind the anthrax attacks. And civil libertarians and liberals shuddered to think that this right-wing ideologue would be in charge of administering new antiterrorist laws that gave the government new powers of search and seizure, detention, and prosecution. In the war against the Taliban and Al Qaeda, the U.S. Taliban was determining policy and the consequences were worrisome.

Tom Ridge and John Potter, on the other hand, appeared as pudgy and overage football players who would be more at home reliving their glory days on the gridiron over a couple of beers than having to deal with complex scientific health and public relations issues. The Postal Service was severely criticized for failing to test its employees when government and media employees exposed to anthrax had been tested and, if necessary, given drugs and medical treatment. Commentators noted that there had been a prompt response for politicians and media personnel exposed to anthrax and a slower one for postal workers. For good reason, postal workers' unions were suing the government, and the country increased its panic when anthrax exposures started appearing in people not in proximity to the previously noted anthrax-saturated letters. The awkward Potter was hardly reassuring when he admitted that the Post Office could not guarantee that customer mail was safe, and Ridge seemed out of his element as he mumbled and bumbled day after day, trying to assure a nervous public when it was obvious that the Bush administration was stumped by the anthrax mystery. When the FBI director begged the public to help them solve the anthrax problem, it was clear that the U.S. government was unable to do its job.

Thus Bush administration officials such as Ridge, Thompson, and Potter began to look more and more like the Three Stooges as they lurched daily through their briefings, gave out contradictory messages, and signaled the incompetence of Bush administration's Stupid White Men to deal with the grave national domestic crisis. Part of the problem with the failure of Bush administration officials to deal with domestic terrorism is that they did not have the intelligence, credentials, or capability to do the job. As the days went by, the dim-bulb Ashcroft became dimmer, his eyes haunted by unseen demons and his voice ever trembling. Hands shaking, his nasal-droning voice and grim visage became the face of the Bush administration's inability to competently deal with the anthrax crisis. This was the price of the Bush administration's ideological cronyism by which Bush and his handlers chose conservative white men to carry out important government jobs, the kind of men that Bush Junior was comfortable with and who were inclined to support hard-right conservative policies and give favors to the corporate donors who would keep the cash flowing to Republican troughs. But the country was paying heavily for the cronyism and corruption that put unqualified conservative men in jobs that they were obviously not competent to handle.[16]

Put into historical context, the anthrax attacks could also be read as blowback from the insanity of the Cold War and the failure of the superpowers and global community to control the spread of instruments of biological terror. Both the United States and the Soviet Union had developed massive chemical weapons programs utilizing lethal substances like anthrax, and although its production and use had been banned, there had not been sufficient attention paid to controlling and containing the circulation of the product—or, for that matter, other lethal viruses like smallpox that had been eradicated as a medical danger by a successful worldwide vaccination program. But the anthrax, smallpox, and other deadly viruses had continued to be cultivated in U.S. research labs, perhaps for use in government biological weapons programs, and there were fears that such viruses had been stolen by terrorists or rogue agents and would be used against the American public.

Indeed, the Bush administration had blocked U.S. ratification of international treaties regulating biochemical weapons and evidently had been promising to allow the military to do biochemical research that had been forbidden by previous treaties. Reports eventually leaked that the U.S. wanted to continue to develop biochemical weapons, and there was no evidence that the Bush administration was taking steps to close down possibly illegal biochemical weapons facilities.[17]

The country was also experiencing blowback from decades of FBI incompetence and mediocrity. Obviously, the FBI had failed to prevent the September 11 attacks, although eventually reports would surface that FBI memos had warned the Bush administration about impending terrorist attacks. As noted in the introduction, in May 2002, a memo was released that an FBI agent from Phoenix, Arizona, was suspicious of Middle Eastern men taking flying lessons. It also warned that Al Qaeda could use hijacked airplanes in terrorist attacks, but this memo was lost in the bureaucracy. In late August, there had been an arrest in Minnesota of Zacarias Moussaouri, later labeled the twentieth hijacker, who had been taking flying lessons and acting suspiciously, but the FBI never put together the accounts despite getting warnings from French intelligence that he was an Al Qaeda member (see Brisard and Dasquie 2002). Moreover, many stories spread concerning FBI agents who desperately tried to warn the agency about imminent Al Qaeda terrorist attacks but were rebuffed, and there were also many accounts of private citizens who also tried to alert the FBI or U.S. government in vain.[18]

Thus, despite copious warnings that many foreign and domestic agencies had informed the U.S. government about forthcoming terrorist attacks in the near future, there was obviously no competent centralized intelligence and no one qualified to process the data, and so the intelligence services failed to serve the nation that had so liberally funded them. Although Vice President Dick Cheney had been put in charge of task forces to study terrorism, energy policy, and global warning in the summer of 2001, it appeared that Cheney had done nothing to coordinate U.S. policy against terrorism and had dedicated his time to working to get favors for his friends in the oil and energy business.

Thus, serious questions should have been raised to Cheney concerning what he did and did not do as head of the Bush administration task force on terrorism. Obviously, there was no apparent coordination of information in the Bush administration on responses to terrorism before September 11, and if Cheney was head of the task force that was supposed to deal with terrorism, it is disgraceful that he did not establish a group to centralize information and construct viable responses. There were several congressional reports over the years that had called for a centralization of information on terrorism and more intelligent government policy, including a report by former Senators Gary Hart and Howard Rudman in early 2001, but Cheney and the Bush administration failed to act on these recommendations. It is also revealing that Cheney himself allegedly pleaded several times with Democratic

Party Senate Majority Leader Tom Daschle not to launch an investigation in U.S. intelligence failures prior to September 11. Such an inquiry would no doubt point a finger at Cheney himself, but as of the end of 2002, the spineless media and Democratic party were not targeting Cheney, although there were many calls to investigate the failure of the U.S. government in order to provide a defense against the September 11 terror attacks.

In fall 2001, after the terrorist attacks and then the anthrax scare, the FBI was again appearing to blunder in the anthrax investigation and was failing to make arrests in either the terrorist attacks or the anthrax episodes that decisively caught the perpetrators. Although the U.S. government had arrested over 1,200 suspects in conjunction with the September 11 events, the *Los Angeles Times* reported that as of November 16, "None Jailed Linked to Attacks." Part of the problem was that the conservative white FBI agents that were traditionally the core of the agency had no cultural ability to interact with people of color, and there were few agents who grasped the complexity of Middle Eastern culture, could speak or read Arabic, or otherwise cleverly interrogate suspects. Moreover, there were acute basic questions about FBI competency and intelligence.

Earlier in 2001, the FBI had been implicated in a series of scandals in which the agency botched major investigations, including revelations that it had lost loads of documents involved in the Timothy McVeigh Oklahoma City bombings, surely the most publicized bureau case of the 1990s. It turned out that the FBI had no centralized computer records, and had no centralized computer databases with federal law enforcement agencies, the INS, or other government agencies. In a hi-tech era, the FBI was clearly technologically challenged.[19] In fact, it was revealed in a congressional investigation of the anthrax exposures that the government had destroyed many of the original samples and types of anthrax before they could be properly analyzed. And in a November 2001 congressional hearing, an FBI agent was forced to admit that the FBI really did not know who had access to anthrax in labs in the U.S., which labs were experimenting with it, what sort of clearance lab workers had, and what strains had been available to different labs.

On the weekend of November 10–11, reports indicated that "Anthrax Letters Likely Sent by Angry Male Loner, FBI Says" (*Washington Post*, Nov. 10, 2001). Based on handwriting analysis of the three letters sent to NBC, the *New York Post*, and Tom Daschle, the FBI was now concluding, "We have a lone individual operating in these incidents." If true, the U.S. was facing a Unabomber situation, a case that had taken eighteen years to solve before catching the sender of mail bombs that had killed and maimed many. This hypothesis seemed to be strengthened by the revelation on November 16 that a newly discovered letter was found sent to liberal Democratic Senator Patrick Leahy. If it was true that an extremist loner was the anthrax attack culprit, as the FBI again suggested, then one wonders on what basis George W. Bush had repeatedly insinuated that the anthrax was being sent by Al Qaeda, although the paralyzing effects and terror of the anthrax exposure due to

hysterical media presentation had no doubt sent the message to many terrorist enemies of the U.S. that this would be an effective instrument of terror.

Eventually, some very frightening stories leaked out that indicated that the Ames
anthrax strain (so called because it came from an Iowa State lab in Ames, Iowa) used
in the attacks on Washington liberal politicians and New York media had been in
the hands of the CIA. Summarizing several news reports, Richard Ochs writes:

> The CIA has cultures of the Ames strain. The Agency has been conducting secret experi-
> ments with powdered germs since 1997 at Battelle Memorial Institute in Ohio. Battelle
> received the Ames strain from Fort Detrick in May of 2001. The CIA said it was trying
> to develop defenses against anthrax, but did not explain why it was doing what other
> defense labs were set up to do. As of December 16, 2001, one FBI investigator said that
> the CIA's anthrax project was the "best lead they have at this point."[20]

As noted above, the FBI admitted that they allowed the Iowa State lab to destroy
the original batch of the Ames strain, making tracing the type of anthrax more difficult and giving rise to speculation that destroying the original strain was part of a
cover-up to protect individuals inside the U.S. government who had access to the
anthrax. In retrospect, it is also suspicious that the anthrax attacks happened at a
time when Congress was discussing the USA Patriot Act and that it was sent to two
Democrat senators, Tom Daschle and Patrick Leahy, who had reservations about
the legislation. Furthermore , it was suspicious that a leading U.S. bioscientist who
might have information concerning the anthrax attacks mysteriously died. In Ochs's
summary:

> A leading anthrax expert, Dr. Don C. Wiley, who may have been in a position to know
> of such a cover-up, died under suspicious circumstances a month after the attacks began.
> According to Memphis police officials, the bridge which Dr. Wiley fell off on Novem-
> ber 15, 2001, had a railing "high enough that even the 6'3" Wiley could not have
> accidentally fallen over without assistance." The local police suspicion of homicide was
> overruled by the FBI "and other U.S. agencies," who insisted it was a suicide.
> Would a U.S. agency kill a non-cooperator? According to former South African
> National Intelligence Agency deputy director Michael Kennedy, when another top bio-
> weapons expert Dr. Wouter Basson refused a job offer, the CIA allegedly threatened to
> kill him.[21]

A strange *New York Times* article by Lisa Belkin, "The Odds of That" (August
11, 2002), notes how at about the same time that Wiley disappeared another bio-
chemicist who specialized in germ warfare, Benito Que, was found dead in his car in
Miami, while the following week another bioweapons scientist collapsed in London,
apparently of a stroke. Belkins continues: "This list would grow to nearly a dozen
in the space of four nerve-jangling months. Stabbed in Leesburg, Va. Suffocated in
an air-locked lab in Geelong, Australia. Found wedged under a chair, naked from
the waist down, in a blood-splattered apartment in Norwich, England. Hit by a car

while jogging. Killed in a private plane crash. Shot dead while a pizza delivery man served as a decoy."

Rather than speculate on what might have led to these strings of murders, worthy of a Hollywood political conspiracy film, Belkins discusses coincidence, probability, and paranoia, suggesting that "a lot of things have 'just happened.'" For more skeptical minds, chilling possibilities emerged that the anthrax attacks originated from within the U.S. government itself and were used to create hysteria to enable the Bush administration to push through its quasi-fascistic USA Patriot Act; to invade Afghanistan with maximum force; and to increase vastly the budgets of the Pentagon, intelligence services, and National Security State. If the U.S. government had foreknowledge of the September 11 terror attacks and a plan to intensify the fear and hysteria through anthrax attacks that would enable them to push through a right-wing agenda, this would be the greatest crime in U.S. history.[22]

Or maybe it just happened that way. In any case, a couple of weeks after the September 11 attack and in the heat of the anthrax anxiety, public confidence was declining in the government's ability to manage the crisis at home and abroad. Washington, D.C., had never been under such bizarre and unpredictable attacks in the history of the Republic, and its citizens were ever more anxious and fearful of lethal terrorist attacks, the imminence of which Attorney General John Ashcroft continually warned the people. His pinched face and monotonous, flat voice were becoming icons of impending doom, and whenever he appeared on television, the public rightfully became alarmed that malevolent forces were adrift in the land, and that all was not well with such characters in government who were unlikely to protect the public and would no doubt make things worse.

Some unsightly tensions begin to emerge on the home front. On November 2, New York firefighters held demonstrations when they heard that officials had apparently decided that once the missing gold and silver ingots stored in a vault belonging to the Bank of Nova Scotia that were buried in the rubble under collapsed Building 4 of the WTC were found, the careful hunt for bodies and material would halt and bulldozers would be used to clean up the rest of the rubble. Firefighters were angry, however, because there were still some of their comrades lost in the debris and they had been ordered away from the site while they wanted to continue to dig for human remains. In an ugly clash with police, several firefighters were arrested, though New York City officials tried to paper over the conflict and did allow the firefighters to continue to search for missing bodies that were carefully removed and not bulldozed.[23]

There were reports that scams were emerging whereby people falsely claimed to lose loved ones in the New York City tragedy in order to gain dispersal of victim funds. There were also electronic swindles whereby telemarketers called to solicit donations for "disaster relief" with money travelling to bogus websites. Reports also surfaced of wholesale robberies of ATM machines in the World Trade Center area during the chaos of the attack. Moreover, stories circulated of remains of a fire truck buried underground full of piles of new jeans apparently stolen by the firefighters from an apparel store.[24] Thus, although initially the best of heroism and bravery of the common people was evident in the response to the tragedy of New York's police, firefighters, and ordinary citizens, more negative representations of crooks, scam artists, and heartless bureaucrats began to emerge. There were also doubts that the Bush administration would provide promised relief to help New York City recover, and although there was a brief attempt by the Bushites to waffle and worm out, public pressure forced them to make good on their promises.

As tensions continued to multiply on the domestic front and no good news emerged from the battlefront, pundits were quietly calling Bush's war "Operation Infinite Disaster." As the war entered its third week, there was already talk of a "quagmire" à la Vietnam, and there were worries that the U.S. strategy was not working, that the Arab world was pulling behind the Taliban and radical Islam, creating hoards of future enemies, and that the Bush administration and Pentagon strategy of bombing without having U.S. troops on the ground was not working. The following chapters will tell the story of the shaky start in the first month of the Afghan Terror War, the dramatic collapse of the Taliban, and the uncertain aftermath of the Bush administration Afghan intervention. The war story will be interweaved with narratives of revelations of the biggest corporate scandals in U.S. history, intense political battles on the domestic front, and vigorous debate over the Bush administration's unilateralistic foreign policy and cowboy capitalist domestic policy in one of the most extraordinary periods in U.S. history.

4

❖

Special Operations, Bombing, and Propaganda War

After two weeks of bombing, the results were not clear. Old-fashioned B-52s saturated large areas with explosive munitions and carpet bombing while winged B-2 bombers aloft for days flew from the U.S. to drop bombs directed by Global Positioning System Satellites with mixed results. With their 172-foot wingspan, these giant flying birds deployed Joint Direct Attack Munitions (J-DAM) to fire an array of weapons. Heavy AC-130 gunships armed with howitzers, cannon, and machine guns blasted alleged Taliban camps and material, while land-based F-15Es hit Taliban or Al Qaeda positions, with giant fuel-air explosive "bunker bombs" used to blow up munitions dumps and possible mountain and tunnel hideouts.

Military theoreticians described the conflict as "asymmetrical," as the Taliban had no sophisticated weaponry or modern military organization. Although the U.S. military claimed that they were destroying Taliban "command and control" centers, there was really no command or control in the sense usually used by the contemporary military. The videos showed in U.S. military briefings depicted U.S. bombs hitting obscure buildings or vehicles, but it wasn't clear that these were really military targets, or that the Taliban had a military force in the conventional sense, or that real progress was being made in the daily bombing attacks.

Moreover, whereas during the first two weeks of bombing the U.S. attacks had destroyed many seemingly military targets on the ground in Afghanistan, it had also hit many civilian facilities, including a Red Cross and UN supplies depot, generating many pictures of wounded or dead Afghan children and destroyed civilian houses. These pictures appeared daily throughout the world and were turning global public opinion against the U.S. intervention, especially in the Islamic world where large antiwar demonstrations were a regular feature of everyday life and threats against Americans in the area escalated. Likewise, the flood of refugees was producing heartbreaking images of people fleeing war and facing disease and starvation. Aid agencies continued to plea for a bombing halt so that food could be delivered to refugees, but the bombing continued unabated into a third and then a fourth and fifth week, with apparent setbacks for the U.S.-backed Northern Alliance forces and few appreciable gains.

On the weekend of October 20–21, drama in the theater of war intensified with accounts of helicopter assaults on Taliban positions, Special Ops forces landing to seek Taliban and Al Qaeda forces, and the beginning of an expanded U.S. intervention. There was much speculation that this was the beginning of a ground war in which U.S. troops would rout the Taliban, but later reports indicated that the Special Ops troops had not garnered significant intelligence in the raid and that the U.S. forces were having difficulty in locating the most important Taliban and Al Qaeda forces and leadership. Later, Bob Woodward would report (2002) that U.S. Special Forces were on the ground in northern and southern Afghanistan, using millions to buy off warlords and Taliban defectors, and organizing opposition to the Taliban regime.

On October 21, there was media buzz about an article in *The New Yorker* by Seymour Hersh that a U.S. Special Operations group had attacked a Taliban complex that held a house used by Mullah Omar, the Taliban leader, but had suffered heavy Taliban fire, which wounded many and helped discourage further operations. The failure raised questions concerning the efficacy of Special Operation units, with one Delta Force soldier telling a colleague that "the planners 'think we can perform fucking magic. We can't. Don't put us in an environment we weren't prepared for. Next time, we're going to lose a company'" (November 12, 2001). Eventually, however, Special Operations would be an important part of the overthrow of the Taliban regime.

There were few solid accounts of what was happening on the ground, but it was clear that the daily bombing was ongoing and civilian casualties continued to mount. AC-130s were equipped with loudspeakers telling the Taliban that they would be destroyed if they did not surrender. "You will be attacked by land, sea, and air. . . . Resistance is futile," the messages boomed, sounding like the *Star Trek* Borg warning mere humans of imminent destruction from the cyberneticized horde. New armed unmanned aircraft, the RQ-1 Predators, were allegedly in the field armed with Hellfire antitank missiles, although stories indicated that bad weather was limiting their effectiveness and some were crashing. Reports that an even larger and longer-range unmanned surveillance aircraft armed with missiles, the RQ-4A Global Hawk, which could bring weapons from the United States to the other side of the world, might be in action. Obviously, Afghanistan would be a testing ground for new weapons and strategies that would help to replace actual men with machines such as satellite-guided planes, taking "postmodern war" and the "revolution in military affairs" to a higher level.[1]

There were stories that the Taliban was disintegrating under the military attacks, but counter-rumors persisted that they were strong and defiant. There were also media reports that the anti-Taliban Northern Alliance was ready to march on Kabul and take over the capital city. Rumsfeld, however, stated in an October 19 press conference that the Northern Alliance rebels were not yet strong enough to defeat the Taliban, that the U.S. connections with anti-Taliban forces were not tight enough, and that the Taliban was appearing stronger than anticipated in their resistance. Moreover, when asked if the war against terrorism would have to be fought in countries outside of Afghanistan, Rumsfeld answered, "There's no doubt in my mind," thus promising that World War Three would be a long and violent one.

HEARTS AND MINDS

When, on October 21, U.S. assaults on the Taliban front lines intensified, speculation began that the Northern Alliance was preparing for an offensive on Kabul. As the fighting increased, streams of refugees headed for the Pakistan border and a human crisis was building as 15,000 Afghans trapped at the border were denied entry to Pakistan. Preparing for the long haul and a lot of bad publicity, the Pentagon hired the public relations firm Rendon Group to try to spin a more positive image to win the hearts and minds of the Afghan people. Rendon Group had previously worked for the Kuwaiti government, the Iraqi National Congress, and corporations like Monsanto that had PR problems. The Pentagon was paying the group "to monitor news media in 79 countries; conduct focus groups; create a counterterrorism Web site that will provide information on terrorist groups and the U.S. campaign against terrorism; and recommend ways the U.S. military can counter disinformation and improve its own public communications."[2]

In addition, the U.S. government hired advertising agency executive Charlotte Beers to serve as an undersecretary of state for public diplomacy to help fine-tune world public opinion. The Office of Public Diplomacy had been originally established during the Reagan administration to pressure the press and the public into supporting covert operations in Central America such as the Nicaraguan contras who, with U.S. support, were trying to overthrow the Sandinista government. The office was thus connected with propaganda and disreputable U.S. interventions. Beers, for her part, had specialized in shaping brand names for big corporations and there was speculation concerning how the new U.S.A. brand would be defined.

So far, U.S. attempts at molding world opinion had been disastrous. Although the initial U.S. spin was that the Afghan operation was dropping bread and bombs, combining military with humanitarian operations, the food effort had been a dismal failure with few of the food packets reaching the population, according to aid agencies on the ground, while starvation and famine increased. By early November, aid agencies predicted that between 6.0–7.5 million civilians were at risk of starvation with 600,000 on the edge of survival (*Los Angeles Times,* November 3, A11). Moreover, there were daily heartwrenching pictures of dead women and children circulating through the global media, producing a very negative image of the U.S. intervention. As *Salon* commentators noted:

> The AP photos that appeared in the *New York Times* on Monday were heartbreaking: Afghan men, including a father, weeping over the lifeless bodies of four small children, killed by errant American bombs. Coming on top of last week's reports that American planes had accidentally bombed a Red Cross facility in Kabul for the second time in as many weeks, the images forced the world to confront one of the most painful issues connected with any war—and an extraordinarily sensitive one in this war—civilian casualties.
>
> To date, human rights groups have confirmed that American bombs dropped on Afghanistan have resulted in at least 48 civilian deaths. America's enemy, the Taliban, has claimed hundreds if not thousands have been killed—figures the United States asserts are vastly exaggerated for propaganda purposes. But for much of the Islamic world, already deeply suspicious of America's motives and rectitude, any civilian casualties are evidence that the U.S. campaign is not against terrorism but against Islam itself. (November 1, 2001)

The world media were full of reports of the U.S. bombing and killing of innocent civilians throughout Afghanistan, with the Human Rights Watch claiming that twenty-three noncombatants died on October 21 in the village of Thori, six hours from Kandahar.[3] Shockingly, there were stories and pictures of U.S. cluster bombs being dropped on Afghan villages, killing people with unexploded shells. Cluster bombs expel as many as 200 small bomblets scattered over a large area the size of two football fields to maximize killing. Many of the bomblets do not explode upon landing and later kill people who have the bad fortune to encounter them, much as with unexploded land mines. Unexploded cluster bomb shells were still killing people years later in Iraq and Kosovo and many international agencies, such as Amnesty International, had called for the banning of the bombs; the Geneva Convention had outlawed cluster bombs, and a 1999 Ottawa agreement signed by Britain, France, and 140 other nations banned the antipersonnel weapons. When interrogated about the United States' use of these vicious devices, Donald Rumsfeld gruffly replied that of course we are using cluster bombs, and of course the purpose is "to try to kill them . . . to be perfectly blunt," as if the very question was an impertinence (*Washington Post,* November 2, A01).[4]

The cluster bomb problem, however, was significant enough for the U.S. propagandists to send leaflets advising the Afghan people not to pick up unexploded yellow cluster bombs, and telling them how to distinguish cylinder-shaped cluster bombs from the rectangular food packages, which were also yellow. The semiotics division decided to resolve the problem by changing the color of the food packets rather than by discontinuing the use of cluster bombs, munitions that were leading to mounting protests over the tactics and weapons being used by U.S. forces to the harm of Afghan civilians.

There were also reports that the U.S. was using depleted uranium, a low-level nuclear waste product, in its bombs, as it did in Iraq and Yugoslavia. In his *World War 3 Report,* Bill Weinberg presents a summary of world press accounts, "Radioactive Bombs Rain Down on Asia":

> "The use of reprocessed nuclear waste in the US air strikes against the Taliban poses a serious risk of radiation poisoning to the human lives in Afghanistan and Pakistan," said the Pakistan *Weekly Independent* last Nov. Added *Dawn,* Pakistan's English-language paper, on Nov. 12: "A leading military expert told *Dawn* that since Oct. 7 the United States Air Force has been raining down depleted uranium shells at targets inside Afghanistan, especially against the Taliban front lines in the north. . . . 'There is widespread radiation in many areas that could adversely affect tens and thousands of people . . . for generations to come,' he said."
>
> A 1994 report to Congress by the secretary of the army said, "Like naturally occurring uranium, DU has toxicological and radiological health risks. . . . Based on the lessons learned in Desert Storm, the army is developing procedures to better manage the internal exposure potential for DU during combat." The report mentioned tungsten as a possible alternative.[5]

A senior citizens' home outside of the western Afghanistan city of Herat was bombed on October 23 and the Red Cross facility in Kabul that had earlier been bombed was hit again on October 26. A Red Crescent facility, the Islamic equivalent of the Red Cross, was destroyed, as was a bus, killing eight or ten civilians. And on October 31, there were reports that U.S. jets had damaged a Kandahar hospital. By the end of October, it was claimed that the United States was targeting electricity plants, water facilities, and transportation, which would return Afghanistan to premodern conditions.

There was a disconnect between Pentagon briefings, with their generally upbeat assessments and meaningless showing of videos hitting obscure targets, and the daily pictures of civilian Afghan casualties and the sufferings of refugees. The juxtaposition of Rumsfeld and his Pentagon generals bragging about military exploits, or explaining away their mishaps, over and against pictures of suffering Afghans created extremely negative images of the U.S. Masters of War for the global public and especially the Arab and Muslim worlds. Rumsfeld especially was alternately testy and arrogant with reporters, as if any questioning of the wisdom of the U.S. military was out of line—a position also taken by conservative commentators. Moreover, as Senator Joe Biden (D-Del.) courageously stated, the United States was appearing as "high-tech bullies" against the primitively armed Taliban, with innocent Afghan civilians as the victims, by bombing them day after day without risking U.S. ground troops.

CIVILIAN CASUALTIES AND GROWING CRITICISM OF U.S. MILITARY POLICY

There was extensive media coverage at the end of October that the U.S. bombing had destroyed an entire village, Chowkar-Karez, in the vicinity of Kandahar. The

Taliban took international journalists on a tour of the village and there were many pictures of destroyed buildings, families mourning their dead, and outrage at the U.S. bombing. The Pentagon at first refused to comment and then said that they had reports that there was a significant Taliban meeting going on and that they had seen a caravan of cars driving to the village. But a local resident said that he and his family were escaping from Kandahar due to intensive U.S. bombing, and that the vehicles were civilian and not military, creating another public relations disaster for the U.S.[6]

Pursuing this story, a British *Guardian* reporter wrote: "After US AC-130 gunships strafed the farming village of Chowkar-Karez in October, killing at least 93 civilians, a Pentagon official felt able to remark: 'the people there are dead because we wanted them dead,' while Rumsfeld commented: 'I cannot deal with that particular village.'"[7] CNN reported in turn that an anonymous U.S. military source told them: "We hit what we wanted to hit" and that the village was "a Taliban encampment." Residents of the village, however, said that the convoy consisted of people escaping the bombing of Kandahar. In the fog of war, the truth is hard to see, but clearly the bombing of civilians was becoming a public relations disaster for the U.S. throughout much of the world.

In neighboring Pakistan, the world was horrified on Sunday, October 28, when sixteen Christians were massacred by Islamic militants during a church service. Hatred was obviously boiling over and the danger was growing that the military conflict could explode into war between Muslims, Christians, and Jews worldwide. Bin Laden continued to issue calls for Muslims to engage in Jihad and members of the Taliban repeated the call.

Things were also not going well for U.S. forces in the battlefield. On October 26, it was announced that fabled Afghan warrior Abdul Haq had been killed while trying to organize his tribesmen in eastern Afghanistan against the Taliban. Declared a "heroic freedom fighter" by Ronald Reagan, Haq was a leader of *mujahedeen* resistance against the Soviets and was one of the major hopes for Americans in helping to create a government structure after the envisaged fall of the Taliban. On October 23, Haq and some associates crossed the Pakistan border, sneaking into Afghanistan to rally opposition to the Taliban. On October 25, Haq and a small band were surrounded by the Taliban and a fierce fight broke out. Haq telephoned his associates in Pakistan, who called contacts in the U.S. and sought to get U.S. military help to save him from capture. Although there were reports of an armed drone firing at the Taliban, Haq was taken into custody and murdered, a poignant symbol of the American inability to control the situation in Afghanistan and organize a viable political alternative.[8]

Reports began to appear again that thousands of volunteers were pouring into Afghanistan for Holy War against the U.S. and that anti-Muslim outrage against the U.S. intervention was growing both from within the U.S. and Europe and in the Muslim world. Pakistanis shot down a U.S. military helicopter inside Pakistan, and there were worries that escalating hostility to the U.S. bombing campaign within

Pakistan could destabilize the Pakistani government. Obviously, U.S. troops in Pakistan were in constant danger, and there would be periodic attacks on the U.S. military in Pakistan and assassinations of Westerners for months to come.

It was not clear, moreover, that the U.S. was making any real progress in destroying Al Qaeda. On October 24, in a *USA Today* interview, Rumsfeld admitted that they did not know if they would ever find bin Laden and that it was like "looking for a needle in a haystack." Soon after, however, Rumsfeld backtracked and said that "we hope and we expect to get him." Moreover, Bush continued to bluster that they were going to "smoke out" the "evil ones" from their caves and "bring them to justice" or "to bring justice to them," a euphemism for murder.

Criticisms were beginning to mount from the right concerning what was interpreted as the insufficiency and failures of the U.S. campaign. Senator John McCain (R-Az.) argued that the U.S. needed to send in a significant amount of ground troops against the Taliban and not just rely on air war. Conservative columnist William Kristol criticized the Bush administration for trying to fight a war with "half measures" and a writer for the liberal *New Republic* called upon the U.S. to first and foremost "destroy the instrument of aggression" and then worry about the political situation in Afghanistan. One-time liberal Geraldo Rivera cajoled Henry Kissinger that the U.S. was not being tough enough in going after the terrorists, and announced in early November that he was quitting his cushy MSNBC cable job to become a war correspondent for Fox News in the Afghan crusade.

Military analysts remarked that the U.S. operation appeared almost identical to the air wars fought in Iraq and Kosovo, with daily heavy bombings from the air, mounting civilian casualties, uncertainty concerning how the bombing campaign would end, and worries that there was no well-thought-out endgame. Various stories noted that there was an "intelligence vacuum" on the ground concerning the whereabouts of Taliban and Al Qaeda leaders, and bad weather seemed to be blocking Special Operations troops from working effectively within the country. There were criticisms that the head of the U.S. military intervention in Afghanistan, General Tommy Franks, was "plodding and unimaginative," and that "the overall effort seems slow off the mark and pretty inadequate." There were also reports that in England, "senior ministers" spoke "disparagingly" of Franks, dismissing him as "an artillery man" reluctant to commit infantry.[9]

When U.S. President George W. Bush was confronted with problems of the U.S. intervention in Afghanistan, he would huff and puff and direct all questions to General Tommy Franks, refusing to take responsibility for setbacks or mishaps. There were also growing complaints from the Northern Alliance forces in Afghanistan that the U.S. was not doing enough and that the U.S. bombing was not really helping them in their efforts to overthrow the Taliban. When the U.S. started to use B-52s for carpet bombing of Taliban positions in early November, the Northern Alliance claimed that the bombs were poorly targeted and missed key Taliban forces. One Alliance leader had the temerity to complain that the American use of heavy bombers to strike Taliban positions "was a largely futile enterprise. He said the American officials planning the campaign appeared to be disregarding the advice of the Afghans who know better. 'Mr. Rumsfeld chooses the target in America. . . . This is our country. We know it best. If I were the defense minister of America, I could use his weapons better than he.' "¹⁰

The United States was equally critical of the Northern Alliance, which had not gained much ground on the Taliban since the U.S. had begun its bombing campaign a month before. U.S. forces complained that the Northern Alliance was not showing significant initiative, claiming that they had overestimated their Afghan allies' abilities, and that the Northern Alliance had been "underwhelming" in the fight so far. When asked if the U.S. trusted the Northern Alliance, Tommy Franks responded, "We're not sure," and there was constant bickering between the supposed allies that was leaked to the world press, starved for any frontline news about the progress of the war.

Britain's Prime Minister Tony Blair, the major U.S. cheerleader, had also had a bad week in what was seen as a disastrous trip to the Middle East. While in a joint press conference with Syria's President Assad on November 1, Blair was forced to hear a lecture, played on television throughout the world, that the U.S./Britain bombing campaign was causing "thousands" of civilian casualties, while Assad lauded Palestinian terrorists as "freedom fighters." After similarly unproductive trips to Saudi Arabia and Jordan, Blair was received frostily in Israel, where the Sharon administration refused to back his call for an end to the "cycle of violence" between the Israelis and the Palestinians, which many believed would be one of the ultimate keys to a lasting Middle Eastern settlement. The Bush administration had been singularly uninvolved in resolving this dispute, but the well-meaning Blair did not seem to have the clout to be an effective mediator.

The same week in England, there was a 12-point drop in support for the war according to one opinion poll, with 54 percent saying that there should be a pause in the bombing. In addition, a speech by Sir Michael Howard, the eminent British historian, was widely reproduced and discussed. Howard argued that it was "a terrible and irrevocable error" to refer to the current campaign against terrorism as a "war" rather than a criminal action, since it bestowed unwarranted legitimacy on the terrorists, mythologized them within the Arab and Western world, and created unrealistic expectations for successful military action and victory. Describing the American bombing as "like trying to eradicate cancer cells with a blowtorch," Howard argued that a "police operation conducted under the auspices of the United Nations" would have been far preferable.¹¹

With the Islamic Ramadan religious holidays approaching in mid-November, there was speculation that the U.S. might halt the daily bombing of Afghanistan, which was creating rising casualties and public relations problems with Muslims and others. Ever crude and blunt, Rumsfeld stated that *"that religion"* did not require the cessation of military activities during Ramadan, reminding audiences of Bill Clinton's contemptuous reference to "that woman." Condoleezza Rice announced on November 2 that there would be no pause in bombing during the Muslim holy month, a point repeated the next day by President Bush.

Inevitably, comparisons with Vietnam and references to the Afghanistan "quagmire" began to appear in the press. The CIA was blamed by "well-placed sources in Washington" for "total failure" in the south of Afghanistan, and Pentagon hawk Richard Perle was alleged to have made critical remarks about the campaign before a TV interview, stating: "I don't know if it looks to you from the outside like indecisiveness and insanity reigns, but let me tell you, it looks even worse from the inside."[12] Pakistan's beleaguered President Musharraf warned the United States that he hoped that the war "was not becoming a quagmire" and pleaded for the bombing to come to a quick end. But apparently the Taliban was digging in for a long fight and an endgame was not yet in sight.

Moreover, Dick Cheney's comments that there would be "more casualties likely at home than abroad" were not reassuring, nor were his comments that the "heightened threat of terrorism might need to be confronted for decades." Some were disquieted that Cheney was sequestered in an "undisclosed secure location," out of the public eye. He was rumored to be hiding in a mountain bunker secure from nuclear attack. Indeed, there was a bizarre parallelism of the sinister Cheney hiding out in a cave in the United States, plotting murder and mayhem in the Middle East so that his friends could have more control of oil supplies and could profit from the war,[13] while the sinister bin Laden hid in caves of Afghanistan, plotting terror against Americans. Meanwhile, Cheney's right-wing Republican allies were scheming in Congress how to steal more federal funds for their wealthy supporters and to push through a law-and-order agenda.

BACK TO POLITICS: WELCOME TO 1984

Although partisan politics had been suspended for a month or so after the September 11 terrorist activists, Washington was returning to the bitter political divisions that had marked U.S. politics for the past decade. Since the hijacking of the airplanes used in the unprecedented terrorist attacks on September 11, there had been intense national concern and federal debate over how best to improve airport security. The ability of four teams of hijackers to get through security with their weapons, fake bombs, and in some cases false identity papers on September 11 raised serious questions concerning airport security in the United States. Obviously, the system had totally failed, much like the system of voting technology in Election 2000, a devastating event that had apparently condemned the world to years of war and the destruction of the polity and economy by the Bush-Cheney gang.

There was consensus that something needed to be done to improve airline security, but significant partisan differences over what to do. The Democrats reasonably concluded that the airport security workers, who were paid minimum wage and were hired and administered by private companies, were poorly trained and the privatized system had dramatically failed. Thus, the Senate, led by the Democratic Party initiative, passed a unanimous 100–0 vote to federalize airport security workers. This meant that they would be better trained and supervised, and would have longer job tenure and security, thus reversing the trend in the privatization of airport security that had led to rapid job turnover and dissatisfaction. One major corporation, Argenbright Security, in charge of airport security in about 40 percent of U.S. airports, had been cited for hiring criminals, providing mediocre training, and failing to pass minimum security requirements and tests.[14] Yet the Republican-dominated Congress continued to block all Democratic Party proposals for federalized airline security, on the ideological grounds that this would increase Big Government. Despite continued shocking breaches of the airport security system, Congress failed to pass reasonable security measures until November 15, under the pressure of a plane crash in New York City that killed hundreds, as I describe in the next section.

As the global and U.S. economy careened into ever-deepening recession, thousands of jobs were lost weekly and the economic outlook continued to worsen. There was consensus that something needed to be done, but partisan battles raged in Congress over solutions. Bush immediately rushed through a $15 billion bailout to the airlines that benefited the corporations but not the workers, and proposed ways that the government would help shoulder insurers' losses from terrorist attacks. The $90-billion economic stimulus package urged in October by the Bush administration and the Republican-dominated Congress included handouts in tax rebates to major U.S. corporations, including $1.4 billion for IBM, $833 million for General Motors, $671 million for General Electric, $572 million for ChevronTexaco, $254 million for Enron, and millions more for other favored Republican Party corporate contributors. There were no provisions in the Republican stimulus package for job retraining or unemployment insurance for those who lost their jobs, no healthcare provisions, and no plans to get more money into the hands of consumers. Although the Republican package was perceived as war profiteering that would not simulate the economy, Republicans in the House approved the package, on a virtual party-line vote, ending the spirit of bipartisan cooperation in Congress and setting the stage for bitter battles over the economy and budget.

Most disturbing to many, the Bush administration relentlessly pushed right-wing antiterrorism policies that threatened civil liberties and the open society that had been the pride of the United States. For years, hard-right conservatives had yearned for harsher criminal laws involving the expanded use of wiretapping, arrest and detention of suspects, restrictions on immigration, and a range of curtailment of civil liberties. U.S. Attorney General John Ashcroft was a longtime extremist advocate of tougher law and order, and he eagerly pursued the right's wish list assault on civil liberties. The Bush administration pushed through a compliant Congress a frightening bill, euphemistically titled the USA Patriot Act, passed by Congress with little significant opposition on October 25 and signed the next day by President Bush with Dick Cheney, John Ashcroft, and other right-wing extremists barely able to control their glee. The act considerably expanded the power of the FBI to spy on wireless telephone calls and the Internet, to circulate the information obtained to other government agencies, and to detain immigrants on the orders of the attorney general, all without court review.

The Bush administration's new White House Office of Homeland Security established an antiterrorism agency answerable only to the president, bypassing Congress completely. The Bush administration also instructed the Pentagon to create an office of the commander-in-chief for homeland defense and to involve the military in domestic affairs. There was talk of putting aside a 150-year-old statute, known as the Posse Comitatus Act, which keeps the military out of the business of domestic law enforcement, thus paving the way for a further militarization of society. In addition, the FBI was refashioned from an agency to fight crime to a government arm of the war against terrorism, providing instruments of domestic repression and a police state.

On October 31, Attorney General Ashcroft ruled that the government could eavesdrop on phone calls between lawyers and clients if it was judged there was "reasonable suspicion" to justify such a move. By November, over 1,200 people had been arrested and detained, usually Arabs or Muslims and mostly without legal representation. When these massive detentions failed to produce any new evidence of the Al Qaeda network or terrorist plots, a discussion began about whether the U.S. should engage in torture to extract knowledge from suspects.[15]

The Bush administration was thus carrying out a Jihad on civil liberties, and those who had supported the appointment of the Talibanesque John Ashcroft as head of the Justice Department were complicit in the systematic assault on democracy and constitutional balance of powers. Ashcroft claimed, like the Taliban, that he never read newspapers or watched television and that he began the day with group prayers and Bible readings with his close associates. The attorney general reserved for himself and his rightist associates to determine who was a terrorist; whose e-mail, telephone, and computer communications could be monitored; who could be arrested without warrant and held without charges; whose conversations with their lawyers could be monitored; and who in effect would lose all civil liberties if suspected of being a terrorist.

On November 14, the U.S. moved closer to a police state when the Bush administration summarily announced that it was going to hold military trials for any foreign terrorists, which would not be subject to the legalities of the U.S. judicial system. This decision, as with Bush's other draconian curtailing of civil liberties, was not done with consultation with Congress, and many feared that a drastic abrogation of the division of powers and further erosion of constitutional democracy was underway. The conservative columnist William Safire wrote in a hard-hitting op-ed piece, "Seizing Dictatorial Power" (*New York Times,* November 15, 2001), "Misadvised by a frustrated and panic-stricken attorney general, a president of the United States has just assumed what amounts to dictatorial power to jail or execute aliens." Other critics decried the coming of Star chambers, kangaroo courts, the emergence of a

Talibanesque legal system, and Jihad against civil liberties undertaken by the Bush administration.

Ashcroft and the Bush administration were attacking civil liberties, the judicial system, and the open society in other ways as well. When Ashcroft was nominated as attorney general, he promised to apply the law objectively and not to follow his well-known right-wing ideological and religious prejudices. But in a stunning use of legal muscle in November 2001, he overturned citizens' initiatives in California and Oregon by cracking down on medical use of marijuana that had been approved by ballot, and outlawed the right of doctors to participate in a terminally ill patient's suicide, which had been approved in Oregon elections. Moreover, Ashcroft put restrictions on use of the Freedom of Information Act, while Bush signed an executive order inhibiting access to presidential records. Bush had blocked access to his own papers as governor of Texas, where he had systematically engaged in sleazy deals with friends and contributors, wrecked the economy of the state, undid environmental regulations, and engaged in a record number of capital punishments. Critics suspected that his halt of scrutiny of presidential papers was not only an expression of his family's proclivities for secrecy, but was also to protect the many dubious activities of his father and others in his current administration who had served in previous Reagan-Bush regimes and had been caught up in the Iran-Contra scandals, various covert activities, and domestic corruption. Brazenly sealing presidential papers and other records, Bush was making it clear that the open society was a relic of history and that Orwellian state secrecy and control of information were the order of the day.

One could only yearn for the good old days of the open and free society as the Bush administration relentlessly deconstructed the scaffolding of centuries of carefully constructed constitutional democracy in order to create a dictatorial police state. This state of affairs was almost totally ignored by the TV channels, which were increasingly becoming propaganda instruments of the Bush administration, and were equally subservient to the wishes of the Texas Führer as the fascist media had been to the dictates of the Third Reich. As it rapidly disappeared, it became clear what a fine liberal, free, and open society the United States had been. With hysteria over terrorism, however, the deeply antidemocratic right-wing forces that controlled the Bush administration were pushing through legislation that was inconceivable months before.

In some ways, the Afghan intervention was the perfect war for the Bush administration. They could push their failing domestic agenda of tax cuts for the rich, increased spending for the military, repressive right-wing law-and-order policies, and a conservative social agenda. Such policies, unthinkable before September 11, were advanced with the assent of a traumatized country, that was willing to follow the leader in a time of crisis. A dramatic downturning of the economy and failures in the battlefield did not seem to harm Bush's popularity, which continued to hover between 85–90 percent in polls taken in early November. Trillions were lost in a declining stock market, thousands of jobs were disappearing, the federal deficit was soaring, and the national and global economy were in decline, but the worsening economic situation was not yet associated with Bush administration policies and his popularity remained high.

The Bush administration had, prior to September 11, already planned to push a patriotic agenda in the fall to identify the Republicans with the flag, patriotism, and nationalism, and Bush and his handlers used the terrorism crisis to push school pledge of allegiance measures and nationalist ideology. In the midst of one of the most frightening crises in U.S. history, it was startling how many visits Bush paid to schools and how often he used photo opportunities to present himself talking to children. Evidently, Bush's handlers thought it best to treat the U.S. public as children, to present Bush as Father, and to flood the media with Bush providing simple explanations to children of the national crisis. Moreover, in his few exchanges with the press, Bush himself appeared ever more childlike, repeating the propaganda line of the day over and over. When asked a complex question, he would wrinkle his brow as if engaged in deep thought and then spit out a simplistic answer like, "We are fighting terrorists. They are evil. We will defeat the evildoers."

On the whole, Bush had reverted into the Alfred E. Newman "What, me worry?" mode that had characterized his short but successful political career. His handlers endlessly told the press that Bush continued to get up before dawn, do his daily workout (including a four-mile jog), and get to sleep early. While he had planned to go frequently to his ranch in Texas for R&R, Bush was reportedly pleased with his weekend getaways at Camp David and appeared generally well-rested and relaxed. Some critics, however, made unflattering comparisons between the easygoing Bush and hardworking New York City Mayor Rudy Giuliani, who continued to labor mightily with New York's problems, or British Prime Minister Tony Blair, who endlessly traveled over the world to bolster the U.S.-led coalition and was starting to appear tired and weary.

Continuing to duel for public opinion, both bin Laden and Bush provided speeches to their constituents. The bin Laden videotape, released on November 3, contained another rambling diatribe against the West, singling out the UN, Pakistan, and other groups that had sided with the West for his threats. The text and video were almost completely ignored by the Western media and one had to go to the BBC website to find the text. A November 9 BBC commentary described the rant as a "bin Laden PR blunder," claiming that bin Laden's extremist fumings were beginning to embarrass Arabs and Muslims who did not want their grievances to be expressed in such a fashion or to be associated with terrorism. Many Middle Eastern and Islamic commentators were beginning to criticize bin Laden more sharply and found especially offensive his attack on the UN as an enemy and its secretary-general, Kofi Annan, as a criminal.

On the public relations war, the Bush administration was intensifying its efforts. It persuaded the Pakistanis to shut down its daily briefing by the Taliban ambassador, whose accusations of crime against the U.S., tirades, and jokes were spreading widely through the Middle East, providing a Taliban version of the day's events hours before the U.S. and Britain could respond. Accordingly, propagandists from Britain and the U.S. got together to form a PR offensive that would begin early in the day in London, so that the U.S.-Britain perspective could circulate throughout the East, and then five hours later Washington would take over the efforts in "public diplomacy," drawing on the talents of Bush administration spindoctors and former advertising guru Charlotte Beers, who was still devising ways to sell the U.S. to the Arab world.

There was also a well-publicized meeting in Hollywood on November 11 organized by Karl Rove, Bush's political advisor, who had made a career out of sliming political opponents and getting favors for corporate campaign donors. Rove met with the cinema community to discuss how they could aid in the war against terrorism, providing a PowerPoint presentation to the Hollywood moguls as if they were high school students. The industry leaders, mostly liberal Democrats, grimly posed for a photo op with the ultraright Bush operative Rove, who beamed at the lens during his moment of Hollywood glitter.

Rove and Hughes specialized in producing and spreading stories that would slander their opponents, and they were concocting a campaign to "demonize" bin Laden, already the most reviled individual in the world. As part of this PR spin offensive, George W. Bush announced in a November 6 speech to Eastern European leaders that bin Laden was trying to get weapons of mass destruction and thus threatened the existence of the entire world. This was well-known news that Bush delivered as if he were pronouncing it for the very first time, and a couple of days later bin Laden played into Bush's plan to make him a bogeyman by announcing that he already had nuclear weapons and was prepared to use them against the U.S.

Indeed, the daring bin Laden had summoned a Pakistani editor who had written a book on him to disseminate his latest round of messages, which were released on the weekend of November 10–11. In addition to claiming, "We have chemical and nuclear weapons as a deterrent and if America used them against us, we reserve the right to use them," bin Laden justified the terrorist attacks, claiming that "Muslims have the right to attack America in reprisal." Although bin Laden had not yet actually admitted to involvement in the September 11 attacks, his interviews and communiqués were identifying him with terrorism and Arab leaders were beginning to criticize him, insisting that his views were not those of conventional Islam.

Bush and bin Laden appeared equally bullying and off-putting to those who were not part of their respective constituencies and propaganda bases. Bush's "you're either with us or against us" position was experienced as arrogant blustering by much of the world, whereas bin Laden's ranting was leading to speculation that the guy had been locked up in a cave too long and was losing it.

The Bush administration planned another prime time television spectacular for November 8, billing his "reassuring" speech to the nation as his most important one in seven weeks. The TV networks, however, failed to go along with the hype, with only one network, ABC, playing the speech. Abandoned even by his ever-faithful conservative Fox Network, Bush got very low ratings, getting trounced by *Friends,*

Survivor Africa, and even the World Federation of Wrestling, suggesting, perhaps, that U.S. citizens were eager to return to normal and were becoming tired of Bush's exploiting the terrorism crisis for his own political benefit. For his part, Bush asked citizens to form local civil defense teams in the war against terrorism, although he offered no specifics and it was not clear that this idea was going to go anywhere.

On the whole, however, the U.S. broadcast media were prime propagandists for the U.S. war against Afghanistan. CNN reproduced a memo, leaked to the press, that its news talking heads must always present reminders of the terrorist attacks on September 11 when reporting civilian casualties and other U.S. military mishaps. The order really didn't need to be circulated, as CNN was almost completely a propaganda network, as were the other U.S. TV networks. Whereas the BBC, Canadian broadcasting, the world press, the Internet, and other broadcasting institutions highlighted footage of Afghanistan civilian casualties and U.S. military blunders, the American television networks continued to focus on the anthrax scare, new terror threats, and invocations of the September 11 bombing. ABC President David Westin apologized for a mild statement that he did not have an opinion on whether the Pentagon was a legitimate target, explaining that his job was to report the news and not explain it. Dan Rather continued to get teary-eyed as he would close his *CBS News* report with remembrances of the losses of September 11, and Tom Brokaw was surrounded by flags as he carried out his daily boosting of the war on the NBC/GE/Military-Industrial Complex network; moreover, NBC now carried a flag logo in its network image on the right-hand side of the screen, identifying the network with patriotism and the nation.

But CNN was perhaps the most aggressive in pursuing the propaganda/patriotism sweepstakes during the first months of what was being touted as a long-term and ongoing U.S. war against terrorism. By November, CNN had developed an introductory news collage of patriotic images that identify the U.S., war, Bush, and CNN in a harmonious unity of patriotism and goodness. The medley of various military and patriotic images was about thirty seconds long, appeared after the commercial break before the next cycle of news stories, and was accompanied by loud background military and patriotic music. The collage begins with an image of the destroyed World Trade Center and the heroic firefighters and police officers working to save their comrades, then cuts to an image of Tony Blair and the slogan "A New Spirit" across an American flag. This signals the global unity of the free world against the terrorist crimes and the rebirth of the spirit of crusading and patriotic Western militancy out of the tragedy of September 11. In fact, Britain's prime minister is the only major world leader enthusiastically defending the American crusade, and the unity and "new spirit" is neither as solid nor as salutary as CNN would like it.

After presenting the U.S. as innocent victims of a violent attack, CNN's collage next cuts to the evil enemy, Osama bin Laden, followed by two pictures of American soldiers with the flag as a background and the slogan "Trust" scrolling across the screen. These images set up opposition between good American soldiers and the evil bin Laden with the message to trust in our forces and leaders. The next collage juxta-poses an image of Bush with one of journalists busy producing news, with "CNN" embedded in the background twice and the slogan "Experience" scrolled across the screen. The fast flow of images identifies both "Trust" and "Experience" with CNN and Bush, also signaling how CNN has become a mere propaganda conduit for Bush. Thus, although CNN has "experience" in producing global news, we can no longer trust it to produce anything but military and political propaganda. As for Bush, one can trust him to do and say whatever his handlers tell him and to act on behalf of the perceived interests of the corporate and military interests behind his administration. But in a volatile and complex political situation, obviously he does not have the experience to cope with the multiplying problems, thus requiring blind trust and faith in believers that the Bush administration will pull us out of the crisis rather than make it worse.

The dramatic opening collage is followed by the words "A New War," with the flag as a background cutting to an image of U.S. troops on the ground with an airplane taking off and the slogan "Global" embedded in the screen. A quick flow of images show a midnight air strike on Afghanistan, CNN broadcasting the drama, a mourning couple, and demonstrating Islamic people with an American flag splat-tered over them, concluding with another American flag with the graphics "CNN" and "Depend On" blazoned across the screen. The final images position CNN as the source of news and images of the "new war" with all its drama, tragedy, and excitement, concluding with the equation of CNN and America, wrapped in the advertising slogan "Depend On," playing off their longtime logo, "Depend on CNN." The collage, in effect, marks the end of CNN as a neutral global news orga-nization.

Labeled the Clinton News Network during the Ted Turner days because of its supposed liberal slant (which was not true; it was centrist), CNN had a reputation as the best global network for worldwide news. During the Gulf War, CNN had the widest range of views broadcast, including Peter Arnett in Baghdad and a broad array of Arab and other critics of the war. During the Afghan Terror War, however, playing to a perceived conservative hegemony and replicating war hysteria, it became a one-dimensional funnel for the views of the Bush administration and Pentagon. Moreover, it incited domestic hysteria with its all-anthrax-all-the-time coverage, overload of tirades against terrorism, and propagandistic coverage of the war. And whereas during the Gulf War, CNN footage and reports were used throughout the world to frame the events, in the Afghan war it was Britain's BBC and ITN and the Arab Al Jazeera that got the scoops and footage that beamed through the global village.

In addition to the propagandistic collage that introduced CNN's news summa-ries, the reports were often overlaid with the same type of hokey melodramatic music in the background as the UBN and Fox Networks use. Also, CNN follows Fox with a constant stream of graphic headlines at the bottom of the screen, trumpeting each anthrax attack over and over and generating increased war hysteria and terror. These are clear signs of the tabloidization of CNN, which is going for the lowest manipulative denominator of patriotism. Each weekend, CNN loaded its schedule with documentaries legitimating the war and replaying September 11 tragedies with interviews with families who lost members to the crime, as well as documentaries attacking the bin Laden terrorist network.

Part of the reason for the conservative hegemony and propagandistic nature of American television was the pressure put on the television networks by right-wing audiences and those crazed with war hysteria. Reproducing the frenzy that U.S. network coverage was producing, audiences responded with fury whenever criticism of the U.S. military, Bush administration, or U.S. policy was mentioned, and many strenuously objected to any showing of Afghan or other civilian casualties resulting from the U.S. bombing. There were well-organized right-wing e-mail and phone campaigns to attack any network that was critical of the Bush administration or Pentagon, and the craven networks bowed to public pressures, becoming conduits of war propaganda.

On November 11, there was a protest in Atlanta against CNN's news coverage, with demonstrators chanting, "CNN: half the story, all the time." The protestors said that millions of Afghans faced starvation because of the bombing, but CNN was not reporting the story—nor were the other U.S. television networks. In fact, whereas the CNN president had ordered his minions to mention the enormity of the September 11 tragedy whenever reporting on civilian casualties from the U.S. bombing in Afghanistan, in a November 5 Fox News Network panel discussion, Fox "Managing Editor and Manager" Brit Hume questioned whether civilian casualties should even be a part of the news, since they are "historically, by definition, a part of war, really." Hume's Fox colleagues assented, while Fox anchors and commentators still wore the flag label pins identical to those worn by the Bush administration, as did NBC anchors (ABC ordered its employees not to wear the pins on camera).

British television, by contrast, as with the Canadian Broadcasting Network, had daily coverage of the ups and downs of the war in Afghanistan, including reports that were critical of the civilian casualties, refugee problems, and dangers of starvation in Afghanistan. The BBC also had occasional sober accounts of the difficulties in rooting out the Taliban and Al Qaeda network, as well as stories on growing British, European, and worldwide opposition to the U.S. bombing strategies. Thus, watching BBC or the Canadian CBC contrasted to American networks presented two sharply different views of the Afghan Terror War, with foreign news sources presenting critical perspectives, debates over policy, and disturbing images, while the U.S. broadcast media censored negative images or views and was purely propagandistic in its presentation and defense of whatever the Bush administration was doing, much like Orwell's propagandistic media in *1984*. As the U.S. intervention began its second month, the war itself was not going well, although you would not know it from U.S. corporate media television coverage.

5

❖

Vicissitudes of Terror War

On Sunday, November 4, one month after the beginning of U.S. bombing of Afghanistan, leading British newspapers claimed that that a major allied offensive was in the works. The *Telegraph* predicted a "ferocious escalation" of ground war, while the *Sunday Times* of London headlined, "Thousands of troops in big Afghan push 'within weeks,'" claiming that "British and American forces are about to mount the first significant ground offensive of the war in Afghanistan in an attempt to establish a 'humanitarian bridgehead' that would bring winter relief [to] hundreds of thousands of refugees" (November 4, 2001). The story suggested that ground troops in the north would drive the Taliban south to establish an area where refugees could be taken care of. Furthermore, the British *Guardian* published a story, "U.S. flies in arms for rebel onslaught," claiming that a massive airlift was about to take place "to supply Afghanistan's rebel forces with arms and ammunition for a major ground offensive against the Taliban." The airlift of supplies was to be accompanied by an influx of U.S. advisors to coordinate the operation, suggesting an accelerated involvement by U.S. troops.

Earlier, on November 2, the *Washington Post* had published a story titled, "Big Ground Forces Seen As Necessary to Defeat Taliban. Bombing Has Left Missiles Largely Intact." This report suggested that the U.S. was concluding that the Northern Alliance could not itself undertake a campaign against the Taliban and that U.S. ground troops would be needed. Interestingly, the *Post* story highlighted the relatively small-scale nature of the U.S. intervention, noting: "The average daily number of combat sorties over Afghanistan is 63, Pentagon officials said. That is just more than one-tenth of the 500 allied sorties flown daily against infrastructure and troops during the 1999 war to expel Serb forces from Kosovo and a tiny fraction of the 1,500 daily missions against Iraqi forces during the Persian Gulf War in 1991."

Other wire service reports over the weekend stressed the U.S. saturation-bombing on Taliban positions and that the U.S. was increasing the dropping of supplies to Northern Alliance troops. But a November 4 *New York Times* story, "Afghan Rebels

Seem a Reluctant Force so Far," was pessimistic concerning the Northern Alliance, indicating that they refused to train when light rain started and played volleyball while the U.S. bombed the Taliban. Another *New York Times* article on November 4 focused on "A Vigorous Debate on U.S. War Tactics" and implied that the Bush administration was deeply split over what to do next. And another article, "More and More, War is Viewed As America's," acknowledged that world public opinion was turning against U.S. policy after initially being sympathetic. The article indicated that the Bush administration was planning a flurry of presidential appearances and speeches the coming week to try to re-persuade the public that its policies were correct.

On Monday, November 5, 2001, American gunship helicopters attacked Taliban military positions near Kabul while U.S. warplanes, including B-52 bombers, blasted a variety of targets in Afghanistan. This was the first time it was alleged that helicopter gunships were used in the campaign and signaled a more aggressive role for the U.S. Likewise, the use of 15,000-pound "daisy-cutter" bombs suggested augmented U.S. military involvement.

A revealing article in the *Los Angeles Times* on the same day interviewed Afghanistan refugees in Pakistan and concluded, "With the rising civilian deaths, a nation once regarded as a savior is increasingly being seen as the enemy—and the Taliban as a victim" (November 5, 2001, A3). The article, by Alissa J. Rubin, collected a series of quotations from war refugees who claimed that they had previously been anti-Taliban and pro-U.S., but that the month of sustained U.S. bombing had made them anti-American and created sympathy for the Taliban. A similar article appeared in the *Washington Post* a few days later by Rajiv Chandrasekaran, "Support Deepens for the Taliban, Refugees Report: U.S. Errors Fuel Sympathy" (November 8, 2001, 1). Obviously, the hearts and minds of the Afghan people were not being won by the bombing campaign and despite increased U.S. propaganda, the anti-Taliban forces would have to soon begin winning victories to avoid growing opposition to the U.S. bombing campaign. A November 8 story, "Taliban Suicide Squads Primed for Action," suggested that Islamic fanatics were willing to engage in suicide missions against U.S. or Northern Alliance forces, a disquieting prospect in the light of other suicide attacks against the U.S. that seemed to bear the mark of Al Qaeda (*The Guardian*, November 8, 2001).

American corporate television, however, ignored accounts of Afghan civilian casualties or any disquieting news concerning the war. A *New York Times* article by Caryn James (November 9, 2001) noted that hundreds of thousands of U.S. viewers were turning to the British BBC and ITN broadcasts to get hard news on the progress of the war and how it was seen by other parts of the world.[1] James remarked that "after two months, American television's cautious approach has turned into kneejerk pandering to the public, reflecting a mood of patriotism rather than informing viewers of the complex, sometimes harsh realities they need to know." Indeed, many critics were noting that the BBC, Canadian CBC, and other foreign broadcasters were providing a much broader international perspective and focusing on disquieting issues such as the humanitarian dimension of Afghanistan refugees; the fallout from U.S. bombing of civilians; growing criticism of the U.S. bombing in the Arab and Islamic worlds; strains within the U.S. coalition; and growing dangers of an escalation of the Israeli-Palestinian conflict, which the Bush administration continued to ignore and that continued to fester, soon to explode.

The media were not just manipulated during the Afghan Terror War, but were a willing and compliant part of the war team, eager to promote U.S. propaganda, to attack the "enemy," and to show that they were part of Team USA. In the process, they made war fashionable again, and normalized military retaliation as the appropriate response to terrorism, thus helping to produce a more violent and dangerous world. A *Sydney Morning Herald* critique of U.S. television coverage noted, "Jingoistic, sugar-coated, superficial—those are just some of the criticisms leveled at US television networks' coverage of the conflict in Afghanistan in recent days—and not just by the foreign competition."[2] In a Newsworld conference in Barcelona, the director of Canada's CBC News said, "It's depressing to see the jingoism" in American TV news, and that watching U.S. news and European network coverage was like watching "two different wars" (*Guardian*, November 14, 2001).

This was indeed my own experience of monitoring the war. Everyday I would catch CNN and the U.S. networks' coverage of the war and compare it with BBC, Canadian CBC, and other international news that I was able to get on my Los Angeles cable and satellite systems. These sources and various newspaper accounts, found easily on the Internet, provided a completely different picture of the Afghanistan war than was being presented on U.S. television networks. U.S. television had degenerated into mere propaganda outlets for the Bush administration and Pentagon, providing relentlessly upbeat accounts of the successes of the Terror War and castigating anyone who raised any critical questions concerning the carrying out of the war and its effects.

As in the Gulf War, the Pentagon heavily controlled media access to the U.S. troops in Afghanistan, and very few U.S. reporters went out in the field to discover what was really happening. It was, indeed, highly dangerous for journalists in Afghanistan, and eight foreign journalists were killed trying to cover the story during a seventeen-day period in November. The Bush administration, notorious for its secrecy, was more restrictive concerning press access to the military than at any other period in history, according to many commentators. Although guidelines were established for media coverage of the military in 1992 after the Gulf War, these were thrown aside during the Afghan Terror War and new restrictions were placed on the media concerning what they could and could not report. The Pentagon threatened reporters with jail if they did not follow their marching orders.[3]

THE FALL OF MAZAR-I-SHARIF AND KABUL

On November 9, Associated Press wire services announced that Northern Alliance troops were declaring that they had captured Mazar-i-Sharif, a key site on the road

from Uzbekistan and Tajikistan to Kabul, which the Northern Alliance had struggled for weeks to take against allegedly fierce Taliban resistance. The increased U.S.
bombing in the area and Special Forces on the ground seemed to be finally taking a
toll on the Taliban, who reportedly fled from the city as the Northern Alliance
troops entered. Or perhaps the Taliban could have easily been dislodged from this
region, where they had no popular support, much earlier if the U.S. had properly
supported Northern Alliance troops in the area and had a better plan to rout them.

In any case, U.S. officials cautiously proclaimed that if the city of Mazar-i-Sharif
had fallen to the opposition, it could serve as a "land bridge" by providing supply
routes to the north and a staging base for assaults on Kabul and south Afghanistan.
But for the first time reports emerged, largely from the British media, that splits
were opening in the UK-U.S. alliance (*The Guardian,* November 9, 2001). British
ministers expressed frustration concerning the U.S. bombing strategy, the lack of
consultation with allies, insufficient U.S. focus on the humanitarian crisis, and the
U.S. failure to seriously address the Israeli-Palestine conflict. Although the British
had been promised that U.S. Secretary of State Colin Powell would make a long-
promised speech at the UN calling for a Palestinian state and taking a tough line on
Israel, this was cancelled, even though the Israelis had recently insulted the U.S. by
using the analogy of "appeasement" to the Nazis in response to U.S. pressures to
reach a settlement with the Palestinians and to halt violence against them.

U.S. news reports over the weekend of November 10–11 were largely triumphalist, celebrating the capture by the Northern Alliance of Mazar-i-Sharif and five
Northern provinces, which gave the anti-Taliban forces control of about one-third
of Afghanistan and an open road to march on Kabul. Alarmed that their entry into
Kabul would cause chaos before a multiforce governing body was formed, the Bush
administration urged the Northern Alliance troops to declare Kabul a free city but
not to enter it. There were also warnings that the West should not trust the Northern Alliance, which had killed thousands and raped and plundered the last time it
had captured Mazar-i-Sharif, while the Pakistanis also obviously did not want the
Northern Alliance to gain too much power in Afghanistan.[4]

Whereas most of the newspapers, wire services, and TV reports on November 11
had the Northern Alliance routing the Taliban, whose forces were allegedly fleeing
Mazar-i-Sharif and other Northern provinces and being taken prisoner or killed,
there was a report in the *Los Angeles Times* that about 1,000 Taliban fighters and
their Islamic Arab supporters were refusing to surrender in Mazar-i-Sharif, had taken
hostages, and were engaged in a bloody battle for control of the city.[5] By November
12, however, the Northern Alliance was claiming that it had captured the northeastern city of Taliqan, was moving toward Herat, now controlled the northern half of
Afghanistan, and was ready to move into the capital city of Kabul.

It appeared for the first time that the U.S. and allied forces in Afghanistan were
seizing ground and initiative, and that it would be possible to establish U.S. bases
in northern Afghanistan, to enable transportation and distribution of humanitarian
supplies, and to establish a territory in which they could go after the Taliban and Al

Qaeda. Whereas for the previous five weeks the Northern Alliance had severely criticized U.S. bombing strategies, now they were praising its precision and effectiveness. Perhaps, as many had suggested, it required U.S. troops on the ground to liaison with the Northern Alliance, provide onsite intelligence, and coordinate bombing with troop movements. It remained to be seen, of course, whether an intelligent military and political campaign would evolve and whether U.S. power would be used effectively.[6] As it turned out, the Taliban would soon collapse, but Afghanistan would be thrown into chaos and the main forces of Al Qaeda and the Taliban, including its top leaders, would escape.

Indeed, the Afghan Terror War was becoming increasingly bloody and chaotic. Disturbing stories about civilian casualties proliferated, including claims that the U.S. had bombed caves housing civilians, killing scores, and had destroyed a Muslim shrine in a small village far from the main cities. It was not possible to know at the moment if these were desperate Taliban propaganda stories or if the U.S. was continuing to bomb civilian targets that would erode support for its efforts.

The weekend of November 10–11 seemed to mark the accelerating advance of Northern Alliance troops and the beginning of the end for the Taliban as a governing force. To the surprise of many, it appeared that the Taliban was surrendering power much more easily than anyone had anticipated. Rather than defending Kabul, the capital city, the Taliban fled, leaving a power vacuum. Although the Bush administration told the Northern Alliance not to go into the city of Kabul, they elatedly entered over the weekend, on the grounds that their troops were required to stop chaos and looting and to maintain order.

In a cute media spin, BBC reporter John Simpson claimed to have "liberated" Kabul, marching into the city with his crew and picking up young street urchins to accompany him on his jubilant march to the capital.[7] Although the Taliban had apparently abandoned the city, the U.S. sent in a cruise missile that hit the Al Jazeera broadcasting studio. During the same attack, an explosion blasted through the wall of the BBC studio, reproduced in oft-played broadcast pictures. Soon after, Al Jazeera claimed that the U.S. deliberately targeted its studio, which was seen by many as a mouthpiece for the Taliban and anti-American propaganda.[8]

Britain's BBC and ITN footage of Kabul after the collapse of the Taliban was quite stunning, portraying not only the joy of liberation and freedom to play music and cut beards after Taliban prohibition, but also the atrocities and the devastation of war. U.S. television, by contrast, largely played upbeat imagery, and the Brits seemed to have scooped the Americans completely on the story; ABC was largely rebroadcasting BBC footage and the other U.S. networks were mostly Bush administration and Pentagon propaganda conduits with no original footage or reporting.

A *New York Times* story, "Savoring Strength in the North, U.S. Worries about Weakness in the South" (November 12, 2001), signaled precisely the problem now facing the U.S. military. Although the Northern Alliance controlled the part of the country where their tribal groups were dominant, the Taliban was rooted in the tribal culture of the south and seemed to have strong support. Media accounts claimed that the Taliban, after escaping from Kabul and northern Afghanistan, were fleeing from the south to Pakistan, and that local southern Afghan warlords and their armies were arresting or chasing the Taliban away, and in some cases killing them.

The main story highlighted that the Taliban "spiritual center" of Kandahar was under siege from Northern Alliance troops and southern forces rebelling against the Taliban. Oppositional forces claimed that they had taken the airport in Kandahar and that the city was in chaos. Moreover, the Taliban (or Northern Alliance troops) had looted all international aid and food agencies in Mazar-i-Sharif, and hundreds of young Pakistani volunteers who had been abandoned by the Taliban and were supposed to fight the Northern Alliance were reportedly massacred. Pictures showed victorious rebel troops killing the Taliban and their Arab supporters. In particular, the BBC broadcast video of Northern Alliance forces killing Pakistani and other Taliban volunteers, stealing their wallets, and holding up their identity cards to gleefully proclaim that they were "foreigners" and deserved to be killed. Taliban supporters were also being arrested in Kabul and other cities, and the BBC and ITN broadcast video showing their arrest, their detention in prisons that looked like animal cages, and in some cases their deaths. Hundreds were killed in the fighting of the past few days, and revenge, looting, and disorder were spreading throughout the country.

The U.S. released statements that bin Laden, Al Qaeda, and the Taliban leadership "were on the move" and that U.S. intelligence was targeting them. Taliban support in the south was also rapidly eroding, with southern tribal groups and militia turning on the Taliban and changing sides, a practice described as a longtime Afghan tradition. The question of the moment, however, seemed to be whether political order and stability could be imposed on the rapidly evolving political situation in Afghanistan and what would be the Al Qaeda response to the routing of the Taliban.

TRAGEDY AND FEAR:
WELCOME TO THE TERROR AGE

On Monday, November 11, Veteran's Day was being celebrated in the United States while reports came in from Afghanistan that the Northern Alliance had just taken the key western city of Herat and now controlled over half of the country, with the Taliban in retreat and flight throughout Afghanistan. Yet news from New York overshadowed the Afghanistan story. Early morning reports announced, "American Airline Jet Crashes in New York" and "Homes in Queens on Fire." Minutes after taking off from John F. Kennedy Airport on Long Island, New York, American Airlines flight 587 crashed in the Rockaway section of Queens, a New York working-class borough where many firefighters and police who died in the World Trade Center attack had lived. Witnesses reported seeing an explosion in the air, whereas others saw one of the engines slipping off, generating speculation as to whether a terrorist bombing or sabotage had caused the crash.

It was not immediately known what the cause of the airline crash had been, giving rise to proliferating conjecture. America was living in constant fear. Once again, it was all-terror-all-the-time on the television networks. Two hundred fifty-five passengers and crew on the plane were dead, forty-four fire trucks and 200 firefighters were sent to Queens where houses were burning, and the rituals of terror were being repeated once again. There was wall-to-wall television coverage of the tragedy site, interviews with eyewitnesses, and press conferences with Rudy Giuliani.

Statements from the White House indicated initially that they had no information on the crash and then claimed that they believed it was not terrorist-related. Since it was not clear what actually happened, and as since I write at the end of 2002 it is still unclear, it is impossible to know why the Bush administration was pushing the interpretation that the tragedy was not terrorist-related. The Bush administration stuck to this position throughout the day and for days to come, suggesting that its spin on events was governed more by perceived political exigency rather than by a desire to level with the public and tell the truth.[9]

There were two other major stories in the news on December 11 concerning the dramatic twists of the Afghan war and the results of a consortium's inspection of the thousands of votes never counted in the 2000 presidential election. Yet in the new era of "breaking news," the U.S. cable channels continuously played the New York plane disaster, ignoring everything else. Using on-the-scene reporting, "expert testimony," and government interviews, the airplane crash took over the day's news, spreading fear that once again terror had struck and showing how New York was hit by yet another tragedy.

"Breaking news" TV has become a form of "reality television" in which TV capitalizes on the "you are there" dimension of television as a window into unfolding events. Endlessly repeating the key dramatic footage of the spectacle of the moment, the television cable networks breathlessly present new bulletins as important developments to keep the audience hooked on the story. Breaking news television assembles its "experts," who circulate the same-old same-old stale opinions and "official" establishment line. Some of the "experts" are government spinners who reproduce whatever "opinion" the image managers at the White House are concocting. On this occasion, and for reasons not completely clear, the Bush administration was relentlessly spinning the line that the cause of the crash was mechanical and that it was not related to terrorism, a conclusion that seemed rather hasty given that the plane had not even been inspected and that sabotage was certainly a distinct possibility.

Hence, the Bush administration throughout the day downplayed the possibility of terrorism and officials claimed that "mechanical failure" was the source. Moreover, every hypothesis was quickly shot down by the Bush administration and suspicions mounted that there could have been sabotage. In fact, the possibilities of a catastrophic mechanical failure or terrorist sabotage were equally disquieting, and there was speculation that American Airlines, the biggest national air corporation and a major Bush administration supporter, might go bankrupt—or be bailed out once again by its friends in the Bush administration, who seemed eager to bail out its big corporate supporters but were reluctant to provide increased healthcare or welfare benefits for workers out of a job.

Just when there was progress for the first time in the Afghan war, the world was once again shown the horrible consequences of a life in terror, in which the technologies of everyday life can be "repurposed," sabotaged, or simply fail, causing massive tragedy. The Terror War was giving Americans lessons in the fragility and contingency of life and what it felt like to be confronted with the possibility of instant and violent death at any moment. It was a harsh lesson and America had lost its innocence, although it was not yet clear what the American people would learn from the national traumas nor how long the national trials and tribulations would go on and under what form.

It was arguably a perfect time to halt the bombing in Afghanistan, to call for a peace campaign, and to discover new ways to fight the international menace of terrorism—although no major politician or pundit made this suggestion in the war-crazed and terror hysteria saturated country. But consider: The U.S.-backed Northern Alliance had just won an impressive string of military victories in their home, the north of Afghanistan, and the Taliban seemed to be collapsing in the south. Yet world public opinion had been turning against the U.S. bombing campaign, and with the month of Ramadan mounting Afghan casualties could turn many in the Muslim world against America and breed fertile ground for new terrorists. Moreover, influential voices in the Arab world were beginning to be sharply critical of bin Laden and Al Qaeda, and it would be possible to isolate the terrorist networks, to expose their vicious activity to the harsh scrutiny of world public opinion, and thus to promote eventual arrests and shutdown.

Furthermore, there were rising concerns over the humanitarian problem in Afghanistan, with millions of refugees facing starvation and sickness throughout its refugee and civilian population, and aid agencies facing the impossible task of addressing their needs during the bombing and political chaos. Although the Northern Alliance's control of the north could make it possible to house and feed part of the country, there was still the question of the ultimate fate of the Taliban, bin Laden, and Al Qaeda, who were rumored to be prepared for guerilla war in the mountains. There was also the question of stabilizing an obviously chaotic political situation, and no one could guess how many innocents would be the victims of unremitting fighting. Reports spread that millions of Afghans were continuing to flee, some from the north fearing Northern Alliance retaliation, some to the north seeking refuge from the Taliban, and some not knowing where to go. There were also reports from the UN of executions in Mazar-i-Sharif and of killing, looting, and general pandemonium throughout the country.

It was therefore an arguably appropriate time to call for a truce and declare a cease-fire as Ramadan was approaching, and to begin a long and difficult period of reconciliation between the U.S. and the Muslim/Arab world. A general amnesty could be promised to all of the Taliban who surrendered, laid down their arms, agreed to a reconciliation and unity government, and pledged to help seek and root out Al Qaeda, while Taliban leaders who had committed crimes could be brought to justice. In fact, it had been generally overlooked in the terror and war frenzy that respected UN High Commissioner for Human Rights Mary Robinson had released a report on Taliban war crimes just as the U.S. was starting its military operations. The report documented Taliban mass killings of civilian villagers and other war crimes, such as were committed in Bosnia, thus establishing the basis for an international tribunal for Taliban leaders responsible for these crimes and for supporting the terrorist crimes of Al Qaeda.[10]

The UN report could be the basis of criminalization for those in Al Qaeda and the Taliban who were culpable of crimes against humanity, and more evidence was surfacing daily of Taliban crimes. Moreover, in his various videotapes and interviews since September 11, bin Laden had all but admitted responsibility for the terrorist attacks, and there was a story disseminated in mid-November that Britain had gotten hold of a recent bin Laden communiqué to Al Qaeda that confessed his responsibility for the September 11 acts and that called for more such acts. Indeed, on November 13 the British government released new documents on its government website indicating bin Laden's confession of guilt in the September 11 terrorist acts, including a video that showed him gloating over the crimes, saying, "It is what we instigated for a while, in self-defense. If avenging the killing of our people is terrorism, let history be a witness that we are terrorists."

On the basis of evidence of Taliban and Al Qaeda crimes, it would be simple to criminalize bin Laden and Al Qaeda, to demand their surrender, and to send in UN-guided troops and perhaps Special Forces from around the world to get them if they refused to surrender. Such actions would give significant legitimacy to an international campaign against terrorism and could provide the basis for a reconciliation of the U.S. and the Islamic world, as well as strike a significant blow against global terrorism and move to stabilize the political situation in Afghanistan. Terrorism was obviously a global problem and required a global solution. As long as the U.S. kept its military intervention at a fever-hot pitch, however, it was clear that Islamic terrorism would continue to gain recruits and carry out daring and lethal attacks against the U.S. and its citizens. In a perpetual terror war, all would live in fear and there would be no peace or security in the West or in the Islamic world.

There could, in fact, be no total military victory against terrorism, and although the Taliban, bin Laden, and Al Qaeda might be defeated, the dangers were that new networks would grow out of the ashes of the old. Cycles of violence and retribution seemed to perpetuate themselves and the hoary metaphor of the mythical Hydra, the monster who grew ten new heads as each old head was cut off, warned that terrorism could not be eliminated by the crushing of one group. The right-wing militarists, of course, made this same argument, which they used to urge on the continuation of the Terror War Jihad to Iraq, Syria, or wherever else terrorists might be held. The issue therefore was whether a solely U.S.-led military campaign could cripple global terrorism, or whether this feat would require a multilateral and multi-dimensional global campaign.

Questions also surfaced as to whether the U.S. could afford to bear the expenses of waging war forever. Costs were now estimated at $1 billion per month for continuation of the Afghan war. By contrast, the bombing campaign in Yugoslavia had cost $3 billion, while the Gulf War bore a price tag of over $61 billion in military expenses, with U.S. allies footing most of the bill. In a situation of worldwide recession, it was unlikely that there could be much sharing of the costs of war and it was not clear how long the U.S. could sustain such expenses itself.[11]

There was no evidence that the Bush administration was contemplating any ceasing of its military activities. The Pentagon was giddy with the success of their bombing campaign and Dick Cheney briefly emerged from his hideout to gloat over the rout of the Taliban and to attack all of those who had criticized his military adventure. Earlier in the week, Cheney's wife Lynne and other rightists who claimed to be the "Defense of Civilization Fund" had circulated a chilling bulletin, attacking university professors and protestors who had spoken out against the Cheney-Bush-Rumsfeld military campaign.[12] The same week, the Bush administration had declared that foreign terrorists would be tried by military tribunal and continued to pass the sort of ultra-hard-right law-and-order conservatism beloved by Cheney and his cabal. Democracy was as clearly under siege in the U.S. as survival was at stake for the Afghans.

IRONIES OF THE COLD WAR AND THE BUSH–BIN LADEN CONNECTIONS

Meanwhile, back at the ranch in Crawford, Texas, George W. Bush entertained his soulmate Vladimir Putin, the president of Russia, by taking him on a pick-up truck tour of his ranchette and treating him to a Texas barbecue. Putin had reportedly taken horseback riding lessons so that he could traverse Texas-style with Bush, but it turns out that the Andover president is no Reagan when it comes to the equestrian arts. Reportedly, the two world leaders had agreed not to discuss touchy issues like the U.S. desire to throw aside all nuclear test ban treaties and go gung-ho for its Star Wars missile "defense" system. Putin must have been tempted, however, by a new series of reports that suggested that Star Wars II couldn't work, was prohibitively expensive, and would lead to the militarization of space and new dangers in the future of getting zapped by space satellites. The Pentagon Masters of War relentlessly pushed their folly, the compliant Bush went along with the fantasy, and Putin zipped his mouth, at least in public.[13]

The meeting between the presidents of the United States and Russia during a crucial phase of the Afghan war was truly a marvelous and surreal spectacle of dialectical reversal. A mere two decades earlier, the U.S. and Soviet Union had been involved in the last great battle of the Cold War in Afghanistan. After Carter's National Security Advisor Zbignew Brzezinski had begun a covert project in 1978 to arm the Islamic *mujahedeen* to overthrow a leftist government in Afghanistan that was friendly to the Soviet Union, the Russians responded with a military invasion of their own and established a puppet government after the previous Afghan regime was overthrown in 1979. A mere twenty years ago, in 1981, George Bush Senior, former head of the CIA and then Reagan's vice president, was conspiring with William Casey and the CIA to train Islamic radicals to fight the Soviets, providing the Jihadists with billions of dollars of aid, up-to-date Stinger missiles, tanks, rockets, and weapons to fight the Russians. Bush Senior and the CIA were generously establishing training camps to make the "freedom fighters" more effective Jihad warriors against the Soviets. Bush/CIA allies in this project included Osama bin Laden and the Islamic radicals who formed Al Qaeda, the Taliban, and the other terrorist networks now set on destroying the U.S.

Moreover, over the past decades, the Bush family had long been in business with the bin Ladens and other Saudi families who supported Islamic Jihad. Bush Senior had been friendly with various bin Ladens over the years, although eyebrows were raised when bin Laden's oldest brother Salem, said to be close to Bush Senior, died in a plane crash in Texas that was never explained. The bin Laden family had reportedly invested in Bush Junior's failed Arbusto oil company and the bin Ladens continued until just after September 11 to be close business associates of the Bush-Baker syndicate.[14]

In particular, Bush, Baker, the bin Ladens, and other highly placed government and business executives were major investors in the Carlyle Group, one of the biggest holders of defense industry stocks, an area that promised to mushroom in profits from the Terror War that their respective sons were in charge of (see chapter 1). Such a story could hardly be imagined by the world's greatest writers, but there you have it. Putin and Bush, whose countries were a short while ago on opposites sides of the Afghan war, were having a friendly barbecue in Texas. Meanwhile, bin Laden and the Al Qaeda, having been trained, financed, and armed by Bush Senior's Reagan administration and CIA, were being chased and bombed by the very forces that had originally helped set them up. And to make it personal, Osama, the black sheep of the bin Laden family, was being pursued by George W. Bush, the one-time black sheep son of his family, continuing longtime complex and shadowy relationships between the Bush and bin Laden clans.

As noted in chapter 1, FBI officials leaked a memo claiming that the agency had been given instructions to halt investigations into connections between the bin Laden family and Al Qaeda when Bush Junior took over as president in January 2001, after his successful election theft. The FBI had been warned to take their hands off of the bin Ladens and other Saudis suspected of supporting terrorism, no doubt because they were such close business allies of the Bush syndicate, and the clans apparently had further business and political interests to pursue.

Thus, the man whom Bush Junior called "the Evil One" was in fact part of a family close to the Bush clan. Hence, it turns out that the Us/Them dichotomy that the Bush administration had been perpetuating is more complicated that one-dimensional patriots would have it. In fact, They are Us, We are Them, and the Bushes and bin Ladens have long been partners in crime before becoming bitter rivals. The Bush–bin Laden Terror War is an old story writ large of feuding and overlapping families. The two families have been involved in business deals and intrigue for decades and a still-unknown story is behind the complex family histories and the current fight between George W. Bush and Osama bin Laden.

In fact, it is rarely acknowledged that earlier Bush interfamily squabbles had also exploded into public during Bush Senior's reign, in the forms of the Panama invasion and Gulf War. In these events, Bush Senior turned with fury on two men whom he had been associated with during his CIA-Reagan-Bush administration years. Many believed that Manuel Noriega of Panama was a longtime CIA asset, and there were many reports of meetings over the years between Bush and Noriega. It was widely believed that Noriega was working with Bush and a covert team in the Reagan administration to illegally supply weapons to the Nicaraguan contras after Congress had banned U.S. support; allegedly, Noriega was embarrassingly involved in the drug business and was using a contra support network to move drugs and launder money. Hence, these or other unspecified reasons led Bush to turn on his one-time ally Noriega in the 1989 Panama Invasion, just as Bush Junior was turning on bin Laden after the September 11 terrorist attacks.[15]

Bush Senior was also point man for Saddam Hussein during the Reagan era, helping him get intelligence and arms for his war against Iran in the 1980s; Bush allegedly approved billions of loans for Saddam that enabled him to build up his military and weapons program, and then turned on his former ally after Iraq invaded Kuwait in 1990, leading to the Gulf War (see Kellner 1992). Such are the things that great novels, films, and documentaries are made of, but our supine, ignorant, and cowardly historians and whores of the culture industry had long failed to take on the challenge of the amazing tales of the Bush clan. Hopefully, sooner or later, the world will get wise to the now clearly confirmed fact that Bush presidencies bring on war and economic devastation. The record is clear that the Bush gang will continue to rob the federal treasuries for their friends, allies, and funders; wage fierce Jihad against what is left of American democracy; and try to control and exploit what is left of the world economy. Until they are exposed and dealt with, there will continue to be war, terrorism, upheaval, and the erection of a military-police state with the hardcore right firmly in charge.

In any case, few historians or media pundits grasped the irony of the Bush-Putin relationship and the ideological flip-flop and contortions of U.S.-Russia relations since the end of the earlier Afghanistan war and subsequent collapse of the Soviet Union barely ten years before. As I documented earlier, the U.S. had armed the Islamic groups, which had driven the Soviet Union out of Afghanistan, contributed to its collapse, and then turned on its U.S. sponsors and declared Jihad against America. This time, the Russians appeared to be on the same side of the Terror War as the Americans, but there were in fact rather different economic and political interests behind the façade of the dramatic events in Afghanistan.

As noted earlier, Afghanistan and its neighboring Central Asian Republics were major sources of gas and oil, and behind the front of Bush-Putin smiles loomed an intense competition to dominate the flow of the enormous energy reserves of the region. The Russians wanted to control the energy resources of the region and to use Russian technology and pipelines to export the energy to both the West and the East. Obviously, the Bush-Cheney group wanted U.S. energy corporations to exploit these resources, build pipelines, and control the flow and sale of oil (see chapter 1).

Hence, behind the bizarre events of Terror War was a titanic struggle for control of energy supplies. As Bush met with Putin on his ranch, some commentators speculated that while it appeared that the U.S. was gaining momentum in the Great Game in Afghanistan for control of energy and its flow, the Russians were really winning ground since the Northern Alliance that was emerging as the major political force in Afghanistan was actually more closely connected with the Russians and would ultimately enable the Russians to gain the upper hand in Afghanistan. Other commentators saw the U.S.'s unilateral military intervention as a naked power play to guarantee U.S. control of the region and its energy sources. Time, of course, will tell which way the Great Game will go; it was, and still is, too soon to say who is really winning, or even what the real stakes of the conflict are.

AFGHAN CHAOS

Despite the rapid collapse of the Taliban in northern Afghanistan and the fall of Kabul, the Afghan Terror War was far from over. United Press International (UPI) announced on November 14 that Dick Cheney continued to change his "secret, undisclosed" residency "because the United States fears a decapitation attack by terrorists armed with weapons of mass destruction." *The Times* of London reported that bin Laden's nuclear secrets had been found in the Al Qaeda headquarters in Kabul, which had been abandoned (November 15, 2001). The safe house contained partly burnt documents that "give detailed designs for missiles, bombs and nuclear weapons," perhaps providing credence to bin Laden's boast that Al Qaeda possessed nuclear weapons that would be used in self-defense; as the Taliban collapsed, the moment of truth might be nearing or the nuclear threat might be hot air.[16]

To add to the terror equation, Mullah Omar told the BBC (which, as usual, was getting all the scoops) that the Taliban would fight to the end and "choose death" rather than surrender. He promised to counterattack soon and said that his forces have "a big plan" for the destruction of America, boasts echoed by bin Laden (*This London,* November 14, 2001). Another underground Al Qaeda laboratory was uncovered on November 15 that contained foul-smelling materials, and U.S. officials speculated that it could have been a chemical weapons factory (although later inquiries have so far unearthed no facilities for major weapons of mass destruction in Afghanistan).

The Pentagon was in victory mode on November 15 and circulated pictures of U.S. Special Forces troops riding on horseback with the Northern Alliance in pursuit of the Taliban. The genuinely loony Rumsfeld grinned his crazed smile from ear to ear as he showed reporters a photograph of a donkey used by the Northern Alliance to transport food and ammunition and described signing orders for saddles, bridles, and horse feed. The combination of hi-tech and premodern war was indeed surreal and the movie might be entertaining if we knew the conclusion.

Unfortunately, the U.S. was also forced to admit that it had bombed a mosque in the eastern town of Khost on the first day of Ramadan, although it denied a report that stray bombs had killed sixty-two civilians in the village. The British *Independent* reported that U.S. "Carpet Bombing 'Kills 150 Civilians' in Frontline Town" (November 19, 2001), and BBC interviewed families complaining of being bombed in their village by the U.S. after they had evicted the Taliban. Such stories did not appear on U.S. television or even in its press. U.S. audiences went ballistic every time there were reports of civilian casualties or any criticism of the U.S. military or Bush administration, showering the offending media source with indignant e-mail, telephone calls, letters, and threats to boycott. The networks went along with the popular mood and provided a highly sanitized and idealized view of the Afghan war, forcing TV audiences who wanted to really know what was happening to turn to British or Canadian television, widely available in U.S. cable and satellite systems, or to the foreign press, easily accessible on the Internet to those adept in information literacy.

The weekend of November 16–17 was opened by contradictory reports. The big story of the previous day had been that Mohammed Atef, bin Laden's right-hand man, military guru, and heir apparent, had been killed in the U.S. bombing of Kabul. It was also reported that Mullah Omar, head of the hardcore Taliban, had cut a deal and was going to depart Kandahar in exchange for his safe passage. Yet on November 17, Reuters claimed, "Taliban Denies Report of Kandahar Pullout," and stated that heavy fighting was going on in the city and in Kunduz, the two remaining Taliban strongholds, a contradictory situation that remained through the weekend.

The political situation on the ground in Afghanistan was also extremely confusing. On November 15, British troops arrived unannounced in the Russian-built Bagram airbase in north Afghanistan. No one had apparently informed the Northern Alliance, who immediately proclaimed that foreign troops were not needed to maintain order and should leave at once, leading British newspapers to nervously tut-tut about the fate of its troops and Britain to delay sending more forces. The Northern Alliance was assuming the functions of a new administration throughout the northern half of the country, to the alarm of many in the West (and Pakistan). But there were also reports that various Afghan warlords were seizing power and it was not clear that there was a coherent plan in place to stop the alleged revenge killing, power struggles, looting, and chaos throughout the country. Western reporters, who now had access to the country, were describing the disturbing situation in sometimes-grisly detail.

There were conflicting rumors on November 16 as to whether bin Laden had left Afghanistan, though the Pentagon believed he had not and continued to heavily bomb the remaining Taliban positions and intensify the hunt for Al Qaeda leaders. Laura Bush, not previously known for her feminism, gave her first national radio address in which she "fired the first salvo in what she called 'a worldwide effort to focus on the brutality against women and children' by the Taliban and the terrorists believed to be operating from Afghanistan's remote areas" (www.cnn.com, November 16, 2001). And it was leaked that the National Security Agency was going to launch a campaign to "keep it zipped," based on the World War II message that "loose lips might sink ships." U.S. citizens were told to be careful of giving terrorists any information that would help them plan their attacks. Already, the U.S. government had taken reams of information off of its government websites and now citizens were supposed to do the same. The much touted "information society" was evidently temporarily waylaid as Operation Enduring War relentlessly forged a new military-police state.

Pundits and armchair generals were ferociously debating the military strategy deployed and attacking those who worried about "quagmire," conclusions somewhat premature as the war on terrorism had hardly been won, and the Pentagon and Bush administration were indeed saying over and over that the war had just begun. CIA apologist Bob Woodward wrote in the *Washington Post* that "Secret CIA Units [were] Playing a Central Role" (November 18, 2001). Woodward's sources had leaked to him that CIA secret paramilitary units had been in Afghanistan since the beginning, and with Predator surveillance unmanned drones in the sky were providing key intelligence for the U.S. airstrikes. No doubt, soon afterwards, someone from the U.S. Special Forces would float a story that it was *their* guys who were the real heroes. And top level Air Force officials informed Thomas E. Ricks in the *Washington Post* that "Target Approval Delays Irk Air Force Officials" (November 18, 2001), claiming that at least ten times they had top Taliban and Al Qaeda officials in their crosshairs but the U.S. Central Command had held up approval, slowing down progress in the war.

Washington Post editorialists had been particularly bloodthirsty during the entire war, calling for intensified bombing, ground troops, and expanding the war to include states supporting terrorism, like Iraq. Writers for the neoliberal *New Republic* had also become extremely militaristic and hawkish. Its editor, Peter Beinart, had persistently attacked critics of the war and even as the routing of the Taliban was underway, the *New Republic* editors called for U.S. ground troops ("Hit the Ground," November 8, 2001).

While the U.S. press played out its military quarrels, the British press provided in-depth looks at the vicissitudes of the military campaign. A long two-part analysis in the *Guardian,* "The Rout of the Taliban" (November 18, 2001), claimed that there had been a fierce debate within allied U.S. and British military circles whether they should go for a fast campaign, using heavy bombing, U.S. ground forces, and Northern Alliance forces, or a slower, more systematic bombing campaign that would then draw upon the Northern Alliance and, if necessary, U.S. ground forces. Obviously, the latter strategy had been decided upon, and when Northern Alliance forces were apparently sufficient to rout the Taliban, U.S. ground forces were considered unnecessary—although after the U.S. failed to apprehend the top al Qaeda and Taliban leadership, military experts argued that the U.S. *should* have used ground troops.

A story by Cole Moreton in the *Independent*, "The Bloody Road to Kandahar" (November 18, 2001), documented the heavy fighting between Taliban and Northern Alliance forces and the incredibly bloody aftermath with countless revenge killings, both of which were downplayed in the U.S. press. Although Pentagon officials had noted that they were systematically attacking Taliban troops who were fleeing the cities they had abandoned, there were no estimates of how many had been killed and how many had escaped. There were also questions concerning how many U.S. troops had been killed. UPI released a bulletin on November 18 that an anonymous Bush administration source estimated that between twenty-five and forty U.S. Special Forces troops had been killed in heavy fighting on the ground. The report also indicated that the Pentagon had forged a policy of not announcing U.S. casualty figures. Secretary of Defense Donald Rumsfeld had announced earlier, "This is the last time I'm telling you the truth," and apparently he meant it. At one press conference, after admitting that U.S. forces were involved in ground operations, Rumsfeld said that none had been killed, a remark a State Department official regarded as "crazy."[17]

It appears that the U.S. had been impressed with Britain's policy of not announcing casualties in Special Operations forces and the U.S. seemed to be following suit. The Pentagon also appeared to be following the standard Bush administration policy of systematic lying and sacrificing truth to the political exigencies of the moment. Conservatives had once valued truth as a lofty value, but for Bushspeak the end was to manipulate the public and promote the Bush agenda, and anything said or done that promoted the agenda was justified. Evidently, the Pentagon, never an agent for truth, was pursuing Bushspeak for its own agenda, and lies and evasion were piling up as high as dead bodies in Afghanistan.[18]

Political chaos in Afghanistan was so striking that even the U.S. media were forced to deal with it. It appeared that the old Afghan warlords had returned to power and that renewed fighting between the competing power blocs and ethnic divisions was likely. As various coalitions of local Afghan forces fought the Taliban and the Taliban's Arab allies in their remaining strongholds of Kandahar and Kunduz, warlords seized power in their old fiefdoms, spheres of influence were divided up, and often-armed rival groupings faced each other.

But in southern Afghanistan, there was a human tragedy that the British and U.S. media were presenting in entirely differently ways. Fleeing from the heavy fighting in Kandahar, the last major stronghold of the Taliban, as many as 100,000 Afghans were refugees in the sand-swept desert, often without tents, food, or shelter of any sort. Curiously, ABC news used BBC footage of the camp, but the voice-overs by the BBC and ABC correspondents were totally different: British media presented the camp as consisting of refugees from U.S. bombing who said that fear of the daily bombing attacks had driven them out of the city, whereas U.S. media presented the camps as containing refugees from Taliban oppression and the dangers of civil war. Probably, there were many reasons for the refugees to flee to the camps, but it was symptomatic of U.S. television reports that it was now forbidden to say anything critical of the U.S. military campaign and to allege that U.S. bombing was causing civilian casualties or problems for the people in Afghanistan, leading to a disconnect between U.S. and world media representations in press and television.[19]

Meanwhile, media attention focused on the fate of bin Laden, Al Qaeda, and the rapidly dispersed Taliban leadership linked to them. *The Times* of London had reported on November 17 that the Taliban was in total collapse after Mullah Omar agreed to surrender Kandahar, its last power base. Evidently, this had been impossible as fanatic Taliban components and their Arab allies, linked to Al Qaeda, refused to give up the fight and were reportedly killing Taliban who were surrendering. In addition, the London *Independent* reported, "Taliban Abandon Surrender Plan after 'Prophetic Dream'" (November 20, 2001). Evidently, Mullah Omar, the one-eyed former commander and head of the Taliban, had "a dream in which I am in charge for as long as I live," and thus told Northern Alliance contacts, who passed on the story to the press, that he had decided not to surrender but to fight on.

The Times reported on November 19 that "Taleban Abandon bin Laden," claiming that the Taliban leadership had declared that bin Laden no longer enjoyed their protection. There were also stories that the Taliban and others were joining the U.S. and British in searching for bin Laden who reportedly was fleeing from cave to cave. Indeed, the U.S. was plastering Afghanistan with leaflets promising giant rewards for bin Laden's capture, was broadcasting radio messages with the same promise, and was dispensing great loads of Afghan money to tribal leaders who were being hired to search the vast number of caves for the elusive Al Qaeda terrorist leader.

One of the greatest manhunts in history was thus underway, with British and U.S. Special Forces joining the search for bin Laden. Press reports buzzed with the latest tittle-tattle of bin Laden's whereabouts, and speculation raged concerning his fate and what his followers would do to avenge him if he were killed. *Newsweek* claimed that bin Laden was now seen in many parts of the Middle East as a "loser" and an embarrassment to Islam and Arabs (November 26, 2001), but no one really knew what would happen after bin Laden's capture or murder.

A split seemed to be widening at this crucial moment between the Bush administration on one side and Britain and its European allies on the other. European nations, UN spokespeople, and various humanitarian aid groups were calling for an immediate addressing of the Afghan humanitarian situation, wanting to get aid efforts underway for the starving and brutalized Afghan people who were dying daily in refugee camps without adequate food, healthcare, or shelter. The U.S., it seemed, was solely focused on the war effort, on getting bin Laden and finishing up the Taliban. Britain had sent an advance group of troops to Balgram to begin clearing the way for the aid effort and rebuilding Afghanistan and had thousands more ready to come, as did many European and other countries. The Northern Alliance, however, seemed not to want more foreign troops in the country as they secured their bases of power, and the U.S. seemed to support this effort, publicly rebuking the British for sending troops and wanting to begin the humanitarian effort before conditions were ready.

A *Washington Post* report on November 22 that "Blair Denies Split over War" reveals, between the lines, that in fact serious fissures had developed between Britain and Washington over military tactics, the next stage of the terror war, when humanitarian efforts and nation-building should be started in Afghanistan, and how they should be carried out. Meanwhile, the remaining Taliban and Al Qaeda forces were playing cat and mouse with the Northern Alliance and United States in the last Taliban strongholds of Kunduz and Kandahar. Mullah Omar's photogenic new spokesperson pledged a fight to the death in Kandahar and told the world to "forget about September 11" deaths and focus on those being killed in Afghanistan by the U.S. bombings, a number he said to be around "2,000 civilians," which British analysts accepted as "probable after seven weeks of attacks" (*Guardian*, November 22, 2001).

While claims of a cease-fire negotiation between the Northern Alliance and Taliban in Kunduz had been floating all week, on November 22 fighting broke out. Although conflicting tales circulated that a deal had been cut and that the fighting was due to "miscommunication," Northern Alliance troops attacked the Taliban, who were simultaneously shelling Taliban front lines at the same time that other Taliban were surrendering. Donald Rumsfeld had said that the rumored 10,000 or so Al Qaeda and Arab "fighters" holed up in Kunduz could not have safe passage, and many believed that they would fight to the end and that there would be a bloodbath in the area.

In fact, while Rumsfeld blustered that there would be no safe passage or escape allowed of Al Qaeda and Taliban forces, thousands were escaping and, in retrospect, failure to apprehend their leadership and key fighting forces was a major failure of the U.S. military intervention in Afghanistan. On the eve of Thanksgiving Day on November 21, George W. Bush told thousands of cheering troops at Fort Campbell, Kentucky, that "Afghanistan is just the beginning of the war against terror. . . . The most difficult steps in this mission still lie ahead," Bush warned, since "there are other terrorists who threaten America and our friends, and there are other nations willing to sponsor them." Evoking the prospects of a long and bloody war and expounding on the "Bush doctrine," the born-again militarist president vowed to go after any nation that harbors, trains, funds, or supports terrorists. This meant long and protracted battles ahead, which would require "sacrifices by our men and women in uniform," but that would result in "complete" triumph over "evil." Welcome to the brave new millennium of unending terror war.

6

❖

Collapse of the Taliban

Although the Taliban regime was rapidly disintegrating, the situation in Afghanistan was increasingly chaotic. The situation was very dangerous for the press, and eight foreign journalists were killed during a short period in November. Yet more and more journalists entered the war zone as Taliban control over Afghanistan evaporated and the U.S. began setting up camps in various areas of the country. Access was tightly controlled by the U.S. military, and strict regulations guided what could and could not be released; thus, in the fog of war, it was difficult to perceive what was really going on. The Afghan war, however, was extremely dramatic and continued to be the focus of intense attention in the U.S. and throughout the world.

THE BATTLE FOR KUNDUZ AND PRISON UPRISING

The battle for the northeastern Afghan city of Kunduz raged on November 23 and reports of the plights of refugees, bloody atrocities on both sides, and a savage battle in the beleaguered city spread, especially in the British and world media. Curiously, in the 1980s, the CIA had helped construct camps and fortifications in the Kunduz area that were used by the Islamic radicals that the CIA supported to fight the Soviet Union, just as the CIA had helped construct cave fortifications in the Tora Bora area where bin Laden would allegedly hide out and apparently escape from. There were daily reports of the uncovering of Taliban atrocities and Northern Alliance revenge killings. Pockets of the Taliban continued to fight on in the mountains and gangs roamed through the country, robbing and killing journalists, travelers, and others who set out on their dangerous roads. Some relief agencies were able to deliver supplies to the north, but in most of the country aid convoys continued to be robbed and controlled by local militia, and were soon shut down.

On November 24, many Taliban surrendered in Kunduz, but the fate of the foreign fighters was still at issue. Stories spread that Pakistani helicopters were arriving in Kunduz to take some of their citizens out of the country, even though the U.S. had demanded that none of the foreign Islamic fundamentalist warriors associated with the Taliban and Al Qaeda be allowed to escape. The Pentagon denied that they had themselves sent in helicopters to extricate Pakistanis, despite repeated reports by journalists who saw helicopters fly in and then leave, full of what appeared to be Pakistani fighters. Perhaps the U.S. had allowed Pakistan itself to extricate some of its citizens as a payoff for support in the Afghanistan war. Pakistan had been extremely upset by seeing its client Taliban regime collapse and their rival Northern Alliance forces take power in Afghanistan. One senior Pakistani official had told the *New York Times* that U.S. Secretary of Defense Donald "Rumsfeld's been extremely callous" in his refusal to allow negotiations for the surrender of the foreign fighters (November 25, 2001), but although Rumsfeld blustered on and on about not wanting to allow Islamist fighters to escape, it appears that the U.S. was allowing Pakistan to take out many of its militants.[1]

Senior British officials also criticized the "belligerent" language of Rumsfeld, who had insisted that the U.S. was "not inclined to negotiate surrenders" and did not want to allow Islamic fighters to escape, a position that British officials claimed sent a message to the Northern Alliance that they had carte blanche to slaughter foreign troops. Indeed, "foreigners" were being blamed by many Afghan groups for its country's troubles and there were discoveries of mass graves in which slaughtered foreign troops had been buried, including one in Mazar-i-Sharif that reportedly contained over 600 bodies (*Guardian,* November 24, 2001).

There were accounts that some of the Arab allies of the Taliban were fighting to the end in Kunduz and that they had held the families of Taliban fighters in ransom, threatening to kill them if the Taliban surrendered or defected. There were also widespread stories that the Arab fighters had killed members of the Taliban in Kunduz who had chosen to surrender. Hence, fears of a bloodbath continued to intensify, even as some Taliban forces gave up the fight. In addition, stories continued to circulate of heavy civilian casualties from U.S. bombing in the Kunduz area, with growing number of reports of villagers being bombed by the Americans and even Northern Alliance troops getting hit (*Independent,* November 24, 2001). Al Jazeera, the Arab satellite TV network whose office had been bombed and destroyed in Kabul, reported that the U.S. had bombed suspected Taliban camps in Pakistan and that some bombs had gone astray and killed civilians—a story later confirmed by Western journalists and reluctantly admitted by Pentagon officials.[2]

On November 25 in Kunduz, hundreds of Taliban and "foreign fighters" surrendered and were taken to the Qala Jangi fortress outside of Mazar-i-Sharif. Other Al Qaeda and Taliban forces were negotiating surrender with representatives of U.S. ally and regional warlord General Abdul Rashid Dostrum, one of Afghanistan's most ruthless and powerful leaders. General Dostrum reportedly agreed to allow Afghan fighters to go home to their villages, Pakistanis to return home after the U.S. picked out Al Qaeda operatives, and other foreign fighters to be turned over to the UN.

Four hundred hardcore fighters ran away, heading west, but the large majority surrendered at Yerganak, a desert spot about five miles from Kunduz.

According to the writers of a front-page *Newsweek* story ("The Death Convoy of Afghanistan," August 26, 2002), Dostrum, accompanied by U.S. Special Forces, accepted the surrender and arranged for a number of container trucks to drive the prisoners from Kunduz to a prison at Sheberghan. Witnesses claimed that hundreds died of suffocation and that Northern Alliance troops fired into the containers, killing many more. In what became the biggest-known massacre of the war, witnesses also saw American troops telling the Northern Alliance to get rid of the bodies and saw the containers were taken into the desert and buried in a mass grave that could hold thousands of executed prisoners. According to a large number of reports, hundreds died in the container trucks, which did not have ventilation holes and were like an oven in the hot desert, and were buried in mass graves in the desert expanse of Dasht-e Leili.

Previous to the *Newsweek* story, Irish documentary filmmaker Jamie Doran had released a film, *"Massacre at Mazar,"* and shown segments to the German and European parliaments, and the story of mass deaths and graves was widely disseminated in Europe. The Boston-based Physicians for Human Rights had also been fighting to preserve the gravesite and to have official UN investigations of the atrocity. The issue is sensitive because there were allegedly U.S. Special Forces who helped supervise the rounding up of the prisoners, their incarceration in the trucks, and their deadly transport to horrendous deaths by suffocation. Doran claimed that he had filmed witnesses who observed American soldiers torturing prisoners, working with the Northern Alliance to dispose of bodies, and being implicated in the massacre. It remains to be seen if there will be further inquiries into war crimes in Afghanistan or if the climate of general terror hysteria will preclude such inquiries.

The Pentagon officially denied any knowledge of the mass murder and graves, and the UN special representative in Afghanistan said at the end of August 2002 that there would be no UN investigation because of the sensitivity of the issue to the Afghan government (and, no doubt, the U.S.).[3] In any case, after twelve days of siege and several days of bloody fighting, Kunduz had surrendered on November 26. Northern Alliance troops began marching into the city when it appeared that thousands of Taliban and foreign fighters had surrendered, with many of the former embracing their Northern Alliance "brothers" and pledging, if necessary, to kill Taliban fighters in the city, who had been on their side the day before!

Opposing Northern Alliance forces entered Kunduz from the east and west and competed for spoils, of which trucks were the prime target. Bands of Taliban fighters resisted and were summarily murdered; in house to house operations, other Taliban forces were arrested and the streets were full of dead bodies, some with their hands tied behind their backs and probably executed. British firsthand newspaper accounts stressed the revenge killings and atrocities, while U.S. papers highlighted jubilation that the Taliban had again been routed and a city "liberated."[4]

A chilling story by Justin Huggler in *The Independent* reported on November 27 of devastation from U.S. bombing of the town on Khanabad. After describing hearing the shock of an explosion and seeing a dazed old man helplessly looking at a bloody and unconscious fifteen-year-old boy who had just been gravely injured by an exploding cluster bomblet, Huggler describes the results of U.S. bombing of a town said to be a Taliban stronghold but whose residents claimed they were largely civilian:

> The Americans killed more than 100 unarmed civilians in Khanabad in the last two weeks, relentlessly bombing heavily populated residential areas in the town, one of the last under Taliban control. *The Independent* first reported allegations of civilian deaths made by fleeing refugees a week ago. Yesterday, after the Taliban left, those claims were confirmed.
>
> Whole suburbs—such as Charikari, where we were—had been destroyed, with giant holes and rubble where houses had stood. We found a man, Juma Khan, digging with a shovel in a crater where 15 members of his family had died. His wife and six of his children, his brother and all of his brother's children were killed when a bomb hit their house at 8 A.M. "I was just sitting there. The next thing I knew, people were digging me out of the rubble," Mr Khan said.
>
> He saw them dig out his 11-year-old daughter, Gulshan, the only other survivor. She has severe head injuries. "I don't know who to blame," said Mr Khan. He didn't even know it was the Americans who killed his family. "Maybe it was the Taliban," he said. "But whoever bombed me is my enemy."
>
> Another man beckoned us towards a pile of rubble, the remains of his house. It wasn't until we had climbed onto it that he told us we were standing on an unexploded bomb. "I was knocked over by the blast," he said. "When I came to, I staggered out of the house, but then I felt my legs give way and I fainted again."[5]

Meanwhile, a prison revolt had erupted in the Qala Jangi prison fortress, also controlled by General Dostrum with the help of U.S. Special Forces; the fortress lay outside of Mazar-i-Sharif, where a group of foreign fighters who had surrendered from Kunduz had been taken. A preview of trouble brewing ahead occurred on November 25, when one of the arrested Arab Islamists exploded a grenade, killing two top Northern Alliance commanders and wounding a British ITN journalist. The next day, in one of the more bizarre and grisly episodes of the war, a prison riot erupted, the prisoners took over weapons from an armory, and a bloodbath was on, with U.S. and British Special Forces firing on the rebelling prisoners, calling in airstrikes, and working closely with the Northern Alliance to crush the revolt that continued into the next week. Reporters on the scene predicted that "hundreds" of the prisoners were being killed in one of the bloodier events of the war, and the Pentagon confirmed this estimate later in the day, while denying reports that a U.S. soldier had been killed in the fight.

Over the weekend, sporadic fighting in Kunduz continued and the violent prison uprising went on through a second and into a third day. U.S. and British special forces were called in to help quell the insurrection in the Northern Alliance prison fortress, and U.S. observers called in military strikes that killed many of the insurgent Arabs but also wounded Americans and killed Northern Alliance troops in "friendly fire." The U.S. military admitted that five of its men had been wounded when a bomb went astray, a CIA employee was killed as the revolt unfolded, and the Northern Alliance lost about forty soldiers, while hundreds of the prisoners were put to death.

Initial accounts from a *Time* magazine reporter on the scene indicated that the Northern Alliance prisoners first seized a British newspaper journalist and then rioted. Yet a later report claimed that prisoners were enraged when an American CIA official started interrogating them, leading to a riot and seizure of arms in the prison fortress. There was also speculation that the Northern Alliance forces had allowed the uprising to take place so that they could slaughter the Islamist fighters, although others alleged that the arrested fighters had planned a suicidal uprising all along. Retrospective reports, however, which were confirmed by several news sources, suggested that the foreign fighters had been told in Kunduz, where they had surrendered, that they would be taken to Kandahar, where the Taliban were still holding out, and were outraged when they learned that they would be incarcerated in a Northern Alliance prison.[6]

After three days of fighting, tanks were brought in to fire on the remaining rebel prisoners and reporters came in and photographed scores of dead bodies. Both the Red Cross and Amnesty International called for an investigation of the uprising and its bloody suppression, and the global media reproduced gruesome pictures of mutilated bodies and hair-raising accounts of the bloody uprising and its suppression. But the macabre story refused to die. The following day, as Red Cross workers gathered the corpses for identification and burial, there was shooting from the fortress's basement, two of the Red Cross workers were slightly wounded and forced to flee, and a third was captured. Initial reports were of a lone gunman hiding in the basement, who had survived the violent assault on the fortress, but two more days of exchanged gunshots and fighting suggested more prisoner survivors. Finally, almost a week after the uprising began, the Northern Alliance flooded with water the basement where foreign fighters had holed up, after bombs, grenades, and even boiling oil had failed to roust them from their sanctuary.

On December 1, more than eighty wounded, famished, and near-dying foreign Islamic fighters emerged from the basement of the fortress with horrible tales of the siege. One fighter, Yaser Esam Hamdi, claimed to be from Baton Rouge, Louisiana, and many were shellshocked and dying.[7] Reporters on the scene prevented Northern Alliance troops from killing some of them immediately, and the Red Cross arrived to give them food and medical care as they were carted off to hospitals and prisons, no doubt capable of a tale worthy of Dostoevsky or Conrad.

THE AMERICAN TALIBAN

Indeed, a bizarre story emerged when U.S. Special Forces operatives approached an alleged American in a Northern Alliance hospital and whisked him away for interrogation. A CNN stringer interviewed the young man, who said he was John Walker, a U.S. citizen from Washington, D.C., who had gone to study Islam in Pakistan and joined the Taliban.[8] When his parents recognized him in the video, they affirmed that he was indeed John Philip Walker Lindh and that they had not heard from him since early in the year. A *Los Angeles Times* story identified him as "a sweet, shy kid from Marin County" who had grown up in the San Francisco area (December 3, 2001). No doubt, his adventures with the Taliban would generate countless tabloid stories and perhaps a TV movie.

The tale of the American Taliban generated tremendous media attention in the U.S. and elsewhere, and was clearly one of the more peculiar events of the surreal Terror War. Later accounts claimed that Walker Lindh, as a teenager in California, was infatuated with the Internet and hip-hop culture, taking on a "wigger" identity in Internet chat rooms and emulating white teenagers who take a black identity. The teenager became interested in Islam and reportedly converted after reading the *Autobiography of Malcolm X*. After studying Arabic and Islam in San Francisco, Walker Lindh traveled to Yemen to pursue his Arabic studies, then went to a religious school in Pakistan where he was recruited to the Taliban, who sent him to Afghanistan where he ended up a survivor from the Qala Jangi prison uprising.

The son of divorced parents, John Walker Lindh took on his mother's maiden name and allegedly received his first name as homage to John Lennon. Clearly, the American Taliban was acting out Lennon's song "Imagine," but gave short shrift to "Give Peace a Chance." Walker Lindh was obviously a poster child of hybridized postmodern identities, moving from hip-hop to Malcolm X to Islam and an especially virulent Al Qaeda fundamentalism. The Internet leaves a long trail and there was evidence that at one point in his hip-hop phase, Walker Lindh appeared to pose as an African American, writing: "Our blackness should not make white people hate us." From wigger, Walker Lindh mutated into a convert to Islam, querying a hip-hop site in 1997 that if the rapper Nas "is indeed a 'God,'" then "why does he smoke blunts, drink Moet, fornicate, and make dukey music? That's a rather pathetic 'god' if you ask me" (cited from *Newsweek,* December 17, 2001).

Walker Lindh's conversion to Islam took him to Yemen and then Pakistan, and he allegedly attempted to memorize as much as he could from the Koran and to intently study Islam. The dramatic switch of identities, which took him to fight with the Taliban in Afghanistan and to emerge barely alive from the prison uprising, illustrates a postmodern mutation and hybridization of identities. In the contemporary era, media and global culture offer the youth of the world a wide range of identities, which can be discarded and recalibrated at will. The American Taliban suggests that postmodern identity is unstable, flexible, and a construct that can be easily changed, refined, and fine-tuned. Presumably, as Walker Lindh faced death in Afghanistan, he realized that reconstituting himself as an American would help his survival, and in the days to come he would reportedly cooperate with U.S. intelligence, but did not initially interact with the U.S. troops who guarded him as a prisoner.

After news of Walker Lindh's arrest, his father frequently went on television to defend his son and hired a lawyer to help him with his legal difficulties. There was a fierce debate over whether the American Taliban was a traitor and should be tried for treason or was just a confused "poor fellow," as the compassionate conservative George W. Bush at first suggested. Bush's father was less compassionate and, in a rare television appearance on ABC's *Good Morning America,* was shaking with rage as he blurted out that he has "absolutely no sympathy" for the "Taliboy teenager" and was sick of "liberal Marin County hot tubbers." The uncompassionate senior Bush exclaimed: "I thought of a unique penalty: Make [John Lindh] leave his hair the way it is and his face as dirty as it is and let him go wandering around this country and see what kind of sympathy he would get."[9]

Many other hysterics went against Walker Lindh with a vengeance, calling for his death. Former prosecutor Nancy Grace went on television repeatedly calling for Walker Lindh's execution, even though she did not know the facts of his story. Andrew Sullivan used the Walker Lindh saga to savage liberal California culture, making the American Taliban a bad-boy poster child for permissive education and mindless liberalism. Sullivan created an extreme comparison between Walker Lindh, who he dismissed as a freak of California liberalism, in comparison to the "heroic" CIA agent, Johnny Spann, who interviewed Walker Lindh just before the prison uprising and his own murder; the interview had been taped by Afghan TV and was later shown throughout the world. Sullivan presented Spann as a paradigm of American conservative small-town rectitude and goodness.[10] Such comparisons are absolutely ludicrous, of course, since Sullivan could not possibly have known the complexities of both lives. Moreover, such a simplistic good/evil dichotomy is precisely the glaring sore and sign of the stupidity of contemporary conservativism, that constantly dichotomizes the world into good versus evil, as also seen with Sullivan's hero George W. Bush.

Walker Lindh was also used to attack liberal pedagogy, when the Associated Press, falsely as it turns out, quoted his high school principal, Marcie Miller, as saying that she was "proud" of her former student. This led to a series of vicious attacks on Miller and a whole arsenal of right-wing assaults on permissive liberal education. As it turned out, Miller had merely said that she was "proud" of the fine students that her school system had turned out, and had never praised Walker Lindh in particular.[11]

Later, it was claimed that Walker Lindh's biological father had come out as gay,[12] creating another wave of commentary on dysfunctional liberal families and covert attacks on gays. Walker Lindh was put in custody with the American military; questioned concerning his knowledge of Al Qaeda; and became a subject of intense debate with the military, the Bush administration, and the public.

In some of the first public interrogations whose results were leaked to the press, Walker Lindh was said to warn of dire Al Qaeda biological terrorist attacks imminently planned on the U.S., culminating in a major apocalypse that would "destroy America," though such threats were dismissed as "Taliban fire-talk." Walker Lindh allegedly later claimed that he had undergone Al Qaeda training and had even met the great man, Osama bin Laden himself. This led conservatives to describe him as the "crown jewel in the Al Qaeda arsenal" or a "pet" of bin Laden, who was being groomed for diabolical attacks on the U.S. Another account, however, claimed that Walker Lindh had told investigators that he chose to fight with the Taliban rather than choose "martyrdom training," which would involve potential terrorist attacks. In any case, the American Taliban's adventures with Al Qaeda undermined the argument put out by Western intelligence apologists, who defended their failures to anticipate the September 11 terrorist attacks by claiming that Al Qaeda could not be infiltrated, as Walker Lindh obviously had.[13]

Another very strange story in early December recounted how ten Uzbek Taliban warriors who had surrendered with the fall of Kunduz had been sent to a hospital in Taliqan for medical treatment, arousing the suspicions of a Northern Alliance officer who searched them and found hand grenades and other weapons. Evidently, the Uzbek's had been trying to get major Northern Alliance officials and the media to talk to them and had planned a suicide mission (*Washington Post,* December 3, 2001). One wondered indeed how many former Taliban fighters were wandering around Afghanistan and what mayhem they would unleash.

Meanwhile, new anecdotes indicated that U.S. Special Forces, who were widely roaming through Afghanistan, were "licensed to kill," and had allegedly executed hundreds.[14] The manhunt to catch bin Laden continued with the U.S. bringing in more troops and bringing ships to patrol the coast, and there were pictures broadcast on BBC television of U.S. officials doling out packages of U.S. dollars to pay Afghans to search the caves for bin Laden, with estimated costs of the operation reaching a cool $1 billion. Bin Laden sightings continued and rumors that he was fleeing on horseback were bandied about. Other stories claimed that Al Qaeda had ten bin Laden lookalikes who were appearing throughout Afghanistan to confuse his hunters.

A FEW HONORABLE PEOPLE

The honorable people of the UN made their first airlift of food and humanitarian supplies in a race against time in northern Afghanistan in late November. As winter relentlessly approached, starving and freezing refugees received food, blankets, and other essentials. Many international aid agencies were prepared to deliver supplies, emphasizing that the need was crucial, and criticized the U.S. for not helping to facilitate deliveries. U.S. ration packets continued to be yellow, the same color as cluster bombs, "which has meant many Afghans are too terrified to approach them" (*Independent,* November 24, 2001). And there was a report that a parachuted U.S. aid pallet smashed into a house, wrecking the building (*Los Angeles Times,* November 24, 2001, A16).

A major split had emerged between Britain/Europe and the U.S. on the continued strategy for waging war in Afghanistan. Many leaders in Britain and Europe were urging that humanitarian supplies be delivered immediately to the millions of starving and homeless people in refugee camps in Afghanistan, some in quite desperate straits, as press and non-U.S. broadcasting made clear in dramatic reports. The Bush administration and Pentagon, however, made it clear that they were not going to allow humanitarian efforts until the military phase was over. There were several reports that the U.S. commander of the operation, Tommy Franks, was strongly opposed to humanitarian efforts, which he believed would complicate his campaign, and that the Pentagon and Bush administration supported him. Accordingly, U.S. officials came out formally against humanitarian efforts on November 30, making it clear that the U.S. had subordinated aid efforts to the military campaign.

A *New York Times* story by Elizabeth Becker, "Level of Food Aid to Afghan Drops" (November 29, 2001), detailed the difficulties in getting relief supplies to the Afghan people, the decline in deliveries due to the chaotic situation of war, and the desperate need for supplies. The British had sent troops to Afghanistan in mid-November to begin what was intended as a securing of conditions to make possible major relief efforts. But both the Northern Alliance and U.S. opposed putting European or foreign troops in Afghanistan at present for humanitarian goals, underlining the unilateral and militarist nature of the Afghan war and questioning the seriousness of the U.S.'s commitment to the Afghan people.

On the domestic front, a few honorable people resisted the police state antiterrorist policies set forth by the Bush administration. Oregon police refused to question hundreds of young Muslims put on a list for interrogations with no specific reasons spelled out. Some U.S. senators were starting to question the attorney general, Ayatollah Ashcroft, who had detained 1,200 people and refused to even give a list of the suspects' names to Congress. In a ceremony in Washington, D.C., to dedicate the Justice Department building to Robert Kennedy, one of his daughters said in a well-publicized statement: "My daughter, Cara, is here today. Cara, if anyone tries to tell you this is the type of justice your grandpa would embrace, don't you believe it," presenting a sharp rebuke to the Bush administration.

Spain was refusing to turn over eight men suspected in the September 11 attacks until the U.S. assured them that they were to be given an open trial and not subjected to the kangaroo court military trials that the Bush administration was planning for "terrorist" suspects. Europeans were becoming more and more critical of the Bush administration's proposals to deal with the legal-judicial dimensions of the terrorist problem. Political commentators attacked the U.S. attorney general for rewriting laws of the so-called "USA Patriot Act" without consulting Congress; abridging by decree the Freedom of Information Act, allowing eavesdropping on conversations between lawyers and clients suspected of terrorism, and justifying military tribunals for suspects while refusing to meet with Congress to explain his police state measures.[15]

Meanwhile, television pundits became especially exercised over the closure of the White House to tourists over the holidays for security reasons. On the CNN program *Capital Gang,* for instance, on November 24 both liberal and conservative pundits went on and on about the threat to the open society and concessions to terrorism involved in shutting down the White House to tourists over the holidays, while failing to engage the more serious issues. The next day on *CrossFire,* only the most conservative member, Robert Novack, took the Bush administration to task for their Jihad against civil liberties.

In a revealing column, the usually liberal Maureen Dowd explained reluctance on behalf of the liberal establishment to criticize Ashcroft and the Bush administration's assault on civil liberties as an expression of genuine fear and a belief that extreme measures were necessary to fight the terrorist threat. Dowd's confession uncovered U.S. liberals' half-hearted commitment to an open and free society and their cowardly failure to attack the agents and instruments of the Bush police-military state.[16] The next day, conservative *New York Times* columnist William Safire, however, wrote a stinging attack against "kangaroo courts," arguing that the Bush administration was carrying out a "dismaying departure from due process" and endangering legal prosecution of the war against terrorism by driving Spain and European Union countries to distance themselves from U.S. legal extremism, thus undermining the international coalition against global terrorism (November 26, 2001).

The honorable U.S. Senator Patrick Leahy (D-Vt.) scheduled Senate Judiciary Committee hearings to deal with the Bush administration's assault on civil liberties. The hearings were highly publicized but inconclusive, although there was much criticism of Attorney General John Ashcroft, who Ralph Neas of the People for the American Way called "the most dangerous threat to civil liberties in the federal government," who was waging a "relentless assault on constitutional rights and civil liberties." Ashcroft himself appeared in a press conference on November 27, saying of the 1,200 or so arrested terrorist suspects that 538 remained in federal custody. Ashcroft refused to give out the names of those not yet charged (on the grounds that it would be a "blacklist") and claimed that Al Qaeda members were among the detainees, although some were skeptical.

Continuing to intensify his relentless assault on civil liberties and the open society, the Ayatollah Ashcroft announced on November 29 that his "Justice" Department was offering "incentives" for foreigners interested in U.S. citizenship to provide useful information on terrorists. With the Orwellian title of "responsible cooperators program," Ashcroft offered "visa assistance" and a "pathway to citizenship" for those who provided information on terrorists. Cooperative informers would be eligible for the "S visa," sometimes referred to as the "snitch visa," offering would-be stoolies privileged access to the much-desired and hard-to-get green card and U.S. citizenship.

Even more disturbing, on December 1 it was reported in the *New York Times* that Ashcroft was "Seeking to Free FBI to Spy on Groups" (December 1, 2001). Ashcroft was reportedly moving to undo restrictions on the FBI established to curb their abuses in domestic spying in the 1960s and 1970s, when J. Edgar Hoover used a "Cointelpro" program against antiwar activists, Martin Luther King Jr. and other civil rights leaders, and other domestic groups. It has been astonishing that no major figure has come out and called for Ashcroft's resignation. A highly controversial right-wing extremist, Ashcroft has gone further than any government official in U.S. history to cut back on civil liberties and he is now a clear and present danger to the survival of U.S. democracy. It is a sign of the contempt that the Bush administration holds for democracy and pluralism that they chose the ultraright and Talibanesque Ashcroft as U.S. attorney general and allow him to push the most extreme reactionary policies in a time of national crisis.[17]

The problem, of course, is that George W. Bush and key players in his administration are themselves hard-right extremists, and Ashcroft is an expression of the dominant Bush administration's ideology and its deeply antidemocratic tendencies. Commentators began talking of the Bush reign as an "imperial presidency," one that has relentlessly and quickly undone the balance of power within federal branches, seizing power for the presidency that was unthinkable in the past. Bush vigorously defended his war tribunals scheme on November 29, which would allow him personally to choose who would be subject to secret military tribunals set up to deal with terrorists.

It is highly ironic that the most imperial presidency of recent times would be constructed for a man who many judge to be the most incompetent, unqualified, and partisan president in memory. Previously, George W. Bush was perceived as highly disengaged, not interested in the details of foreign or domestic policy, and more committed to his compulsive daily exercise regime and long weekends and holidays than to affairs of state. Of course, Bush has always served as a figurehead for the small group of individuals who surround him and program his every move and gesture; his political handlers, such as Dick Cheney and other right-wing extremists, are the ones who are formulating the hard-right policies that Bush claims to represent.

In any case, U.S. democracy entered a highly perilous stage as the Bush administration continued to seize and augment presidential power, upsetting the delicate balance of power upon which democracy depends. The mainstream corporate broadcasting media continued to promote patriotism and war fever, while disquieting analyses of the threat to democracy spread through the international press and Internet. Indeed, U.S. television had become largely a mouthpiece for the Bush administration and Pentagon, while Internet and print media began questioning the Bush Terror War policy.

On the dishonorable front, bellicose armchair warriors urged the Bush administration to take on Iraq to get rid of Saddam Hussein; this included Dick Morris, Clinton's one-time pollster, who was thrown out of office when it was revealed that he regularly rented a hotel room to suck prostitute's toes as he briefed Clinton on the domestic implications of foreign policy.[18] Wire services reported on November 25, however, that the next phase of the Bush administration war against terrorism would probably involve strikes against suspected Al Qaeda–related terrorist camps in Somalia, Sudan, Yemen, and perhaps the Philippines. Yet in an especially bellicose public statement on November 26, Bush threatened action against countries like Iraq, who were producing "weapons of mass destruction" and threatened Iraq with military attack, insisting that Afghanistan "is just the beginning."

As for the anthrax wars, scientists had concluded that the deadly Ames strain had certainly originated in U.S. Defense Department chemical weapons facilities, although it still wasn't clear who had sent the letters (*Washington Post*, November 25, 2001). Thus, the anthrax that had caused deaths in Washington and New York and had panicked the nation originated from dangerous U.S. weapons programs, one more blowback of Cold War lunacy.[19] Eventually, by December 17, Bush administration officials themselves were forced to admit that the anthrax had originated in U.S. government labs, and agencies like the CIA and other defense institutions scrambled to deny that they had allowed the release of the highly toxic and dangerous anthrax strain that continued to infest the U.S. Senate building and that had taken at least five victims.

The anthrax hysteria provided in retrospect a Rorschach test in which protagonists could project their preferred villains as the culprits. George W. Bush recklessly insinuated that the culprits were bin Laden and Al Qaeda, further demonizing the "Evil One" who has so far eluded Bush's grasp. Those in the Bush administration and elsewhere who desired war against Iraq were leaking misinformation that the anthrax had the fingerprints of Saddam Hussein on it. Leftists were convinced that it was a U.S. right-wing extremist militia group that had sent it, since largely liberal senators and media organizations were targeted. The FBI was concluding that a lone lunatic like the Unabomber was responsible, whereas the German Greenpeace reported that they had received information that the anthrax was sent by someone in the biochemical weapons establishment to secure more funds and attention for their programs. Anti-Bush conspiracy theorists saw it as a weapon of the Bush administration to wipe out liberal senators and media and to create hysteria that would help in carrying out their Terror War and Jihad against civil liberties and the constitution.

Anthrax jitters continued to spread as hoaxers sent white powder and as occasional spores showed up here and there, an outgrowth, perhaps, of the potent earlier dissemination. Anthrax vaccines were strongly urged for government officials, who were also considering a national smallpox vaccination program. Furthermore, officials were also worrying over the disappearance of a Harvard University biology professor, who was an expert in potentially deadly viruses such as Ebola (*Boston Globe*, November 24, 2001).[20]

Domestic weirdness continued to multiply. A man from India and his wife who had survived the World Trade Center bombings were popular on the evangelical belt as the man told rapt listeners how Jesus saved him from disaster.[21] A pastor in Idaho put up an anti-Muslim church sign that read: "The spirit of Islam is the spirit of the antichrist" (*The Idaho Statesman*, November 22, 2001). The "Reverend" Jerry Falwell kicked in with some choice and well-publicized remarks that identified Islam with hate and terrorism, exhibiting a less-than-compassionate conservativism and a

Christianity defective in love and intelligence. And a *New York Times* article documented that "Apocalyptic Theology Revitalized by Attacks" (November 23, 2001), encouraging speculation that the end of the world war was near and Jesus' Second Coming was on the horizon.

Strangeness and horror continued to emanate from Afghanistan as well. As anti-Taliban troops surrounded the remaining Taliban stronghold of Kandahar, Mullah Omar released increasingly hysterical and shrill calls for Jihad against the Americans and demands that his followers fight to the death and not surrender, at a time when rational Taliban forces in Kandahar were allegedly negotiating surrender with local Pashtun tribes and foreign Islamic fighters were attempting to flee from the city. Mullah Omar allegedly had also put out a $50,000 bounty on the heads of foreign journalists and it was indeed dangerous for journalists in Afghanistan, with several getting killed in late November and the BBC pulling its staff from the north of the country because of rising violence.

There were also reports (perhaps U.S. misinformation) that bin Laden was becoming increasingly paranoid, that he might fall victim to Afghan betrayal, and that his end was near. One could only imagine what was going through the Al Qaeda leader's head as bombing intensified in Kandahar and southern Afghanistan. One could also wonder what was going on in Dick Cheney's head as the vice president hid in his undisclosed retreat, plotting the next stage in Bush administration robbery of federal funds for their corporate clients. Cheney had reportedly been paid severance of $31–36 million when he left the Halliburton corporation to become vice president, and he repaid the company and defense industry with many favors during his months in office (see Kellner 2001). When Enron president Ken Lay complained that the powerful energy regulatory agency Federal Energy Regulatory Commission (FERC) was not responsive to his demands, according to a PBS *Frontline* documentary and several news accounts, Cheney removed the head of the energy regulatory agency and put in a more compliant one.

Cheney had also allowed Enron President Lay and other big energy company officials to sit in and determine U.S. energy policy and thus served his former industry big time. But in November, the once-mighty energy company Enron collapsed in one of the major meltdowns in U.S. financial history, and George W. Bush and Dick Cheney's good friend Ken Lay, perhaps the biggest financial supporter of the Bush administration, were in disgrace. Did Cheney worry that he too could be undone at any moment, with exposure of his own many shady maneuvers on behalf of the oil and defense industries? As the president of Halliburton, Cheney had received a spectacular severance pay to make sure he would view the interests of the energy and defense industry giant positively and act accordingly. While CEO of Halliburton, Cheney had made highly questionable business deals with Iraq, which was on a prohibited enemy list; lied about it to the media; and faced exposure for his Iraq dealings. As Cheney assembled the Bush administration team, he made sure that personnel sympathetic to the interests of his favorite corporations and industries, the biggest Bush-Cheney campaign contributors, would receive favors and in the first months of the Bush administration provided stunning largesse and payback (see Kellner 2001, Chapter 11).

If the media ever focused on Cheney's business and political career, Cheney would be ruined. Knowing the morass of slime, corruption, and crime that he, Enron, Halliburton, and the many members of the Bush administration that criss-crossed between big business and big politics were mired in must have created sleep-less nights and worrisome days; one wonders what medications Cheney and Bush were on to manage their anxiety levels. And as bin Laden's health declined in his retreat, how was Cheney, who had four major heart attacks, holding up under pres-sure? What demons drove the demonic bin Laden to carry out such a mad Jihad, and what drove Cheney to such a ferocious battle on behalf of the right wing and for the energy corporations? Both of these figures represented the extremes of con-tending factions of the contemporary era, Islamic Jihad versus right-wing militarist and corporate capital, locked in fierce battle with the world as their playground.

In Afghanistan, possible endgames were emerging for the U.S. military interven-tion. Shortly after the fall of Kunduz, it was announced on November 26 that over 1,000 Marines had landed north of Kandahar and that the U.S. "owned a piece of Afghanistan," establishing a beachhead for military action against Kandahar and surveillance of roads leading from the city. Reports circulated that the Taliban had given up the Afghan border city of Spin Boldak, and that anti-Taliban troops now controlled most of the roads from Kandahar, which was becoming surrounded by all sides. Southern tribal leaders negotiated with Taliban friends in Kandahar for peaceful surrender, although it was rumored that Mullah Omar, his Taliban faithful, and the foreign fighters would go down swinging.

For people of honor, once again an opportunity for a splendid exit was offered. Negotiations were underway in the south of Afghanistan to surrender Kandahar and representatives of the people of Afghanistan were in Germany opening a conference to negotiate a peaceful future for the country. The Taliban were collapsing, bin Laden and Al Qaeda were on the run, and now was the time to criminalize them and send in Special Forces from around the world to arrest the Al Qaeda and Taliban leaders guilty of crimes against humanity. There was a long list of crimes committed by both groups, and documentation of their domestic crimes and planned terrorist activities were being assembled throughout the country. It would be very instructive for the world to get a clear picture of the vicious reign of the Taliban and diabolical Al Qaeda terrorist plots, in particular showing the Islamic world that these groups were harming Islam and were antithetical to its spirit and teachings.

The United States was lucky (so far!) that the Jihad movement had not been more explosive, that support for bin Laden and the Taliban was isolated, and that the Islamic world seemed to be turning against the Al Qaeda Jihadists as more and more of their actual and planned crimes were being documented. Now was the time to make bin Laden and the Al Qaeda outcasts in the Muslim world and into global bandits who were an embarrassment to Islam. Now was the time to begin dealing seriously with the Afghan refugee problem and to begin rebuilding the country.

Crucially, now was the time for the U.S. to begin mending its fences with the Arab and Muslim world rather than present itself as the world policeman and murderer of Arabs, as many Middle Eastern papers were doing as they continued to reproduce pictures and stories of U.S. bombing damage on Arab and Muslim civilians.

But instead of helping to negotiate a peace and mend relations between the U.S. and the Arab-Islamic world, Bush became more and more bellicose, warning the U.S. that it was entering a "dangerous period" and stressing that Afghanistan is "just the beginning" in the war on terrorism. In bragging mode, Bush said that "we're smoking them out" and warned Iraq that it was next if it did not allow UN inspectors back in to check if it had truly dismantled its weapons of mass destruction program. Political commentators noted that delivering an ultimatum is not a good way to begin serious negotiations and as Iraq rejected Bush's challenge, U.S. warplanes attacked Iraq's "no-fly" zone on November 27 (see chapter 11 for Bush's shifting Iraq policy).

Obviously, the Bush administration wanted to continue and widen the war and keep it going. Although the situation in Afghanistan was hardly stabilized and Taliban and Al Qaeda leaders remained at large, speculation buzzed about who the U.S. would bomb next and how long it would be until Saddam Hussein was in Bush's crosshairs. Of course, there was still much unfinished business in Afghanistan to deal with first, as bin Laden and the Al Qaeda leadership remained at large and there remained dangerous Taliban forces roaming around the country.

THE FALL OF KANDAHAR

By November 27, the Afghanistan border town of Spin Boldak's control was in question and in a fight with Taliban troops, four British Special Troops were wounded in a gun battle north of Kandahar. U.S. Marines who were setting up camp near the Kandahar airport also engaged Taliban fighters and the Pentagon announced that warplanes bombed a compound southeast of Kandahar said to be used by leaders of the Taliban, Al Qaeda, and Al Wafa, an Islamic foundation accused of terrorist activities. The Pentagon claimed that they had discovered forty sites where chemical, biological, and nuclear weapons might be produced and were investigating to see what had actually been produced at these sites.

But there were also disquieting and proliferating reports that civilian casualties from U.S. bombing were on the rise in Afghanistan. Moreover, more and more displaced civilians were blaming U.S. bombing for their plight, creating dangers of future anti-Americanism and assaults on Americans as payback for the bloody Afghan wars, and raising the specter of possibly intensifying anti-Americanism throughout the Arab world. An article by Rory McCarthy in the British *Guardian*, "U.S. Planes Rain Death on the Innocent" (December 1, 2001), tells how earlier bombings in the Kabul area destroyed villages and killed scores of civilians near the Afghan capital, leading the journalist to conclude: "Evidence of destruction on the ground and accounts from dozens of witnesses point to a devastating pattern of inaccuracy by U.S. bombers, in sharp contrast to Pentagon assertions of precision bombing."

Horrifying stories proliferated through the world media on December 2 concerning the extensive bombing of civilians in the Tora Bora area, where bin Laden was said by some to be holed up in caves and underground tunnels partly built by the CIA when they supported Islamic extremists in the battle against the Soviet-backed Afghan government in the 1980s. Accounts in various media listed the civilian victims of Tora Bora U.S. bombings to be 20 to 200 dead and scores wounded. Although the U.S. military claimed that they checked their records and had not bombed the villages in question, global television showed scores of victims in Jalalabad hospitals.

Northern Alliance Foreign Minister Abdullah Abdullah announced the same day that his sources indicated that bin Laden was not in the Tora Bora cave complexes, but around Kandahar where anti-Taliban forces had surrounded the city and were preparing for what they hoped was the final offensive. There were reports of intensified fighting on December 2, of U.S. and British Special Forces fighting in the area, and that U.S. ground troops might be brought in to take Kandahar.

A story by Paul Harris in the *Observer* (December 2, 2001), "Warlords Bring New Terrors," described the chaos in southern Afghanistan where warlords had returned to a reign of robbery, rape, and murder. The dogs of war had been unleashed and they were snapping in fury. There had been reports that the U.S. had investigated the alleged execution of 160 Taliban fighters by Northern Alliance forces in the Kandahar area in the presence of U.S. Special Forces (*Independent*, November 29, 2001). Although a Pentagon spokesperson said that they concluded no evidence of a massacre had been ascertained, it was clear that the war had let loose an orgy of bloodshed, retaliation, and barbarism, implicating the U.S. in one of the most violent episodes in recent history.

Moreover, an article by Paul Watson and Lisa Getter, "Silent Peril Lies in Wait for Afghanistan's People" (*Los Angeles Times*, December 1, 2001), documented continued civilian casualties by unexploded cluster bombs, noting that the U.S. had dropped 600 of these highly dangerous bombs, each of which had 202 bomblets, thus leaving thousands of "potential deathtraps on the ground." Reacting against excessive U.S. use of cluster bombs, several groups, including Landmine Action and Princess Diana's Memorial Fund, called for international controls on the use of cluster bombs.

The intense bombing of Kandahar continued as anti-Taliban forces approached the city from each side, refugees fled, and the area was said to be enveloped in an all-encompassing cloud of dust raised by the continuously pounding bombing. Reports came out as well that "U.S. bombs hit [the] wrong target for [the] second time in two days" (*Independent*, December 3, 2001): "A senior mujahedeen commander said U.S. strikes killed more than 100 civilians around Agam, 25 miles south of Jalalabad, on top of at least 70 killed in air raids on Saturday night. At least eight of the latest victims were guards and government officials of the Eastern Shura, the council of anti-Taliban mujahedeen leaders who now hold eastern Afghanistan." Once again, the U.S. seemed to have made a grievous targeting error, and a global television spectacle over the weekend was full of images of maimed bodies and wounded civilians hit by U.S. bombing mistakes. Once again, the Pentagon denied the claims of mistaken targeting. As reported in the *New York Times* (December 3, 2001):

> Claims of significant civilian casualties from errant weapons in that region this weekend were again denied today by the United States Central Command. A senior military spokesman at the command's headquarters in Tampa, Fla., said that surveillance and intelligence reports had been re-examined, and that no weapons had gone off-target. "We have reviewed all targets that were struck over the past 24 hours or so in this area, roughly from Jalalabad to the Pakistan border," said Rear Adm. Craig R. Quigley, the deputy Pentagon spokesman. "We hit everything that we have shot at. No weapons went awry. We struck no unintentional targets."

But news from a multitude of sources asserted that the U.S. had bombed at least four villages in error, with confirmation of these accounts by reporters and copious television broadcasts of interviews with Afghan civilians seriously wounded by U.S. bombing, all suggesting that targeting errors had been made. In an article, for instance, "A Village Is Destroyed. And America Says Nothing Happened," Richard Lloyd Parry visited the village of Kama Ado, in the Tora Bora area, and gave vivid descriptions of the destruction of a village upon which American B-52s unloaded a dozen bombs that allegedly killed 115 men, women, and children (*Independent*, December 4, 2001).

A *Washington Post* article reported on "mounting outrage over the U.S. bombing campaign. At a council of tribal elders in Jalalabad's central mosque, the assembled leaders passed a resolution condemning the attacks and demanding an immediate end to the bombings. Said Jamal, a deputy to Jalalabad's mayor, said local authorities have been overwhelmed with complaints in recent days from villagers demanding a halt to the air attacks. 'People are very unhappy about this American bombardment against civilians,' he said. 'They are very angry. Now they are saying they don't like Americans'" (December 4, 2001). Once again a Pentagon spokesperson, Rear Adm. John D. Stufflebeem, insisted: "We know there were no off-target hits, so there were no collateral damage worries in this series of strikes. I don't have any reports of any villages being struck. And all reports I have is that all of our weapons have been on target."

Disturbingly, U.S. military officials were entering the lying and denial mode as they had so many times before in Vietnam, the Gulf War, and other interventions (see Knightly 1975 and Kellner 1992). Of course, lying and treachery were norms in Afghanistan, so the specific civilian casualty stories in question could be misinformation. However, reputable reporters from U.S., British, and other newspapers and television networks had carefully documented many of the reports, raising the question of why the U.S. military did not simply admit to making targeting mistakes and apologize for civilian casualties rather than obfuscating. Evidently, the U.S. military had been told that Taliban or Al Qaeda officials were in the villages bombed, but it was becoming increasingly apparent that local Afghans were using U.S. bombs to get at age-old enemies and that the accelerating bombing of Afghan civilians by the U.S. was becoming highly embarrassing and could eventually turn Afghans against the Americans, as well as produce new Arab enemies as images of dead Afghan civilians were disseminated throughout the world.

Meanwhile, more and more U.S. troops, as well as some from Britain and other countries, poured into the undisclosed U.S. camp in the vicinity of Kandahar. This build-up of troops raised speculation that U.S. and allied forces would be used in an assault on or a sweep of Kandahar if anti-Taliban Afghan groups could not negotiate surrender or capture the city itself. U.S. officials repeated their insistence that Mullah Omar and top Taliban and Al Qaeda leaders could not negotiate release and would be held accountable by the U.S., and the world waited to see the fate of the Taliban regime unfold.

Over the weekend of December 2–3, Israel experienced its most deadly 24-hour period of terror in years, with a half-dozen major attacks, including suicide bombings in Jerusalem and Haifa that left at least twenty-six dead and scores injured. There were fierce calls for retaliation, intense pressure on Arafat and the PLO to arrest the perpetrators, and an immediate Israeli military response that created a situation in which Israel and the Middle East could explode into major war at any moment. There were speculations that Palestinian groups like Hamas were linked to Al Qaeda and were promoting bin Laden's dream of an all-out war of Muslims versus Jews, Christians, and the West. The stakes in Middle Eastern politics were raised, Israelis booed the Bush administration's peace mediator General Anthony Zinni, and the long-term failures to create peace between Israel and Palestine, coupled with the new war against terrorism, had created a situation of unparalleled danger.

Not surprisingly, negotiations in Bonn, Germany, between competing Afghan forces were multiplying problems and complexities. There appeared to be a split in the Northern Alliance between the Old Guard, centered around Dr. Burahanuddin Rabbani, the president of Afghanistan from 1992 to 1996 before the Taliban took over and recognized as president by the UN, and the younger members who appeared more flexible and accommodating. Rabbani had created obstacles earlier in the week when he insisted that key decisions could not be made in Bonn but must be ratified in Kabul, and he had made it clear that he did not want a large international peacekeeping force. His younger Northern Alliance colleagues appeared ready to ratify agreements in Bonn, insisted that Rabbani would not be imposed as president, and were open to negotiations, while many major foreign leaders called Rabbani, begging and threatening him not to create obstacles to a peace agreement. On December 2, however, he floated "new ideas on Afghan future" that were certain to cause controversy. Rabbani suggested, among other things, that Omar, bin Laden, and top Taliban and Al Qaeda leaders not be handed over to the U.S. for trial but should be tried in Afghanistan (*Washington Post,* December 3, 2001). Obviously, a major split was in the making within the Northern Alliance, and its differences with other Afghan ethnic and tribal groupings created an incredibly complex situation.

On December 4, the hopeful news circulated that the conference in Bonn had reached provisional consensus concerning a new government in Afghanistan with Hamid Karzai, a Pashtun leader and U.S. ally who was appointed to be provisional leader. But later that day there were reports that the U.S. "friendly fire" near Kandahar had killed three U.S. servicemen and wounded nineteen, as well as killing five members of the southern anti-Taliban opposition forces and wounding several others, including the new head of the interim Afghanistan administration, Hamid Karzai! Evidently, a satellite-directed U.S. missile went astray when U.S. ground troops were working with anti-Taliban Afghan units to help capture Kandahar.[22]

Fortunately, Karzai was only lightly wounded, for the next day it was announced that Taliban leader Mullah Omar had agreed to "surrender Kandahar," to hand over weapons, and thus to admit defeat. A murky deal was made between Omar and Karzai that would allow Omar to surrender and live "in dignity." In Karzai's version, if Omar renounced terrorism and agreed to give up Osama bin Laden, he could receive amnesty. The feisty Donald Rumsfeld, however, would have none of this and barely contained his anger when he blurted out that if any of "those people" gave Omar or other Al Qaeda and Taliban leaders amnesty, U.S. "cooperation and assistance" would "take a turn to the south."

Conflict between Rumsfeld and Karzai was not to unfold, however, as Taliban troops fled Kandahar with their weapons the night before the announced Friday surrender. Mullah Omar himself, who had repeatedly called upon his followers to fight to the death, quickly disappeared without renouncing terrorism, enabling Karzai to declare that Omar was "a fugitive from justice" and state, "I want to arrest him."

With the collapse of the Taliban regime, Kandahar erupted into chaos. Opposing factions of the anti-Taliban forces entered the city and fought to take control of arms and institutions. Looting was widespread and there were few reports of celebration as shellshocked residents coped with their new situation. U.S. soldiers tried to patrol roads leading out of Kandahar and reportedly attacked one Taliban convoy, killing seven. But no one knew how many of the Taliban and its foreign Islamic supporters successfully fled the city, and there were incriminations that "it was worse than careless to let the terrorists slip away" (*The Times,* December 8, 2001).

On the other hand, as pictures of the roads from Kandahar to the Pakistan border showed when television crews were allowed to enter the city, many vehicles and individuals fleeing the city had been bombed or shot. The road was littered with ruins of tanks, trucks, animals, and human bodies, so obviously many Taliban or Islamic fighters had been slaughtered on the flight from Kandahar.

The interim President Karzai called upon Afghans to hunt for bin Laden, while tribal groups organized forces to storm the caves where he was believed to be hiding in the Tora Bora area. The U.S. intensified bombing around the caves. There were claims that bin Laden was seen riding around on horseback in the area, and another on December 8 that Mullah Omar was "captured," though this turned out to be untrue. Donald Rumsfeld declared that the war was far from over, that the new situation was fraught with dangers, and that the U.S. intervention was entering a complex and dangerous stage.

There were also the dangers of mass starvation of Afghan refugees and victims of the postwar anarchy. At a conference on donor aid to Afghanistan in Bonn on December 9, UN representatives and the German Foreign Minister Joschka Fischer, pleading for international aid efforts and stability, noted that postwar chaos and famine threatened millions. The Bush administration had still not announced any step-up in humanitarian missions and there were broad hints that the U.S. mission was largely military and that others would have to take responsibility for stabilizing Afghanistan and providing humanitarian relief. Colin Powell did announce, however, that the bridge from Uzbekistan to Afghanistan had been opened, and trucks started to bring badly needed food and clothing into the northern part of the country. But the center of the U.S. military effort was on catching Osama bin Laden himself.

7

The Hunt for bin Laden

Attention now focused on the caves of Tora Bora where bin Laden was believed to be hiding. Local villagers reported seeing him riding on horseback in recent days and the U.S. military said that they believed that he was in the vicinity. The U.S. organized three groups of local tribal militia to hunt for bin Laden and the Al Qaeda leadership in the Tora Bora mountain region, and they were accompanied by unspecified numbers of U.S. and British Special Forces.

The first efforts of Afghan tribal groups to flush out Al Qaeda from the caves were not encouraging. Perhaps 1,000 or more well-armed and organized Al Qaeda fighters in the area suppressed the first attempts by the barely trained local militia to assault the mountain fortresses. Over the weekend of December 8–9, U.S. bombing of the White Mountains intensified and the roughly 2,500 Afghan fighters continued their attempts to assault the stronghold, but their six-day campaign had made little headway in the face of heavy Al Qaeda resistance. Moreover, the *Washington Post* reported that over the weekend, a U.S. bomb took the lives of three allied Afghan attackers, "bringing to 20 the number of Afghan attackers killed by the United States near Tora Bora. 'We're very angry,' [one of the local militia leaders] Zaman said" (December 10, 2001).

In southern Afghanistan, U.S. "hunter killer teams" roamed the Kandahar area looking for Al Qaeda or recalcitrant Taliban fighters. U.S. forces fought one band of retreating pro-Taliban Arabs, reportedly killing seven, and moved into the outskirts of the city. U.S. Special Forces accompanied Afghans to Mullah Omar's former headquarters that revealed what some Afghans saw as "opulence," marveling over (and pinching) its luxury items. But most Western reporters described it as rather tacky with its pink-tiled toilets, golden chandeliers, gaudy murals, a brightly colored mosque, and large living quarters, replete with stables and grounds for horses and camels. Omar himself was in hiding with a $10 million bounty on his head.

The Kandahar area remained dangerous, and no aid organizations were able initially to get access to the city. Interim President Hamid Karzai received visitors in

Omar's former palace, but as soon as he left for Kabul, gunshots were reported throughout the city and it remained a site of danger and violence. On December 13, U.S. forces drove into Kandahar and secured the airport, but unspecified threats of attack put them on high alert and postponed efforts to begin using the airport for flights.

The focus of world attention, however, was on Tora Bora. On December 11, the U.S. dropped a 15,000-pound daisy-cutter bomb on the entrance of a cave in an effort to flush out or kill senior Al Qaeda leadership. The Arab and Al Qaeda fighters in the area had been subjected to days of bombing and were reportedly ready for surrender. According to *The Times* of London, as of December 11, "the eight-day bombardment" was "equivalent to all the explosives dropped on Dresden in 1945. It seems that Tora Bora took about a third of all the American explosives dropped on Afghanistan in the past two months."

The ragtag Afghan forces, now referred to as the "eastern alliance," were able to take over an Al Qaeda training camp and some caves after the heavy U.S. bombing, as the bin Laden forces scurried out and moved higher into the mountains. The caves themselves appeared in TV and photo images as rather barren and not the fortified and modern headquarters sketched out in simulacra of the caves that had appeared in newspapers and TV. There were reports that one of the three Afghan leaders of the militia assault forces had negotiated a surrender for the Al Qaeda and Arab fighters, but the U.S. rejected terms of surrender and continued to bomb the caves. This angered the faction of the Afghan militia forces attempting to negotiate, who complained that the U.S. scuttled the deal, a claim that the Pentagon rejected. However, other competing Afghan militia groups insisted that the negotiated cease-fire and purported negotiations were ploys to help provide time for the bin Laden forces to regroup or to escape to Pakistan.

AT HOME WITH BIN LADEN AND THE SAUDIS

There were indeed rumors on December 12, published in the *Christian Science Monitor,* that bin Laden himself had escaped, according to Abu Jaffer, a bin Laden associate from Saudi Arabia who said that the Al Qaeda leader had fled to Pakistan ten days ago. U.S. military officials, nonetheless, continued to affirm reports that bin Laden was still holed up in the Tora Bora mountain fortress. The major event of the week, however, was the release of a home videotape of bin Laden and associates laughing about and celebrating the September 11 terror attacks on the United States. The videotape had been found in a house in Jalalabad in November, and it recorded bin Laden, a Saudi sheik visiting the area, and various associates reminiscing about the success of the September 11 attacks. It was presented by the Bush administration and media as a "smoking gun" in which bin Laden claimed responsibility for the attacks, pre-knowledge of them, and joy in what he saw as their success. Yet, even before the tapes were released, skeptics claimed that a good lawyer could argue that bin Laden might be merely bragging and might be illicitly claiming responsibility, so that the legal status of the tape was unclear.

The history of the bin Laden video was somewhat murky. Reportedly, anti-Taliban Afghans found the tape in Jalalabad after Taliban forces fled the area. It was shown to Bush and others in his administration in late November and came to the public's attention on December 8, when a story leaked to the *Washington Post* mentioned its existence and significance. The next day, Vice President Cheney admitted possession of the tape on a talk show and said that the Bush administration had not decided whether to release it or not. There were then reports early in the week that copies of the tape would be given out to the media, but that their release was being delayed to ensure accurate translation. The story surely generated intense media interest, but also some skepticism as to why the Bush administration had delayed release of the tape for so long and in so circuitous a fashion.

Some argued that the bin Laden tape might have tremendous propaganda value as an antidote to those in the Middle East and elsewhere who continued to believe that bin Laden was innocent and was being scapegoated for the attacks. The tapes also reportedly made bin Laden look extremely callous and cynical and might help create a more negative image of him in the Arab world. In preparation for the release of the tapes, first Dick Cheney and then various other officials who were shown the tapes claimed that they revealed how cruel and vicious bin Laden was for allegedly being shown gloating over the deaths on September 11. The most extravagant response was that of George W. Bush, who claimed: "For those who see this tape, they'll realize that not only is he guilty of incredible murder, he has no conscience and no soul—that he represents the worst of civilization."

The soulgazer Bush looked into Russian President Putin's eyes and saw his soul and, behold, Putin's a soulman; Bush stared into bin Laden's evasive eyes and perceived that he has no soul. This soulgazing ability assumes that Bush himself has a soul somewhere in the cauldron of greed, guilt, anxiety, aggression, pettiness, spite, confusion, and emptiness that constitutes his own subjectivity. Yet, Bush seemed to have forgotten that, according to his own catechism, bin Laden represents the antithesis rather than just "the worst of civilization."

The tape itself was released on December 13 and dominated the television networks and buzz of the day. The Bush administration held the tape several days, to assure accurate translation but also to build up anticipation (and maybe to doctor the tape). The story also pushed off the news agenda reports that Bush had the previous day pulled out of the antiballistic missile treaty, a move that Russian leader Putin called a "mistake" and that had the Chinese and others up in arms and ready for a missile race. Moreover, Bush had invoked "executive privilege" to keep Congress from seeking a wide range of prosecutors' decision-making documents, leading conservative Congressman Phil Burton (R-Ind.) to complain, "This is not a monarchy." No Phil, it's just a democracy being flushed down the tubes with the media broadcasting the spectacle of the day to cover over the relentless attack on democracy and seizure of presidential power by the Bush administration under the cover of Terror War.[1]

The bin Laden tape was fascinating and revealing, disclosing intimate details of the September 11 terror acts and showing bin Laden's delight in the results and belief that the attacks were sanctioned by God and evidenced God's blessing. The discussion revealed the geopolitical sweep of Al Qaeda, which had strong support in the Islamic world, and the fanatic religious ideology that permeated their every reference. The historical and religious allusions made clear that the Saudi Wahabbi religion provided the ideological basis of Al Qaeda. The conversation was replete with mention of dreams, visions, and omens of the September 11 terror attacks, as if they were a mandate of God and in line with Islam folk mythology. The discourse showed the premodern interpretation of Islam that permeated the Al Qaeda mindset. It combined quotations from the Koran, Islamic poetry, and folk sayings with discussions of the great joy and power of the September 11 terror attacks. According to the conversation, the success of the September 11 attacks was creating an enormous surge of interest and conversion to Islam in Holland and elsewhere, claims not supported by empirical evidence that put on display the propensity to elevate fantasy over fact in the bin Laden circle.

One chilling exchange, however, compared Muslims' joy in the killings to sports events, as when one is excited about the victory and success of one's team. The Saudi sheik effervesced with enthusiasm to bin Laden about the cheers and exultation felt by the Saudi followers of Team Jihad when they viewed pictures of the attacks on the World Trade Center and the Pentagon.

Moreover, the tape showed the deep complicity of Saudi Arabia in Al Qaeda and its financial, organizational, and personal support of bin Laden in his adopted country. The Saudi sheik whom bin Laden was speaking with, and who dominated the conversation, was later identified, as were several mullahs referred to in the banter. Bin Laden seemed extremely anxious to hear about Saudi support for his terror acts and appeared exceedingly pleased to hear of his backing in a number of mosques and that Saudi Arabians were generally ecstatic about the results of the terror attacks and regarded bin Laden a national hero.

One wonders if the deep interconnection between bin Laden, Saudi Arabia, the September 11 events, and the Bush family will ever come to light and how the public will view the close relationships between the Saudis, the Bushes, and their business partners. If the Bush doctrine were logically applied, the U.S. would be forced to go after Saudi Arabia, obviously the country that most markedly produced, financed, and supported the Al Qaeda network, supplying fifteen of the nineteen terrorists as well as bin Laden and other top Al Qaeda leadership.

Acknowledging the crucial role of Saudi Arabia in global terrorism, however, would force the Bush administration to go against a country that Bush's family and friends had long been deeply implicated in themselves. Revealing aspects of Saudi Arabia's connections with the Bush group were spelled out in some articles published in the *Boston Herald* on December 10 and 11, 2001. The articles recounted

that Saudi Arabia had refused to let the U.S. use Saudi bases for the military operations in Afghanistan, had balked at freezing of assets linked to bin Laden, and had
provided many of the foot soldiers who had taken part in the September 11 terrorist
attacks. The *Boston Herald* stories document the ways that the Bush family, Dick
Cheney, and other major Bush administration supporters have been themselves
involved with Saudi oil business, arms sales, construction projects, and other business deals, suggesting a tight interconnection between the Bush administration and
Saudi Arabia. The conclusion is that extremely close connections between the Saudis
and Bush administration officials and supporters have helped produce the anger and
rage in the Arab world that has promoted terrorism against the U.S., and that
although the Bush administration arguably had leverage with their Saudi friends to
fight terrorism, they seemed not to utilize it and overlooked the deep complicity
between the Saudis and the Islamic terror networks.

As for the so-called Arab street, it was not impressed with the bin Laden video,
believing that the tape was a fraud. Qatar's Al Jazeera television broadcast commentators immediately insisted that the "tape has been fabricated, it's not real." The
father of condemned terrorist Mohammed Atta dismissed the tape as a "forgery" to
an Associated Press journalist. Obviously, some Arabs were so bound to belief in bin
Laden that they could not recognize the cynicism and viciousness in his distortion
of Islam, while others so distrusted and hated the U.S. that it was unlikely they
would believe anything released by the Great Satan. Moreover, BBC reported that
not only did many Arabs question the authenticity of the tape, but they were also
angry at the timing of its release:

> Some Saudis questioned whether the man on the tape really is bin Laden. They say he
> is not thin enough, that he is a different person from the gaunt, turbaned figure who
> released his own videotaped messages a few weeks ago. In Cairo, some Egyptian Islam-
> ists are suggesting that the US government has spent the last few days concocting the
> tape to fool the world. But in London, a leading Saudi dissident, who asked not to be
> named, told the BBC he was sure the tape was genuine because of the language used
> and topics discussed.
>
> **Unfortunate timing**
> However, he said the tape's release would only increase popular Arab support for bin
> Laden, proving, he said, that he had the power to hurt America. The timing of the
> tape's release is certainly unfortunate for Washington, coming as it does amidst massive
> Israeli retaliation against the Palestinians. The tape's potential effect, therefore, is largely
> lost on an angry Arab public.
>
> Even though many moderate Arabs may now be convinced of bin Laden's guilt, their
> attentions are more focused on the misfortunes of the Palestinians today than on what
> happened in New York three months ago. (December 13, 2001)

Many Arab newspapers downplayed or ignored the bin Laden tape and many
Arab TV viewers complained that they could not understand the Arabic, especially
that of bin Laden, whose voice was muffled during the recording and whose mouth

was often shrouded in darkness, making it difficult to see his lips, thus encouraging speculation that his voice was at least partially dubbed. Sensing Arab frustration with the poor sound, and seemingly shocked by the largely negative Arab response, the Bush administration's PR bumblers decided to release the videotape again, this time with Arabic subtitles, as if Washington's translators were going to change Arab hearts and minds about the Terror War.

The U.S. response to the bin Laden tape was, not surprisingly, ferocious. Large segments of the public were visibly angered, called for bin Laden's head, and came to demonize the demon of terror even more. Bin Laden's gloating and laughing over the September 11 deaths curdled the blood of many in the U.S. audience and evoked copious calls for retribution. This response, of course, raises the stakes in actually capturing or killing bin Laden to claim success in the Terror War. Bin Laden emerged clearly as the number-one figure in global terrorism, a sworn enemy of the U.S. with a network of support and adulation. If he was not brought to justice, the campaign could be judged a failure, or at least closure would not really have been achieved.

Although George W. Bush blustered on December 14 that it was "preposterous" that anyone could doubt the authenticity of the bin Laden tape, in fact there were fierce debates over its production, meaning, and mode of release. The critical discussion of the tape indirectly demonstrated the sophisticated hermeneutical capacities of audiences and critics through the world, thus vindicating the position long argued by British cultural studies that different audiences produce different interpretations of a given text. Special effects experts in London said "[that a] fake would be relatively easy to make" (*Guardian*, December 15, 2001). But experts in the U.S. from Bell Labs and MIT concluded that "technology [is] not yet good enough to fake bin Laden tape" (Associated Press, December 15, 2001).

The response to the tape confirmed French theorist Jean Baudrillard's position that we are currently living in an era of simulation, in which it is impossible to tell the difference between the real and fake, between reality and simulation. As Hollywood films use more and more computerized scenes—as rock stars digitally "cleanse" their image, such as when Michael Jackson uses it to wipe away sweat from a vigorous performance or make himself more black to blend in with his brothers on stage, and as politicians use political image production and spectacle to sell themselves—the difference between the authentic and the fake is harder and harder to determine. Is George W. Bush a real president, or is he just acting out the sound bites fed him by his handlers, performing a scripted daily political act that he does not fully understand? Are the frequent warnings of impending terrorist attacks genuine or just a ploy to keep the public on edge to accept more reactionary right-wing law-and-order politics? Is the terrorist danger as dire as the National Security State claims, or are they hyping threats to raise their budgets and power? In an era of simulation, it is impossible to clearly answer these questions as we do not have access to the "real," which in any case is complex, overdetermined, intricately constructed, and in some cases, as Kant discerned in his distinction between phenomenon and noumenon, ultimately impossible to specify.

Yet the hermeneutical challenge that I am undertaking in these studies is to capture as much of the events and significance of the September 11 attacks and subsequent Terror War as is possible at this point in time. Many others are participating in this project. Indeed, there was close scrutiny of every word and image of the bin Laden video, with some claiming that bin Laden had never worn a ring such as was present on his finger, which was supposedly unusual for him and Islamists in general. Other Islamic experts said that the words, images, sequence, and nature of the tape had the aura of veracity, ensuring that the tape would be one of the most closely scrutinized and interpreted texts in media history.

As for its origins, an article in the *Observer* by Ed Vulliamy and Jason Burke claimed that the "bin Laden videotape was result of a sting" (December 16, 2001). "Intelligence sources" confirmed to the reporters that "curious circumstances" surrounded the Saudi sheik who was receiving bin Laden, and there was speculation that he was part of a sting operation that set bin Laden up to make the confession on video by playing on his egotism and narcissism. Of course, in the weird world of misinformation, it could be leaked that the Saudi sheik was part of a bin Laden sting precisely to discredit and endanger the Saudi, who appeared to be an all-out Jihadist.

Others wondered why the circumspect bin Laden would allow a tape to be made of what was perceived as a confession, whereas others speculated that the cunning bin Laden left the tape behind purposely to construct a legacy that would encourage others to follow his example. And legal experts concluded that release of the bin Laden video would help future Al Qaeda defense teams, who could cite the tape by indicating that bin Laden had said that the "martyrdom" teams had no information as to their tasks until the last minute. Thus, the Bush administration unwittingly helped to provide a defense to terrorists, rendering the release of the tapes highly problematic (*The Times,* December 16, 2001).

THE ASSAULT ON TORA BORA
AND BIN LADEN'S ESCAPE

On December 14, the night of the broadcasting of the bin Laden tape, the Pentagon told CNN that they now believed that they had bin Laden and his Al Qaeda forces surrounded in the Tora Bora mountain fortresses. Three groups of eastern Afghan fighters were advancing up the mountain where the Al Qaeda forces were believed to be sequestered, accompanied by U.S. and British Special Forces. Resistance from the Al Qaeda fighters was fierce, leading the Pentagon to conclude that they were protecting "something valuable," perhaps bin Laden himself. The possibility of capturing or destroying Al Qaeda leadership led to intensified bombing, the sending of more U.S. troops to the scene, and attempts to block exit roads from the mountains to neighboring Pakistan. There was some pressure to get bin Laden before the weekend, as a three-day festival of Eid, which ends the Muslim holy month of Ramadan, was about to begin and there was belief that the Arab militia fighting Al Qaeda would go home for the weekend. It was also turning cold and had snowed, making military operations more complex.

The Afghan tribal soldiers were also complaining again, claiming that "the American bombs disturbed our negotiations." A *Los Angeles Times* report indicated that as Afghan tribal leaders squabbled about whether they should or should not negotiate with Al Qaeda fighters, "the cold and hungry soldiers had grown disgruntled and abandoned their posts. Late that night, Al Qaeda fighters swarmed forward to seize back crucial stretches of the Milawa valley. Tribal soldiers were still battling to regain the area Thursday" (December 14, 2001, A14).

On the weekend of December 14–15, stories continued to circulate of fierce fighting in Tora Bora, the retreat and surrender of Al Qaeda troops, and speculation as to whether bin Laden was in the mountain fortresses being attacked. U.S. troops were reportedly heavily involved in the fighting, bombing was intense, and there were accounts of some U.S. troops being wounded in battle. One eastern Afghan leader complained that he was negotiating with Al Qaeda troops, demanding unconditional surrender, but "he doubted the United States would accept any deal with Al Qaeda. 'In my opinion,' he said, 'the Americans want to kill them'" (*Washington Post,* December 15, 2001).

The main story of the weekend, however, was that Pentagon officials had leaked to CNN that they had audiotapes, which suggested that bin Laden himself was in the caves directing the military operations. Expectations of bin Laden's imminent capture thus intensified, although some military analysts told CNN that it was standard operating procedure to use tapes to confuse the enemy during retreat. The haunting specter of the inability to determine between reality and simulation arose in speculation that the supposed bin Laden voice could have been from an audiotape used to deflect attention from the flight of Al Qaeda fighters from the caves into Pakistan.

Indeed, there were reports that hundreds of bin Laden's forces had left for Pakistan and that sixty-one fleeing Al Qaeda fighters had been captured by the Pakistan border patrol. A UPI filing by Amaud de Borchgrave, however, suggested that the Pakistan border was highly porous, that hundreds of Al Qaeda troops had escaped, and that the local tribes were largely sympathetic to them (December 14, 2001). There was, of course, speculation that bin Laden himself had already escaped in this fashion, and in a *Washington Post* interview Donald Rumsfeld confessed that there are "hundreds" of tunnels from the caves in Afghanistan to Pakistan, thus creating many possible escape routes.

The Tora Bora Al Qaeda forces, however, seemed to be crumbling and there were reports on December 16 that hundreds had fled, many had been captured, and scores had been killed. There were reportedly few troops left in the caves after sixteen days of intense bombing and intermittent heavy fighting. A *Washington Post* story by Molly Moore and Susan B. Glasser surprisingly revealed that the remaining Afghan fighters had a sense of humor (December 16, 2001):

> The radio traffic also offered a glimpse of the confusion surrounding the final hunt for the bin Laden loyalists, as Afghan fighters cautiously advanced toward remaining Al Qaeda positions, anxiously called off U.S. warplanes and searched in vain for enemies they fear might have already fled to Pakistan.
>
> Some of the voices over the radio were plaintive, some eager, some humorous. "The weather is very cold," one Afghan fighter radioed this morning. "Tell the Americans to continue the bombardment. I cannot fire."
>
> After reporting the presence of only a few Al Qaeda fighters, he joked: "Tell the Americans to use gas to finish them. . . . I'm very cold."

By December 17, it appeared that the Al Qaeda fighters in Tora Bora had been soundly routed, although it would turn out that many escaped. The eastern alliance claimed victory over Al Qaeda, admitted they had no idea where bin Laden was, and begged the United States to stop bombing, claiming that the night before three of its own fighters were killed by U.S. bombs. When queried by reporters in the Pentagon where bin Laden might be, Rear Adm. John D. Stufflebeem remarked that the hunt was "like searching for fleas on a dog. If you see one and you focus on that one, you don't know how many others are getting away." The racist admiral was referring to Afghanistan as a dog with fleas, reducing Arabs to animals much as the U.S. military had done in the Iraqi "turkey shoot" that they bragged about at the end of the Gulf War (see Kellner 1992).

The U.S. military admitted that there was no more electronic "chatter" from Al Qaeda Tora Bora communications, and the eastern alliance was searching the caves, finding old weapons and wretched living conditions. But, crucially for the U.S., it appeared that bin Laden had escaped, perhaps to Pakistan where it would be tricky to dislodge him. The forlorn Afghans and the Al Qaeda fighters captured in the battle for Tora Bora appeared utterly shellshocked and pathetic, as the Al Qaeda troops pleaded with the Afghans not to turn them over to the U.S. and as they were paraded in front of the world media.

OMAR UNDER THE GUN, AFGHANS BOMBED, AND A NEW PRESIDENT

On December 18, Afghan forces indicated that they had located Mullah Omar in a mountain hideout in southern Afghanistan with 500 fighters, and that they planned to attack "and lynch him" (*Guardian,* December 18, 2001). Unable to get bin Laden, the Bush Terror War needed another high-profile target. Yet the Afghan forces who claimed that they knew where Omar was hiding seemed reluctant to go after him, maintaining that they first needed to provide security for the city of Kandahar, which was still subject to acts of violence and full of one-time Taliban and perhaps Al Qaeda fighters.

Pakistan claimed that it had captured about 188 Al Qaeda guerillas fleeing from Tora Bora, but on December 20, a group of forty-two prisoners overpowered their guards, commandeered four vans, and in the ensuing melee killed at least ten people and allowed an indeterminate number of Al Qaeda fighters to escape. A *New York Times* story reported that "Taliban Chiefs Prove Elusive" (December 20, 2001), noting that most of the top Taliban leadership had gotten away, either assimilating themselves in Afghanistan or fleeing to Pakistan, where many had luxurious villas.

Focus shifted to Kabul and the installation of the new interim leader, Hamid Karzai, in a dramatic inauguration ceremony. The celebration was marred by reports that a convoy of village elders from the Khost area, on the way to the ceremony in Kabul on December 20, had been bombed when U.S. planes swept down on a caravan of 15–20 vehicles, killing sixty people according to initial reports. The U.S. immediately claimed that they had correctly targeted a caravan of Al Qaeda and Taliban leaders. As details leaked out to Reuters and Western news sources, a story emerged that Pacha Khan, a local rival warlord, had blocked the caravan's route and diverted it to an alternative one. The warlord then reportedly relayed to the Americans that the group was Al Qaeda and it was immediately bombed out.[2]

Put on the defensive on the day of the Afghanistan presidential swearing-in, U.S. General Tommy Franks claimed that hand-to-shoulder missiles were fired at the U.S. planes and that made the caravan a legitimate "enemy" target. Western news sources interviewed locals in hospitals who had survived or witnessed the U.S. air attack, all of whom insisted that those "in the convoy were supporters of the new administration" and demanded that the interim Afghanistan government investigate and take action against the American attacks on Afghan villagers.

In fact, there were reports some weeks previously that the U.S. had bombed several civilian villages in the Tora Bora area. The U.S. military denied repeatedly that the targets were civilian, but reporters who interviewed locals insisted that the U.S. had bombed innocent villagers not connected to Al Qaeda. Yet the issue was dropped in the frenzy of the bin Laden videotape and final assault on Tora Bora. Evidently, being an American general means never having to say you are sorry, no matter how gross the misdeed. As Salmon Rushdie put it in his novel *Fury* (2001): "What's wrong is wrong, and because of the immense goddam *power* of America, the immense fucking *seduction* of America, those bastards in charge get away with" lies, evasions, and crimes.

Interim President Karzai's swearing-in ceremony on December 22 revealed pictures of the martyred Northern Alliance hero Masoud plastered everywhere, while speakers profusely lauded the Northern Alliance hero killed by Al Qaeda assassins just before September 11.[3] *The Times* of London noted that despite a phalanx of U.S. officials in the audience, there were no references in any of the speeches to the U.S., which the paper claimed was "snubbed" by Afghans not happy about the ambiguous U.S. role in their country (December 23, 2001).

In Tora Bora, local Afghan fighters seemed reluctant to continue searching through the caves, many of which were badly bombed, for the remnants of Al Qaeda members or for useful material left behind. After hauling away truckloads of old weapons and other material from the Tora Bora caves, most of the local fighters left to go home, leaving the U.S. with the dirty work of inspecting the caves, which were perhaps booby-trapped by Al Qaeda and weakened from heavy U.S. bombing. Tommy Franks ordered hundreds more U.S. troops to search the caves to locate potential Al Qaeda fighters, dead or alive, and a report claimed that one of their duties was to cut off the fingers of dead Al Qaeda fighters to search for DNA match-ups for the leadership, few of whom had been found.[4]

During the days to come, however, the U.S. decided to use U.S. Special Forces and local Afghans to search the caves, rather than a major U.S. military force. Meanwhile, bin Laden seemed to have disappeared. Some locals and military analysts believed that the voices of bin Laden heard in the Tora Bora caves were audiotapes that were played over radio transmission systems to create the impression of bin Laden's presence in the caves. There were claims that he'd escaped to Pakistan, although the Pakistani President Musharraf said it was unlikely that he'd crossed the Pakistan border and could be dead in the Tora Bora caves. Other stories had bin Laden escaping to Iran with friendly supporters, and no doubt there would be bin Laden sightings throughout the world until he was apprehended. George W. Bush insisted that bin Laden would be captured by the U.S., but there was no discernible evidence that anyone had the slightest idea where he had slithered away to.

Terror War took some new forms as reports circulated that bin Laden had an armada of twenty or so "terror ships" that could be loaded with explosives and wreak havoc in crowded Western harbors. One suspect ship was boarded off of England on December 21, held for some days and thoroughly searched, but no lethal contents showed up. Shoreline security in England and elsewhere was beefed up, and there was fear that the next Al Qaeda assault would be a coastal attack via ship (although as of the end of 2002, no terror ships have appeared). On December 20, the U.S. had mistakenly entered an Iranian oil tanker, thinking that it was an Iraqi vessel smuggling oil; two Iranians were allegedly hurt and Iran lodged a formal protest to the U.S. to demand an explanation.

A bizarre incident on December 23, moreover, indicated that airline security was far from reasonably competent. A tall man without checked luggage got on an American Airlines flight from Paris to Miami, although he had been kept off of a flight the day before because of suspicious behavior and demeanor. On the flight, he tried to ignite his shoe to set off explosives to presumably blow up the plane, but was stopped by a vigilant air steward and passengers.

Although initial reports claimed that the man was not connected to Al Qaeda, later testimony from Al Qaeda prisoners indicated that the would-be bomber had been seen in bin Laden training camps. Moreover, it appeared he had been travelling around Europe and Israel without visible means of support, creating suspicions of connections to terror networks. Evidently, the suspect, Richard Reid, had gotten a new British passport that erased records of his travels, had been detained by French police because of suspicions, but was allowed to pass through security and board the flight the next day. The episode revealed that neither state authorities nor airline corporations had markedly improved security and that more attacks on airlines could be expected.

The explosive that Reid carried was highly sensitive and dangerous, leading intelligence experts to conclude that he must have been networked to a terror group in order to have such sophisticated weapons and to travel so often. The Richard Reid incident suggested the existence of sleeper cells still operative and that European and other countries, and the airlines industry, had a long way to go to guarantee security against terror attacks.

Another bin Laden video was distributed on December 28, which featured a pale and gaunt Osama, who had apparently aged since his last video. The tape seemed to suggest that bin Laden was alive as of early December, but he appeared more fatalistic, insisting that his Jihad would go on after his death, that the U.S. was carrying out a "crusader" war against Islam, and that Islam would triumph.

As December and the year 2001 came to an end, there was one more disturbing report that a U.S. bombing raid on the village of Qalaye Niazi in Paktia province in the early hours of December 20 had killed 107–170 local civilians. The Pentagon insisted that the village was a hideout for Al Qaeda fighters, but reporters from the BBC and various British newspapers gave vivid descriptions of the carnage and testimonies from villagers that the victims were civilians.[5]

On December 31, there were reports that groups of U.S. Marines were on the way to go after Mullah Omar. But the next day it was claimed that the excursion had been targeting a Taliban headquarters that was said to hold intelligence and might still be used by Al Qaeda or Taliban rebels. The Pentagon claimed that the Marines had raided the compound and seized materials, but had not confronted any Taliban or Al Qaeda forces nor found significant intelligence.

As the new year began, there were intensified accusations that the U.S. bombing had been killing civilians at an alarming rate. According to the *Independent* (January 1, 2002):

> Villagers in Qalaye Niazi, four miles north of the eastern city of Gardez, said several US warplanes and helicopters took part in the pre-dawn strikes on Sunday. A villager, Janat Gul, who claimed 24 members of his family were killed, told Reuters: "People are very upset. . . . There are no al-Qa'ida or Taliban people here."
>
> Witnesses said at least 12 houses had been flattened and that the village was littered with scraps of flesh, pools of blood and clumps of what appeared to be human hair. There were a number of large craters in the village. US forces were invited to examine the damage and to find out what happened.

Once again, the U.S. claimed that they had hit a military target, a compound used by the Al Qaeda and Taliban, and claimed that there was no "collateral damage."[6] A disturbing pattern was emerging, noted in the British and foreign press but not in the U.S. media. There were proliferating accounts that significant civilian casualties followed U.S. bombing in eastern Afghanistan, and in all cases the U.S. military aggressively argued that they had hit military targets, discounting reports of civilian casualties. Each time, however, independent journalists confirmed the civilian deaths. In the Qalaye Niazi incident, the Pentagon admitted that further inquiry had indicated civilian residences next to the alleged military depot that they had bombed, but despite many press reports they refused to admit that U.S. bombing had created civilian casualties in the incident and claimed that the Qalaye Niazi bombing was still under investigation.

On January 2, 2002, *The Times* of London reported, "'Precision Weapons' Fail to Prevent Mass Casualties," claiming that "American bombers may have caused twice as many civilian deaths in Afghanistan in the past 87 days as NATO did in the 78-day air war against the former Yugoslavia in 1999." The weekend's toll, the story indicated, raised conservative estimates of Afghan civilians killed by American bombing to as high as 1,000, while one "recent unofficial report by an American academic said that the death toll among civilians could be closer to 4,000." *The Times* then summarized accounts of civilian casualties from U.S. bombing:

> During heavy airstrikes in the Tora Bora region in eastern Afghanistan last month local Mujahidin commanders said that more than 170 people were killed over several days, including civilians and a number of their own fighters.
>
> In another bombing raid in November local people said that about 150 civilians died in Kunduz and Khanabad.
>
> Earlier in November it was claimed that up to 35 civilians had died in the village of Chokar-Karez, 25 miles north of Kandahar, during an attack by an American gunship. The Pentagon said that there had been a legitimate military target in the village.
>
> Up to 60 people were killed last month in an attack on a convoy of vehicles. The Americans said that they were Taleban and al-Qaeda fighters, but Afghans insisted that they were tribal elders on their way for the inauguration of the new Government in Kabul.
>
> There have been dozens of other incidents in which small numbers of civilians have died, including four workers at a United Nations demining centre in Kabul in October.

A CBS multipart news report indicated that part of the problem with the misguided bombs and missiles was defective batteries made at the Eagle-Picher Technologies Plant in Joplin, Missouri (December 6 and 7, 2001; January 7 and 9, 2002). Workers at the plant testified to CBS that they had encountered faked tests, defective products, and corporate cover-up "not on thousands, but on millions of batteries that they sold." The workers worried that this endangered U.S. national security and called for investigations.

Afghan leaders continued to give out contradictory signals concerning their response to claims of U.S. bombs killing Afghan civilians, with some sharply condemning the U.S. attacks, confirming villagers' reports concerning civilian casualties, and demanding a halt to U.S. bombing. Others in the Afghan government defended the U.S. attacks, including President Hamid Karzai, who stated that the U.S. could continue bombing as long as it was necessary to eradicate terrorism. But obviously there were significant segments of Afghan society who were outraged by the continued U.S. bombing of civilians and would agitate to end the U.S. military intervention.

Meanwhile, on January 2, once again reports proliferated indicating that U.S. troops were engaged in a huge manhunt for Mullah Omar in a mountain village in southern Afghanistan that was suspected of harboring the leader. The hunt expanded after the publication in the *New York Times* that Al Qaeda leader Ayman al-Zawahiri had written a manual, found by U.S. intelligence, that urged key members of the Al Qaeda group to flee early to avoid destruction of the group and to prepare to regroup. Local Afghan politicians were trying to negotiate surrender of a large number of Taliban forces around Omar and the U.S. was worried that once again he'd get away, as he had when Afghan forces negotiated the surrender of Kandahar, and threatened tribal forces that they would face U.S. bombing if Omar was not handed over (Associated Press, January 2, 2001).

On January 4, rumors buzzed in Kabul that Mullah Omar was about to be captured and the *Guardian* headlined a January 5 story, "U.S. and Afghan Forces Pin down Mullah Omar." A coalition of U.S. and anti-Taliban forces (ATF) "closed in on villages in the central highlands yesterday where the interim Afghan government claimed that the Taliban leader, Mullah Mohammed Omar, and about 1,500 supporters were making their last stand." The Pentagon asserted that the "action focused on two areas near the towns of Baghran and Deh Rawud, in the mountains north of Kandahar. Afghan and U.S. Special Forces were reported to have taken up positions around the towns, with U.S. marines behind them cutting off escape routes."

In a separate operation further east near the town of Khost, a few miles from the Pakistan border, the U.S. suffered its first (admitted) combat casualty when a special forces soldier was shot dead while on patrol near the town of Gardez. A CIA agent was wounded in the incident, which one officer described as an ambush. A few days later, it was reported that a fourteen-year-old Afghan boy had shot the American with unclear motives, and as tribal elders discussed what to do with the alleged teenage shooter, he escaped.

In the same region, the Pentagon had been heavily bombing a major Al Qaeda training camp at Zhawar that had been the target of a 1998 U.S. cruise missile attack that was intended to kill Osama bin Laden. The camp had been attacked previously in the Afghan war, and the Pentagon claimed that there had been reports that Al Qaeda forces were meeting there again, to regroup, and the Pentagon bombed the camp repeatedly. But evidently once again the Al Qaeda forces had escaped, and nothing was found except destroyed military equipment. Local villagers, however, were angered by the intensity of the bombing and claimed once again that there were civilian casualties, including the killing of local individuals who had nothing to do with Al Qaeda or the Taliban.[7]

There was also discouraging news concerning Mullah Omar. Although he was supposedly close to capture, Reuters reported on January 5 that the "Trail for Omar and bin Laden [was] Growing Cold." Afghan forces claimed that there were no Taliban or Al Qaeda forces in the Baghran area where Omar had purportedly been hiding. Furthermore, a spokesperson for the Kandahar governor said that no clues had been found indicating that Omar had been in the region at all and wondered why it had been assumed he was. A BBC report on the same day indicated that Mullah Omar and a group had escaped the area in a motorcycle convoy.

In any case, the failure to capture Mullah Omar was becoming a major embarrassment for both the interim Afghanistan government and U.S. military forces, as was the escape of bin Laden. By the weekend of January 5–6, it seemed to many that flaws in the U.S. military strategy were responsible for the escape of bin Laden, Mullah Omar, and other major Al Qaeda and Taliban leaders. Critics argued that the U.S. zero-casualty policy and failure to employ ground troops had enabled top enemy leaders to escape. Just as the U.S. relied on Northern Alliance troops to capture the northern part of Afghanistan and rout the Taliban, so too did the U.S. rely on southern and eastern ATF. But whereas the Northern Alliance was an organized military operation of sorts and strongly anti-Taliban, the ATF were tribal organizations who were often of the same Pashtun tribe as many Taliban forces. Moreover, the local tribes and militias had questionable allegiance to U.S. goals and had grudges of their own against regional tribal enemies to pursue, for which U.S. forces were used to harm ancient rivals. Moreover, some of the groups were notoriously treacherous and easily guided by Taliban or Al Qaeda bribes to let their leaders escape.

U.S. General Tommy Franks, as if responding to criticisms of his failed strategy while in charge of the operation, justified reliance on Afghan tribal forces on January 5 by claiming that he was avoiding the mistake of the Soviets in Afghanistan. The Soviets, he insisted, were seen as an invading force, but by working with local groups the U.S. was overcoming this negative perception. This answer, of course, is evasive and begs the question. Clearly, one can work with local groups *and* put a significant amount of one's own troops on the ground in key operations.

Eventually, a series of stories described how ineffectual U.S. policy allowed bin Laden, Omar, and much of the Al Qaeda and Taliban hardcore leaders and fighters to get away, and within military circles as well there was much criticism of the Pentagon and Bush administration's Afghan strategy. In retrospect, it is obvious that large numbers of U.S. troops should have been deployed in the Kandahar surrender to increase the chances of capturing Mullah Omar and major Taliban leaders. Likewise, more U.S. troops should have been put into the Tora Bora region to bottle up escape routes for Al Qaeda forces and perhaps even get bin Laden.[8] But instead of a "noose" and a "net," words that the U.S. military had used to describe their imminent capture of bin Laden, it was clear that the operation was a sieve with big holes. This was due in large part to the problematic prohibition against deploying major numbers of U.S. troops on the ground for military operations and partly due to reliance on Afghan and Pakistani allies and other proxy forces. Hence, analysts eventually concluded that "the Afghanistan war made al Qaeda harder to stop, by compelling it to regroup as a mass of decentralised cells which tend to carry out their own attacks, rather than wait for instructions of prepared plans from the leadership."[9]

8

❖

The New Barbarism:
World in Turmoil

As the hunt for bin Laden and Omar escalated, all hell broke loose in the Middle East as the Israelis and Palestinians continued to wage terror war against each other. After the Palestinian suicide attacks of December 2, the Israelis struck back with a series of assaults on Palestinian targets, with one missile going astray on December 12 and killing two Palestinian children. Palestinians retaliated once again with an attack that killed ten Israelis living in the Gaza settlements, and on December 13 Israel broke off contact with Yasser Arafat and announced a stepped-up military campaign to arrest Palestinian militants and confiscate weapons. Israel then showered Palestinian territories with missiles, tank assaults, and military attacks, leading to the occupation of Arafat's compound some weeks later and the intensification of the Israeli-Palestinian conflict throughout 2002, without any serious mediation efforts of behalf of the Bush administration.

It was now perfectly clear that one of the consequences of the Bush doctrine, which proclaimed the right of a country hit by terror to go after the government of the country where the terrorists lived, was to legitimate military aggression and political repression. This barbaric "doctrine" could be used to justify war against "terrorists" anywhere in the world, anytime that a government wanted to strike out at enemies. The Bush doctrine thus effectively provided carte blanche for military retaliation in which the law of the jungle would replace international law, diplomacy, and negotiation. As the new millennium unfolded, centuries of diplomatic progress were put aside as the New Barbarians took the world into the dangerous space of Operation Enduring Terror War.

REGRESSION, REACTION, AND BARBARISM AMOK

The bin Laden terror network and the Bush administration's response arguably represent societal regression on a massive historical scale. Deploying the weapons of

163

terror and war instead of diplomacy and legality, Al Qaeda and the Bush administration put force before negotiation and barbarism before civilization, unleashing an era of unrestrained militarism, terror, and aggression.

Whereas bin Laden has emerged as a figurehead for radical Islamic fundamentalism and terror, George W. Bush has emerged as a figurehead for unrestrained military action, conservative economic policies, assaults on civil liberties and the open society, and aggressive assertion of U.S. power politics. Throughout the Afghan campaign, the U.S. had subordinated humanitarian issues to military ones and generated tensions with its closest ally, Great Britain, which intensified as the days went by.

In effect, the Bush administration was carrying out a primarily unilateral military campaign, using cluster bombs, killing thousands of civilians, and driving hundreds of thousands of Afghan people from their homes with little effort to provide humanitarian shelter or protection for the innocents.[1] The U.S. had also failed to provide adequate prisoner of war facilities for surrendering Al Qaeda troops, leading the U.S. to participate in, or observe, massacres of hundreds of surrendered troops, events that could be construed as war crimes. But such was the barbarism and war hysteria that the major U.S. television networks solely celebrated the military victories without dwelling on the "collateral damage." A new barbarism had become fashionable, with U.S. Secretary of Defense Donald Rumsfeld and other tough-guy military spokespeople becoming national celebrities, while armchair pundits outfrothed each other in efforts to appear properly tough and martial.

Another negative consequence came to the fore from Bush barbarism as the noose tightened around the necks of bin Laden and the Al Qaeda leadership. UK Defense Secretary Geoff Hoon announced that Britain opposed the execution of Osama bin Laden and argued that international law dictated that he be given a fair trial. This was an explicit slam at the Bush administration, which was a strong supporter of the death penalty and was calling for secret military tribunals. As U.S. Attorney General John Ashcroft traveled to Europe, many Europeans were angry that Ashcroft was urging them to drop their objections to the death penalty in favor of giving the U.S. an unrestrained hand in carrying out trials and executions as they saw fit. Under the guise of fighting terrorism, the Bush administration was thus pushing its barbaric efforts to legitimate capital punishment and promote highly antidemocratic legal policies.

On December 17, while defusing mines at the Kandahar airport, one U.S. Marine had his foot blown off and two others were injured. This called attention to the barbarism of land mines, which saturated Afghanistan after twenty years of war. It also highlighted the gross savagery of the Bush administration's opposition to the land mine treaty that much of the world had endorsed. Land mines are an utterly barbaric instrument that are highly anticivilian, as they are often buried and hidden and sometimes only explode many years later. There is no excuse in a civilized world to continue this excessively violent technology and it should be eliminated immediately. Afghanistan, for example, had from 640,000 to twenty million unexploded land mines, with an average of eighty-eight mine casualties per month, according to the Halo Trust, a British organization that has been destroying land mines and unexploded munitions in Afghanistan since 1988.[2]

A revealing British speech given on December 11, generally ignored by U.S. media, was also significant. Admiral Sir Michael Boyce, chief of the Defence Staff, cited a significant divergence between Britain and the U.S. in the prosecution of the Afghan campaign. As I have noted, whereas the U.S. wanted to focus primarily on military aims, Britain was eager to carry out humanitarian aims, to put in place peacekeeping troops to maintain order, to enable food and other necessities to be delivered, and to enable the process of the reconstruction of Afghanistan to begin. For some weeks, the U.S. had rebuffed British demands to get on with the humanitarian program and Boyce reflected growing British impatience, stating: " *We* have to consider whether we wish to follow the United States' singleminded aim to finish Osama bin Laden and Al Qaeda . . . or to involve ourselves in creating the conditions for nation-building or reconstruction as well" (*The [London] Times,* December 13, 2001).

As if to confirm the wisdom of British calls for immediate peacekeeping forces in Afghanistan and the folly of the Bush administration's resistance to them, there were reports that "Unpaid Soldiers Spark[ed] Crimewave in Kabul" (*Guardian,* December 15, 2001). Allegedly, unpaid and desperate Northern Alliance soldiers were looting wealthier Kabul neighborhoods and even killing people who resisted their robberies. The Northern Alliance troops complained, in turn, of not being paid for months and not being able to afford life in Kabul, calling attention to the immediate need for an international brigade of peacekeeping troops throughout Afghanistan and stepped-up humanitarian aid efforts.

While U.S. media and the Bush administration were gloating over their military successes in Afghanistan, many critics argued that until bin Laden, Mullah Omar, and top Taliban and Al Qaeda leadership were arrested or eliminated, the U.S. could not really claim victory because the stated war aims had been to go after Al Qaeda leadership and not just to overthrow the Taliban. Although most people in Afghanistan seemed to be happy to be rid of the Taliban, some critics said that people were not yet really better off, that many former Taliban leaders and corrupt warlords had returned to power, that suffering in the country had increased as a result of the war, and that chaos and uncertainty prevailed. Others, like the British and many Europeans, were distressed that the U.S. had not played a stronger role in humanitarian aid and were skeptical of U.S. commitment to Afghan reconstruction. Europeans were also becoming increasingly disturbed with what was obviously the unilateralist and militarist nature of the Bush administration's war on terror, with the U.S. going it alone as the world policeman against global terrorism, unleashing a New Barbarism and unending terror war.

Arabs were increasingly angry over the number and extent of civilian casualties in Afghanistan and the fierce attacks of Israel against Palestinians. The U.S. seemed to walk away from Israel-Palestine negotiations as they pulled out their diplomat General Anthony Zinni and refused to publicly rebuke Israel for their daily assaults on the Palestinians. On December 15, the U.S. vetoed a UN Security Council resolution that condemned acts of terror against Israelis and Palestinians, that demanded an end to nearly fifteen months of escalating violence, and that established a "monitoring mechanism" to bring in observers. Israel evidently opposed the latter condition and the U.S. thus killed an effort to bring in the UN to help produce peace, angering the Arab world and causing tension with close European allies and other civilized nations who supported the resolution. It was hard to imagine how there could be peace in the Middle East between Israel and Palestine without UN intervention, as obviously conditions were spinning out of control, but the Bush administration was clearly more intent on waging enduring terror war than promoting peace and security.

The U.S. Lone Ranger and Wild West approaches to global terrorism were threatening to position the U.S. as the number-one target for those who felt aggrieved and wretched, assuring a host of enemies and retribution for years to come. Bush's Terror War thus unleashed an era of militarism and barbarism that would not only create an ever more insecure and violent world, but would also produce more enemies of the U.S. who would resent the constant assertion of U.S. military power and its blocking of serious efforts for peace, global responses and solutions to global problems like terrorism, and an end to the Middle East conflict between Israel and the Palestinians.

One media spin on U.S. unilateralism was that key members of the Bush administration genuinely believed in U.S. superiority and its mission to play a major global role. Critics saw the unilateralism as a naked U.S. power grab and desire to play the role of the new sole superpower and policeman of the world. The Bush administration was, however, playing a dangerous game, for its aggressive military posture was destabilizing many regions and giving various groups an excuse or cause to create turmoil.

Jumping into the New Barbarism, terrorists in India attacked the Parliament in the bloodiest assault on India's democracy in its history. China executed Muslim separatists and the U.S. sent troops into the Philippines to help exterminate oppositional Islamic groups. CIA forces entered Somalia, preparing for more U.S. military attacks, and the United States set up support bases in Kenya for operations in Africa. In a *New Yorker* article, "The Iraq Hawks" (December 16, 2001), Seymour Hersh documented a new war plan for Iraq that was being developed by the Bush administration and would follow the Afghanistan model of heavy bombardment of Iraqi targets and U.S. support of oppositional groups inside and outside Iraq. Critics questioned the Iraq/Afghanistan analogy and doubted that Iraqi opposition to Saddam Hussein was as extensive and well-organized as were the Taliban's Afghan opposition, which easily overthrew a poorly armed and barely functional Taliban military.

In China, a bizarre act of barbarism was reported the same day: A suicide bomber had entered a McDonald's in China and detonated the explosive, killing himself and wounding others; was this an act of sheer madness, of culinary critique, or an antiglobalization protest? In the U.S., a fake grenade rolled down the aisle of an American Airlines flight and caused mayhem at a San Diego airport, forcing evacuations, grounding flights and closing streets. It turns out that Lolita Austria, age fifty-seven, had stolen a small shopping bag belonging to an airport security screener, which contained a fake grenade that was used to test security. Earlier, an additional American barbarian closed down the Atlanta airport when he jumped over a security barricade to avoid missing a connecting flight to a football game.[3]

The New Barbarism was visible every day on American television, running 24/7 on the Fox Network and dominating CNN and the NBC cable networks. The barbaric bourgeois boob Bill O'Reilly, on his December 16 *No Spin Zone* spinfest, reduced the issue of the bin Laden videotape to a litmus test as to whether you were a patriot or traitor, according to whether you believed it was a smoking gun or did not decisively prove bin Laden's guilt. Although there were few serious doubts that bin Laden and Al Qaeda were guilty of the September 11 bombing, the tape had its fishy elements and it was highly offensive for the simplistic O'Reilly to use any Bush administration argument as a litmus test for patriotism. Indeed, the highly reactionary U.S. Attorney General John Ashcroft had used the same tactic the week before in congressional hearings, where he argued that anyone who questioned military trials for terrorists or questioned his barbaric antiterrorist policies were aiding and abetting the terrorist enemy. This was, of course, the same tone and argument that had been adopted by the most rabid anticommunists in the 1950s, an earlier era of U.S. political barbarism.

The Fox Network, as mentioned before, was owned by Australian right-wing barbarian Rupert Murdoch and was run by the grossly barbaric Roger Ailes, a Republican spinmeister, professional liar, and perfect poster man for the New Barbarism. Fox pundits oozed barbarism from every pore: blaring graphics and creepy crawlers; ruling out mention of civilian casualties from news reports; and bringing on an unending parade of bellicose, barely literate military "analysts," who parroted the Pentagon's line of the day, and antiterrorist "experts," who outdid each other with belligerence and hostility.[4]

An ultraright media attack-dog group, The Media Research Center, sent out an e-mail on December 13 revealing the deeply antidemocratic thrust of the New Barbarism. It made clear that anyone who opposed the Bush administration and Pentagon's policies would be subject to a witch hunt and that any media criticism of Bush and company would not be tolerated. The right-wing thugs promised that they would launch an attack on any journalist or media outlet that did not follow the politically correct Bush administration's line on terrorism. It was unlikely, however, that the conformist broadcast media needed any attack dogs. Prohibitions against the mention of civilian casualties had already circulated throughout the media; there were few, if any, reports on the television networks of military misdeeds, such as the use of cluster bombs; and reports of the killing of Afghan civilians were barely visible on U.S. TV. But the right-wing New Barbarians wanted *total control* of the news media, total censorship of military news, and total conformity to the demands of ongoing and total war.

On December 16, a disturbing story circulated about how the publisher of *The Sacramento Bee,* speaking before a California State University graduation ceremony, was heckled. Janis Healey's speech was overwhelmed by boos and shouting when she voiced concerns about racial profiling, the suspension of civil rights of suspects in the September 11 attacks, and the establishment of military tribunals. Another ugly crowd scene took place on December 17 in the Cleveland Brown's football stadium. An unpopular referee decision in the final minutes of a close game sent off a crowd reaction, during which barbarian fans heaved thousands of beer bottles, garbage, and miscellaneous items at the referees, hitting players of both teams and other fans. The president of the team franchise explained that most of the beer bottles were plastic and "don't carry much of a wallop." Besides, "I like the fact that our fans cared." The owner of the team brushed it off, saying that "it wasn't World War III," thus in effect legitimating the crowd's barbaric behavior.[5]

At the end of December 2001 in Australia, fires swept through New South Wales, ringing Sydney, and twelve young boys were arrested on suspicion of arson, while BBC reported looting and showed firefighters whose engines and belongings had been stolen as they fought the fire.[6] Argentina's economy collapsed, in part due to political corruption and incompetence in the country and in part because of barbaric IMF requirements that required excessive cutbacks in the state sector and social services to pay back exorbitant interest on loans. The destructive effects of capitalist globalization were clear and one hoped that in the future countries would be intelligent enough to resist the barbarism of predatory capitalism and construct states and a public sector able to produce more prosperity and social justice.

Promising that the New Barbarism would continue in the new year, Barbarian-in-Chief George W. Bush pledged that 2002 would be a "war year" in an end of the year radio address. As the economic crisis in the U.S. intensified, U.S. Labor Department statistics indicated that 1.1 million American citizens had lost their jobs in the last year since Bush stole the presidency, and the United States had the highest unemployment statistics in years. With worsening economic conditions, the Bush administration needed distraction from the U.S.'s economic woes and would no doubt concoct military adventures in the coming year. The Democrats were talking of making the failed U.S. economy and Bush's tax giveaway to the rich, which had eaten up healthy budget surpluses, a big issue in the 2002 elections, so Bush obviously wanted to keep focus on the Terror War to sidetrack attention from the economy.

Nazi, Communist, and other oppressive regimes had frequently used a "state of emergency" to repress opponents, deflect criticism, and augment power, and the Bush Barbarians were doing precisely this, using the legitimate fear of terrorism to push through their right-wing policies. Moreover, in the months ahead, whenever they faced serious criticism, there would be a rash of warnings of imminent terrorist attacks, and those criticizing Bush administration policies would be accused of aiding and abetting the enemy. The world was indeed in a state of emergency, but Bush administration policies were arguably making the situation more perilous rather than providing productive solutions to the problems of terrorism and the way to a more peaceful world.[7]

It was also clear by the beginning of 2002 that the Terror War was being used to justify a variety of types of repression. In an article, "U.N. Fears Abuse of Terror Mandate," William Orme notes how "the anti-terrorism campaign has been used by authoritarian governments to justify moves to clamp down on moderate opponents, outlaw criticism of rulers and expand the use of capital punishment" (*Los Angeles Times*, January 2, 2001). Orme notes how UN officials and human rights advocates were becoming increasingly concerned that the war on terror was legitimating both military aggression and domestic repression on a frightening scale. In a joint letter to Bush, for instance, "Eight leading American human rights groups said his order authorizing the tribunals—which could impose the death penalty—will be cited by foreign dictators for 'decades to come' as a justification for summary executions."

The Guardian presented a revealing portrait of the New Barbarism in an article by Julian Borger, "Washington Hawks Get Power Boost" (December 17, 2001). It reported on a recent dinner at an expensive Washington hotel to officially honor the "Keepers of the Flame," who were "U.S. security officials deemed by their more conservative colleagues to have fought the good fight for bigger defence budgets and tougher policies." "'It's taken us 13 years to get here, but we've arrived,' the evening's host, Frank Gaffney, the head of a hawkish Washington thinktank, declared to applause and murmurs of agreement." (Gaffney was cited earlier in this book for earning the derision of a Canadian audience as he suggested expanding the Terror War to every Arab country imaginable and their "sponsors" in China and Russia.) The celebration marked the victory of hawks Donald Rumsfeld and his wolfish deputy Paul Wolfowitz over Colin Powell's multilateralist approach to foreign policy and the secretary of state's "attempts to keep negotiations going with Moscow over missile defence," which were "abruptly brought to an end last week with the announcement that the United States would withdraw from the antiballistic missile (ABM) treaty." The New Barbarians "are capturing key squares on the chessboard of Washington power, at the expense of the moderates at state" and "almost certain to win" the right wing's "battle to pursue the war of terrorism into Iraq and suspected terrorist havens across the world." Providing a useful catalog of the New Barbarians who were taking over the Bush administration and leading the world into an era of unending Terror War, *The Guardian* listed:

AMERICA'S TOP SABRE-RATTLERS

Donald Rumsfeld—A veteran of the cold war chosen by the vice-president, Dick Cheney, in the face of opposition from Colin Powell, now secretary of state. His radical policies and abrasive manner initially provoked resistance from the Pentagon generals. But the war on terrorism has made him the most powerful member of the cabinet and he is expanding his influence into foreign policy fields normally managed by the secretary of state.

Paul Wolfowitz—Mr Rumsfeld's deputy, and the foremost exponent of a new war against Saddam Hussein. He is a former academic with a wide-ranging network of travellers and sympathisers, commonly referred to in Washington as the "Wolfowitz cabal."
Doug Feith—The Pentagon's policy supremo and a former director of the Centre for Security Policy (CSP), who has led the charge for a more pro-Israel Middle East policy.
Frank Gaffney—A former defence policy official and Rumsfeld acolyte who now runs the CSP—a thinktank and ideological seminary for young hawks. He advocates the scrapping of the Oslo peace process, the forceful promotion of the national missile defence system, and a settling of scores with Baghdad.
Richard Perle—Known as Ronald Reagan's "prince of darkness" for his distaste for disarmament treaties, and his hawkish attitude towards the Soviet Union. Mr Perle retains an important role in the defence policy board, a Pentagon thinktank which he chairs.
John Bolton—The hawks' man inside the state department. Despite the objections of Colin Powell, he was appointed undersecretary of state for arms control, non-proliferation and international security, even though he is a committed unilateralist who opposes global arms treaties on principle.
Zalmay Khalilzad—The top Afghan-American in the administration. Three years ago, he signed a joint letter with Donald Rumsfeld and other hawks, calling on the Clinton administration to topple Saddam. He is seeking to take over the Middle East portfolio when Bruce Reidel steps down later this month.

As 2001 came to an end, not much had been heard recently from Barbarian-behind-the-Throne Dick Cheney, who was reportedly still hiding in his "undisclosed location" while Osama seemed to have left his cave. *The Guardian,* however, published a news brief, "Cheney shows himself for cash" (December 17, 2001). The entry claimed that Dick Cheney "has been quietly out and about raising $500,000 in Texas and Oklahoma for Republican congressional candidates," no doubt so that the Repugs can front more barbaric boosters for the barons of oil that Cheney so blatantly represents. Speaking of oil, *The Times* of London was one of the few to point out that Donald Rumsfeld's visit to Azerbaijan, Georgia, and Armenia over the weekend, and the United States' renewed military aid and cutback of sanctions to these countries for previous ill deeds, ended an "economic embargo [that] has hindered U.S. oil companies from developing Caspian Sea fields, which they now have encouragement from Washington to try to do" (December 17, 2001).

Dialectical thought makes the connections, and exploring oil and politics will reveal that Dick Cheney, the Bush family, James Baker, and their friends had long cultivated connections with Caspian Sea oil exploration and the countries in the area that allegedly have oil reserves greater than those of Saudi Arabia. The New Barbarism is thus in part a front for good old greed and desire to exploit and control oil supplies and markets. It intersects with the interests of the military-industrial-propaganda complex to expand and assert U.S. geopolitical domination, as well as to promote Carlyle Fund stocks held by the Bush family and their friends in the defense industries. And New Barbarism and the Terror War help the Bush administration keep the public in a state of frenzy to create conditions in which it can ram its hard-right policies down their throats and further its attempts to undo centuries of American democracy and decades of diplomacy.

The Terror War in Afghanistan could thus be the opening salvo of the New Barbarism, enabling George W. Bush and his administration to militarize U.S. society, embark on endless military adventures, scare the public into hysteria, and use war fever to carry out their hard-right agenda, stealing wealth for the corporate sectors that fund their campaigns and of which they are a part. Of course, wars need antagonists, and Osama bin Laden and Al Qaeda provided the perfect villains, the embodiments of "evil," with Saddam Hussein and other latent villains to be constructed to legitimate the next stages of Terror War as the Bush Barbarians plot their enduring wars.

Yet, in some ways, Terror War is not a war at all in a conventional sense with well-defined enemies, territories, and goals. Eradicating evil from the world, as George W. Bush had proclaimed at the beginning of his era of military adventure, is a dangerous fantasy and will perhaps in the end promote what it was supposed to eliminate. But the Terror War was highly useful for the Bush-Cheney gang, who could exploit the crimes of terrorism to deflect attention from their own corporate and political misdeeds and those of their friends such as the Enron Corporation, whose scandalous collapse was beginning to get media attention by the end of 2001 and would get much more, as I note in later discussions of what became one of the defining stories of the era. Manipulated into hysteria and inflamed by sensationalistic media, the U.S. public was ready for the next assault on terrorism and was a willing spectator of the New Barbarism and relentless expansion of the military-industrial complex.

BUSH MILITARISM: SKY-ROCKETING BUDGETS, MILITARY SHIELDS, AND PREEMPTIVE STRIKES

The U.S. Commission on National Security for the 21st Century maintained that "Outer Space and cyberspace are the main arteries of the world's evolving systems. Through technical and diplomatic means, the U.S. needs to guard against the possibility of 'breakout' capabilities in space and cyberspace that would endanger U.S. survival or critical interests."[8] In his first speech on military affairs after announcing his candidacy for president in 1999, George W. Bush affirmed the concept of a "Revolution in Military Affairs" (RMA) and was soon touting the virtues of a National Missile Defense (NMD) shield. Upon obtaining the presidency through a highly controversial electoral process, Bush called for a dramatic increase in military spending and pushed the space missile NMD program, popularly known as Star Wars II. The Bush administration also undermined collective security based on multilateral negotiations and treaties over weapons control by renouncing nuclear weapons treaties and attempts to regulate nuclear testing, biological and chemical weapons, small arms trading, land mines, and environmental treaties, which had been carefully nurtured by decades of diplomacy.

The Cold Warriors from Bush's father's circles who surround the figurehead and control policy are key representatives of the virulent military-industrial complex and are promoting a plethora of new weapons systems, as well as unparalleled expansion of the U.S. military budget and scope of military intervention. The Bush administration initially proposed $310 billion in military spending for 2001, with much more expected for a missile-defense system that was the pet project of his Secretary of Defense, Donald Rumsfeld. In mid-February 2001, Bush announced he was seeking an addition $2.6 billion for hi-tech weapons and by the end of the month would detail further requests for hikes in the Pentagon budget beyond the $310 billion already targeted. By summer 2001, the Pentagon budget was up to $324 billion, while Bush's 2002 budget proposed a 6 percent boost in spending to raise the Pentagon budget to $330 billion, eventually going up to $355 billion. And for fiscal year 2003, Bush proposed a record $48 billion increase, with Congress eventually passing in October 2002 a record $355.1 billion budget.[9]

The dramatically increased military spending to develop a space-based "National Missile Defense" system (Reagan's "Star Wars" program reborn) threatened not only to expand the military budget but to accelerate both a new arms race and the militarization of space.[10] Before assuming office Bush spoke of "American responsibilities" and the "promise of America," while promising a "humble" U.S. foreign policy that eschewed "nation-building." Once in office, however, Bush pursued a highly irresponsible politics of unilateralism that renounced global environmental treaties, rejected arms limitations treaties, pushed ahead to build a missile defense system strongly opposed by U.S. allies, and accelerated tensions with Iraq, Iran, North Korea, China, and Russia, generating "enemies" that would justify a missile defense system and increased military spending.

During its first nine months the Bush administration pursued a hardline foreign policy reminiscent of the Cold War at its peak. In the opening weeks Bush bombed Iraq and heightened tensions in the Middle East, threatened China, told Russia to expect reduced aid, and alienated Japan when a Navy submarine giving Republican financial supporters a demonstration sank a Japanese fishing boat, killing nine people. The Bush administration worried much of Europe with its aggressive approach to national missile defense (NMD), making it clear that it does not intend to pursue constructive negotiations with North Korea. Even before September 11, the Bush administration returned the world to the Cold War paranoid universe of the military-industrial complex, while Dr. Strangelove seemed to be alive and well in the U.S. Defense Department, concocting Star Wars missile systems that will cost trillions of dollars and have yet to be proved functional.

Bush, Cheney, and Rumsfeld had also resurrected the concept of "rogue state," a notion jettisoned by the Clinton administration, that was sure to increase tensions and the possibility of war. Dangers of an aggressive new Bush foreign policy were soon evident. On March 24, 2001, the *Washington Post* published a report that Bush had a meeting two days before with defense Secretary Rumsfeld who was preparing a report that China had supplanted the USSR as its Number One Enemy and should be the focus of U.S. military policy. Some days later, an "accident" occurred when a Chinese plane and U.S. spy plane off the Chinese coast collided and the U.S. plane, loaded with hi-tech surveillance equipment and the latest in military computers, crash-landed on a Chinese offshore island, after which the crew was held hostage for eleven tense days while its release was negotiated.

Critics claim that "corporate payback" is the "defining trait" of the Bush administration and major force in determining its hard-right policies. Abrogation of the Kyoto Treaty and the Bush-Cheney energy policy were payback for the more than $50 million contributed by the oil and energy industries. The former director of the Star Wars program under Reagan, Dr. Robert W. Bowman, makes a similar argument in terms of Bush's military policy. Star Wars II, Bowman argues, will "line the pockets of weapons manufacturers for decades" at the expense of "optional" programs like health, education, the environment, and welfare. Moreover, it gives "the multinational corporations and banks absolute military superiority for their 'gunboat diplomacy around the world.'"[11]

The militarization of space constitutes yet another troubling dimension of Bush administration pursuit of a space-based missile program and unilateral foreign policy.[12] UN treaties have called for the demilitarization of space and the renunciation of space-based military programs. The Bush administration, however, has made clear that it plans to deploy weapons in space with a land, sea, air, and space-based Star Wars II system. The Pentagon has revived the Reagan-era plan for "Brilliant Pebbles," a scheme that would place thousands of missile interceptors in space, raising the possibility of space wars and accidental mishaps. Another piece of Reagan's SDI, "Brilliant Eyes," has been resurrected, consisting of a series of low-flying satellites geared to tracking missiles or presumed weapons.

Maintaining a weapons-free space, however, is crucial to a hi-tech economy that depends on communications satellites for its functionality, as well as increasing the hopes for global peace. The more weapons flying around in space, the greater chance of their misuse or an accident. It is also tragic that the militarization of space has supplanted efforts for the scientific exploration of space, as the Star Wars II budget is now twice that of the entire NASA budget. The destiny of the human race depends on the peaceful exploration of space, while its militarization could threaten the very survival of the human species.[13]

The Bush administration has undermined every single arms control treaty it has faced since coming to power. When it rejected a pact to enforce a biological weapons ban in July 2001, a British commentator noted: "America's lone, wanton wrecking of long-running negotiations to enforce the 1972 treaty banning biological or germs weapons is an insult to the pact's 142 other signatories, a body-blow for the treaty itself and a major setback for international efforts to agree to practical curbs on the proliferation of weapons of mass destruction."[14] Bush stood condemned as "proliferator-in-chief" of dangerous weapons, one whose presidency "confirms a pattern of reckless, unilateralist behavior on arms control, as on environmental and other issues."[15]

Once again Bush carried out the wishes of his main campaign supporters, as it was the biotech and pharmaceutical industries that opposed the inspection program called for in the biological weapons treaty. Although biological weapons are deemed a disturbing threat to the entire world, the U.S. found itself in a minority of one in opposing the treaty, putting U.S. corporate interests before those of global security. Similarly, the U.S. was the sole nation out of 178 to renounce ratification of the Kyoto treaty to combat global warming during a July 2001 meeting in Bonn.

The frightening marriage of the Bush administration and its "revolution in military affairs" with enduring terror war poses renewed threats to global security and world peace. Even before September 11, the Bush administration had undermined multilateral frameworks for controlling arms, and maintaining global peace and security through the regulation of chemical, biological, nuclear, and other weapons of mass destruction. Its pursuit of what is in effect a unilateral military policy in Afghanistan and beyond completely controlled by the U.S. threatens to create an era of intensifying warfare. Bush militarism is thus part of a New Barbarism that threatens a militarist future with permanent war and terrorism in a deadly cycle of violence. Bush's New Barbarism is also evident in Pentagon military policy following the Afghanistan war.

PRISONERS, NEW U.S. MILITARY BASES, AND PROXY WAR

It appeared that the interrogation of captured Taliban and Al Qaeda forces was now a major focus of U.S. efforts in Afghanistan. The U.S. claimed to have captured one of the top twenty Al Qaeda leaders, said to be in charge of training camps for bin Laden. The U.S. now held over 270 Taliban and Al Qaeda fighters who were under intense interrogation, including the American Taliban, John Walker Lindh. No doubt under U.S. pressure, Pakistan handed over the former Taliban ambassador to Pakistan, Mullah Abdul Salam Zaeef. This bespectacled and clever Taliban leader had been the public face of the Taliban regime, holding daily conferences and slyly attacking the Americans to the delight of a large global Arab audience. Obviously, the U.S. wanted to chat up this fellow and threaten him with long imprisonment and harassment if he did not spill the beans about Mullah Omar and the Al Qaeda connection.

Donald Rumsfeld said that those Taliban and Al Qaeda prisoners under interrogation were going to be sent to the U.S. military base in Guantanamo Bay, Cuba, one of the relics of the Cold War. Although there were reports that this move was protested by Cuba's President Fidel Castro, who had long vilified the continued U.S. occupation of a military base on Cuban soil, American senators visited Cuba and then claimed that Castro now gave his permission. Accordingly, a makeshift detention center was produced in Cuba and on January 11, the first batch of around twenty prisoners were flown to the camp, in hoods and shackles and in some cases under sedation, accompanied by a phalanx of U.S. guards. Amnesty International worried about their treatment and requested meeting with the prisoners to assure that they were being treated humanely. The U.S. was not treating these forces as prisoners of war, who are protected by the Geneva Convention, and was going to interrogate and try them on non-U.S. soil to avoid lawsuits in the U.S. over the Bush administration's controversial military trials policy.

The *Los Angeles Times* reported on January 6 that the U.S. was also building military bases in many countries around Afghanistan, with a string of tent cities and new bases that have sprung up in thirteen locations and nine countries in the Afghanistan region. Altogether, according to this article, "More than 60,000 U.S. military personnel now live and work at these forward bases." The article suggested that these bases were likely to outrage Islamic fundamentalists, as bin Laden had been incensed by the U.S. bases in Saudi Arabia after the Gulf War. This could also be a dangerous assignment for U.S. troops, who would be subject to terrorist attacks in the host countries.

There were reports that Pakistan was pressuring the U.S. to close down some of its bases in their country and that the U.S. was considering complying by building up a permanent encampment in Kandahar and multiplying U.S. military camps in other countries in the region. Some countries were beginning to question U.S. military presence in their territory, and on January 19 the *Washington Post* and various British newspapers published a story indicating that the Saudis were about to ask U.S. military forces to leave the country. Within days, however, U.S. Secretary of State Colin Powell insisted that U.S.-Saudi relations were fine and that the U.S. had not been asked to close down their bases, although obviously a debate was going on in both countries and there were clearly serious problems between the U.S. and the Saudis.

The possibility of imminent U.S. military action against Iraq was temporarily lessened in January 2002, when it was reported that the Bush administration was no longer funding the Iraqi National Congress (INC), the major exile-based Iraqi opposition group. The INC had reportedly not provided adequate accounting for monies already allocated; in other words, millions received from the U.S. was not properly accounted for and the group, based in London, had not provided any tangible efforts.[16] This, of course, infuriated militarists who wanted Iraqi blood for their Sunday afternoon enjoyment and would be forced to satisfy their aggressions elsewhere. Throwing some meat to these dogs, Senator John McCain shouted out after a trip to Afghanistan to meet the U.S. troops, "Next stop, Baghdad!"

Meanwhile, the relentless Afghan winter intensified and there were worries about starvation and poor conditions at refugee camps. The State Department had claimed on January 3 that a surge of food aid deliveries had averted the threat of widespread famine in Afghanistan. Yet stories in the *New York Times* on January 4 and 6 questioned claims of famine avoidance. In large sectors of the country, warlords were stealing food; in other parts, continued violence and banditry prevented aid agencies from delivering food or medical supplies, so Afghanistan was still in a crisis situation, according to many.[17]

Shockingly, although this was not widely reported in the U.S. media, the U.S. was not supporting food and humanitarian deliveries throughout Afghanistan, and had been actively hampering efforts that it believed were conflicting with its military endeavors. Although the U.S. eventually allowed Britain and the Europeans to establish a police-security force in Afghanistan, it was limited to Kabul, supposedly because the U.S. wanted to continue to focus upon military action against remaining Al Qaeda and Taliban forces in other parts of the country. This policy condemned thousands of Afghans to starvation and raised the question of why humanitarian and military operations could not be carried out simultaneously.

Highlighting dangers to the ongoing military operations in Afghanistan, on January 9, a U.S. jet crashed in Pakistan, killing all seven aboard; it was later claimed that pilot error was responsible for the jet crashing into a mountain. In another setback for the U.S., it was announced that three major Taliban leaders, including the notorious Defense Minister and Minister of Justice Mullah Turabi, had surrendered to Afghan forces and then were given amnesty, despite Washington's claims that they wanted these men detained and tried. Clearly, there were diverse political forces in Afghanistan, and many were hostile to the U.S. and not prepared to cooperate with either the central Afghan regime in Kabul or with Washington.

It was indeed not clear exactly what the U.S. military could accomplish in Afghanistan, as it was not certain that other major Taliban or Al Qaeda leaders were still in the country. The continued reports of bin Laden and other terrorist sleeper cells throughout the world indicated that terrorism remained a major problem, but it appeared to many that the war on terror was no longer primarily a military issue. Instead, many agreed that terrorism is more productively interpreted as a global criminal issue that requires a combination of international military, police, and legal solutions grounded in criminalizing, arresting, and shutting down terrorist networks. To effectively fight terror would require using a wide array of global legal, financial, police, and military organizations, rather than depending on the U.S. military as the superpoliceman of the world.

Although shutting down the Taliban support of the Al Qaeda network, eliminating some Al Qaeda forces in Afghanistan, and finding intelligence in the country had clearly provided a material blow against the Islamic terrorist network, it was less spectacular efforts throughout the world that were beginning to systematically undermine the Al Qaeda network. Its operatives were arrested in Britain, France, Germany, Spain, and many European countries, and terrorist activities by members of these groups were prevented. In Indonesia, Malaysia, the Philippines, and other countries, there were reports that Al Qaeda members were incarcerated and there were global efforts to cut off the financial sources that had allowed flow of funds to support the Al Qaeda organization and projects. The war against terrorism was just starting and it appeared that continued major U.S. military interventions, as in Afghanistan, would not alone suffice to shut down the terror networks, and that more multilateral global efforts would be needed.

In addition, it was doubtful that U.S. military efforts were going to win the hearts and minds of Arabs and Muslims throughout the world and prevent the rise of further terrorist networks and attacks, and it was probable that excessive U.S. military intervention would create new enemies and assure future attacks. Most critics believed that the U.S. was losing the propaganda war, especially in the Muslim world, which viewed continued military attacks in Afghanistan and elsewhere as assaults against Islam.[18] Moreover, as I discuss in the next section, there was growing controversy over U.S. handling of prisoners of war that was creating international debate and criticism of U.S. policies.

The U.S. was suggesting that it was intending to carry out a series of wars by proxy, using local militia forces to fight alleged terrorists in places like Somalia, Sudan, the Philippines and elsewhere in order to go after terror networks. This strategy, however, seemed highly problematical in the light of the Afghan war and the situation of the countries named as candidates for proxy wars. The U.S. failure in Afghanistan to capture major Al Qaeda and Taliban leaders had largely resulted from relying on proxy troops. The forces that the U.S. had depended on in the Kandahar region and Tora Bora caves had been highly unreliable and allowed many Taliban and Al Qaeda leaders to escape. Without major deployments of U.S. military forces on the ground to do the work, any results would be highly unpredictable and ambiguous, as in the Afghan war.

There was growing evidence that indeed the proxy strategy was failing in Afghanistan and meeting resistance elsewhere. In mid-January, there were reports that tribal groups in Afghanistan were refusing to participate further in exploring caves, a major focus of the U.S. effort to seek evidence of Al Qaeda membership, tactics, and plans in caves, military sites, and training houses. During the same week, when U.S. troops were sent to the Philippines to help the government go after rebel forces there, large demonstrations against the U.S. military presence erupted, there were calls for the impeachment of the Philippines' president who had invited U.S. troops, and so it was announced that U.S. forces would not actually be sent into the fields but would serve solely in training and advising capacities.

The presence of U.S. troops in the Philippines evoked memories of an earlier U.S. occupation of the country, and some commentators noted that the sending of U.S. military advisors and Special Forces paralleled the Vietnam intervention that proved so disastrous. Once U.S. soldiers become involved in the complex dynamics of local situations, control over the situation becomes increasingly complex, U.S. forces are subject to constant danger, and the results might not be what are intended.[19] Likewise, critics of planned U.S. military deployments by proxy in Sudan and Somalia pointed out that these regions were in a state of chaos, were highly dangerous and unpredictable, and would be difficult terrain to navigate and control.

"DETAINEES," "UNLAWFUL COMBATANTS," AND
THE GUANTANAMO BAY FIASCO

The perception that the U.S. was treating Arabs in a dehumanizing way was intensified with coverage of U.S. handling of members of the Taliban and Al Qaeda who were captured during the Afghan war. From the beginning, engaging in Orwellian Bushspeak, the U.S. refused to call those who were captured "prisoners of war." Instead, the Bush/Pentagon gang insisted that the detainees were "unlawful combatants" who would not be subject to the Geneva Convention, leading to a hailstorm of international criticism. Pictures were shown in the *New York Times,* British papers, and throughout the world depicting the prisoners in Afghanistan with bags over their heads and in chains and shackles. These pictures received little commentary or mention in the U.S. media, although there were some criticisms in foreign journalism circles.[20]

Images, however, of the prisoners taken from Afghanistan and landing in Cuba in fluorescent orange jumpsuits, blacked-out plastic goggles, turquoise face masks around their mouths and noses, knit hats pulled over their heads, ear cups to block out sound, mittens encompassing their hands, and shackles on their legs created intense controversy, leading to claims that the prisoners were being submitted to excessive sensory deprivation. Likewise reports that the prisoners were shaven of their beards and hair, which were part of their religious identity, and were housed in concentration camps, exposed to the weather, lit at night with beaming florescent lamps, forced to sleep on concrete slabs, and made to live in a glare of publicity created a debate about the conditions under which the prisoners were housed. There was also criticism of the food, which included bagels and cream cheese as well as "Islamic" prepackaged TV dinners and Fruit Loops. Called "Camp X-Ray" by the American military prison guards, because you could see right through it into the skeletons of human beings rapidly being stripped of their humanity, the camp elicited a thunderstorm of criticism, mostly, however, in diplomatic circles and the foreign press.

The British government and media were extremely upset with the conditions of incarceration and treatment of the prisoners, and there were reports that the barbaric situation was creating a serious chasm between the two major allies in the war against terrorism. British Foreign Minister Jack Cross was particularly perturbed, and Tony Blair reportedly called Bush to tell him that Britain expected more humane treatment of the prisoners. European Union External Relations Commissioner Chris Patten said that the West was in danger of losing international support and the moral high ground if prisoners were mistreated or executed. Lord David Russell-Johnston, president of the Council of Europe's parliamentary assembly, said that pictures of the captives published over the weekend raised troubling questions about their treatment: "We're supposed to be better than terrorists," he said. Javier Solana, secretary-general of the European council, German Foreign Minister Joschka Fischer, and the Netherlands urged the United States to treat the captives according to the Geneva Convention and international law. And ambassadors from the countries where the prisoners originated were demanding humane treatment for their citizens and criticizing the U.S. military prison.[21]

On January 14, the International Committee of the Red Cross (ICRC) argued that those being held by American forces must be counted as prisoners of war under the Geneva Convention and were entitled to the full protection offered by it. They also insisted that the U.S. euphemism "battlefield detainees" had no legal meaning, a criticism also made by many of the next buzzword of "unlawful combatants," which the U.S. propaganda ministers cooked up to justify the U.S.'s refusal to follow international guidelines and legal requirements. The ICRC declared as well that prisoners being held in Kandahar, Afghanistan, were being kept in unsheltered stockades in the bitterly cold winter and without privacy.[22]

The U.S. military, especially Donald Rumsfeld, feistily defended the prison conditions. Rumsfeld made the obvious arguments that there "are among these prisoners people who are perfectly willing to kill themselves and other people." This is true and points to a serious security issue, but does not answer the question of whether the specific conditions of detention were necessary or justified, why the prisoners should not be treated according to the Geneva Convention, and why the U.S. chose Guantanamo Bay in the first place.

More racist overtones were heard in the Pentagon's justification for treatment of the prisoners during their transportation from the U.S. to Cuba and their incarceration in what appeared to many to be concentration camp conditions. One Pentagon general asserted that the prisoners were so dangerous that they could "cut through hydraulic cables" with their teeth! And eventually even the *Washington Post*, which had so far strongly supported the Afghan war and the U.S. military intervention, suggested that Guantanamo "has been a public relations . . . debacle." It criticized Rumsfeld in particular, "whose handling of the prisoner issue has done much to ignite the international controversy. The globally broadcast misinformation about which he complains stems largely from his own policy of strictly limiting media access to Guantanamo while offering accounts of U.S. handling of the prisoners that have been by turns vague, flippant or simply wrong" (January 25, 2002, A24).

The Red Cross maintained on January 21 that distribution of the pictures of the prisoners bound and blindfolded, and the subsequent publicity, contravened the Geneva Convention's article that forbid prisoners to be displayed for publicity and required their detainers to protect their privacy. The United States' treatment, according to its critics, also disregarded the Geneva Convention requirement that prisoners be kept under similar conditions as their detainers and be treated with dignity and humanity. The Red Cross persuaded the U.S. to allow them to regularly inspect the prisoners, to register them, and to help improve treatment. Human Rights Watch claimed that the U.S. was violating international law by avoiding the POW label, while a team of American lawyers led by former U.S. Attorney General Ramsey Clark filed a petition in Los Angeles requiring the U.S. government to bring the detainees at Guantanamo Bay before a civil court to define the charges against them and to provide them with legal representation.

Granting that the Al Qaeda and Taliban prisoners might be hard cases and dangerous, on pragmatic and instrumental grounds, as well as moral and legal ones, it was not clear what the positive benefit was of treating the prisoners in a controversial and arguably barbaric fashion. The war against terrorism, as I have argued throughout this study, is largely a global one and the primary challenge is for the U.S. to gain allies in what is shaping up to be an epochal struggle. This requires changing the U.S. image and perception in the Arab and Muslim world, bringing developing countries into modernity and the global world, and isolating Islamic fundamentalist terrorist extremists of the ilk of bin Laden and his network. From this perspective, the U.S. handling of the Afghanistan war prisoners has been a public relations disaster and a major U.S. setback in the Terror War. From the legal perspective, critics claimed that the U.S. was violating international law and standards in handling prisoners of war, opening U.S. military personnel to future barbaric treatment, and encouraging barbarians all over the world to dismiss humane treatment of those perceived as their enemies. International legal authorities maintained that the U.S. violated the rights of the prisoners in the first place by deciding that they were indeed war criminals rather than allowing an international body, or recognized court, to determine if those detained were indeed combatants and thus prisoners of war.

From a moral point of view, the U.S. treatment of the prisoners is promoting and spreading barbarism and undermining civilization, making the world a more ugly, dangerous, and violent place. Human Rights Watch put out a devastating 660-page report that U.S.-style repressive legal and military policies were already being used by the governments of Russia, China, Israel, Saudi Arabia, Egypt, Zimbabwe, and elsewhere to justify brutal treatment of political prisoners, intensifying a New Barbarism throughout the world. The War on Terrorism was allowing repressive governments everywhere to declare its critics and opposition as "terrorists," to imprison them without basic legal rights, and to treat them as they wished—exactly as the Bush administration was doing with its prisoners.

Moreover, pragmatically speaking, pictures of the wretched treatment of Arab prisoners were generating hatred of the U.S. around the world, guaranteeing revenge and Jihad, and portending that innocent civilians in the U.S. and elsewhere will once again pay the price for a barbaric and out-of-control U.S. military and political administration. What, indeed, is positively accomplished by the maltreatment of these prisoners; the failure to label them as what they obviously are, "prisoners of war"; and the failure to treat them according to the Geneva Convention? Likewise, failure to provide them with basic legal and human rights and to judge the prisoners according to accepted law and practices, preferably in an open court, could only turn large segments of the world against the U.S. by causing it to be perceived as an aggressive and vicious bully, thus creating more enemies for the U.S. and guaranteeing future retaliation.

There was also the irony that the prisoners were being held in Guantanamo Bay,

Cuba, a hangover from an earlier era of U.S. imperialism and a relic of the Cold War. The U.S. had seized the base in 1898 during the Spanish American War and formally leased the land around Guantanamo Bay in a 1903 treaty with Cuba, which was renewed in 1934 by a right-wing and corrupt government that was eventually overthrown by Fidel Castro and his merry band of revolutionaries. Castro had repeatedly told the U.S. that he wanted them off the island and a Cold War standoff had emerged. Putting the prisoners in this contested historical space was a highly unusual decision and points to the surreality and lack of good common sense that are characteristic of the Bush administration and U.S. military, which has surely presided over one of the most bizarre and incredible years in U.S. history.[23]

Thus, on the pragmatic level of what the U.S. was actually going to do with these prisoners, the fruits of the strange Bush administration and Pentagon policy were becoming an international embarrassment and growing public relations problem. A British minister told the London *Times* (January 20, 2001): "Picking people up, giving them a good going over and sticking them on a plane to Cuba isn't what our police and security services would do. Our forces would have gone through the whole thing on the ground much more closely in terms of following through the contacts of the individuals, where they are based and witnesses and so on." Indeed, what did the U.S. think it would gain by bringing these prisoners to Cuba? Wouldn't it have been better to set up detention centers in Afghanistan or within the region, to carefully question them, to find out as much as they could about the individual prisoner's networks and connections, to try to reeducate the prisoners in terms of proper Islam, and perhaps to turn over some of the prisoners as informants? Certainly, hard cases were not going to bend, but they could be turned over to their home countries that could probably deal with them in a more effective manner than the bumbling U.S. military did. It indeed appeared that the U.S. had no real plan or strategy to use the prisoners in any way that might advance the war against terrorism; the U.S.'s barbaric treatment was only likely to gain more enemies for the West.

A report circulated on January 23 that the Bush administration expected to "send most detainees home" raised questions about the rationality of the policy, which had obviously caused more harm than good, in the first place. The same day it was announced that the U.S. was planning to review its treatment of the prisoners, had temporarily suspended the incarceration of more prisoners, and was rethinking the whole affair. The Canadian Broadcasting Company (CBC) reported on January 23 that Canada, which was currently engaged in police and military activity with the U.S. in Afghanistan, was having serious reservations concerning turning over prisoners to the U.S. There was concern in Canada that prisoners would be held under controversial conditions and subject to the death penalty in military trials. Furthermore, British Foreign Minister Jack Straw straight-out declared that any British citizens held under conditions not governed by the Geneva Convention should be returned for incarceration and trial in Britain. The response of close U.S. allies to the Bush administration's refusal to recognize the importance of holding prisoners under international law pointed to a potential collapse in the supposed coalition against terrorism, which appeared more and more to be a unilateralist project of the Bush administration and Pentagon.

The Bush administration and the majority of U.S. pundits assaulted the European criticisms, put forth "war is hell" arguments, and claimed that since Al Qaeda does not play by the rules, there is no reason that they should be treated according to international law. These thuggish arguments miss the point that if the Terror War is a struggle between civilization and barbarism, international law should be affirmed and the prisoners should be treated in a way that is above criticism; in other words, one side needs to act civilized. There is also a human and legal rights argument that individuals imprisoned during wartime conditions should have a "competent tribunal" judge them, make charges, and provide a fair trial. This is another ground on which there is legitimate cause for concern, as many allies in the war against terror do not approve of Bush's military tribunals and oppose the death penalty.

Recognizing the dangers of a public relations fiasco, members of the Bush administration provided assurances that most of the prisoners would be sent to their home countries after interrogation. In addition, a memo was leaked to the *Washington Times* on January 27 that Colin Powell had recommended a review of the Pentagon policy, suggesting that the prisoners be interviewed, with some labeled as prisoners of war and with a commitment to treat them under the Geneva Convention to show respect for international law.[24] The same day, however, Donald Rumsfeld visited the Guantanamo Bay camp and once again affirmed that the detainees would not be referred to as POWs, nor would the Geneva Convention apply, leading the U.S. media to discuss a Powell-Rumsfeld split while foreign observers worried again about the "Rumsfeld problem."[25]

Pressure continued for months to release prisoners from the Guantanamo Bay camp from Britain, Kuwait, Saudi Arabia, Afghanistan, and other countries whose citizens were being held. There was a major Kuwaiti campaign that got a lot of publicity in the world media by claiming that its citizens held as prisoners were studying Islam and were not Islamic Jihadists. Eventually, several prisoners were released with one Afghan man claiming to be over 100 and others also of advanced age. At the same time, the Pentagon was outraged when a picture circulated of a new batch of "detainees" coming into the camp bound, tied, gagged, and hooded like the earlier group whose photos circulated around the world.[26]

Negative effects on U.S. citizens and potential problems for U.S. troops from the POW controversy surfaced when *Wall Street Journal* reporter Daniel Pearl was kidnapped in Pakistan. The *Journal* and other news sources received an e-mail from a group declaring that Mr. Pearl was being held "in very inhuman circumstances quite similar to the way Pakistanis and nationals of other sovereign countries are being kept in Cuba by the American army. If the Americans keep our countrymen in better conditions, than we will better the conditions of Mr. Pearl and all other Americans that we capture" (cited in *Guardian,* January 28, 2001). For the next weeks, the Pakistani group played cat-and-mouse with their detainee, declaring that he would be executed within twenty-four hours if the kidnapper's demands were not met, then extending the deadline. Another communiqué proclaimed that Pearl had been killed and that Bush could find his body in the graveyards of Karachi. Taunting the U.S., the group proclaimed that Pearl was "collateral damage" and that they were "thirsty for the blood of another American," frightening journalists and other Americans in Pakistan. Eventually, Pearl was murdered and the killers disseminated the dramatic picture of his death, making it clear that Americans in many parts of the world were not safe and that the Bush administration's policies would produce many casualties.

There were also emerging criticisms that a U.S. military assault on Somalia would be "a waste of effort." A U.S. government advisor, Ken Enkhaus, declared that only 10–12 Somalis had significant links to the bin Laden network and that reliable U.S. intelligence was "exceedingly low," increasing the risk of a repeat of the botched American intervention in 1993. Interestingly, this debacle was being given a positive spin as an episode of U.S. heroism in the film *Black Hawk Down* (2001), which was exciting audiences throughout the world. In the U.S., there were criticisms that the movie sugarcoated the actual problems with the U.S. military intervention in Somalia and there were worries that a future U.S. adventure by the Bush administration and Pentagon would meet similar problems. There were reports that in Somalian cinemas, there were loud cheers as the Somalians in the film shot down the U.S. helicopter and pursued and killed the American soldiers, attesting to growing anti-American sentiment in the Muslim world against Bush administration policies.

Meanwhile, political wars at home erupted as the biggest scandal in modern U.S. history emerged with the collapse of Enron, the corporation that was a major financial supporter of the Bush administration and that had helped produce the energy, deregulatory, and tax policies that were the Bush-Cheney gang's hallmark. The crisis galvanized the attention of the media and political class, and generated extreme dangers for the Bush administration, whose scandals, policies, corruption, and history might be exposed at last to media scrutiny.

9

❖

The War at Home: Political Battles and the Enron Scandal

As Congress reconvened in January 2002 after the Christmas break, it was clear that the Bush economic stimulus package had stalled. The Bush administration continued to insist that tax breaks for the rich and its big corporate supporters like Enron would provide a stimulus for economic recovery. The Democrats weren't buying this, and every reputable economist agreed that current economic difficulties were due to a conjuncture of the Bush tax giveaway, the 9/11 attacks and resulting military intervention, and the downturning of the U.S. and global economy. There was a consensus that further tax breaks for the wealthy would make a bad situation worse. Although the Democrats made reasonable proposals for a stimulus package that would put government resources in the hands of those in economic need and workers who had lost their jobs, the Bush administration would not budge and a stalemate on the economic stimulus issue was reached.

Putting on display his blatant demagoguery and basic dishonesty in a January 6 speech, Bush blamed the political standstill on the Democrats. He claimed that their policy was to raise taxes and in a memorable Bushism declared with force: "And I challenge their economics when they say raising taxes will help the country recover. Not over my dead body will they raise your taxes." This, of course, was a blatant lie, as no Democrat had called for tax increases and were merely suggesting that Congress rescind the criminally irresponsible trillion dollar-plus in tax cuts for the wealthy set to kick in over the next ten years that the Bush gang had pushed through Congress.

Congressional budget figures revealed that the healthy surpluses of the Clinton era were giving way to disturbing $100 billion dollar–plus deficits in the first Bush year with more alarming deficit forecasts for the future. After there had been a bipartisan consensus in the Clinton era to cut back on the debt and to responsibly fiscally manage the economy, Bushonomics would raise the national debt dramatically

185

higher. Consequently, accountable members of Congress were saying that it would be reckless to institute future Bush tax cuts for the superrich in the years to come in such a perilous economic situation.

Indeed, there were forecasts that by the end of 2001 there would be hundreds of thousands more Americans out of work, thanks in part to Bushonomics. The brazenness of Bush's false claim that Democrats wanted merely to raise taxes and his hyperbolic malapropism "not over my dead body" pointed to growing desperation and hysteria in the Bush administration that was about to be confronted with its worst crisis yet. I noted earlier that the collapse of the Enron Corporation in November 2001 and its declared bankruptcy on December 2 created potential embarrassment and corrosive scandal for the Bush administration. The Enron Corporation had been one of George W. Bush's biggest contributors in Grand Theft 2000 and had helped finance the heist of the election in the Florida recount wars. Ken Lay was also a major contributor to Bush's inauguration, as well as having been a longtime supporter of both the Bush I and Bush II regimes, as I document in Kellner (2001) and in the following section.

FAMILY FRIENDS:
BUSH ADMINISTRATIONS AND ENRON

Certainly, Enron and the Bushes went way back. Bush affectionately dubbed Enron President Ken Lay "Kenny Boy," and Enron had not only supported the gubernatorial and presidential campaigns of George W. Bush, but was also a major supporter of George H. W. Bush. Ken Lay had long been a close family friend of the Bushes in the Houston business community that included election theft manager and Bush consigliere James Baker. Bush père, Baker, and their close friend Bob Mosbacher had been involved with Enron in both business deals and political campaigns, so that the Bush-Baker-Enron nexus was deep and far-reaching. Enron was a strong supporter of Bush Senior in the 1988 presidential election, and Bush I rewarded Enron by calling the Argentine minister of public works to get an Enron pipeline in Argentina. The Argentine president, Carlos Menem, himself a highly corrupt crony capitalist and a personal friend of the Bush family, obliged, making a sweetheart deal with Enron that freed the company of tariffs and taxes.

From 1988 to 1992, the Enron Corporation continued to be a major corporate supporter of the Bush presidency, and Bush Senior repaid the favors by asking Lay to co-chair a July 1990 G-7 economic summit in Houston and appointing him to his export council in 1990. The earlier Bush administration included in its energy act of 1992 provisions to oblige utility companies to carry and transmit Enron energy. Moreover, in Kevin Phillips's useful summary:

> In December 1992, Bush's Commodity Futures Trading Commission, chaired by Wendy L. Gramm, wife of Texas GOP Sen. Phil Gramm, created a legal exemption

that allowed Enron to begin trading energy derivatives—a further growth enhancer for the company. When Bush left the White House in 1993, Enron made Wendy Gramm a company director and signed a joint consulting and investing agreement with James A. Baker III, Bush's secretary of state, and Robert A. Mosbacher, his Commerce secretary. The two were to do Enron's global deal-making for natural-gas projects."[1]

Disclosing the close economic and political connections between the Bush gang and Enron, in 1992 Ken Lay was named co-chair of the Bush Senior election team and host in Houston to the Republican National Convention. Despite his attempts to distance himself from Lay and Enron, George W. Bush was also deeply connected with Enron. Lay was a key supporter of George W. Bush's 1994 election in Texas, with Lay and Joe B. Allen (of Vinson & Elkin, Enron's Houston law firm) the top fundraisers. Lay chaired Governor Bush's Business Council and received favor after favor from Bush during his two governorships. For instance, in 1997, Bush urged then–Pennsylvania governor Tom Ridge, now head of Bush's Homeland Security department, to support an Enron-backed energy deregulation plan for the state and pushed through a similar deregulatory scheme in Texas.

The Bush-Enron connection intensified during Bush's run for the president in Election 2000. During the 2000 campaign, not only was Lay a major financial supporter of the Bush campaign, but Bush, his family, and friends had Ken Lay's personal jet at their disposal. During the Florida recount wars, Lay and Enron helped defray the costs. And, as would soon become clear, many key players in the Bush administration had close ties with Enron, including Vice President Dick Cheney.

In early January 2002, the tale of the Enron collapse was emerging as a story of the biggest business scandal in U.S. history. Every day new dramatic tales circulated of offshore island dummy corporations (with names like Jedi and Chewco from *Star Wars*), false bank accounts, tax-dodging schemes, stock swindles, insider trading of the declining stock while top executives sold off their shares, accounting and auditing outrages, document shredding to cover up its misdeeds, and daily revelations of the scandal's connections to Bush administration officials.

As the stories unfolded, Ken Lay was becoming synonymous with Big Business flimflam, and George W. Bush saw fit to distance himself from Lay and Enron, claiming that Lay had supported Democratic Governor Ann Richards in the 1994 governor's race and only became acquainted with him afterwards. This was a blatant lie as Lay had supported Bush family campaigns for years and knew Bush father and son extremely well. As noted, Lay was a major supporter of both George W. Bush governor races in Texas, was a major funder of the Bush 2000 presidential campaign, and had long been closely associated with the Bush family and others in the Bush administration.

Bush's blatant lie was quickly uncovered as Ken Lay himself admitted that he was a close friend of the Bush family for years and supported George W. Bush since 1994 in his bid for the Texas governor race against Ann Richards. The episode of Bush brazenly lying about his own personal history is all-too-typical of Bush's mendaciousness and his propensity for revising his past. Bush had repeatedly denied well-documented stories of his business scandals, his association with a number of dubious characters, the sins and disgraces of his business life, and a large number of embarrassing questions about his personal life. Constantly revising the image of his past had been a defining feature of the short but successful public life of George W. Bush, and he was caught red-handed in his lying about his Ken Lay and Enron connections.

Indeed, George W. Bush had been a lifetime recipient of the favors of the sort of crony and corrupt capitalism that Enron and Lay represented. Bush's failed oil companies had been sustained by his father's friends, relatives, and people interested in buying political connections. Young Bush, like Enron executives, had been accused of insider trading when he sold his Harken Energy shares just before a report of declining profits lowered the stock value, and then failed to properly register his sale with the SEC.[2] As a politician, Bush repaid favors to his cronies and economic and political investors and was part of a family that embodied the very ethos of corrupt crony capitalism.

Moreover, Bush's lies about his Enron relations dramatize what I have called "Bushspeak," a distinctively George W. Bush way of speaking with a purely instrumental relation to truth.[3] The political discourse of Bush and his handlers is intended solely to promote his own political ends, rather than to honestly or accurately answer questions or state positions. Bush has lied about himself his entire life and his staff of spinners, especially Karl Rove and Karen Hughes, have helped construct the tissue of lies that constitutes his official biography and current policy positions. Bush's corrupt past and present have been spun by his spin machine so many ways and in such duplicitous fashion that it is probable that Bush himself no longer knows the difference between truth and lie, and thus is able to blurt out blatant whoppers such as his embarrassing attempt to cover over his close connection with Ken Lay.

ENRON, THE S&L SCANDAL, AND THE BUSH FAMILY

The Enron collapse is a major political and economic scandal, one of the defining events of the epoch. In fact, it is amazing that George W. Bush has been caught up in three defining spectacles of the Third Millennium, events that are among the most stunning in U.S. history and that happened within a single twelve-month period: the stealing of a presidential election in Grand Theft 2000, 9/11 and the subsequent Terror War, and the collapse of Enron and uncovering of its shocking history. The Enron scandals are especially important since they reveal the failure and catastrophic effects of Bushonomics; the amazing history of Bush and his partners in corruption and crime; and the fatal flaws of a system that would allow Enron and Bush and his cronies to flourish, loot the economy in startling ways, and assume the very pinnacle of economic and political power.

It is clear that the Enron scandals reveal the utter unworkability and dangerous consequences of the Reagan-Bush-Cheney conservative pro-market economic policy that deregulates the economy; allows a Wild West capitalism to flourish; and eliminates regulation, law, and accountability in the economic realm while placing the state in the service of the most corrupt and greedy corporations. As governor of Texas and president of the United States, George W. Bush and his associates had done everything possible to deregulate oil and energy corporations and to provide windfall tax benefits and other financial favors to his corporate and wealthy supporters. Hence, Enron, for instance, not only did not have to pay taxes, but also got back millions in rebates. Laws and regulations governing banking and accountability of corporations were thrown out the window and the way was open for Enron and Wild West capital to loot the system and undermine the economy, with substantial payoffs to the Bush administration and other politicians to look the other way and aid and abet the corporate theft.

A similar looting of the system had taken place earlier and a parallel cast of characters had been involved in a previous scandal: the Savings and Loan scam of the 1980s Reagan and Bush administrations, when banking, savings and loans, and other financial institutions had been deregulated and multitudes of corporate crooks stepped in and robbed the financial system, costing taxpayers, according to some estimates, from $500 billion to over $1.3 trillion (see Pizzo 1989 and Lewis 1990). In a way, this systematic corporate crime bonanza was bigger than the Enron robbery and the perpetrators largely got away with it. The S&L thievery surely should have alerted government and corporate officials that deregulation and laissez-faire policy are extremely dangerous and open the doors to large-scale corruption and crime.

The S&L scandal should have also alerted politicians, the media, and the public to the sort of scam and corruption that the Bush family has engaged in for generations. Architects of the S&L deregulation policy included then–Vice President George H. W. Bush and Reagan's Chief of Staff and Treasury Secretary James Baker, who also served in other offices in an astounding career that has so far escaped widespread public scrutiny. A book by former *Houston Post* reporter Pete Brewton (1992), however, documents how friends and family members of the Bush and Baker family, as well as the Mafia and CIA, took over S&L institutions, looted them, and left the public with the bill.

The crimes of the S&L looting and Enron debacle are in some ways similar. After Reagan-Baker-Bush deregulation, the scammers of the S&Ls went on an orgy of corruption, taking out funds from the S&Ls, for example, and investing them in a variety of schemes and scams that enabled the S&L managers, such as Neil Bush, to skim off big bucks for themselves and their cronies. Enron used the openings of deregulation to set up dummy businesses for their con operations, to hide money, to avoid taxes, to employ tricks to hide debt and losses, and to inflate the value of their stock prices. As the scandal unfolds, no doubt other inventive business maneuvers will come to light.

Both the S&L institutions and Enron threw money at politicians as they scammed the system, making sure that they had political friends in high places. The corporate players in the respective crimes spent money outrageously to buy friends and supporters, ranging from lavish entertainment that often included prostitutes, booze, and drugs to purchases of a wide range of goods and services that bought goodwill and kept money flowing (many Enron creditors, as were shown nightly on television for some weeks, were left with outstanding bills for products and services rendered that could bankrupt many small businesses). And Enron even bought journalists and intellectuals, paying them outrageously high fees to speak or consult with the corporation, financing, for instance, an Enron Chair in James Baker's institute at Rice University.

Not only does the Enron debacle show that the kind of Wild West capitalism that George W. Bush and his cronies advocate does not work, but it also reveals the appalling connections and histories of the Bush family, especially if seen in connection with the S&L scandal. Enron-Bush connections are multiple, beginning with a history of favors to the Texas-based energy corporation from successive Bush administrations: in George H. W. Bush's presidency, in George W. Bush's two terms as governor of Texas, and in his short but eventful term as president. While in Texas, Bush pushed through the Enron agenda by creating the most deregulatory environment imaginable, in which the energy companies had almost no state regulation or requirements, to the detriment of the state's environment, economy, and eventually the people of Texas, who had to pay for the Bush-Enron excesses—indeed, given the collapse of Enron stock and the large number of investors who lost billions, the entire country had to pay for Bushonomics and the shenanigans of his supporters, friends, and associates.[4]

The epic story of Dick Cheney, oil, and Enron is similarly mind-boggling. Cheney admittedly met with Enron executives six times while developing energy, tax, and economic policy. Moreover, there are allegations that Cheney replaced the head of the energy department regulation (FERC), Curtis Hubert, with Patrick H. Wood, a crony of George W. Bush's from Texas who was previously head of the Texas Public Utilities Commission and who would be more pliable to Enron's demands.[5] Throughout 2002, there have been demands that Cheney hand over notes and documents pertaining to his Enron meetings, but so far he has stonewalled these requests, opening the way to potential Senate hearings or trials that will perhaps provide a media spectacle equivalent to Watergate—or maybe even better.[6]

The entire Bush administration is, in fact, saturated with oil and energy connections and ties to Enron. Cheney, National Security Advisor Condoleezza Rice, Commerce Secretary and former Bush campaign manager Don Evans, economic advisor Lawrence Lindsey, Trade Representative Robert B. Zoellick, and many others in the Bush administration come straight from the oil and energy industries. Moreover, Cheney, Evans, Lindsey, Zoellick, and others have close Enron connections and were engaged in conversations with Lay and other top Enron officials during its collapse. John Ashcroft has had to recuse himself from the Enron investigations because of campaign contributions from Enron and close connections with the corporation, as have other top Justice Department officials. Texas Senator Phil Gramm helped write the rules that deregulated energy production and enabled Enron to create its offshore entities, avoiding public scrutiny and tax liabilities; Gramm's wife Wendy had served on Enron's corporate board; and both Gramms received bundles from Enron (perhaps leading Phil Gramm to decide not to run for reelection, knowing that he'd excessively scammed the tainted Enron money box).

Bush's top policy advisor, Karl Rove, always on the take and on the make, had major stock investments in Enron, which he was forced to sell when reports leaked out that Rove owned large blocks of stock in Enron, Intel, Dell Computers, tobacco firms, and other corporations that had pending government business and demands. Rove reportedly sold the stock but continued to provide lavish favors to those who contributed to Bush campaigns. It was also leaked to the press on January 26 that Rove had recommended Christian fundamentalist leader Ralph Reed to Enron; Reed was employed for years with the corporation in an advisory capacity. Rove wanted Reed's support, which he got, for Bush's run for the presidency in the year 2000, but did not want Reed directly on Bush's staff as the plan was to package Bush as a moderate "compassionate conservative," and not a hard-right Christian fundamentalist à la Reed.

Top Enron employees had close connections with the Bush administration; for example, the Army Secretary Thomas E. White, who Bush appointed to bring corporate management skills to the military, came from Enron. White is a typical representative of the "revolving door" from the public to the private sector and back, and is a poster boy for Bush-Enron connections. While army secretary, White had been pushing the privatization of energy production for military bases, a move that would immensely benefit Enron. He also held onto his Enron stocks although he was supposed to divest, and was caught up in a web of scandal that threatened to force his resignation.

White ran Enron Energy Services, one of the divisions most caught up in fraud and corruption. Under White, the division systematically inflated its profits by exaggerating the value of its contracts and business, showing the division as turning a profit when it was not. While White claimed innocence of his division's malfeasance, documents obtained by *Salon* indicated that White was caught up in the various schemes and helped create off-the-books partnerships and various fuzzy accounting scams.[7]

And so the Bush administration is caught up from head to toe in an economic scandal that could be bigger than Teapot Dome in the 1920s and a political scandal that could have been larger than Watergate. The Bush administration strategy has been to claim that Enron is an economic affair and not a political one, but in terms of policies and players, the economic and the political overlap and tightly connect Bush administration policies and personnel with Enron. Because millions of people will be seriously harmed by the Enron-Bush scandals, and perhaps the economy will be further weakened, one gazes in amazement at the scale of the corruption and crime. The Enron-Bush scandals boggle the imagination in immensity and scale, and no doubt we've only seen the tip of the iceberg. It will be interesting to see if, once again, George W. Bush will escape the taint of scandal and political destruction. Or will the Bushgate flood open in a spectacle that will keep the public entertained and the media, lawyers, and judges busy for years to come?

In any case, the pattern of Bush family politics should be perfectly clear, although as of late 2002 the media and political class still didn't seem to quite get it. Bush politics involve the extraction of large corporate funds to finance political campaigns and then the providing of government largesse and favors in return. Like the Mafia, you reward your friends and punish your enemies. Moreover, you are brazen, daring, aggressive, and without scruples or limits. Indeed, in the midst of the Enron scandals throughout 2002 Bush continued to push for tax breaks for the rich as an economic stimulus package, including a $254 million tax giveaway to Enron! And Bush still extolled the virtues of "free markets" and attacked government regulation the same days that new Enron scandals were heating up, which, in fact, demonstrated the need for regulation, management, and oversight of market activity.

Indeed, the Enron scandal not only revealed the fallacies of laissez-faire market-centric economic politics and the scandalous corporate interconnections of the Bush administration and Enron, but also disclosed deeply rooted failures in the political and economic system—just as *Grand Theft 2000* disclosed the failures of the U.S. voting, political, and legal system[8] and the September 11 terrorist attacks revealed the limitations of U.S. intelligence and domestic security, creating a triadic matrix of systemic problems.

Not only did lax government policies enable Enron to pull off its misdeeds, but the entire system of oversight and regulation failed dramatically. Enron's auditor, Arthur Andersen, one of the country's major accounting firms and a further top Republican and Bush contributor, totally failed in its oversight and auditing responsibility. Arthur Andersen turned out to be part and parcel of the Enron scandals with overlapping interests and officials going from one company to another. Thanks to a change in finance and auditing laws, Arthur Andersen was both hired as a consulting firm with Enron while they were auditing the company, a clear conflict of interests. Embarrassingly for the Bush administration, their allies had blocked legislation that the Clinton administration had been pushing to separate accounting and consulting work. The Republican-led blocking of legislation that would have separated auditing and consulting work helped generate one of the largest and most expensive scandals in the history of the accounting industry, one that eventually brought down the Andersen company.

The Securities and Exchange Commission (SEC) failed to properly oversee the Enron stock frauds, and the business press and top Wall Street security firms had been touting the Enron stock for years: As it ascended to number seven on the Fortune 500, year after year Enron was voted the most innovative company in the U.S. and the business press lavished praise on its innovation, leadership, quality of product, and success, while the stock price shot up thanks to its support by leading Wall Street firms and investors. Although the Bush administration proposed tighter regulation of stocks, overall it had been pushing deregulation and was responsible for the lax atmosphere in which security transactions took place.

The Bush gang, for instance, had chosen Harvey Pitts to run the SEC. Pitts was a lawyer who represented firms fighting the government agency and who himself was a fanatic foe of regulation of the stock markets. Drawing on Bush Senior's imagery, Pitts promised a "kinder and gentler SEC," sending out, in effect, the message that anything goes when the foxes are minding the henhouse. As one corporate scandal after another unfolded in the spring and summer of 2002, under intense political pressures and spotlights Pitts promised more effective SEC regulation, but few seriously believed that he would reform an extremely corrupt and out-of-control investment system.[9]

Revelations of the flimflam and scandal concerning how Enron made its money, hid its losses, and bamboozled investors and the public disclosed serious flaws in the top institutions of the economy. The bogus corporation was an expert in fictive capital, creating phony satellite companies, borrowing money to finance them, presenting the debt from the loan as a profit for the company, gaining tax credits, covering losses, and inflating stock prices. This shell game fooled the investing world, which praised the company and bought the stock, driving its value up, up, and up, despite the fact that it was a house of cards that one day would come crashing down, down, down.

While the Enron story buzzed through the press with new daily revelations and scandals, in an outrageous display of cronyism and partisanship, Bush appointed the highly controversial Otto Reich to a position in the State Department as secretary for Latin American affairs and the appointment of Eugene Scalia, the son of ultra-right U.S. Supreme Court Justice Antonin Scalia, for an important Labor Department solicitor post. Reich had long been associated with Cuban and Nicaraguan anticommunist terrorists and had been strongly opposed by Democratic senators, and Eugene Scalia was strongly opposed by Democrats and labor leaders for his anti-labor positions. When the Senate had refused to ratify their appointments, the brazen Bush pushed their nominations through by executive order as Congress was in recess, creating outrage among those who understood such matters.[10]

PRETZELS, THE ENRON COLLAPSE, AND BUSH'S INSIDER TRADING

On Sunday, January 13, one of the more bizarre episodes of the incredibly surreal Bush presidency occurred when President George W. Bush fainted while allegedly eating a pretzel as he watched a football game alone in his bedroom. If the story were true, one would feel sorry for poor George, reduced to watching football by himself in his bedroom on a Sunday afternoon while his wife Laura reportedly was reading in a different room, or talking on the telephone, depending on the spin. Medical experts quickly appeared on television to provide deeply serious, but unintentionally comical, technical explanations of how a wayward pretzel could momentarily decrease a heart rate and lead to fainting. But Bush watchers on the Internet speculated that the wayward president had gone off the wagon again, as Bush appeared to have a few days after the deadlocked election in November 2001, when he appeared slightly dazed from the previous night's activities with a red swollen nose and large Band-Aids covering what his spinmasters said was a pesky boil that had exploded.[11]

Bush's appearance the day after his fainting episode was none too reassuring, as once again he had a swollen red nose and gaping cuts on his face that were said to be a result of the spill after the pretzel fainting episode. Bush gamely went on the road to talk up his economic program, but critics noted that this was one of his weaker weeks, that he was unable to muster enthusiasm for his unpopular economic programs, and that he appeared lackluster and disconnected.

Meanwhile, every day there was a new revelation in the Enron scandal of documents being shredded, disclosures of phone calls to the Bush administration pleading for help, information on connections between Enron and the Bush administration, and ongoing economic consequences of one of the top ten Fortune 500 corporations collapsing in disgrace. Enron employees, investors, and those left with billions of unpaid debts for services rendered were obviously outraged. As a response, there were multiplying lawsuits by the day to get hold of whatever resources Enron would have left and perhaps extract some of the billions made by top Enron executives who sold their stock just before its value collapsed.

Many of these people pursuing lawsuits had documents and replications of incriminating Enron e-mail, bundles of shredded documents, and leaks from Enron employees into the endless ocean of crime and corruption that had marked the corporation's infamous history. Tales of Enron infamy circulated daily through the media. E-mails and videos showed that Ken Lay had assured employees that Enron was in good financial shape and urged them to buy stock at the same time that he was engaged in selling his own stock, an example of obvious insider trading and manipulation of his own employees.

During the first few months of the Enron scandals, the media had not bothered to look into allegations that George W. Bush had himself assimilated his initial nest egg through insider trading (see chapter 1). Would, indeed, the stories of George W. Bush's financial scandals ever come out in public, or would Bush Jr., like his father, manage to avoid general disclosure of his unbelievable personal and business history? Would Terror War be manipulated to focus attention away from Bush scandals or would the problems with the economy and public outrage over Enron and other Bush administration scandals focus anger on Bush himself and his astonishingly corrupt family and cronies? The survival of U.S. democracy, the global and U.S. economy, and perhaps the future of the human race rested on the answers to these questions, as Bush barbarism could push the world into historical regression and possible destruction if it was not stopped.

ENRON IN THE PUBLIC EYE

The stakes were raised as a media spectacle when on January 25 dramatic reports erupted that a top former Enron executive had apparently committed suicide. The body of former Enron Vice Chairman J. Clifford Baxter was found in his car, apparently dead from a gunshot wound to his head, with the pistol and a suicide note beside him. An Enron whistleblower had claimed that Baxter had engaged in a feud with then–Chief Enron Executive Jeffrey Skilling about the off-balance sheet deals that the company was using to hide billions in debt and that would eventually bring them down. Baxter was scheduled to testify in congressional hearings in Washington the following week and was a defendant in many lawsuits. Obviously, he was despondent over this state of affairs, but the fact that the police did not release immediately the suicide note and the crime drama aura to the whole Enron story inevitably created Internet and media speculation that perhaps foul play was involved. In any case, precisely this sort of human drama catches the attention of publics that have difficulty understanding complex economic and political issues, and the human drama helped to keep the Enron saga on the front burner of media attention.

As the Enron wars heated up, there were dangers for the Bush administration that the entire web of entanglements with Enron and other shady corporations would become unraveled. If the shocking program of deregulation pushed by Bush-Cheney, favors to corporate contributors, and failure to provide security for the U.S. economy and polity, which were making the U.S. vulnerable to terror attacks and the economic collapse of its major corporate allies like Enron, were brought to the light of day, the Bush administration would suffer the consequences. Indeed, attention was focusing on Dick Cheney's role in the Bush administration's meetings with Enron and his chairing of a Bush administration commission on energy policy that had devised a program that energy corporations like Enron had helped to write.

Vice President Dick Cheney had allegedly met with members of the Enron Corporation at least six times as he was overseeing U.S. energy policy, a task that no doubt preoccupied him when he was supposed to be chairing an antiterrorist task force. It seemed that Cheney's priority was to get as many favors as he could for his oil and energy corporation buddies. In his stunningly regressive program, Cheney urged increased production of oil, coal, and nuclear energy, cutbacks in environmental regulation, and privatization and deregulation of energy throughout the U.S. Furthermore, the Bush-Cheney tax policy was to give breaks to its major corporate funders, rewarding obsolete fossil fuel, nuclear energy companies, and energy traders like Enron at the expense of developing alternative sources of energy, thus making the U.S. energy system dependent on rapidly depleting fossil fuels, predatory energy traders, and oil supplies from an increasingly unstable Middle East. Revealing the entanglements of the Bush administration and energy industry and the dangerously irresponsible and corrupt energy policy worked out by Cheney and his corporate allies could be a major scandal for the Bush administration.

The General Accounting Office (GAO) and congressional committees had been requesting from Cheney a list of who he had met with, which individuals and corporations had put what input into the energy plan, and how he had generally proceeded. Cheney had been stonewalling these requests, but the intensity of the Enron scandals, and allegations by California Democrat Congressman Henry Waxman that Enron had written in at least fifteen proposals into the final Bush energy plan, had led to renewed focus on the Cheney energy policy group. There was also interest in a variety of other energy corporations whom Cheney had met with and what provisions he wrote in his policy to meet their needs.

The GAO had been threatening Cheney with lawsuits if he did not divulge the information, and both Bush and Cheney had made it clear that they were not surrendering information, leading the GAO to announce in early February 2002 that they were going to sue the U.S. government for the documents and information required. Cheney claimed, as is always the case with these scoundrels, "executive privilege" and said that he wanted to leave the office of vice president stronger and did not want to weaken it. These high-sounding principles smelled suspiciously of the stink of Cheney's deep and corrupt involvement with the energy industries. Interestingly, not only did the liberal press push Cheney to give up the information, but so too did political conservatives, fearing that failure to disclose would create a public fight, bad publicity, and increased embarrassment for the Bush administration. There were also criticisms of Cheney's deceptive response to the media when queried about his stonewalling, whereby Cheney tended to position a Democratic congressman as the source of the issue as if it were a mere partisan political attack, whereas it had been the GAO, led by a Republican, who was pushing for Cheney's notes and response.

Major battles over U.S. domestic politics also loomed on the horizon. Both Bush and Cheney urged Senate Majority Leader Tom Daschle not to hold hearings or look too closely into the intelligence failures that had caused the U.S. not to be prepared for the September 11 attacks. Cheney had been put in charge in May 2001 of a domestic security antiterrorist group, but had obviously done little of import. The inevitable question concerning possible preknowledge of the September 11 terror attacks by U.S. or foreign intelligence service emerged: what did Cheney know and when did he know it? What, if anything, had he done? If nothing, why not?

If he knew nothing—if Cheney himself were not responsible for gathering and analyzing reports of possible terrorist attacks on the U.S.—then this is a mighty failure of leadership by Cheney and the Bush administration. If Cheney had received word of the score of warnings from multiple domestic and foreign sources of the danger of a September attack by the bin Laden network, Cheney should resign immediately, as this blunder would be one of the biggest in U.S. political history.

In any case, so far Cheney has taken no responsibility for his failures in protecting the U.S. from the September 11 attacks and few critics have pinned this upon him. Perhaps, although he was appointed head of a domestic security antiterrorist group, and although there were at least five reports on terrorist dangers that Cheney should have reviewed, he was apparently not engaged in these issues. Cheney appeared to have focused instead on energy policy and making sure that Enron and other major contributors to the Bush-Cheney campaign, including his other oil-energy friends and allies, got all that they wanted in energy deregulation and policy. Of course, the Enron collapse highlighted the scandalous role of the Bush administration in producing energy policy that had little to do with U.S. needs, the environment, or the global economy and everything to do with the interests of the Bush administration's corporate funders and allies. This itself is a major scandal and should mean that Cheney's life in the Bush administration will be short and unsweet, although so far Cheney has gotten away with astonishing corporate scams and political scandal without significant media focus or political debate.

Another set of upcoming political battles and scandals were revealed in a *Washington Post* story by Eric Pianin, "Bush Budget about to Show Its Darker Side" (February 3, 2002, A01). While Bush was proposing the most fiscally irresponsible budget in U.S. history that would raise military spending to astronomical heights, that would provide billions in tax relief and credits to the richest 1 percent and top corporations, and that would increase overall government spending by 9 percent, there were deep cuts for crucial programs. According to the *Post* story, Bush would "seek sharp cuts in highway funding, Army Corps of Engineers water projects, congressional environmental initiatives, job training and scores of other domestic programs, reflecting the darker side of the fiscal 2003 budget that calls for record spending increases for the military and for domestic security."[12]

Bush would thus allow the infrastructure to decay, weakening the U.S. economy and quality of life, while giving unparalleled wealth to his favorites in the energy and defense industries (where Bush, Cheney, and others in the Bush inner circle always had heavy investments). Not only would Bush's economic stimulus package contain nothing for job training, but he would also cut back on existing programs! Moreover, he would dip into Social Security and Medicare to pay for his government handouts to preferred corporate sectors and friends. And when the Bush administration unveiled its $2.13 trillion budget for 2002, it contained a $344 billion tax cut for the rich and a $591 billion giveaway to Bush's wealthy supporters over the next ten years, while the deficit for 2002 was now forecast as $106 billion, with predictions emerging over the summer that the deficit could run over $160 billion, 1.5 percent of the gross national product.[13]

The Bush-Cheney gang used the growing deficit to raid Social Security and Medicare funds, programs that they hoped to radically privatize and cut back. While budget battles loomed on the horizon and Bush threatened perpetual Terror War against the "axis of evil," the Enron scandal continued to threaten the legitimacy of the Bush presidency. Over the weekend of February 3–4, 2002, the Enron wars heated up. A report that Enron had commissioned, written by Dean William Powers of the University of Texas law school, concluded that Enron's collapse was the result of "a systematic and pervasive attempt" to inflate profits and to hide losses, rather than simply a matter of a few rogue employees breaking the rules. Moreover, in congressional testimony on his report, Dean Powers noted: "What we found was appalling. There was a fundamental default of leadership and management. Leadership and management begin at the top, with the CEO, Ken Lay."

The Enron report was widely discussed on the Sunday talk shows and in the press, and Ken Lay's testimony before a Senate committee the following Monday was keenly anticipated. Lay cancelled on Monday morning, however, and his lawyers said that the unfavorable publicity over the weekend and the "prosecutorial" attitude of Congress led Lay to cancel his appearance. The Senate voted to send Lay a subpoena that would force him to testify and, in a press conference after the meeting, Senator Ernest Hollings (D-S.C.) made the sharpest critique of the complicity between Enron and the Bush administration yet to be aired. Hollings accused Bush and his administration of being in Enron's pocket and creating a "culture of government corruption." *The Guardian* (February 5, 2002) provides a useful summary of Hollings's remarks that reportedly infuriated Republicans:

> "I've never seen a better example of cash-and-carry government than this Bush administration and Enron," he said. "Specifically, everyone knows how the Bushes got the cash," he added, referring to Enron as "the largest contributor to the Republican committee running the convention and the inaugural committee and everything else like that."
>
> He recited a list of cabinet members and other administration officials who he claimed had formerly been on the Enron payroll, as employees, advisers or lawyers.
>
> The list included the attorney general, John Ashcroft, whom the senator described as "Enron's man"; the president's economic adviser, Lawrence Lindsey; the army secretary, Thomas White; and the energy secretary, Spencer Abraham. He accused them all of pursuing policies that were favourable to Enron.
>
> The justice department issued a statement rejecting the Democrats' demands for the appointment of a special counsel to look into the Enron scandal. It insisted there was no conflict of interests involved in the inquiry it was conducting.

Ken Lay was now the poster boy for corporate corruption and a villain for our time. The previous week, his wife had appeared with Lisa Meyers on NBC, the GE-owned network always sympathetic to corporate scoundrels. In tears, Mrs. Lay pleaded for the innocence and goodness of her husband and cried about their own financial woes, claiming, "Other than the house we live in, everything else is up for sale."[14] Evidently Hills and Knowlton, the infamous public relations firm that had manufactured Bush I's Gulf War propaganda,[15] had advised Mrs. Lay to try to gain sympathy, but the result was national revulsion. Reporters had a field day discovering that the Lays still owned a bevy of houses, which had not been put on the real estate market as Mrs. Lay had claimed, with one headline noting, "Enron chief down to last dozen houses."

The parallel between Ken Lay and S&L poster boy Charles Keating was striking. Just as Keating had spread the ill-gained wealth from his looting of California S&Ls to family members, so too had Lay provided his children with lucrative positions in

Enron, contracts for business, or other favors. Both the Keatings and the Lays purported to be solid Christians and philanthropic members of the community. Both were conservative Republicans who spread political donations far and wide to both parties, and both received bountiful political favors that, when uncovered, created great embarrassment to recipients (recall the "Keating Five," five senators who had received contributions from the S&L crook, including John McCain and astronaut hero John Glenn [D-Ohio]).

Senator Hollings's connection of Enron with the Bush administration was revealing and was bringing into the open what the Bush administration was trying so hard to hide: that Bush and Enron were closely connected and bound up together in a culture of corruption. Hollings's reference to "cash-and-carry government" makes the point that I made in *Grand Theft 2000* and have been making throughout this study: The basic practice of Bush politics is to receive money from contributors and return the favor with political deals and handouts. Bush had done this systematically with Enron and other major contributors during his days as Texas governor and in his presidential administration. The deal was, "Bring me the cash, and I'll do you the favor, the public be damned!"

It could also be pointed out that Enron and Bush pursue the same practices of lying and hypocrisy while advocating the same brand of market cutthroat capitalism. As I have argued in *Grand Theft 2000* and in this study, Bushspeak is a discourse of lies and hypocrisy. Obviously, Ken Lay and his Enron empire were built on a web of lies and deception that spun out in a panorama of hypocrisy. For years, Enron lived and got away with the Big Lie that they were an innovative corporation that would bring wealth and prosperity to its partners and investors. Bush, of course, was pushing the Big Lie that his brand of unleashing predatory capitalism and providing favors to his benefactors would benefit everyone. Unfortunately, it might well take the bankruptcy and collapse of the U.S. economy to finally cue the public in to the depth of Bushian corruption and catastrophe. In the words of David Vest: "The Bush agenda is to do to the nation what Ken Lay and his cronies did for Enron— loot it for the benefit of the people at the top, loot the economy, loot the environment, loot the public wallet, leaving ordinary citizens to foot the bill and clean up the damage, like ruined Enron employees."[16]

In the meantime, the fall of Ken Lay was breathtaking to behold. One of the most popular, successful, even revered, corporate leaders had turned overnight into a villain and perhaps the most reviled individual in the United States. One could only hope that the Bush family would soon be subject to similar uncovering, revelation, and universal contempt. When people are scammed, they are resentful, and when it is perceived that someone who was trusted is untrustworthy and corrupt, the public's response is anger and the desire for justice.

It was also stunning how the current mutations of corporate capitalism had produced such disastrous results. Early in the twentieth century, German social theorist Max Weber noted that a previous era of capitalism marked by inner-worldly asceticism, rational capital accounting, and moral rectitude was coming to an end, being replaced by a more predatory, amoral, and cutthroat capitalism. In a prescient passage, Weber described:

> In the United States, where it has been given most freedom, acquisitiveness, stripped of its religious and ethical meaning, tends today to be associated with purely competitive passions, which often give it the character of a sporting context. No one knows as yet who will live within these confines in the future . . . [or] whether there will be a state of mechanised petrification, embellished by a kind of frenzied self-importance. In that case it might indeed become true to say of the "last men" of these cultural developments: "specialists without soul, hedonists without heart: this cipher flatters itself that it has reached a stage of humanity never before attained." (Weber 1958, 182)

Weber's prediction of the new capitalist anticipated EnronMan, a completely amoral seeker of wealth, luxury, and power. Whereas the earlier capitalist produced actual goods and services, the new predatory Enron capitalist bought up products, services, and commodities produced by others, as well as buying up stock futures, derivatives, and other fictive investments. Enron capital reproduced by hype and buzz that drove up its stock, enabling it to buy more imaginary businesses, juggle its books, write off loans and losses as profits, and create an imaginary picture of its enterprise. The house of cards was bound to fall, and in so doing discredited an entire mode of capital accumulation.

By February 5, it appeared that Ken Lay was on the lam. A house congressional committee tried to serve him with a subpoena through his lawyer, who said that he could not accept the document for Lay because he did not know where his client was! The House and the media found this "puzzling," although the next day Lay's lawyer confirmed that Lay now had the subpoena and would testify the next week, setting off speculation as to whether Lay would testify or take the Fifth.

Meanwhile, the country saw some of the faces of the key Enron villains. Several Enron executives took the Fifth, but former President Jeff Skilling testified that when he stepped down on August 14, 2001, "I believed the company was in strong financial condition." When told by the chairperson of the committee that when staffers interviewed Skilling in December he had said that when he left Enron "the company was in the best shape it ever was," he continued insisting that he knew nothing of the company's growing problems, the shady deals that would bring it down, and the efforts to cover over the impending collapse.

No one believed Skilling, and over the weekend of Feb. 9–10, congressional members on the weekend talk shows said that Skilling had probably perjured himself and could be subject to prosecution for his testimony. Ken Lay announced that he would take the Fifth and not testify during his summons to Congress, and a grim-faced Lay seethed as he listened to Congress tongue-lash the once high and mighty close friend of the Bush-Cheney gang. The scandal continued to simmer, leading Bush administration spindoctors to desperately try to portray Enron as a mere economic issue and not a political one.

The political nature of the Enron scandal, however, emerged once again when the General Accounting Office (GAO) filed suit against Dick Cheney on February 22, as they had threatened to do, demanding that Cheney hand over notes of his meetings with Enron and other energy industry executives who had helped the Bush administration develop a national energy policy. This was the first suit in the agency's eighty-year history, dramatizing the lawlessness and arrogance of the Bush administration and its propensity for secrecy. Of course, such aggressive behavior led to speculation that Cheney had something to hide. There had been numerous reports that key provisions of the energy bill had been sought by Enron, including by Henry Waxman, demonstrating the close connections between Bush-Cheney and Enron. In a brazen display of their fundamental illegitimacy, the White House announced that it had procured U.S. Solicitor General Theodore B. Olsen, the ultraright activist who had represented the Bush election team in their fateful appearance in the U.S. Supreme Court where the Felonious Five handed Bush a much-disputed and arguably illicit election victory. Once more, there would be legal battles concerning significant issues that would help determine whether U.S. democracy would be restored or continue to be stolen and undermined by right-wing extremist forces.

The pillaging of the Federal Treasury to provide tax breaks for the wealthy and raiding Social Security and Medicare to help pay for the skyrocketing federal deficit constitute perhaps the most outrageous fiscal thefts in history, but it makes perfectly clear the ultimate goals and substance of Bushonomics. Bush obviously wants to destroy government programs like Social Security, Medicare, job training, and other aspects of the welfare state to promote a warfare state in which sectors of the military-industrial complex connected to the Bush gang would prosper and those outside of its influence would suffer. The perpetual Terror War would legitimate this radical restructuring of the U.S. economy and polity, just as it would justify cutbacks in civil liberties and erection of a police state. The Bush plan to rob the federal treasury for its corporate allies and to produce a military-police state for the new millennium is audacious and frightening to behold. Would the pusillanimous Democrats and corporate media stand up to Bush and prevent his destruction of the liberal welfare state, open society, and the U.S. and global economy?

After the Putsch of Grand Theft 2000, it appears that the Bush Reich is the next step. Would the Democrats and media reveal the magnitude of the Bush threats to the Republic and exploitation of Terror War for his own hard-right and corporate agenda? Would the people become informed about what Bush was really up to and turn against him? Would the rest of the world see the dangers of an American Reich to the global economy and world peace? Or would collapse of the world economy and an era of warfare be the fate and perhaps the end of the human species as we entered into a dangerous new era of history?

Thus, although Karl Rove urged Republicans to push Bush's success in the Terror War in the 2002 midterm election, in fact more pressing issues would be Bush's war plans for the future and his destruction of the U.S. economy and political system.

Did the American people want to fight endless wars all over the world against alleged terrorists who may or may not be a threat to the United States? Did the American people want to isolate themselves from the world and serve as the superpoliceman, losing friends and gaining enemies with each intervention? Would Bush be allowed to paper over the scandals of his administration and connections with corrupt corporate allies like the Enron gang with unending war? Answers to these questions would be provided by the unfolding dramas of the present age, ongoing as I write. On the Terror War front, it was clear to many observers, though to few in the U.S. media and political establishment, that the Bush administration's quasi-unilateralism and the continuation of the military campaign in Afghanistan were political disasters, isolating the United States from its allies, eliciting increasing international criticism of U.S. policies, and deeply offending Muslims. Hence, although in the United States the Bush administration's military intervention in the Terror War was considered an overwhelming success, this was not the opinion emerging in more informed sectors throughout the world.

10

❖

The Afghan Nightmare and the "Axis of Evil"

Within Afghanistan, there was a widely circulated view that the bombing raids on Tora Bora and the Al Qaeda complex at Zhawar during December 2001 were largely failures. At Tora Bora, the hesitancy to use U.S. ground troops and the preference to rely on local troops had allowed a large number of Al Qaeda and Taliban fighters to escape, including, perhaps, bin Laden. At Zhawar, although much Al Qaeda and Taliban military equipment was destroyed, the U.S. military also bombed the sites of anti-Taliban fighters without adequate discussion with local authorities. Damage to Afghan civilians and their homes from U.S. bombing was distancing local groups from the U.S. military; local Afghan militia were refusing, for instance, to help the U.S. military search Tora Bora's extensive cave network. In both the Tora Bora and Zhawar regions, there were growing and intensifying anti-American feelings due to the large number of civilian casualties, and there was displeasure throughout Afghanistan with the continuation of the U.S. military intervention.[1]

There were definite limits to what U.S. bombing could achieve in the war on terror and the distinct possibility that excessive bombing of civilians and overly aggressive military interventions could alienate both Afghans and U.S. allies in the struggle against terrorism. Worse, there was the real possibility that the growing anti-Americanism in Afghanistan and throughout the Islamic world as a response to continued U.S. bombing of civilians in Afghanistan, the mistreatment of Islamic prisoners, and threatened interventions throughout the Islamic world could breed a new generation of terrorists reacting against what was perceived as barbaric American attacks against Arabs and inhuman treatment of its prisoners.

U.S. MILITARISM AMOK

A conference in Tokyo on January 20–21, 2002, had raised pledges of about $4 billion of support from various countries for rebuilding the war-torn country of

Afghanistan, although there was disappointment that the U.S. had not contributed more. When U.S. Secretary of State Colin Powell had visited Afghanistan before the Tokyo conference, he was confronted by cabinet minister Sima Samar, the Women's Affairs Minister, who called upon the U.S. to pay for 75 percent of the reconstruction of Afghanistan, noting that "the donations should be equal to the cost of the bombs dropped on Afghanistan" (*The Observer,* January 20, 2001). In fact, although the Bush administration had claimed that their policy would be both military and humanitarian, the latter was obviously subordinated to the former, as the U.S. had blocked for months humanitarian efforts to get aid to civilians. Moreover, there were worries in Afghanistan that the U.S. would once again pull away when their military intervention was concluded, as they did in the earlier Bush administration after the Soviet Union had left the country.

Meanwhile on the military front, the Pentagon announced that there was a skirmish between U.S. forces and supporters of the former Taliban regime sixty miles north of Kandahar that resulted in as many as fifteen Taliban fighters being killed and twenty-seven captured. *The Times* noted that there was a renegade army of up to 5,000 Taliban soldiers with 450 tanks, armored carriers, and pickup trucks in tense skirmishes with U.S. troops (January 25, 2001). *The Guardian* stated the next day that "remnants of Al Qaeda fight on," claiming that hundreds of bin Laden's fighters have blended into the Kandahar region and are preparing for trouble. But, once again, soon after this incident villagers accused the United States of killing anti-Taliban leaders in a recent bombing attack. An article by Rory McCarthy in the *Guardian* (January 28, 2002) noted:

> Villagers yesterday insisted the US troops had been badly misled. They said the victims of the attack at Hazar Qadam were headed by an ethnic-group leader called Haji Sana Gul, who had just disarmed a number of Taliban fighters still holding out in the area.
>
> His brother Bari Gul said the men spent Wednesday night in the local madrassah, or religious seminary. Before dawn the next day US troops swept in, killing several people in the madrassah, including Haji Sana Gul himself.
>
> Two of the dead had their hands tied behind their backs, Bari Gul said. Three more people were killed in a building a mile away.
>
> Yusuf Pashtun, an aide to the Kandahar governor Gul Agha, said he too believed American commandos had struck the wrong targets. "It looks like it was raided by mistake," he said. "The people of the district centre are very much against the Taliban."

It appeared that almost every U.S. bombing raid over the past several weeks had gone awry, killing civilians and anti-Taliban forces rather than Al Qaeda or Taliban forces.[2] The U.S. seemed to be receiving exceptionally bad intelligence and their misguided attacks were becoming a major embarrassment to the interim President Hamid Karzai who was getting pressured by tribal leaders to get the U.S. to stop the military attacks that were largely hitting civilians or even anti-Taliban forces. For about a week after claims that the U.S. had mistakenly killed pro-government forces, the Pentagon finally admitted that they had received bad information, conceding for one of the few times that they had made errors.

There were also disturbing stories that bomblets from cluster bombs were continuing to kill civilians. In a story, "Long after the air raids, bomblets bring more death," Suzanne Goldenberg wrote that "at least 41 people have been killed and 46 injured in Herat and nearby villages by cluster bombs which did not immediately explode when they were unleashed by the U.S. bombers, but nestled in the soil and bided their time" (*The Guardian,* January 28, 2002). Goldenberg's account provides heartwrenching accounts of innocents killed or maimed by the unexploded cluster bombs, raising the question of why the U.S. deployed these deadly antipersonnel munitions in the first place in Afghanistan.[3]

A report published by the Project on Defense Alternatives explained why there were such high casualty rates from U.S. bombing in the Afghan war. Comparing the U.S.-Afghanistan campaign with the Kosovo air war, the group concluded that the rate of civilian casualties was at least four times higher in the Afghanistan war due to greater emphasis on Global Positioning Systems, which are less accurate than laser-guided bombs; that there was heavier use of enormous bomber airplanes in Afghanistan; and there was an increased use of cluster bombs and other antipersonnel devices. Demographic features, like higher population density, and poor intelligence also contributed to the higher casualty figures in Afghanistan.

Thus one of the Big Lies of the Afghan war was Donald Rumsfeld's statement, "No nation in human history has done more to avoid civilian casualties than the United States has in this conflict."[4] Every study so far has discovered hundreds to thousands of civilian casualties and story after story has emerged of U.S. targeting mistakes, reliance on information from Afghanistan forces seeking revenge on enemies, use of cluster bombs and antipersonnel munitions, and other factors that helped produce an extremely high number of civilian casualties.

Interim President Hamid Karzai visited Washington on January 28, the first Afghanistan leader in decades to do so. Since he was trying to get increased aid and support for his country, he did not publicly condemn Washington for its recent attacks on Afghan civilians or criticize U.S. policy. Karzai had pleaded on the eve of his visit for more international security forces in other parts of Afghanistan, but he was not able to get a commitment from the Bush administration to provide security forces or increased humanitarian aide. Instead, George W. Bush offered Afghanistan support to build a military and train police forces. Critics, however, felt that the last thing Afghanistan needed was more military equipment, and worried that training military and police forces might result in instructing forces which would eventually be anti-American, as with the CIA financing and training the Islamic fundamentalists who later became Al Qaeda.

During Karzai's visit, the issue of serious civilian casualties from past and present U.S. military operations in Afghanistan did not come out in public. But Karzai appeared to many observers, and to opponents within his country, as an all-too-compliant American puppet who might not have a long career in the morass of

Afghan politics. During the Karzai visit, however, Bush seemed to equivocate on the status of the U.S. prisoners in Guantanamo Bay. On January 29, his administration stated that they were considering Colin Powell's request to agree to treat the detainees under the Geneva Convention and international law, although they continued to refuse to provide POW status to those incarcerated. Bush himself verbally prevaricated in a White House Rose Garden press conference with Karzai, twice calling the fighters "prisoners" and then excusing himself and substituting the word "detainees." For instance, Bush stated: "We're in total agreement on how these prisoners—or detainees, excuse me—ought to be treated." Bush insisted that he would listen to "all the legalisms, and announce my decision when I make it."[5]

The situation in Afghanistan continued to be dangerous for U.S. forces and new evidence was surfacing of Al Qaeda terrorist plots. CNN reported on January 25 that documents were found in a Kabul house used by Al Qaeda operatives that suggested the organization was building a serious weapons program, with an emphasis on developing a nuclear device. A U.S. prisoner turned over by the Bosnian government was labeled a top Al Qaeda aide. And accounts continued to proliferate concerning new terrorist cells turning up in Singapore, Indonesia, the Philippines, and elsewhere. Clearly, the Al Qaeda network was being pursued on a global level and blocked in at least some of their terrorist projects, but it was equally clear they had not closed down shop and continued to pose threats to the U.S. and its allies.

In a hospital outside of Kandahar, there was a dramatic storming of a section of the building that had been occupied by Al Qaeda fighters who had armed themselves with grenades and threatened to blow themselves up if apprehended. A six-week standoff had resulted, where U.S. Special Forces had ordered that they be starved out, but sympathetic supporters had smuggled in food. On January 29, U.S. Special Forces and Afghan soldiers threw grenades into the occupied ward of the hospital and in a gun battle all six of the foreign fighters were killed. The next day, a Red Cross official claimed that U.S. officials had assured him that there would be no raid on the hospital, which the Red Cross was administrating, and would inform the Red Cross in case of a change of policy but had failed to do so.

While media attention had been focused on U.S.-incarcerated Al Qaeda and Taliban fighters in Guantanamo Bay, Cuba, and their legal status, controversies were also growing concerning the imprisonment of Al Qaeda and Taliban forces in Afghanistan. An inspection team from Physicians for Human Rights claimed that conditions at Shebhargan prison, near Mazar-i-Sharif, were "in grave violation of international standards for those held in detention or as prisoners of war." According to the group, collections of 110 prisoners were being held in cells designated for no more than fifteen "in conditions described as overcrowded and unhygienic, and where inadequate food and medical supplies have led to deaths" (*Independent,* January 29, 2002). In view of the fact that so many Al Qaeda and Taliban fighters had gotten away and many Taliban had negotiated releases, it was awkward that some continued to be incarcerated under questionable conditions.

On January 29, a U.S. helicopter crashed, injuring sixteen, the latest in a series of aviation mishaps that had claimed eleven American lives in the Afghan intervention. The plane went down in the Khost region in eastern Afghanistan, and the crash was attributed to pilot error. Meanwhile, it was announced that the U.S. antiterror campaign in the Philippines would begin with 600 troops due to arrive, including 160 Special Ops forces. Although there had been controversy over the U.S. mission and mixed signals as to whether it would go forth, it appeared that the U.S. was about to embark on another military adventure. On January 30, however, it appeared that there was a glitch concerning whether the U.S. troops would or would not serve under the authority of the Philippines military. There were also large demonstrations in the Philippines against the U.S. troop deployment. But in early February, despite continuing demonstrations against the U.S. intervention in the Philippines, it was agreed that the U.S. troops were going to carry on their mission under the command of the Philippines military. This concession ironically evoked conservative opposition in the U.S. on the grounds that American troops should not be subject to "foreign" military command. As terrorist attacks killed Filipinos at the beginning of the U.S. military intervention, there was talk that the U.S. was returning to the kind of fateful intervention of the Vietnam period and was this time overextending itself throughout the world.

THE "AXIS OF EVIL" AND BUSH'S NEW IMPERIALISM

To assure funding for continued U.S. military interventions into the far future, George W. Bush requested in his January 29 State of the Union address a massive defense hike of $48 billion, the biggest increase in military spending in over twenty years. It appeared that the promises of Donald Rumsfeld to cut unnecessary military spending and programs were put aside in favor of across-the-board hikes in military spending. Programs included the controversial Crusader artillery system, owned by the Carlyle Fund that includes former President Bush and James Baker. Indeed, the Bush budget was full of items that would benefit family, friends, and supporters, and one wondered how long the Bush gang would get away with using national security to enrich their own.

In his televised State of the Union address on January 29, Bush promised an epoch of Terror War, expanding the Bush doctrine to not only go after terrorists and those who harbor terrorist groups, but also to include those countries making weapons of mass destruction. Claiming that Iraq, Iran, and North Korea constituted "an axis of evil, arming to threaten the peace of the world," Bush put the "world's most dangerous regimes" on notice that he was planning to escalate the war on terror. Rattling the saber and making it clear that he was perfectly ready to wag the dog if Enron, domestic scandals, or economic failures threatened his popularity, Bush put "rogue states" and terrorists everywhere on notice that he was prepared to go to war indefinitely against an array of targets in an epoch of escalating Terror War.

As was becoming his norm, Bush's team was able to orchestrate an impressive media event with celebrities like Hamid Karzai in the audience next to Laura Bush, along with members of U.S. military families, New York firemen, and other icons of September 11. Moreover, Bush was learning to read his teleprompter speeches with proper emphasis and pronunciation, but was not able to rid himself of his tell-tale smirk, weird darting eye gestures, and mounting arrogance and self-satisfaction. He also took the occasion to announce new dangers to the U.S. via plans found in Afghanistan to blow up U.S. nuclear installations, public monuments, and other targets.

In fact, these documents had been found weeks before and had already been discussed in the media, so Bush was simply using the threats to legitimate his own militarist agenda and to deflect attention from his own failings at economic policy and the involvement of himself and others in his administration in the Enron scandals. Certainly, terrorism remains a threat to the U.S., but to exaggerate the dangers, to escalate the war, and to engage in excessive rhetoric is arguably not the way to deal with the problem. In a round of TV interviews that preceded Bush's address, one of his advisors, Karen Hughes, claimed that Americans face dangers from up to 100,000 terrorists trained in Afghanistan and deployed worldwide. Eyes bulging and lower lip tremulous, the utterly mendacious Hughes, who has made a career of lying for Bush, made it clear that Terror War would be a major focus of Bush administration policy. Terrorist experts were dumbfounded at the spinmistress's far-fetched fantasizing with Stanley Bedlington, a former CIA terrorism analyst insisting that "Al Qaeda has never had that kind of strength." Bedlington continued: "I just came back from a luncheon with about 15 specialists. If I dropped that like a rock into a stagnant pool, there would be roars of laughter" (Associated Press, January 29, 2002).[6]

Likewise, Bush's rhetoric of "evil" was becoming tiresome and worrisome to many. He used the term "evil" at least five times in his State of the Union address and included countries like Iran, itself undergoing complex domestic changes, in this litany. Furthermore, what Bush did not talk about in the State of the Union speech was also significant. He did not mention Osama bin Laden or the Al Qaeda and Taliban leadership that he had failed to apprehend. Bush did not refer to the sky-rocketing deficits that his fiscal mismanagement had produced, glossing over the reversal in one year from the largest surplus in U.S. history to a stunning $100 billion–plus deficit (with estimates rising by the week).[7] Bush claimed that the "state of the union had never been so good," but in fact during Bush's presidency the nation suffered one of the greatest one-year reversals and declines in U.S. history. The U.S. economy was suffering massive unemployment, the Enron scandal was harming investor confidence and pointing to glaring problems that Bushonomics had helped produce, while the national deficit was escalating out of control.

Moreover, in his State of the Union address, George W. Bush out-voodooed Ronald Reagan in his calls for wildly increased military spending, a jump in home security spending, large tax cuts for the wealthy, *and* a 9 percent increase in basic government programs. Bush was willing to finance this budget with a more than $100 billion deficit for 2002 and an $80 billion budget deficit for 2003—estimates that have since risen.[8] One tries to imagine the uproar this would create if the Democrats had urged such irresponsible deficit funding of the government. It was startlingly clear that the Bush administration was returning to the giant deficit spending that had seen the Reagan years double the national debt, while Bush I, in his failed four years of economic mismanagement, doubled the national debt once again. Every responsible economist believed that it was necessary to keep the deficit and national debt under control to ensure U.S. economic stability, but once again the Bush administration embarked on a rash and dangerous economic policy that could end in catastrophe for the U.S. and global economy.

Looked at more closely, Bush's State of the Union address could be read as a cunning use of Terror War to push through his indefensible domestic programs like the Star Wars missile program, his tax breaks and giveaways for the rich, and his social service programs that would advance a conservative agenda that people and charities would solve social problems and not government. The "evil axis" countries could be used to legitimate producing the Star Wars missile defense system that critics had claimed had not been proven workable. Although on one hand, the very notion of an "axis of evil" suggests the Bush administration's geopolitical confusion and misunderstanding, on the other hand, it opens the way to any military intervention anywhere, for whatever justification the Bush administration sought to concoct. And by calling attention to countries that produce weapons of mass destruction, it could legitimate preemptive strikes against countries that it chose to stigmatize and attack.

Incredibly, Bush was using the Enron collapse to push his tax giveaway program and discredited pension plan. Although Bush did not mention the unmentionable name of "Enron" in his speech, the day after the State of the Union Bush called for pension reform in the light of the Enron collapse, using the national tragedy to push his social security stock scam, telling workers that with improved investment advice and some protection, they would be better off with retirement plans in which they could choose to invest their own savings—as if the Enron and other corporate scandals had not revealed the uncertainty of investment and dangers in the stock market!

The emphasis on care, compassion, sacrifice, national service, and community voluntarism in the State of the Union address gave Bush credence as a compassionate conservative, as opposed to a hard-right ideologue and shameless manipulator of crisis and tragedy for his own political ends. But the emphasis on patriotism, national unity, and moral community function not only to identify his party and policies with patriotism, but also to identify anyone who criticizes his foreign or domestic policies as "unpatriotic." As noted, Lynne Cheney, wife of U.S. Vice President Dick Cheney and a longtime cultural warrior against the Left, circulated texts documenting unpatriotic statements by university professors. Since September 11,

Cheney had been leading an assault against dissidents to Bush administration policy on the grounds that they are not patriotic and supporting the president in a time of war and danger—a position also taken by her husband, Dick. Stressing national unity and patriotism was thus providing a cover for suppressing dissent and for threatening to undermine U.S. democracy, revealing the dangerous antidemocratic proclivities of the Bush-Cheney gang.

Furthermore, appropriating the language of "moral community" for a conservative "homeland defense" against "an axis of evil" and terrorism redefines "community" in conservative terms as those who identify with U.S. government policy. It also subordinates discourses of social justice, civil rights, and democracy to pulling together in the name of national unity, a move that can easily be used to suppress dissent and progressive agendas. It was clear that Bush was using the terrorist attacks and national security to push through his right-wing agenda. The term "homeland" has connotations of National Socialism and conservative nationalism, the German term *"Heimat"* was frequently used by the Nazis to legitimate repressive domestic policy and aggressive foreign policy and was their preferred ideological term for the nation. Homeland defensive forces in Nazi Germany were known as *Heimswehr* or *Heimatschutz.* "Homeland Security" plays on and intensifies fear that one's own home and person will be attacked, and legitimates a government taking over power and control to circumvent rights and freedoms in the name of defending the "homeland."

Despite the reckless, dangerous, and irresponsible tone and thrust of Bush's speech, the U.S. media shamefully and predictably gushed over Bush's performance, failing to criticize it. Throughout the day of the State of the Union, the cable television networks outdid each other in building anticipation for Bush's speech and hyping the president's popularity and brilliant accomplishments. After the speech, CBS's Dan Rather celebrated it as "a solid, even eloquent address," while NBC's Andrea Mitchell found it "amazing." On CNN, William Bennett, the country's self-proclaimed morality czar, praised Bush's "speech of moral confidence," while Rudy Giuliani deemed it "philosophical" and "spiritual." Television commentators from across the board oohed and aahed about how President Bush was "transformed." In fact, Bush usually delivered a pre-prepared speech that he had time to rehearse competently, and there was nothing spiritual or transformed about his bellicose rhetoric, pushing his hard-right agenda with ideological platitudes and pushing buttons in his audiences to gain applause.

The day after, newspaper commentators almost universally applauded the speech. The Hall of Shame for pandering punditry includes *Washington Post* columnist Mary McGory's "Triumphal Oratory" that eulogized Bush's "stunning" speech while babbling about his "phenomenal" popularity. Walter Shapiro, in a *USA Today* piece, gushed over Bush's "awe-inspiring popular support," deeming "Bush more than entitled to enjoy this moment." Bob Herbert in a *New York Times* op-ed piece, "As Bush's Stature Rises," effused over "the bond that is developing between President Bush and the American people," while William Safire in a commentary, "'To

Fight Freedom's Fight,'" praised Bush's speech and urged him on to attack Iraq, Iran, and North Korea!

While the U.S. media and Congress wildly applauded Bush's jingoistic speech, the rest of the world was stunned by the irresponsibility of Bush's barbaric "axis of evil" doctrine. The British *Guardian* cited Bush's "Hate of the Union" and escalation of militarist rhetoric, while an editorial in the paper chided "George Bush's delusion" that the September 11 tragedy gave Bush a free hand to lead the world into infinite war (January 31, 2002). The French paper *Liberation* found Bush's tone "more martial than ever," and *Le Monde* noted that U.S. allies Russia and China were chief suppliers of the "military programs" of the countries Bush singled out. French Foreign Minister Hubert Vedrine criticized Washington's approach to terrorism as "a new simplistic approach that reduces all the problems in the world to the struggle against terrorism," Mr. Vedrine said during a lengthy interview on France-Inter radio. "This is not well thought out." Mr. Vedrine suggested that Europeans would need to speak out more and more because they faced a United States that acted "unilaterally, without consulting others, taking decisions based on its own view of the world and its own interests."

The Russians complained that their allies were being included in the "axis of evil" and that the improving relations with Washington would be subverted if Bush expanded the field of war. Close allies Germany and Japan were put off that Bush used the loaded word "axis," which evoked World War II and the crimes of the Third Reich and Japanese, events that their countries had tried to overcome. A number of countries were irritated by Bush's threat to act unilaterally against terrorism if "some governments were timid in the face of terror." Bush's jibe was aimed against countries like the Philippines, who insisted that they had been resolute and effective allies in the work against terrorism. And, of course, Iran, Iraq, and North Korea were shocked that Bush had collapsed them into "an axis of evil," which inadvertently strengthened the hands of hard-liners within these regimes to resist accommodation with the West and especially the United States, which was threatening them with extinction.

The State of the Union address showed the dangerous demagoguery that was becoming the very essence of George W. Bush. Totally bereft of ideas and insight himself, Bush is an empty vessel programmed by right-wing ideologues and fanatics. The very lunacy of his "axis of evil" shows hysteria, desperation, and a willingness to do anything possible to assert U.S. power and to justify U.S. aggression. The "Bush doctrine" is a demented concretion of his father's "new world order" in which the U.S. is the superpoliceman of the world, positioning itself as the beacon of civilization who is able to define "the axis of evil" and go after whoever it labels in this category. But such discourse serves as a cloak for a project of U.S. domination of the world and global hegemony, promoting the "full spectrum dominance" that certain Pentagon ideologues have long dreamed of.

In the view of European critics, however, Bush's speech showed that "the Bush administration "is not now primarily engaged in a war against terrorism at all" but

U.S. world dominance, thus "abandoning whatever remaining moral high ground the U.S. held onto the wake of September 11."[9] David Talbot commented in *Salon* (February 14, 2002) that Bush's rhetoric is a "flight of idiocy" that reveals how Bush sees the world in the simplistic "black-and-white terms of the born again fundamentalist that he is."

Bush's term "axis of evil" is indeed highly misleading and semantically inaccurate. An "axis" implies a coalition and connection between countries that are embarking on a common project of domination. Iraq and Iran have long been bitter enemies, fighting a vicious war between 1980 and 1988 (in which the U.S. cynically supported both sides covertly, leading to the Iran-Contra affair and helping to produce the Iraqi military machine that invaded Kuwait and prompted the Gulf War; see Kellner 1992). North Korea, of course, is a whole other question, and its neighbors South Korea and Japan as well as other bordering countries were extremely distressed by Bush's rhetoric. Bush's ill-conceived speech reportedly harmed the faction in South Korea trying to moderate North Korea's behavior, while helping the conservative factor wishing to promote a hard line against North Korea.

Choosing Iran as part of the tripartite axis, a throwback to the fascist triadic axis of the 1940s, is an act of stupendous geopolitical stupidity that stunned Iran and others around the world. During the Afghan Terror War, Iran showed great sympathy for the U.S. intervention, strongly condemned the September 11 bombings and the Al Qaeda network (which had long been Iran's strategic enemy), pledged itself to help extricate U.S. servicemen in danger in Afghanistan, and became part of a network of humanitarian aid. Moreover, within Iran there had been pro-American and antigovernment demonstrations in recent months, showing a desire, especially on the part of the young, to reach out to the West. There were, to be sure, recent reports of Iran playing the old strategic game in Afghanistan by arming a warlord on its border to promote Iranian interests, perhaps undermining the central government in the region. Certainly, there were hard-line and anti-American forces in the Iranian government, but there were serious reform movements in Iran that many Western powers were trying to aid and strengthen. Despite all this, Bush's aggressive rhetoric was reinforcing the credibility of conservative and anti-Western factions by demonstrating once again U.S. hostility against Iran.

Moreover, how, in the light of post–September 11 politics, could Iran be deemed part of an "axis of evil" over, say, Saudi Arabia? It was well known that the Al Qaeda network had its strongest financial and personnel support network in Saudi Arabia, where bin Laden's family had long lived. Fifteen of the nineteen terrorists were Saudis, and there were reportedly over 100 Saudis in the Guantanamo Bay camp that had been the focus of controversy, with a Saudi diplomat publicly calling for their release. The controversial "dinner with bin Laden" tape that had been played with such fanfare by the Bush administration (see chapter 7) showed strong support within Saudi Arabia for bin Laden, and a recent poll indicated that 95 percent of the Saudis were sympathetic to bin Laden and his group.

Furthermore, the day after Bush's "axis of evil" speech, the *Guardian* (January 31,

2002) printed articles indicating that there had been at least eight terrorist attacks on Westerners in Saudi Arabia over the last year and that Westerners had been tortured to confess to responsibility, including one British citizen who was himself a victim of a bombing! Yet applying the label of "evil" even to Saudi Arabia is highly problematic. In a series on the troubled relationship between the Saudi Kingdom and the U.S. in the aftermath of September 11, the *Washington Post* revealed the hitherto not discussed Saudi dropping of oil prices immediately after the terrorist attacks, instead of raising them as planned, in order to help the U.S. economy recover (February 14, 2002).

But the main problem with the "axis of evil" discourse is that it is likely to alienate both Arabs and allies. Arabs are extremely incensed over Bush's fast and loose use of the word "evil" to apply to Arab countries, and the "axis of evil" serves to position many Arabs against the West. Moreover, U.S. allies were expressing extreme distress over the term and Bush's speech, which implied a rabid unilateralism that the U.S. would go it alone in its crusade against evil, worrying the rest of the world that U.S. intervention would become increasingly dangerous and destructive.

THE DANGERS OF UNILATERALISM

Thus, whereas a sane global policy against the international threat of terrorism would involve bringing in as many Arab allies and other countries as possible in the war against Islamic extremism, Bush's "doctrine" was likely to alienate both Arabs and allies in the struggle. Furthermore, it positioned the U.S. as the main target of global terrorism and the object of future likely retaliation. Thus, Bush's axis of evil concept is probably the most cockamamie political idea advanced by an U.S. president during my lifetime.

This is not to deny that weapons of mass destruction are a serious issue and that eliminating them would be a rational and highly desirable goal. But in fact it is precisely the Bush administration that has refused to participate in every major treaty to control or eliminate weapons of mass destruction (see Kellner 2001). The U.S. is a rogue nation in terms of developing weapons of mass destruction and blocking treaties that could lead to their elimination. A rational plan to eliminate weapons of mass destruction would be to criminalize their use, to build a coalition of nations that renounced these weapons, and to work to systematically eliminate them.

Although Bush's arrogant posturing was playing well domestically, it was faring ever more poorly in the global arena where it is necessary to gain allies to effectively fight terrorism. Responding to global fears of Bush's bellicose militarism, and to allay worries that Bush's rhetoric was going to lead the world into war, Bush administration spokespeople tried to assure the world that Bush would be restrained in choosing military targets and that his rhetoric was simply to "put on notice" countries that supported terrorism, which would be subject to U.S. intervention. Visiting

British Foreign Minister Jack Straw told the British press that Bush's "evil axis" speech was "vote-getting rhetoric" and for domestic consumption rather than a serious threat of immediate military action.

At first, Bush administration spokespeople seemed to back away from the implications of Bush's speech, saying that he was just sending the "axis of evil" crowd a "message" to "put them on notice" that they were being closely watched. By the end of the week, however, Bush himself played up the rhetoric in domestic speeches and interviews and over the weekend top administration figures, including Colin Powell, defended the axis of evil doctrine as "a wake-up call" to the international community. Condoleezza Rice sternly rebuked Jack Straw, who had said that the phrase was only for domestic political consumption, stating that "when the British government speaks about foreign policy, it's not about British politics."

The problem with Bush's "axis of evil" speech, however, is that it was further angering and alienating those in the Arab world who the U.S. must persuade to renounce terrorism and militant Islam. Bush's rhetoric and use of military force was likely to help recruitment of Islamic militants and to make acts of terrorism against the U.S. more likely. And although a major challenge for U.S. diplomacy was to build a global coalition against terrorism, Bush's aggressive unilateralism was likely to weaken global coalitions and undermine multilateral efforts. Indeed, top European officials at a major NATO security conference over the weekend of February 2–3 came away in despair at Bush's pugnacious unilateralism, fearing that it would destroy NATO and create serious political divisions in the years to come.

Furthermore, the highly respected Chris Patten, British conservative party leader, former governor of Hong Kong, and current European Commissioner for international relations, deemed Bush's doctrine "absolutist and simplistic." The French Prime Minister Lionel Jospin warned the U.S. not to give in to "the strong temptation of unilateralism." European commentators worried that Bush's belligerent rhetoric would alienate allies, isolate the U.S., and snatch defeat from the jaws of victory. Others condemned Bush's continual whipping up of fear of terrorism, leading to the paradoxical syndrome of "arrogance and fear" that Anatole Kaletsky dissected in the London *Times* (February 7, 2002).

Some critics suggested that Bush's "axis of evil" address was intended to draw away focus from his failure to apprehend major Taliban and Al Qaeda leadership, or domestically to make progress in the war against terror. In fact, it has rarely been noted in the U.S. media that global efforts to arrest terrorists have been much more striking and effective elsewhere in the world than in the U.S. It is astonishing that not only has the Bush administration so far failed to apprehend the source of the anthrax attacks and panic that followed the September 11 attacks, but despite thousands of arrests, as of the end of 2002 the U.S. has only charged a few suspects with terrorist involvement and has not publicly or convincingly exposed plans targeted at the U.S. (Zacarias Moussaouri was arrested before the September 11 attacks and later charged when his complicity with Al Qaeda and the actual September 11 attacks was suspected.)

By contrast, the British and European newspapers that I read regularly document arrests of terrorist suspects and the breakup of terrorist groups all over Europe. Likewise, many other countries have also been highly effective in arresting local terrorists, foiling plots, and seriously damaging the terror networks. It seems that this patient intelligence, police, and judicial work is more effective than the blustering posturing of a George W. Bush. Thus, although the overthrow of the Taliban and destruction of the Al Qaeda camps in Afghanistan definitely struck at the bin Laden network, the failure to apprehend top leaders makes the U.S. military intervention a mixed result at best.

Furthermore, continued U.S. military blundering with the murder of Afghan civilians and the fierce global controversy over the treatment of Terror War prisoners is arguably undercutting U.S. authority to lead the war against terrorism and revealing stark limitations of Bush administration policies and personnel. During the first week of February 2002, for instance, there was a stream of revelations of U.S. military mistakes in which the Pentagon made an all-too-rare acknowledgement that they may have killed civilians in recent raids by mistake. The Pentagon admitted, for instance, that the much-criticized raid on a village in Uruzgan province, south of Kandahar, on January 24 had killed civilians. Twenty-seven Afghans held in the raid were released and there were reports that U.S. Special Operations Forces were handing out US$1,000 bills to families of survivors, with ABC news showing tribesmen displaying their bills. Soon after, several of those released claimed that they were beaten and kept in cages by the U.S. troops, suffering serious injury.

Bill Moyers's PBS program *Now* on February 9 featured an Afghan American woman going back to her native country and interviewing relatives who had lost family members because of U.S. bombing errors. On February 11, the Pentagon conceded that a missile strike the previous week at a suspected Al Qaeda hangout had killed peasants and supporters of the Afghan government. Thus, it appeared that continued U.S. military presence in Afghanistan was taking a serious toll and creating international scandal and outrage among the Afghans. The Karzai government tried to minimize the uproar, blaming the problems on poor intelligence and local Afghans using the U.S. to settle ancient hatreds and scores.

Furthermore, President Bush's constant rhetoric of "evil" began wearing thin, as was his administration's failure to come up with rational proposals and policies in the war against terror. Fear was escalating that the Bush administration was becoming a major liability in the global struggle against terror, and the escalation of its unilateralist military interventions will no doubt make matters worse. There were also criticisms beginning to circulate that the Bush administration was manipulating and exaggerating reports about future terror attacks to keep up terror hysteria and to deflect attention from its domestic problems, failures, and growing scandals.

While the Bush administration and U.S. Justice Department has generally failed to produce dramatic domestic results in the war against terror, U.S. Attorney General John Ashcroft struck a blow against the terror of nudity, when he demanded that a nude statue of a twelve-foot-high woman figure of Justice have her breasts covered. Ashcroft was reportedly embarrassed at being photographed with the bare-breasted woman, and the puritanical Talibanesque Attorney General demanded Burka-like coverage to protect him and other like-minded puritans from the dangers of female nudity.

Yet the hypocrisy sweepstakes for the new year goes to the U.S. Supreme Court Justice Anthony Kennedy, who set out with Laura Bush to launch a "morals program" in Washington area high schools to compensate for a lack of "moral outrage" among some high school students following the September 11 terrorist attacks. "I thought this was an attack on the rule of law, and there should be a legal response," Kennedy explained. Justice Kennedy, one of the Felonious Five, who has been accused of committing treason in making a purely partisan judgment in choosing George W. Bush as president in the U.S. Supreme Court's coup d'état, himself launched a wave of moral outrage when he voted to stop the ballot counting in Florida and ratify George W. Bush as president, an event that elicited strong critique in the legal community (see Bugliosi 2001; Dershowitz 2001; and Kellner 2001). It seems that many of the worst scoundrels in the U.S. system are using September 11 to cover over their own sins.

The Bush administration thus systematically proliferated lies and hypocrisy with Dick Cheney refusing to release reports of his meetings with energy groups that helped write energy policies and then covering up his refusal with appeal to lofty principle. The Bush administration masked its attempts to expand its military power and political hegemony with claims it was attacking an "axis of evil." It used the September 11 terrorist attacks to push through a right-wing law-and-order agenda and to provide expanded military budget and favors to its major corporate contributors. Any time critics questioned their policies or the media pressed too hard on Bush and Cheney scandals, as it did in May and June of 2001, the administration released new threats of impending terrorist attacks on the U.S. Meanwhile, although the Bush administration was eager to launch a new military campaign against Iraq, things were not going well in Afghanistan and the Bush administration "war on terrorism" was not proceeding smoothly.[10]

THE BATTLE OF ANACONDA AND
OTHER AFGHAN SKIRMISHES

Back on the Terror War front, during the spring and summer of 2002, the conflict in Afghanistan appeared to be winding down, punctuated with U.S. military search and destroy missions against remnants of Al Qaeda and Taliban troops and what appeared to be an escalating guerilla war against U.S. troops and the Afghan government. As noted in the past several chapters, since the collapse of the Taliban in November, U.S. operations seemed to be killing more anti-Taliban civilians than Al Qaeda and Taliban (AQT) forces and the U.S. was rapidly losing support for their military interventions in Afghanistan. The U.S. had repeatedly refused to support global humanitarian efforts to police and reconstruct Afghanistan, claiming that such efforts would hamper their military activity. The U.S. did allow, however, some Canadian, Australian, and British forces to join in their search and destroy missions, with mixed results.

On March 2, U.S. military commanders launched what they named Operation Anaconda against AQT forces, beginning a major search and destroy operation in the Shahikot valley, a desolate area of eastern Afghanistan south of Gardez. Code-named for a Union Army plan to encircle and strangle the Confederacy as a South American snake crushes its prey, the operation involved more than 1,500 U.S. sol-diers, 100 Australians, 100 other allied soldiers, and 450 Afghan fighters. The plan involved efforts to search and engage large numbers of AQT troops with the U.S.-led forces, which would be supported by U.S. air power and divisions of troops that would seal off the escape routes, preventing the sort of get away of Al Qaeda forces in the Tora Bora region.[11]

Yet the Operation Anaconda metaphor was not really accurate as the valley, tradi-tionally the domain of Afghan resistance fighters, opened to a series of mountain ranges that tower up to 10,000 feet and that unfold all the way to Pakistan. The region also traditionally had well-fortified guerilla positions and a network of caves that could hide weapons and fighters. In earlier eras, many British and Russian troops had lost their lives to Afghan guerillas in this area, a stronghold and sanctuary whose name signifies "place of the king."

The plan involved using friendly local Afghan troops in a three-week-long U.S.-led sweep intended to clear the region of AQT forces. The mission would be sup-ported by seven groups of U.S. Special Forces and elite fighting teams who would be brought into specific areas by helicopter, with U.S. troops set to seal off the southern end of the valley while Afghan fighters would seal off the north. On the morning of March 2, the seven U.S. teams took off for their destinations, but the Afghan troops' advance was stalled when they encountered heavy resistance from AQT fighters in the region. A U.S. Special Forces Warrant Officer, Stanley Harri-man, was killed, along with Afghan fighters, as the Afghan unit tried to fight its way out of what appeared to be an ambush.

The U.S. Special Forces teams were also subject to enemy fire, but six of the seven groups managed to land and position their forces for reconnaissance and fighting AQT in the area. The seventh team, however, involving Navy SEALS in a Chinook helicopter, was heavily assaulted from AQT fighters in the mountains. After repeat-ing bombing the area, the U.S. had sent up the SEALS to the ridgetop of the moun-tain, which they believed to be uninhabited, to have an observation post overlooking the valley.

As the SEALS began to descend the chopper, they were hit by machine-gun fire from several directions and were obviously caught in an ambush. The chopper took off, but a crew member fell off and the badly damaged machine barely was able to get away. The Chinook chopper managed to land a few miles north, its controls freezing and its radio out. In a tense rescue mission, another chopper crew rescued the downed SEAL team, took them back to Gardez, and then set off to the mountain ridge to retrieve the soldier who had fallen off. A Predator drone showed the downed SEAL engaging what appeared to be Al Qaeda troops, then captured and apparently shot.

More Chinooks with U.S. troops were sent to the mountain site, code-named "Ginger," to retrieve the downed SEAL and insert Special Forces to engage the AQT. Two helicopters in the Ginger area unloaded their teams, who encountered heavy fire, with one chopper pulling away while the other was disabled. The Special Forces teams on the mountain scrambled to set up defensive positions, but were fiercely attacked and six more Americans were killed, apparently in the opening moments of the fight.

For twelve hours, the surviving U.S. troops fought on in a mountain version of the "Black Hawk Down" scenario in Somalia. U.S. jet fighters, AC-130 gunships, and attack helicopters flew in nonstop combat, bombarding the AQT troops in the mountain ridges. Bombs dropped included a 2,000-pound BLU-118B, a thermobaric bomb that creates a blast of high pressure inside a cave, triggering off fierce explosions. The next day there was a 7.2 earthquake in the area, and quakes continued in the region as the U.S. continued to drop heavy explosives on the mountains and caves where AQT forces were allegedly hiding.[12]

In early evening, eighteen hours after the mission had begun, the surviving U.S. troops were evacuated by helicopter in what was one of the fiercest battles since Vietnam and Somalia, and it was also the most costly of the war in terms of U.S. casualties. The U.S. continued saturation bombing of the area for the next few days, and on March 18 U.S. General Tommy Franks called Operation Anaconda "an unqualified and absolute success." Critics, however, said that both the Afghan and U.S. forces had been critically ambushed in the operation, that it was poorly planned and executed, that communications failed in the heat of battle, that most of the AQT forces escaped, and that it was in many ways a disaster.

There was also no consensus on how many enemy casualties were inflicted or whether substantial numbers of AQT fighters in the area managed to escape. As Operation Anaconda entered its second week, one U.S. commander claimed that over 800 AQT had been killed and when pressed Donald Rumsfeld testily replied that while he didn't want to get into the "numbers game," that "certainly hundreds" of AQT forces had been killed. A chilling report from a U.S. soldier who had participated in the operation indicated that there were potential scenes of carnage: "We were told that there were no friendly forces. . . . If there was anybody there, they were the enemy. We were told specifically that if there were women and children to kill them."[13] This could have been mere bragging, however, and after the operation, as Afghans and reporters entered the scene, the enemy death toll fluctuated from 800 to 500, 300, 200, and 100, with only twenty confirmed dead and widespread suspicions that most of the AQT had managed to escape.

The bombing of the Shahikot valley region in Operation Anaconda was fierce, including the thermobaric bombs that spread an explosive cloud through caves, igniting deep regions of the caverns that had previously been inaccessible to traditional bombs. In the weeks following Operation Anaconda, there were a series of additional earthquakes in late March, including one that killed over 1,000 Afghans. It is true that earthquakes are common events in the Hindu-Kush region surrounding the battles that comprised Operation Anaconda. But this region has also been targeted recently as one of the most environmentally sensitive mountain ranges in the world by the United Nations University in Japan, and the years of warfare and related environmental destruction were noted as chief reasons as to why these mountains are now prime candidates for natural disasters. The war-damaged and scarred earth had suffered years of drought and when it finally rained in the spring of 2002 there were damaging floods, followed by a plague of locusts.

Therefore, and this went completely unreported by the media, Operation Anaconda did not simply occur on a "mountainslope," but rather the U.S. military chose to stage a "thermobaric" intervention into a drought-ridden, ecologically threatened, geologic region primed for catastrophe. Thus, although the resulting large quakes that followed could not be directly linked to U.S. military actions, it cannot be denied that these bombing campaigns contributed to the further ecological instability of the area. This assault on the ecosystem added to a series of ecodisasters wrought by previous U.S. wars like Vietnam, the Gulf War, and NATO's intervention into Kosovo.[14]

The same day that Tommy Franks proclaimed Operation Anaconda an "unqualified success," there were reports that 1700 British marines were flying to eastern Afghanistan to relieve U.S. forces and to chase down remaining AQT fighters in the area. British papers noted that U.S. troops were not used to fighting in such high altitudes and were not experienced in mountain guerilla fighting. Over the next several months, British troops launched three highly touted operations that they described as "clean and sweep" and not the Vietnam-era "search and destroy" to get AQT. But the British forces had no major encounters and the AQT seemed to have disappeared from the area. In a useful summary, British *Guardian* reporters Kim Sengupta and Colin Brown (May 19, 2002) provided an overview of British operations:

> The development [of thirty-six British servicemen becoming ill with a virus] follows a week of increasing controversy over the British mission, with accusations that the Government was using overwhelming spin to camouflage the fact that three separate operations had achieved little tangible success.
>
> The mission has become mired in recriminations, accusations and confusion. The mood in the heat and dust of Bagram airbase, its headquarters, is fractious. The frustration of the marines at the lack of contact with the enemy was said to have been increased by unrealistic demands from politicians in London and a stormy relationship with the media.
>
> So has the mission been an overwhelming success, as Mr Hoon and the MoD claim, or a failure which should be wound up? This is how the mission unfolded.
>
> *Ptarmigan*
>   The first mission in Afghanistan, which began in the middle of April. Around 400 marines from 45 Commando were deployed in southeast Afghanistan accompanied by

acres of coverage in the media. In reality it was an acclimatization exercise and found little apart from some corpses left over from Anaconda. There was a flurry of excitement when journalists taken up to the hills were told that some sudden explosions were incoming mortar rounds. They turned out to be sheep getting blown to bits after stepping on mines.

Snipe

This one was meant to be for real. In a late-night briefing in a tent, Brigadier Roger Lane, the British commander told a group of us journalists that he was sending 1,000 men into the mountains. The Marines were told to expect up to 1,000 enemy fighters in the targeted area.

By the end of the 13-day mission the enemy had neither been seen nor engaged. Nine caves full of arms and ammunition were, however, found in the Drangkhel Ghar range in Paktika. This was described as an al-Qa'ida arsenal and blown up. A local (allied) warlord claimed the arms were his. The military continued insisting that they were al-Qa'ida's.

Afterwards Brigadier Lane pronounced that the success of the operation should not be counted in the number of "body bags" but the fact that the enemy could no longer use a key base and supply route.

Condor

The Australian SAS became involved in a firefight, killed several gunmen, and requested assistance from Bagram headquarters. At the same time US warplanes bombed "enemy positions," killing 10.

Normally the response to the Australian request for help would have been by the US Army's 101st Airborne, who acts as the Quick Reaction Force. But, according to American sources, the Marines, stung by criticism over lack of contact, demanded that they get the mission. Brigadier Lane announced the mission in an unexpected appearance at the 9am briefing at Bagram.

"It is clear that it is a substantial enemy force," said the Brigadier.

But Afghan officials claimed that the Australians had not, in fact, engaged al-Qa'ida but stumbled into a skirmish for land between two clans. Tribal elders insisted that the American warplanes had bombed a wedding party, which had been firing celebrations shots into the air.

As summer unfolded, there were few successes in the continuing U.S. campaign to try to destroy AQT troops and there was a string of attacks on Afghan civilians, government officials, and U.S. and allied troops. As reported, a June 30 U.S. air strike killed scores of civilians at a wedding party and created a great outcry of protest from the Afghanistan government. The Afghans claimed that forty-six people had been killed and 130 wounded, whereas the U.S. Central Command identified thirty-six dead and fifty wounded. In a report released in September, the United States continued to insist that antiaircraft fire had instigated the bombing, while the Afghans claimed it was wedding celebrants firing off their guns.[15]

The incident, however, deeply angered the Afghans, and the U.S. military was put under more restrictive bombing rules. Moreover, there were major terrorism episodes in Afghanistan in which Afghan government officials were assassinated and U.S. and other foreign troops were attacked by remnants of AQT fighters, making it clear that Afghanistan was far from stable. As we will see in chapter 11, an attempted assassination of Afghan President Hamid Karzai and a series of bombings in Afghanistan in September 2002 revealed how precarious the situation was in that beleaguered country.

The U.S. had also invited Canadian forces to help them search for AQT fighters and, in one highly embarrassing episode on April 18, U.S. planes bombed Canadian troops engaged in training exercises, killing four from "friendly fire."[16] The U.S. press hardly mentioned the episode and while President Bush made several public appearances the day after the "friendly fire" bombings, he made no statement of apology or regret concerning the incident, fiercely angering the Canadians. The next day a contrite Bush made a public apology, but soon thereafter the Canadians announced that they were withdrawing their troops in the summer and the British too were debating whether or not to remain in Afghanistan.

By May 2002, it appeared that the Afghan Terror War had entered a guerilla war phase in which AQT forces had blended into the country or gone to Pakistan for sanctuary. Senior and mid-level leaders of both Al Qaeda and the Taliban remained at large, and the U.S. and its allies had encountered or apprehended few AQT fighters since Operation Anaconda. The U.S. forces continued to search the countryside for AQT forces, and in late May, a U.S. airborne assault on the village Bandi Temur, on the edge of the desert sixty miles from Kandahar, killed the respected 100-year-old village elder and others. A graphic story in the British *Guardian* by Carlotta Gall, "A Raid Enrages Afghan Villagers" (May 27, 2002), presents a disturbing description of the carnage wrote by the U.S. forces and notes:

> The raid has caused Afghans here to compare the tactics of the American-led coalition to brutal raids by the Soviet Army in the 1980's.
> "They are thinking of when the Russians came and killed a lot of people, and they are thinking that the Americans and British will also repeat that," said General Akram, the regional police chief in Kandahar.
> Military officials said the raid on Friday was based on intelligence that the village was a sanctuary for senior Taliban and Al Qaeda figures.

Obviously, if the U.S. continued to make mistakes and attack innocent civilians, guerilla resistance would increase and Afghanistan would indeed become another Vietnam. Some commentators who had supported U.S. military action in Afghanistan were beginning to see that Bush's military intervention had been ill-conceived, beset with blunders, and had failed in significant ways, as I have been arguing from the beginning of this narrative. *Salon* editor David Talbot, for instance, noted that although he initially found Bush's straightforward rhetoric bracing, he came "to think of Bush's rhetoric as part of the problem instead of the solution" and found the "axis of evil" speech to be "a flight of idiocy." Likewise, although he supported

Bush's military attack on Al Qaeda and the Taliban, he worried about future military interventions and argued that the times called for "less swagger and more diplomacy."[17]

There were also reports of continued mistreatment of AQT prisoners in Afghanistan and Guantanamo Bay, Cuba. The Pentagon had admitted in March 2002 that among the 194 prisoners held in Cuba and the hundreds still held in Afghanistan, they had failed to find a single person who they could prosecute as being involved in the September 11 terrorist attacks. An article by Bob Drogin, "No Leaders of al Qaeda Found at Guantanamo" (*Los Angeles Times,* August 18, 2002), for instance, suggested that the imprisonment of the AQT fighters in Cuba had not yielded any significant information or apprehended major leaders, thus raising the question of whether the controversy over the episode was worth the effort. Yet at the end of March, Donald Rumsfeld stated that the Pentagon planned to keep prisoners from the Afghan war in captivity in Cuba indefinitely, even if they are acquitted in military tribunals. The British, by contrast, stated that they would treat AQT fighters captured in Afghanistan as prisoners of war and a group of experienced civil rights lawyers planned to take the U.S. to court for a breach of Camp X-Ray detainees' rights.[18]

As summer 2002 progressed, Afghanistan officials continued to plead for a beefed-up international security force to help maintain order in the country. But until late August the United States refused to add its own peacekeepers, stating instead that their plan was to help build and train an Afghanistan army—a task that would surely take years. Critics noted that the Pentagon was basically running U.S.-Afghan policy, that other agencies of the U.S. government should work with aid groups and other interested parties to help advance reconstructing the country, that the U.S. was largely aiding warlords in the country and contributing to its militarization and long-term instability, and that basically the U.S. lacked completely any political or economic strategy for Afghanistan.[19]

Finally, at the end of August, Pentagon officials who had long opposed expanding the international security forces in Afghanistan agreed that enlarging it and allowing U.S. and other security forces to patrol the countryside out of Kabul would help secure the country and allow U.S. troops to leave sooner. A senior Bush administration official described this as "a mid-course correction," but it called attention to the stupidity of Pentagon policy against expanding the security forces earlier, demands that both the Afghanistan government and U.S. allies had been making for months. However, "American officials said that steps to enlarge the peacekeeping force might not come for months and that finding nations to contribute the forces would not be easy."[20] Earlier, Britain, Canada, and other U.S. allies were eager to furnish security troops, but Bush administration and Pentagon policies had so alienated U.S. allies with their unilateralist approach that it was now hard to find security forces that would agree to work with the imperialist Americans.

It thus appeared that U.S. policy in Afghanistan was largely a failure. The U.S. choice to work with local militia and warlords to overthrow the Taliban and pursue

Al Qaeda and Taliban forces had largely failed. The warlords in the north had easily routed the Taliban, but committed atrocities such as mass murder of young prisoners, as I documented earlier and were a great force of corruption, exercising oppressive power and expanding the drug trade. In southern and eastern sectors of Afghanistan, warlords used the United States to extract vengeance against longtime enemies, causing many civilian casualties and building up resentment toward the U.S. in Afghanistan and in the Muslim and Arab worlds in particular. The U.S. and its warlord allies had failed to capture Osama bin Laden, Mullah Omar, and other key Taliban and Al Qaeda leadership, and many suspected that they had helped the AQT leadership to escape.

Failure to use a multinational coalition and ground troops had thus secured the power of traditionally oppressive warlords in much of Afghanistan, had allowed AQT leadership to escape, and had created a highly unstable situation in Afghanistan. The dispersal of key AQT forces made intensified guerilla war in Afghanistan likely and increased the possibility of terrorist attacks against the U.S. and the West. The U.S. intervention in Afghanistan had produced thousands of casualties, resentment in the country, and negative images throughout the world that was helping to create new enemies for the U.S. that might be involved in future terror attacks. To make matters worse, after Afghanistan the Bush administration beat the war drums for a military attack in Iraq, an adventure sure to create more enemies for the U.S. and disperse the U.S. military in a way that would surely benefit the remnants of the Al Qaeda network. Bush's doctrine of unilateralism and preemptive strikes was thus threatening to involve the U.S. and the world in an epoch of endless war and upheaval.

11

❖

The New Militarism, Lies and Propaganda, and the High Costs of the Bush Presidency

Rarely before had the discourse of an American president received the amount and intensity of worldwide criticism as Bush's "axis of evil" discourse evoked. The very term suggested to the world that the Bush administration was living in a time warp and ideological fantasy world that was out of sync with contemporary complexities. Although the term "axis" accurately described the United States and Europe's adversaries in World War Two, terrorism was a much more dispersed and shadowy opponent and countries like Iran and Iraq had their own conflictual histories, which included a bitter and bloody eight-year war between them from 1980 to 1988. Critics of the "axis of evil" discourse correctly read the term as an expression of American arrogance and blindness that arrogated "good" for itself while projecting "evil" onto its enemies. Given the U.S.'s controversial and much-criticized foreign policy over the past years and the scandals attaching to the Bush-Cheney-Enron administration, it was disingenuous at best and clearly hypocritical for members of this axis of corruption to use lofty moralistic language to define its goodness and the vileness of its defined enemies of the moment.[1]

Someone had to take a hit for this stunning rhetorical and propaganda blunder and, sure enough, it was the speechwriter. Right-wing ideologue David Frum who, according to his wife, coined the phrase, announced his retirement in late February 2002. Yet although the axis of evil hyperbole was obviously a failed political rhetoric on the global scale and a problematic one on the domestic level, it had the pragmatic and instrumental value for the Bush administration, Pentagon, and its corporate allies of promoting a big boost in military spending. Indeed, Bush's "axis of evil" speech, made on the eve of a South Asia trip in late February, could be read as good business promotion for family economic interests and those of Bush's military-industrial complex compadres. The Bush administration had been putting up military bases all thorough Central Asia, and Dick Cheney's Halliburton Corporation was getting the construction contracts. Moreover, one could perceive the U.S. troop positioning around Central Asian countries that had significant oil, gas, and energy resources as a setup to protect the interests of Bush oil and energy industry allies, and to secure protection of future U.S. energy ventures in the region.[2]

Moreover, with the $48 billion in increased military spending, Bush Daddy and his Carlyle Group investors were making stacks of money off of weapons sales and other military investments. So consider this: In his "axis of evil" speech, Bush threatens South Korea with North Korean military attacks, goes to South Korea, and tries to get them to buy a new fleet of Boeing fighter jets that would profit Bush's friends at Boeing and family investment funds. On the trip to China, Bush's Uncle Prescott, his father's brother and the son of the Bush family patriarch Prescott Bush, who managed banks and businesses for Adolph Hitler, has been head of the Chinese-American Chamber of Commerce. In China, then, Bush's tasks for family business interests were to smooth the way for increased U.S. investments and helping out his Uncle Prescott and assorted corporate interests.

The Bush administration's pursuit of their allies and supporters' economic interests are crude and crass, and were brought to embarrassing light by the Enron scandals, but this has not impeded them from carrying out business as usual. For instance, the Bush administration pulled off a scam for the Carlyle Fund that so far has alluded attention. To everyone's surprise, Donald Rumsfeld initially supported the oversized and outdated Crusader artillery system that critics claimed was overpriced and more appropriate to earlier models of war. Bush himself had criticized the Crusader program during the 2000 election and Rumsfeld had earlier also opposed it. With Rumsfeld's seeming support, the Carlyle group put out an IPO (i.e., initial public stock offering) of the company that made the Crusader, and the stock soared in value. They then dumped big chunks of the stock and, lo and behold! Rumsfeld was now against the system in a fierce fight with Pentagon army bureaucrats who wanted it, including the highly disgraced Secretary of the Army Thomas White, whose Enron sins were creating a firestorm of criticism. Bush jumped in and declared himself against the Crusader, no doubt thinking that he could claim he was both for a hi-tech military and was not a shill for family interests, although his father's Carlyle associates had already pocketed their profits from the scam.

Although George W. Bush is a shameless panderer for the economic interests of family, friends, and supporters, there is also a dimension in which a conjunction of Bush's right-wing religious fundamentalism and growing militarism fuel his policies and discourses. On a stopover in Alaska on February 16 to cheer up the troops while he was on the way to visit Japan, South Korea, and China, Bush used the "C" word, telling Canadian troops in the audience that they "stand with us in this incredibly important *crusade* to defend freedom, this campaign to do what is right for our children and our grandchildren" (my emphasis). During his visit to China, Bush went out of his way to stress his religious beliefs and the importance of religious freedom. The same week, U.S. Attorney General John Ashcroft assured a Christian broadcasters' group that God is on our side in the war against terror. No doubt Islamists feel the same way about Allah, and such religious fanaticism would likely assure that Terror War would continue into the foreseeable future.

Thus, Bush combines moralistic and religious rhetoric to support his military adventures. Meanwhile, U.S. allies were becoming extremely agitated by Bush's bellicose "axis of evil" discourse, insistence on the U.S. building a missile defense system that would destabilize existing arms agreements and balance, and the intensifying unilateralism of the Bush administration foreign policy, reaching beyond a mere war on terrorism to embrace U.S. domination of the world. In the revealing Alaska speech, Bush threatened that "this nation won't rest until we have destroyed terrorism, until we have denied the threat of global terrorism." He repeated his "clear message" that "either you're with us or you're against us," and the troops broke into applause. And promising again more military intervention, Bush shouted: "The American people must understand, the best way to secure the homeland is to unleash the United States military!"

Of course, such aggressive rhetoric is partly for domestic consumption and to keep his core supporters at a white-hot intensity of excitement. The rest of the world was not buying Bush's aggressive unilateralism, however. In South Korea, thousands protested Bush's visit with demonstrators carrying signs depicting Bush with demonic horns and bloody fangs, chanting, "Bush go home! Bush go home!" A giant demonstration in Iran carried a sign insisting that "Bush is Dracula," with hundreds of thousands chanting, "Death to America!," suggesting that Americans will die to pay for Bush's rhetorical and other sins. The *New York Times* reported "Europe Seethes As the U.S. Flies Solo in World Affairs" (February 23, 2002), noting that accusations of U.S. "unilateralism, arrogance, bad manners and oversimplification" were flying through European capitals in the wake of Bush's "axis of evil" speech and threats against Iraq.

During his Asian visit, Bush also demonstrated once again his erratic command of the English language and propensity to misspeak, as when he sent the Japanese yen into a tailspin when he confused "deflation" with "devaluation," leading currency traders to think that the U.S. and Japan had negotiated a currency devaluation of the yen whereas in fact the discussion centered on deflation. In a curious potential Freudian slip of passive aggression, Laura Bush chose to read a "Curious George" story to second-graders in a Japanese school. In introducing the stories, she noted that "George is a monkey," and when members of the entourage tittered, she explained that her husband was also named George, although she did not recommend that the students should go to www.smirkingchimp.com or www.bushorchimp.com for images and texts that displayed Bush's resemblance to simian expressions and behaviors.

Although Bush tried to relax the climate during his Asian visit, announcing in South Korea, for instance, that the U.S. had no intention of invading North Korea and wanted peace in the region, his verbal slips muddied the waters. Bush family and supporters had budding economic interests in South Korea and were reportedly angry that Bush's rhetoric had created an uproar on both sides of the Korean peninsula and had strengthened the hand of hard-liners on both sides who favored war. But Bush just couldn't help falling back into his simplistic "evil" discourse in South Korea. When shown axes used by the North Koreans against U.S. troops, Bush righteously intoned that he had just seen evidence that explained why he used "evil" to describe "them." Earlier, Bush had referred to the "Pakis" when discussing problems between Pakistan and India, resurrecting an old racist term from the British Empire, and it appeared that he just could not help using racist and essentializing terms to demean friends and allies alike.

Commentators suggested that Bush's ill-conceived "axis of evil" discourse and botched visit to Korea had imperiled South Korea's "Sunshine policy" and dialogue and rapprochement with the North, while undermining the reelection chances of President Kim Dae Jung. Bush's performance in China was equally incompetent. Instead of engaging the Chinese on democracy, globalization, human rights, and progressive values, Bush lectured the Chinese on religious freedom, emphasized the importance of his personal religion in talks with the Chinese leaders, and failed to gain any appreciable concessions from the Chinese on missile sales or to reach any notable political or economic agreements. Likewise, critics claimed that his visit to Japan had produced no productive dialogue on the economic reform that most believed Japan needed to undergo, nor was there any notable progress in U.S.-Japanese relations.[3]

THE RISE (AND FALL?) OF THE
PENTAGON MINISTRY OF TRUTH
AND THE LIES OF BUSHSPEAK

On the whole, the military and Bush administration did not fare well in the propaganda dimension of Terror War. As mentioned, early in the Afghan war, the Pentagon had hired the public relations firm Rendon Group to try to spin a more positive image with which to win the hearts and minds of the Afghan people and the Bush administration also hired advertising agency executive Charlotte Beers, a former CEO for both the Ogilvy & Mather and J. Walter Thompson advertising giants, to serve as an undersecretary of state for public diplomacy (see chapter 4). As noted earlier, in the public relations war the Bush administration organized propagandists from Britain and the United States to form a PR offensive that would provide a 24/7 spin on the news in the Afghan war. Beers's "public diplomacy" agency was also to provide segments with U.S. celebrities, giving rise to speculation that Michael Jordan might be called up to produce spots telling the world to "be like us." Indeed, Beers gushed that it would be easy to sell the world attractive brands like George W. Bush and Colin Powell.

In testimony to Congress in October 2001 shortly after her confirmation, Beers explained that as undersecretary for public diplomacy and public affairs, she would be "responsible for the overall planning and management" of the global propaganda war against terrorism. She explained all of the ways that her agency was working with world media, using U.S. embassies to circulate positive information, increasing radio services to fifty-three languages, and organizing series of speakers to promote pro-U.S. positions all over the world. Beers noted that she had met with the Ad Council the previous week "to discuss a series of public service announcements, here and overseas, that distill the values and virtues of American democracy and the many good things we have achieved on the international front." American advertising had gone to war.

Yet there was no measurable success in the propaganda war, and whatever information and hype the U.S. reproduced was countered by images of dead or injured Muslims who were victims of U.S. bombing. Nor did the images of Afghan refugees and those displaced by war win hearts and minds for the U.S. Accordingly, after the Afghanistan war wound down in late April 2002, propaganda chief Charlotte Beers asked a House subcommittee for a 5 percent hike in the public diplomacy budget to $595 million. The former advertising CEO said the U.S. has to "improve and magnify the ways in which we are addressing people of the world—not necessarily other world governments—but people." The propaganda outreach would be especially targeted at "disaffected populations" in the Middle East and South Asia, where a poor perception of the U.S. "leads to unrest, an unrest that has proven to be a threat to our national and international security," Beers stated during her April 24 testimony.

Citing a common fixture of political and advertising campaigns, Beers insisted that increased polls would be a necessary component of measuring Arab public opinion and then discerning a strategy to improve communication. Accordingly, Beers told the House panel she wanted to expand polling by the Bureau of Intelligence and Research in "Muslim countries and communities to provide policymakers with information on foreign publics' attitudes, perceptions and opinions so public diplomacy messages can be more effectively targeted." Furthermore, she cited a need to track opinion over time in Afghanistan and in Muslim communities. Polling and focus groups could also be used all over the world to gain information about foreign publics and their attitudes toward the U.S., with studies in Europe to gauge the level of anti-American sentiment and views of missile defense, and targeted polling in the Middle East on a variety of issues.[4]

In addition, Beers said that the State Department is committed to working with foreign broadcasters to produce documentaries that highlight positive aspects of American life, culture, or community. She noted that the State Department was using $15 million from the Emergency Response Fund to purchase "an aggressive campaign of message placement" and was planning to install "American Corners" in Muslim universities. There was much criticism of Beers's PR approach to public diplomacy, and many doubted whether U.S. advertising techniques were the best ways to create more productive relations with the Arab and Muslim worlds.

While the debate over public diplomacy simmered, a stunning leak in the *New York Times* on February 19 revealed that the Pentagon had created a totally Orwellian "Office of Strategic Influence" to systematically convey Pentagon propaganda on a variety of issues. The new office was reportedly promoting classified proposals for aggressive campaigns that would plant stories in foreign media and use the Internet and e-mail to spread information and misinformation from fake addresses not traceable to the Pentagon. Some in the Pentagon were bothered by discussions that the office would systematically lie to foreign countries, as if it were surprising for the U.S. to have a Ministry of Lies. Journalists were up in arms worrying that the Pentagon would systematically deceive them, as if it were not already a vehicle of Pentagon propaganda and lies.

The proposed OSI chief, Brigadier General Simon Worden, indicated that he envisions a broad mission ranging from "black" campaigns that use intentional disinformation to "white" propaganda that would rely on truthful news releases. During the same period, the Pentagon announced two more Orwellian agencies related to information and surveillance, the Information Awareness Office (IAO) and the Information Exploitation Office (IXO). These bureaucracies would develop new electronic espionage technology and analyze intercepted data with a combined budget of $48 billion. Amazingly, the IAO is to be run by Reagan-era National Security Advisor John Poindexter, who had resigned in disgrace for getting caught in Iran-Contra lies and for reportedly being involved in an illegal Contra arms procurement ring connected with drug smuggling. Returning from infamy, Poindexter was to oversee the construction of a computer system "that could create a vast electronic dragnet, searching for personal information as part of the hunt for terrorists around the globe—including the United States."[5]

On February 26, Rumsfeld announced that the Office of Strategic Influence was officially shut down. When Rumsfeld and Bush were publicly pressed, they were forced to declare that they did not officially endorse lying and George W. Bush ended the controversy with the promise, "We'll tell the American people the truth." This is perhaps the most hypocritical statement imaginable, since Bush administration and Pentagon policies had brazenly practiced the arts of deception and lying. In my book *Grand Theft 2000* (Kellner 2001), I argued that Bushspeak constituted a systematic distortion of language and a collapse of the distinction between truth and falsity. Like Orwell's Newspeak, Bushspeak inverts the meaning of language (i.e., "War is Peace," "Slavery is Freedom") and copiously uses the Big Lie as an instrument of public policy. Bush campaigned in Election 2000, for instance, on a platform that he was a "compassionate conservative," whereas in fact, as his record as Texas governor made clear and now his record as U.S. president shows, Bush is a hard-right conservative who carries out the agendas of corporations that grease his palms. Bush lied regularly during the presidential campaign, claiming that he was for a patients' bill of rights whereas he opposed meaningful legislation in that direction, or that his tax cut would benefit everyone whereas the Democrats' tax reforms would only benefit "special interests," while in fact the Bush tax cut benefited largely the top 1 percent while sending the budget into record deficits.[6]

During the Battle for the White House in the Florida Recount wars after the deadlocked election, the Bush campaign lied daily, claiming that all votes were counted many times over, that machines were more reliable than people, that Bush had won fair and square, and that Gore was a "sore loser." Built on a foundation of lies and intrigue, the new Bush administration started out with a Big Lie, claiming that in vacating the White House in January for the new administration, the Clinton staff had trashed the building. Moreover, the new Bush administration leaked stories that the Clintons had stolen gifts from the White House for their personal use, and that Clinton's people had also stolen items from Air Force One on the trip to New York, which appeared for sale on the Internet shortly thereafter. These stories were headlined in the press and endlessly dissected on talk radio, television, and the Internet, overshadowing Bush's early days in the White House.[7]

Bush's misinformation specialist Karl Rove was well-known in Texas politics for his whispering campaigns to smear opponents, and it was clear that the Bush PR strategy was to tar Clinton and his administration to the maximum so that the Bush crew would look good by comparison.[8] Rove's strategy was to open the Bush presidency by presenting a Good versus Evil image, as if the bad Clintonites were vulgar and disrespectful and the new Bush administration was honest and well-behaved. There were investigations by press and government of the allegations, and it turned out that Rove and company's stories of White House vandalism were greatly exaggerated, the claim of theft on Air Force One was pure disinformation, and Clinton's gifts were not significantly larger than those of Reagan and Bush Senior. It was clear that the whole affair had been orchestrated simply to embarrass Clinton as he left office and to elevate Bush to an image of propriety and respectability.[9]

Bush's White House would regularly leak rumors to friendly journalists, or those managing right-wing websites such as the Drudge Report, and the stories would quickly circulate and be taken up by the mainstream media; there would then be days of impassioned discussion, and eventually reputable newspapers like the *New York Times* would publish stories deflating claims, as previously noted, that the departing Clintonites trashed the White House or took mementos from Air Force One. In addition to leaks and rumormongering, the Bushites also regularly practiced the Big Lie. During the 2000 election and its first months in office, the Bush administration systematically lied concerning its tax cut program. If the public knew that the Bush tax cut "plan" would only benefit the top 1 percent of taxpayers, it would be hard to sell to the public, so the Bushites lied by saying that everyone would benefit.

Bush's economic program that he pushed through Congress during his first month in office was based on what Paul Krugman (2001) called "fuzzy math," providing utterly fallacious figures of projected taxes and revenues to make his case for a massive tax cut for the rich. Although Bush claimed to be a "compassionate conservative" who was for education, cheaper prescription medicines for elders, and improved social security, in fact his most deeply felt commitment was to cut taxes, and in a moment of exuberance he even increased his proposed cut from $1.3 trillion to $1.6 trillion. Although economic czar Alan Greenspan, the Ayn Rand enthusiast who many believe runs the U.S. economy, was at first reluctant to support big tax cuts and stressed the importance of continuing to pay off the deficit, he eventually endorsed the tax cut. As the hogs gathered to feed in the federal trough, the main conflict was over how much taxes would be cut and who would receive the benefits of tax reductions.[10]

Although Bush had mendaciously claimed in a debate with Al Gore in fall 2000 that the Democratic Party tax cut reform would just benefit "special people," while Bush's tax cut would benefit everyone, the reverse was the case. As noted, Bush's tax breaks went to the rich and groups that had supported him. The process recalled the first big Reagan tax cut, when budget director David Stockman began devising across-the-board tax cuts for individuals, ending with a corporate greedfest that sent the national debt and interest rates soaring. Later, Stockman recalled: "The hogs were really feeding. The greed level, the level of opportunism just got out of control."[11] Indeed, in pondering Bush's brazen tax giveaway to the rich program, one might recall the effects of the Reagan tax cut, which helped raise unemployment and interest rates while the stock market declined and the federal deficit soared.

As deficits grew out of control with the spending needed to respond to the September 11 terror acts, the Bush administration continued to lie about budget figures, about how the Afghan Terror War and other programs would be paid for, and about the extent of the burgeoning deficit and the worsening economic situation. In one of the most disgusting comments of his presidency, Bush stated while fundraising: "You know, I was campaigning in Chicago and somebody asked me, is there ever any time where the budget might have to go into deficit? I said only if we were at war or had a national emergency or were in recession. (Laughter.) *Little did I realize we'd get the trifecta* [emphasis added]. (Laughter.)"[12] Astonishingly, Bush repeated this snide joke, delivered with his trademark smirk and snortish chuckle, more than fifteen times into June 2002. Critics noted that in fact Bush had never specified these three conditions as justifications for deficit spending or raiding the Social Security fund, and that therefore the whole nasty political ploy was simply a lie, providing another example of the intimate connection between Bushspeak and lying.[13]

The "trifecta" scandal puts on display the true Bush, arrogantly boasting of getting away with his manipulative economic program based on lies and fuzzy math, while making light of the September 11 tragedies that enabled him to justify deficit spending for his special interests. Indeed, the Bushites continued to lie about many things and Bush's press secretary Ari Fleischer became known as a highly skillful dissembler, by his begging questions from reporters, refusal to answer questions by cutting questioners off with dubious premises that invalidated the questions, and flat-out lies with which he manipulated the press.[14]

Bush's communication specialist and key political advisor, Karen Hughes, was also infamous for prevarication. For years, Hughes had lied about Bush's personal life, covering over his sins and helping him hide his many skeletons of youthful indiscretion, shady business deals, and political skullduggery. As noted, Hughes had not distinguished herself as a propagandist in the public opinion dimension of Terror War. According to *Roll Call,* Hughes told a closed-door meeting that "a divine plan" had enabled the Bush team to get through the September 11 catastrophe. As mentioned earlier, she was reportedly "shocked" to learn that the Taliban barred women from schools and outlawed movies, thus displaying total ignorance of Afghanistan, and she raised eyebrows on the occasion of Bush's "axis of evil" speech when she declared that 100,000 terrorists were trained as killers who were threatening the United States.[15]

Yet when Hughes announced that she was leaving Washington to return to Texas with her "homesick" family, she was celebrated as one of Bush's most valued employees and herself spun her leaving as evidence of the Bush administration's concern for families. Cynics noted that Hughes had lied for Bush for years at relatively low pay and could make a bundle taking on corporate board positions, political consulting fees, and lectures. Yet insiders fretted that without the relatively pragmatic and down-to-earth Hughes, right-wing hard-liners and Karl Rove would take over the White House, to Bush's and the country's detriment.[16]

Karl Rove got into Republican Party politics in the 1970s by carrying out dirty tricks against political opponents as a leader of the Young Republicans. Working from the beginning with George W. Bush in his quest for the Texas governorship, Rove was known in Texas as "Bush's Brain" and was nicknamed by Bush himself "Turd Blossom." Also influenced by Bush I political honcho Lee Atwater, Rove was a hardball political operative and right-wing ideologue who brought Nixonian tactics into the Bush administration. Imitating Nixon dirty trickster Murray Chotiner, Rove also refined the technique of the Big Lie, developed by Hitler and Goebbels, against Bush's Democratic opponents in Texas and later in Washington. Rove got into trouble when Bush II went to Washington and Rowe continued to consult with firms like Enron, Intel, Dell, and other companies in which he held stock who had to do business in Washington (the sleazy Rove sold almost a million dollars' worth of stock three weeks after Bush had announced his energy plan, getting his "bounce" before unloading).[17] But Rove survived the scandals and helped push through Bush's hard-right agenda during the first months of his presidency (see Kellner 2001).

In retrospect, Rove can be seen as Richard Nixon's revenge, combining Nixon's Machiavellianism with a complete disregard for truth and integrity, in pursuing a politics of spin, slime, and slander.[18] Since Bush obtained office in Grand Theft 2000, Rove has told a series of Big Lies to characterize Bush's policies. I have earlier documented the absurdity of Rove's claim that the hardcore unilateralist Bush is multilateralist.[19] Indeed, a major thrust of this book is to explicate and critique Bush's dangerous unilateralism. Rove also declared in February 2002 that "President Bush is a populist," claiming that Bush is "economically populist, fiscally conservative, [and] socially moderate."[20] Such a claim is absurd, as Bush is obviously the most pro–big business and antipopulist president in recent history. In fact, during the 2000 campaign, Bush also made a populist pitch that he trusted the people and not government, but when confronted with the recount challenge in Florida, the Bush team insisted that people could not be trusted to count votes—that you could only trust machines, not people (see Kellner 2001). Hence, Bushspeak is populist when it is pitching to the people for votes, corporate when it is giving out favors, and technocratic when it is counting votes (or trying to prevent an accurate tally).

In a rare July 13 TV interview on *Tim Russert,* the shameless Rove told lie after lie about Bush and his administration, beginning with the outrageous claim that for Bush "policy drives politics," as if Bush were interested in specific policies rather than political spin and the political effects of his policies. After an account of the drama of September 11 with Bush on the run across the country, leaving out the Big Lie he'd floated about specific threats to Bush and Air Force One that forced him to fly willy-nilly across the country, Rove then said that after the big event, "I saw a command presence. I saw a firmness and a resolve and clarity and a discipline that was really extraordinary." In fact, this is pure bluff and spin, and attempts to make Bush into great wartime leaders like Churchill or Roosevelt are farcical. Bush is still Bush, which means intellectually lightweight (like Rove himself), hypocritical, programmed, and thoroughly dispensable.

Then Rove, who specialized in sleaze, slander, and dirty tricks in his many campaigns for Bush, made the astonishingly false claim that Bush administration politics would be issue-oriented, about a positive agenda, and would not use negatives against opponents. All summer Rove was trying to resurrect the discredited "compassionate conservative" label, begging Republicans to stop sounding so "mean and greedy," claiming that the Bushites were running "a different kind of politics" that rejects "the blame culture" for a "responsible culture." Then, in what David Corn described as "a great moment in the history of spin," Rove had the audacity to claim that in the just-declared new model of "compassionate conservatism": "It's Ronald Reagan meets Bobby Kennedy."[21]

For Rove, "corporate meltdown," caused arguably by Bush-Rove's right-wing and pro-market deregulatory mania, was a small matter, just "a few bad CEOs of big companies, who, in the excesses of the 90s . . . got outside the rules." Note how the deceptive Rove blames the corporate scandals on the excesses of the Clinton 1990s, refusing to see the links between the economic policies of the Reagan-Bush regimes and the deregulatory Republican Congresses that made it possible for the corporate crimes to take place.

Finally, after trying to impress Russert and the audience with his knowledge of the McKinley administration, the mendacious Rove claims that the Bush administration had "changed the tone" in Washington from partisan attack and slander to civilized discourse. This is pure bovine excrement, and ol' Turd Blossom is a master of dishing up rhetorically sweet but mendacious ideological sound bites. He thinks if he lies about Bush and the Bush administration enough, people will believe the lies, precisely Joseph Goebbels's political philosophy during the Third Reich.

But the major liar in the Bush White House was George W. Bush himself. Bush had lied about his past for decades, a symptom that was embarrassingly evident when he was confronted with his close connections with Enron's Ken Lay. As the Enron scandal was exploding, Bush claimed that Lay had not even supported him for governor and that he had only known Lay since the mid-1990s. In fact, Lay himself admitted that he strongly supported Bush against Ann Richards in 1994 in the race for Texas governor and had known George W. Bush personally since the mid-1980s. How Bush could so blatantly lie about his connection with Lay, which was well known to everyone in the know, is mind-boggling and shows the contempt for truth and the public that defines George W. Bush.

Although Bush claimed that he would bring a "new era of responsibility" to the presidency, Bush had never shown a strong streak in this area and throughout his presidency was refusing to take responsibility for anything that went wrong. As noted, when Bush was confronted with problems of the U.S. intervention in Afghanistan, he would huff and puff and direct all questions to General Tommy Franks, thus refusing to take responsibility for setbacks or mishaps. When the Enron scandal erupted, he denied any personal responsibility or corporate connection that might have contributed to the scandal. When Israeli and Palestine hostilities intensified, Bush blamed Clinton for being too involved and refused to take any responsibility himself, sending CIA head George Tenet, Colin Powell, Anthony Zinni, or others to mediate. When Bush was queried by the press, who was anxious to see if he had a plan or would play a role in mediating the conflicts, Bush referred to the Saudi peace plan or prior U.S. proposals before finally being forced to make a statement on the Israeli-Palestinian conflict in mid-June, after which he then continued to ignore the issue.

Every major commentator on the Middle East, however, knows that until a solution to the Israeli-Palestinian conflict is found, there will be no peace or stability in the region. Most believe that the U.S. alone can mediate a peace by virtue of its influence over Israel. Moreover, as indicated in the introduction and later in this chapter, when confronted with the responsibility of his administration in allowing the September 11 terror attacks to occur, Bush heatedly disavowed any responsibility, attacked critics, and refused to acknowledge any responsibility for failings of his administration or his own lack of involvement in the issue. Likewise, he had never acknowledged any problems with the U.S. intervention in Afghanistan, always celebrated it as a triumph of his administration, and never considered the need for developing more constructive engagement with the problems of Afghanistan, as opposed to primarily military intervention, until late August 2002 when the Bush administration reluctantly committed to international peacekeeping forces throughout Afghanistan.

Hence, although Bush and his minions blather frequently about the importance of "responsibility," Bush himself is the least responsible president in recent memory, choosing to blame others or evade personal responsibility when things go wrong. Hypocrisy and lies ooze from the secretive, evasive, and highly deceptive Bush administration, which pays lip service to conservative discourse and refuses all norms of truth, intellectual integrity, reason, and justice. Instead, Bushspeak is the contemporary equivalent of Orwellian Doublespeak, reducing discourse to political manipulation and serving the interests of a small political and corporate elite.

WAITING FOR THE WAR ON IRAQ AND GROWING BUSH AND CHENEY SCANDALS

In early February 2002, reports circulated that U.S. attacks on Iraq were inevitable. Richard Perle, a senior advisor to U.S. Secretary of Defense Donald Rumsfeld, indicated that war with Iraq was likely even if Baghdad backed down and allowed inspectors back in to hunt for weapons of mass destruction, according to an interview in early February at a Munich Security conference:

> "I don't think there's anything (Iraqi leader) Saddam Hussein could do that would convince us there's no longer any danger coming from Iraq," said Richard Perle, head of the Defense Policy Board of the US Department of Defense. . . . Perle, quoted in an interview with the German edition of the *Financial Times* at the Munich Security Conference, said the only thing that would convince the US regarding Iraq would be a change of regime. US President George W. Bush was now on "a very clear path" heading toward war with Iraq, said Perle.[22]

In March, Vice President Dick Cheney visited eleven countries in the Middle East to garner support for the U.S. war against Iraq, and every country he visited publicly told him that they were against such aggression and chided the United States for not doing more to help with the volatile Israel-Palestine situation. Cheney was publicly lectured and rebuked in every Arab country he visited, all of them insisting that the U.S. should not attack Iraq but should instead put more pressure on Israel. The crown prince of Bahrain, for instance, told Cheney, "The people who are dying today on the streets are not a result of any Iraqi action. . . . The people are dying as a result of an Israeli action. And likewise the people in Israel are dying as a result of actions taken in response." The conservative *Weekly Standard* concluded, "Not since Secretary of State Warren Christopher returned from Europe with egg on his face in May 1993 has a high-ranking American official had such a bad week abroad as Vice President Dick Cheney just spent in the Middle East."[23]

Still, the Bush administration seemed to go ahead with plans for war against Iraq. The British *Guardian* reported that the U.S. had begun preparations to move its Gulf headquarters from Saudi Arabia to Qatar in order to bypass Saudi objections to launching a military attack against Iraq from Saudi soil:

The independent Saudi Information Agency, based in Washington, reported that US military trucks had been seen leaving the base at al Kharj, 50 miles south of Riyadh, and arriving at the border with Qatar in the second week of March. The vast al-Udeid air base in Qatar has become increasingly important to the US air force since the Saudi government refused to allow air raids on Afghanistan to be launched from its soil. The movement of trucks to Qatar may represent a temporary redistribution of resources to pursue the Afghan war, but the request for bids to move sophisticated equipment suggests a more permanent relocation, analysts said.

The move to Qatar, which has been the subject of speculation in Washington for the past few weeks, would allow the US to conduct an air campaign against Iraq in the face of Saudi refusal to collaborate, overcoming a serious obstacle to the second phase of the US "war on terror." There have also been unconfirmed reports, in the US press and from Iraqi opposition groups, of a quiet US military buildup in Kuwait to between 25,000 and 35,000 troops.[24]

By late April, there were reports that the Pentagon was putting final touches on a plan to invade Iraq, perhaps as early as the fall of 2002. But U.S. plans may have been put on hold when a high-ranked U.S. military official leaked that "the uniformed leaders of the U.S. military believe they have persuaded the Pentagon's civilian leadership to put off an invasion of Iraq until next year at the earliest and perhaps not to do it at all, according to senior Pentagon officials." The May 24 *Washington Post* story indicated that the joint chiefs of staff waged a determined "behind-the-scenes campaign to persuade the Bush administration to reconsider an aggressive posture toward Iraq in which war was regarded as all but inevitable," as the Pentagon did not have the troops or material to fight a sustained war against international terror networks and Iraq at the same time. In addition, U.S. allies strongly opposed a U.S. intervention in Iraq due to fears that a military conflict would destabilize the regime and because of concerns over the uncertainties of a post–Saddam Hussein regime.[25]

Meanwhile, the Bush administration had to deal with another contentious issue. As noted in the introduction to this study, on May 15 CBS News broadcast a memo that indicated that the CIA had briefed President George W. Bush some weeks before the September 11 terror attacks indicating the possibility of Al Qaeda assaults on the U.S., and the president evidently did nothing, remaining on vacation in his ranch for the longest presidential vacation in recent memory. For the first time since September 11, there was serious discussion concerning the Bush administration's responsibility for the terrorist bombings, and in the days following there were daily exposés of warnings that had been given to the FBI, the CIA, and various sectors of the Bush administration concerning the dangers of impending Al Qaeda attacks.

Newsweek (May 20, 2002) published a politically explosive cover story concerning how the Bush administration had downplayed efforts by the Clinton administration to stop Al Qaeda and fight terrorism, including Bush cutting Justice Department budgets to fight terrorism, the lack of concern with terrorism by Bush's National Security Advisor Condoleezza Rice, the Bush administration's Treasury Department loosening of controls over money and finance that helped terrorists move money, and how Donald Rumsfeld had shut down a program that attempted to keep a Predator missile aimed at bin Laden for possible retaliation. *Time* provided a cover story some weeks later ("The Secret History," August 4, 2002) that claimed that the Clinton administration had not only urged the importance of fighting bin Laden and terrorism, but also had a plan to take on Al Qaeda that the Bush administration had failed to prioritize until it was too late.

To deflect attention from growing criticism, Vice President Dick Cheney appeared on television warning Democrats "to be very cautious" in ascribing blame to the Bush administration for the September 11 terror attacks. Cheney continued by asserting that it is "thoroughly irresponsible and totally unworthy of national leaders in a time of war" to criticize his administration, saying in effect that it was unpatriotic and abetting the enemy to criticize the Bush administration. Cheney himself had repeatedly warned Senate Majority Leader Tom Daschle against holding hearings concerning how U.S. intelligence and political failures had led to the September 11 attacks.[26] Indeed, Cheney would have good reason to fear such investigation, since he had been put in charge of a Bush administration task force to address issues of terrorism and energy policy in May 2001 and had obviously devoted his energies to gaining energy policy favorable to his friends and Bush administration supporters in the oil and energy industries. Cheney had been asleep at the wheel and his failure should have evoked fierce criticism, although as of the end of 2002 he has eluded scrutiny for his role in heading the Bush antiterrorism task force and failing to put into play measures that could have prevented the September 11 attacks (such as coordinating intelligence operations and connecting the dots concerning the stream of warnings of imminent Al Qaeda attacks).

Bush himself, as usual, refused to face the press concerning what he did or did not know about terrorist attacks on the horizon before September 11. But following his pattern of refusal to take responsibility, in a speech on May 17 to young military forces, Bush blamed the criticism of his pre–September 11 neglect of terrorism on the culture of the capital, claiming that "Washington is the kind of place where second-guessing becomes second-nature." In addition to Cheney's statement and Bush's evasion, National Security Advisor Condoleezza Rice appeared at a press conference on May 16 and insisted that the Bush administration was not more concerned about the August 6 CIA memo because it only had warned about "traditional hijacking" plots, as if this were not sufficiently important to warn airlines and the public. Rice continued her extremely inept explanation, stating: "I don't think anybody could have predicted these people would . . . use an airplane as a missile."

In fact, there were a flurry of reports that since the mid-1990s terrorist groups had contemplated using planes as missiles, a danger warned against in the summer 2001 G-8 conference in Genoa, Italy, that Bush and Rice had attended. For the first time since September 11, notions like "serious credibility gap" were being leveled at the Bush administration and CBS's Dan Rather told the BBC in an interview: "Patriotism became so strong in the United States after 11 September that it prevented U.S. journalists from asking the toughest of the tough questions about the war against terrorism," adding, "I do not except myself from this criticism." Rather went on to note: "It's an obscene comparison . . . but you know there was a time in South Africa that people would put flaming tires around peoples' necks if they dissented. And in some ways the fear is that you will be necklaced here, you will have a flaming tire of lack of patriotism put around your neck."

Yet finally criticism of Bush administration failures regarding terrorism in their pre–September 11 neglect of the issue was accelerating, and to dampen this discourse the Bush administration put out a flurry of warnings concerning dangers of imminent terror attacks. Cheney said that new assaults were "all but inevitable" and likely to come soon, and Condoleezza Rice was all over television talking about an increase in "chatter" from intelligence sources and dangers of more terror attacks, perhaps over the Memorial Day holiday weekend. There were specific warnings that apartment units could be rented and used to blow up buildings, and another flurry of warnings concerned dangers that New York sites like bridges or the Statue of Liberty could be hit. FBI Director Robert Mueller warned of the dangers of suicide bombers of the sort that had plagued Israel for years. Secretary of Defense Donald Rumsfeld warned again of the danger of terrorists using weapons of mass destruction, including nuclear ones. Other reports mentioned more airline hijacking, attacks on malls or sports events, and even dangers from terrorist scuba divers!

Some of these reports came from Al Qaeda officials arrested in Afghanistan or from those held in Guantanamo Bay and elsewhere. Of course, one of the goals of terrorists is to spread terror, so a clever terrorist would want to create anxiety concerning major institutions, sites, and sectors of the economy, and the Bush administration seemed to be helping the terrorists achieve their goal of spreading generalized anxiety through the country. Yet, since there had not been one attack since September 11, despite frequent Bush administration warnings, skepticism was emerging that the Bush gang was exploiting terrorism dangers to push its own right-wing agenda.

In a rare moment of candor, Bush's press secretary Ari Fleischer admitted that the recent raft of terrorist alerts was issued "as a result of all the controversy that took place last week." Fleischer was "referring to reports that the president received a CIA briefing in August [2001] about terror threats, including plans by Osama bin Laden's Al Qaeda network to hijack U.S. commercial airliners." This admission, of course, increased outrage and for the first time since September 11 the Bush administration had a serious public relations crisis to deal with.[27]

After the firestorm of controversy surrounding the Bush administration and U.S. intelligence agencies' apparent pre–September 11 information about an imminent bin Laden attack on the U.S. using airplanes, Bush took off in late May for a trip to Europe. As he prepared to leave the U.S., there was a flurry of reports that Bush's pre–September 11 policy had systematically decentered focus on terrorist operations and cut back budgets and personnel for dealing with terrorism in the Justice Department, FBI, military, and other areas of government, thereby hampering the efforts to deal with bin Laden and terrorism that were begun by Clinton. Whereas British papers, the BBC, and various Internet and foreign sources had long documented that the Bush administration had told U.S. and foreign agencies to "go easy on bin Laden and the Saudis" and had blocked investigations into their activities begun by the Clinton administration, these explosive stories had not yet circulated in U.S. mainstream media.

Meanwhile, on the eve of Bush's European visit, former U.S. Secretary of State Madeleine Albright published a *Washington Post* piece on "Why Europe Doubts" (May 22, 2002), laying out some of the reasons that Europe has become extremely hostile to Bush administration policy and was distancing itself from its policies and actions. In particular, she noted that although Europe appreciated that terrorism was a common problem requiring serious efforts, Europeans were fed up with the Bush administration's unilateralism, which privileged military-led solutions and which failed to allow for either the active participation of NATO forces or any nation not handpicked by the U.S. This, Albright argued, led to the perception by Europeans that U.S. policy showed "an embarrassing unwillingness to use the European military capacities that are relevant." Europeans also were concerned about the Bush-Cheney gang's failures to adequately engage the broader diplomatic, political, legal, and economic dimensions to halting terrorist networks. In addition, Albright claimed that Europeans were angry about Bush administration positions on missile defense and their rejection of global commissions and treaties on biological weapons and arms control, international justice, ecology and climate change, and a wealth of other issues in which the Bush administration exhibited a consistently virulent unilateralism.

Just before Bush's first trip to Russia, U.S. media revealed that Bush's nickname for Russian Prime Minister Vladimir Putin was "Pootie Poo," disclosing once again Bush's embarrassingly juvenile tendency to construct insulting nicknames for his associates and people of importance with whom he had to deal. Although the talks with Putin and the Russians appeared cordial and the two Cold War antagonists signed a planned nuclear weapons reduction treaty, Putin was firm to lecture back to Bush when the American president evoked U.S. concern over Russian support of an Iranian nuclear energy facility. Putin responded by pointing out that Russia and others were concerned about U.S. military deliveries to Taiwan and U.S. support of a nuclear power plant in North Korea; Bush seemed taken by surprise by the latter issue and did not respond.

Defense analysts said although while it was useful to sign a missile reduction treaty, no adequate provisions had been made for protecting and disposing of obsolete missiles, creating dangers that rogue missiles could be sold on the black market or get into dangerous hands. Likewise, on the Bush administration's insistence, the treaty did not call for the immediate destruction of the weapons to be taken down and stored (they could be held for up to ten years), and either side could abrogate the treaty at short notice. Thus, experts believed that the treaty really did not improve nuclear security and was just a cosmetic photo opportunity to give Putin and Bush good spin.

Moreover, the Pentagon had leaked a Nuclear Posture Review report that had called for more flexible nuclear weapons, argued for a resumption of weapons testing, and called for the exploring of "contingencies" that could require nuclear attack on Russia, China, North Korea, Libya, Syria, Iraq, or Iran. These states were not happy to be on a nuclear targeting list and commentators noted that although arguments for tactical use of nuclear weapons are not new, the endorsement of a policy of first-use nuclear strikes marks a dramatic policy shift.[28]

Bush's trip to Germany after his Russian visit revealed his declining stature and how he was held in contempt by large masses of people. There were giant demonstrations against Bush, and when he spoke in the German parliament attacking Iraq and trying to get European support for the venture, he was booed by parliamentarians who held up a peace flag and walked out of the arena, an unparalleled protest within the usually decorous German parliament. There were many comparisons between JFK's "Ich bin ein Berliner" speech and the tumultuous welcome Ronald Reagan received in Germany after the fall of communism, compared to the hostile reception received by Bush.

In France, Bush managed to further embarrass and humiliate himself, clearly demonstrating his inability to govern and represent the U.S. After a two-hour meeting with French President Jacques Chirac, at a long press conference Chirac voiced French and European opposition to Bush administration policy on the Middle East, global warming, the environment, and trade (the Bush administration had just approved steel tariffs and federal aid to farmers that angered the French). Chirac insisted that countries should learn to reduce pollution and the consumption of "resources that cannot be renewed," gaining a blank stare from the U.S. president who had spent much of his entire career before politics in the oil industry. During his press conference with Chirac, Bush stumbled and mumbled, with the French president looking on in astonishment when after Bush rambled incoherently and admitted that he forgot the question, explaining: "That's what happens when you get past 55."[29]

Bush was described by Dana Milbank (*Washington Post,* May 28, 2002), as "in a rather skittish and unfocused mood after a demanding five-day tour to Germany and Russia. He referred twice to Mr. Chirac as 'President Jacques' and pronounced the French president's second name throughout as " 'shrak.' " In an article, "Weary, Bush Mocks Reporter," in the usually Bush-friendly *Washington Times* (May 27, 2002), Bill Sammons wrote:

> In the live-televised question and answer section, Bush testily responded to a question by NBC reporter David Gregory who asked:
> "I wonder why it is you think there are such strong sentiments in Europe against you and against this administration?" the reporter said. "Why, particularly, there's a view that you and your administration are trying to impose America's will on the rest

of the world, particularly when it comes to the Middle East and where the war on terrorism goes next?"

Turning to Mr. Chirac, he added in French: "And, Mr. President, would you maybe
comment on that?"

"Very good," Mr. Bush said sardonically. "The guy memorizes four words, and he
plays like he's intercontinental."

"I can go on," Mr. Gregory offered.

"I'm impressed—que bueno," said Mr. Bush, using the Spanish phrase for "how
wonderful." He deadpanned: "Now I'm literate in two languages."

Continuing his ill-tempered response, Bush accused Gregory of "showing off as
soon as you get in front of a camera," forgetting that performing in front of cameras
and asking critical questions are what TV reporters are supposed to do. Bush's
attempts at humor during his European trip also fell flat, as when he admired the
immaculate grounds of Russian President Putin and commented: "Nice of you to
mow the grass for us." When discussing plans with Putin to dispose of nuclear material, he said industrialized countries would pay $20 million "to help Russian securi-
tize the dismantled nuclear warheads" (whereas the verb "to securitize" means to
turn a commodity into a stock that can be traded). Bush also spoke of "uninalien-
able rights" and continued to finger-wag and pontificate on the dangers of Iraq and
terrorism. Russian television repeatedly played footage of Bush chewing gum upon
entering a meeting with Putin, and then spitting it out in his hand before the press
conference. Bush also practiced what one wit called "robo-tourism," after he raced
through the Kremlin's Cathedral Square, a treasure-house of churches and historical
sites, in seven minutes, tore through the Russian museum in thirty, and attended
an abridged version of "*The Nutcracker*," staged to "accommodate the president's
schedule" (and his short attention span).[30]

Most embarrassingly, the German news magazine *Der Spiegel* (May 19, 2002)
had reported that during a conversation with Brazilian President Fernando Enrique
Cardozo, Bush bewildered his colleague by asking: "Do you have blacks too?"
requiring Condoleezza Rice to point out that Brazil has more blacks than the U.S.
Meanwhile, as the Moron-in-Chief ripped through Europe and embarrassed his
country, violence continued to heat up in the Middle East; Pakistan and India stood
on the brink of nuclear war, with warnings of U.S. and British citizens to leave the
countries immediately; and Afghanistan still did not have a reconstruction plan and
was subject to sporadic U.S. violence, including a May 31 "friendly fire" incident
in which the U.S. killed three pro-Afghanistan government troops, signaling again
the lack of a coherent U.S. policy in Afghanistan. The world was suffering mightily
from having a completely incompetent U.S. president who was becoming a global
as well as national catastrophe.

It was certainly a major tragedy that such an incompetent, irresponsible, and
deeply flawed individual found himself administering a complex Terror War and
dealing with a variety of national and global issues that he could not really handle

or help produce solutions for. It was becoming ever more clear that George W. Bush was a figurehead president run by right-wing extremists and militarists, and that the country and world were suffering the consequences. During the midst of Mideast turmoil, a *Washington Post* reporter noted: "As Israeli troops and tanks stormed Yasser Arafat's compound today, President Bush played with his dogs, went for a jog and worked around his ranch."[31] As India and Pakistan approached the brink of nuclear war, Bush went fundraising and continued business as usual, sending his subordinates to deal with the problem.

Indeed, George W. Bush is the dispensable man. There has probably never been a president in recent U.S. history less qualified to deal with the complexity of contemporary problems and less able to play a constructive role in terms of policies, ideas, or personal diplomatic intervention. Bush's main function is to serve as figurehead and spokesperson for his right-wing handlers. His key role is to be popular and get votes. No one really expects him to have any ideas, engage in serious issues, or make any contribution whatsoever to national political life or culture. Bush is truly dispensable, a man more interested in his Texas ranch and daily workouts than in the problems of the economy or foreign affairs. It is a tragedy that in an era of complex global politics, the U.S. has a mediocre provincial at the ship of state, which has been destined under his unwatchful watch to fall into treacherous global waters.

Curiously, and perhaps to compensate for Bush's deficiencies, his administration constantly speaks of his "leadership." It is striking how often when speaking to the media, Bush's aides constantly refer to "the president's" plan, actions, or leadership. Indeed, critics have pointed to internal Bush administration memos that instruct spokespeople to mention Bush's "leadership" in all contact with the media, as if saying it would create it. In another quaint rhetorical strategy of Bush administration spin, when his spokespeople are pushing to the media unpopular programs like tax cuts that mainly benefit the rich, or his blocking of decent prescription drugs bills to help senior citizens, Bush's minions constantly refer to "the president's position," what "President Bush believes" or the like, seeming to assume that because Bush is popular, whatever unpopular positions that his administration is pushing will sell if they are associated with the president.

Bush himself constantly alludes to his "plan" for this and that, and assures the nation he will make a "decision" when, for instance, it comes time to move against Iraq. In fact, the pro-corporate, unilateralist, and militarist hard-right corps of his administration formulates the plans, makes the decisions, and carries out the policies, with Bush serving as a mere figurehead and cheerleader. Bush's role is to provide sound bites to the public when his handlers have agreed on specific policies and to raise funds for the Republican party—a task at which he is highly successful, breaking Clinton's previous record year in his 2001–2002 fundraising activities and helping his party to gain unprecedented gains in the November 2002 midterm elections.

Bush's performances in summer 2002 were extremely frightening in form and substance. After returning to the U.S. after his disastrous European trip, in a speech to West Point cadets on June 1, Bush proclaimed a new "doctrine" that the U.S. would strike first against enemies. It was soon apparent that this was a major shift in U.S. military policy, replacing the Cold War doctrine of containment and deterrence with a new policy of preemptive strikes, one that could be tried out in Iraq. U.S. allies were extremely upset with this shift in U.S. policy and move toward an aggressive U.S. unilateralism. In an article, "Bush to Formalize a Defense Policy of Hitting First," David E. Sanger wrote in the *New York Times* (June 17, 2002), "The process of including America's allies has only just begun, and administration officials concede that it will be difficult at best. Leaders in Berlin, Paris and Beijing, in particular, have often warned against unilateralism. But Mr. Bush's new policy could amount to ultimate unilateralism, because it reserves the right to determine what constitutes a threat to American security and to act even if that threat is not judged imminent."[32]

The Bush gang was also launching preemptive strikes against its own citizens. On June 10, John Ashcroft dramatically announced from Moscow that the U.S. had arrested a U.S. citizen with suspected ties to Al Qaeda who had planned to bring and explode a "dirty bomb" to the U.S. Although many in the U.S. and other intelligence communities immediately questioned whether the suspect, an Islamic convert born Jose Padilla, was really a major Al Qaeda player, he was arrested, declared an "enemy combatant," and as of the end of 2002 has been denied a lawyer or the usual legal rights enjoyed by U.S. citizens.

As the Bushites rattled their sabers and spread fears of terrorism, the stock market tanked and it was obvious that the economy was in disarray thanks to Bushonomics and Terror War. Summer 2002 would be remembered as a time when some of the most dramatic corporate scandals in history unfolded, when individuals lost vast amounts of savings and investments, when nearly 2 million jobs were lost over the previous twelve months, and in which the economic and political scandals of Bush and Cheney would finally appear in mainstream media and debate. It was now clear that the Bush administration comprised the worst economic managers of the century and had thoroughly messed up the once booming U.S. economy, and that the risk of further war and global insecurity had increased exponentially since the Bush crusade had launched its Terror War.

STOCK MARKET SLUMPS, ECONOMIC
WOES, AND IRAQ DEBATES

The Enron scandal was emerging as the biggest political-economic outrage in U.S. history, but the Bush administration was desperately trying to process it as an economic and not a political scandal. But in fact the economics and politics of the affair were interconnected and pointed to the fundamental flaws of Bush-Cheney ideology and their personal corruption. Enron had been encouraged in its Wild West cowboy capitalist economics by Bush-Cheney laissez-faire policies that urged deregulation of the energy market. When governor of Texas, Bush deregulated the energy market, turning Enron and other companies loose to despoil the environment, rip off customers, and engage in the most audacious criminal wheelin' and dealin' in U.S. corporate history. As discussed earlier, Bush convinced then–Pennsylvania Governor Tom Ridge, later his designate for Homeland Security Führer, of the wondrous benefits of energy deregulation. Hence, Pennsylvania, California, and many other states deregulated their energy markets, bringing in the Enron and other sharks to game the suckers. But ultimately the deregulation pushed by Bush and his allies had generated a morass of scandal that it will take years to sort out and will no doubt produce reams of books and studies.

Moreover, by spring 2002 when the Enron scandal broke there were fifty former Enron executives working in the Bush administration, including Bush's key economic advisor Larry Lindsey and his Secretary of Army Thomas White, who was trying to deregulate the Army and to privatize their energy sources while he was being accused of crimes during his Enron days. Bush and Cheney had been very close personally and politically to Enron, which exemplified the unrestrained capitalism unleashed by Republican pro-market and antideregulation politics.

As it turns out, the Enron disaster was just the tip of the corporate morass that was fast emerging under the scrutiny of the media, federal investigators, and internal revelations of fraud and corruption. In summer 2002, a dazzling array of corporate scandals unfolded, one after another, showing the calamitous results of Bush-Cheney laissez-faire economics and the breathtaking stupidity of the pro-market and antiregulation policies that the right wing has so aggressively been promoting since the age of Reagan and Bush Daddy. The quasi-religious belief that the market could solve all problems, and that regulation was a hindrance to the natural order of things and a well-functioning economy and polity, had been proven disastrously wrong, deflating the most costly ideological fantasy in recent history.

In June 2002, the telecommunication giant WorldCom went bankrupt in one of the biggest corporate collapses in history. Like Enron and Cheney's Halliburton, WorldCom had engaged in accounting tricks to cover over losses such as by making capital gains expenditures appear as profits. But it attempted to hide over $3.8 billion of debt and expenses in an obvious fraud, and later it came out that the company's bookkeeping tricks covered over twice that amount of losses and debt. The result was a dumbfounding collapse of an economic giant (whose bankruptcy cost investors and pension plans uncounted billions) and one of the great corporate crimes in U.S. history.

The Reagan administration had begun aggressive deregulation of the telecommunications industry, pursued by Bush I and Clinton, but the most aggressive pro-market deregulator, Michael Powell, was installed by George W. Bush as FCC commissioner. An example of the nepotism that pervades the Bush administration, Michael is Colin Powell's son and he devoted his energies to waging war on all regulation of media and communication industries. Powell's reign followed and promoted an orgy of mergers in which the relatively small Mississippi-based WorldCom absorbed the telecommunication giant MCI as well as a bevy of smaller companies. Powell and his FCC never saw a merger that they didn't love and they unleashed the telecommunication industry to go on a merger binge, one that opened the door for corporate leaders to pocket billions in merger acquisitions, stock market games, and simple scamming and fraud.[33]

WorldCom's founder and flamboyant chief executive, Bernie Ebbers, was an apostle of deregulation and another big supporter of Bushonomics. Once again, the Andersen accounting firm had allowed the corporate chicanery, and when Ebbers and WorldCom executives were called before Congress to explain their doings, they pleaded the Fifth. In late August, two former WorldCom executives were indicted on securities fraud charges, and three others were said to be ready to plead guilty, producing the setting for another major corporate passion play and media spectacle.

Earlier in the year, the telecommunications powerhouse Global Crossing filed for bankruptcy. Quest Communications, another telecom giant, fell under investigation for its business practices in March, and in June its president was forced out. There were allegations that he had unloaded his stock, knowing that his company was going down, and thus was engaging in insider trading. Just before an announcement that the biotech firm's InClone highly touted cancer drug was not going to receive government approval, its president unloaded his stock and evidently informed his friend, media maven and family home guru Martha Stewart, who sold her stock, bringing in more accusations of insider stock trading to the well-known media personality and thus bringing to a popular audience the complex issue of insider trading.

As a result of the insider trading, executives of Enron, Global Crossing, InClone, and the other corporations that were going under were bagging billions in profits while their employees, pension plans, and stock investors were getting taken to the cleaners. Millions of people suffered from these corporate outrages and there were widespread calls in the public, media, and Congress for reform of the system that had allowed a wave of the major corporate crimes in U.S. history to take place. Most embarrassing for George W. Bush, there was also a return to allegations that he too had amassed his fortune from the sort of insider trading that was being widely publicized and decried. Moreover, there were revelations in July that Bush had received the same sort of loan to buy corporate stock that the Enron, WorldCom, and other corporate criminals were being excoriated for; that Bush's Harken Energy had set up dummy corporations to transform losses into profits like Enron and other companies under attack; and thus that Bush had engaged in exactly the same kind of shady and corrupt practices that were being assailed in the media.

Part of the problem was that financial companies and stockbrokers were deeply implicated in the corporate corruption. The deregulation of financial markets pushed by the Reagan and Bush administrations and by the Republican-dominated Congress during the Clinton administration had created a situation in which wheeling and dealing outside of the constraints of traditional practices was the norm. Consequently, many financial firms were involved in stock offerings and the promotion of the stock of shady corporations and themselves were involved in fraud and scandal. There were investigations of big firms like Merrill-Lynch, which pleaded guilty to and paid a $100 million fine for improper activities of its securities analysts. Further, investigations unfolded of Citigroup and its investment wing Salomon Smith Barney for allowing members of the most corrupt corporations to have insider tracks in buying new stock offerings, and there were also allegations that security analysts at other top firms urged customers to buy stocks that they had interests in.[34]

The Bush administration was forced to demand needed reform of corporate America because of the public outrage and outcry over the scandals, corruption, and economic mess, but it was clear that the Bush-Cheney gang were part of the problem and not the solution. Not surprisingly, after the collapse of major U.S. corporations, the stock market tanked in one of its biggest declines in history. It was becoming apparent that the Bush-Cheney clique comprised the worst economic managers in memory, turning record surpluses from the Clinton years turning into record deficits. On August 31, 2002, ABC News reported that in the past year over 1,800,000 jobs had vanished and that the stock market had lost over $7.7 trillion dollars since March 2001. People lost significant savings, pension plans were threatened, and many people were being financially devastated and losing their jobs. Foreign investors also were pulling their money out of the stock market and one analysis deemed Bush "Twice as bad as Hoover," claiming that "George W. Bush is shattering records for the worst first 18 months in office for a U.S. president as measured by the benchmark Standard & Poor's 500. In his first year-and-a-half in the White House, Bush presided over a 36.9 percent decline, almost twice the percentage drop of Herbert Hoover, the president who led the nation into the Depression."[35]

Obviously the economy was in significant decline with no relief in sight. When Bush gave a rare news conference on July 8, a day before he was to announce his corporate reform package to Wall Street, most of the questions referred to Bush's own alleged insider trading and business record with Harken Energy and he seemed flustered and unable to deal with the questions. When he gave his speech the next day calling for harsher penalties for corporate wrongdoers and mild reform, the stock market went down in a triple-digit plunge, with Bush's speech punctuated by split-screen television frames showing the stock market plunging ever further as Bush prattled on.

Bush and his team were trying to insist that the problems were caused by merely a few bad corrupt corporate executives, but it was evident that the problem was systemic and that Bush and Cheney had engaged in the same kind of practices under scrutiny for years. Dick Cheney was indeed a veritable poster boy for corporate corruption. As CEO of Halliburton, his company had manipulated profit and loss figures just like Enron; Cheney had carried out a disastrous merger with Dresser Industries, a company that the Bush family had long been involved with, and Halliburton's stock plummeted as a result of Cheney's fateful merger in part because Dresser was liable for millions in asbestos lawsuits. But Cheney had unloaded his stock and made over $36 million during his last year as CEO before becoming vice president, surely a paradigmatic example of corporate greed. Moreover, Cheney was being sued by Halliburton stockholders who had lost their savings due to the collapse of the company's stock because of Cheney's questionable and perhaps illegal policies. Ongoing investigations were likely to uncover embarrassing and perhaps criminal actions on Cheney's part. Indeed, the SEC was also probing the methods of accounting used during Cheney's tenure as Halliburton CEO. Cheney was in serious trouble and needed a war in Iraq and big-time victory to deflect attention away from his misdeeds.

The Bush administration needed scapegoats after the revelations of the astonishing corporate corruption that was undermining the U.S. economy and found one with the cable communications giant Adelphia. The company was reputedly in financial trouble and it was alleged that its conservative Christian owner, John Rigas, had simply looted the company for billions to enrich himself and his family. In a televised photo op to demonstrate that the Bush gang was going after the corporate crooks, Rigas and his sons were handcuffed and carried away to jail to be booked for corporate crime.

Needless to say, the Bushites also tried to blame the economic woes of the country on Bill Clinton! Former binge drinker George W. Bush explained the economic situation as a result of a "hangover" after the "economic binge of the 1990s." Stock advisor Bush, in claiming that the economy and stock market were fundamentally healthy, said that people could always invest in bonds, a comment that led to another triple-digit dip in stock prices, anger on Wall Street, and probably regrets that the corporate-financial elite had allowed such a dunce to become president.

There was widespread criticism that Bush was taking another month-long vacation at his ranch in Crawford, Texas, while the economy was going to hell and Terror War still threatened. Accordingly, Bush's handlers organized an "economic forum" at Waco, Texas, for August 13 that would demonstrate that the Bush administration was on top of managing the economy and cared about people's economic concerns. Of course, the Bushites didn't bother to invite any Democrats or major economists, so the event was basically a photo op with Bush, Cheney, some cabinet members and corporate executives, and a few handpicked "common people," all of whom affirmed that the economy was A-OK and Bushonomics was the way to go. Bush and Cheney darted from one session to another, trying to generate photos that they were concerned and making some classic Bushisms, with Bush telling one group: "I promise you I will listen to what has been said here, even though I wasn't here." To another group, the President bubbled: "I can assure you that, even though I won't be sitting through every single moment of the seminars, nor will the vice president, we will look at the summaries."

This less-than-reassuring photo opportunity was roundly derided and soon after, despite pleading by Tony Blair and others, Bush declined to appear at the Earth Summit in Johannesburg, South Africa, that was to take place early in September. Bush's refusal to go called attention to his contempt for the environment, and speakers at the summit from around the world, including many American delegates, roundly denounced Bush, whose administration had blocked all progressive global and national environment policy. Colin Powell made a brief appearance and was booed and jeered, with protestors exhibiting signs reading: "Shame on Bush!" and "Bush: People and Planet, not Big Business." Yet the Bush administration, following the dictates of the oil and energy companies they represented, managed to block calls for renewable energy sources at the summit, thanks to an unconscionable capitulation on behalf of European Union countries who went along with the oil bandits in the Bush regime.[36]

Obviously, when it came to both the economic and environmental crises, the Bush-Cheney gang was part of the problem and could offer no solutions because its key players, regulators, and officials were themselves involved in the corrupt economic and political system that was generating countless scandals. As noted in chapter 9, Bush's SEC Commissioner Harvey Pitt was a fanatic advocate of deregulating financial markets. Also, FCC Commissioner Michael Powell had pushed deregulation and allowed limitless telecommunications mergers to take place that were now imploding; Gale Norton, Bush's secretary of the interior, had long been a tool of corporate anti-environment forces; and Enron, Arthur Andersen, and other major corporations under investigation had long been close to Bush and Cheney.

Interestingly, like S&L crook Charles Keating, the current crop of corporate villains, such as Ken Lay, Bernie Ebbers, John Rigas, and others under indictment, had presented themselves as conservative Christian businessmen. Like Bush, they represented a strange amalgam of conservative Christianity, right-wing market ideology, and a propensity to play fast and loose with the rules of the game to enrich themselves. A stench of hypocrisy thus permeated the whole affair, including the reaction of Congress. Politicians who had passed the deregulatory policies that had made the corruption and crisis possible, and had taken large financial contributions from the corporations now going down, were making sanctimonious noises about the need for reform, accountability, and long jail terms for the wrongdoers.

As the summer of 2002 turned into fall, economic figures got worse and worse. The nonpartisan Congressional Budget Office (CBO) revealed that the deficit for fiscal year 2002 will force the government to borrow $157 billion, with worse deficits to come in the years ahead, in large part due to Bush's tax cuts benefiting the superrich. CBO Director Dan L. Crippen described as "astounding" the reversal in predictions that the government would run a surplus from the years 2003–2012 to predictions that there would be growing deficits for the foreseeable future thanks to the plunge in tax receipts because of the Bush giveaway and a worsening economy. The analysis revealed once again the fallacious figures that the Bush economic team based their policies on and revealed a fiscal crisis of the state so immense that it was difficult to grasp.[37]

Moreover, a report on "The State of Working America 2002–2003" documented that unemployment as of mid-2002 was two percentage points above its level two years before, with "hidden unemployment," scant job growth, a slowing of wage growth, and increasing divisions between rich and poor.[38] The report detailed labor markets stalling with no job growth, retirement lurching out of reach for many, benefits running out for unemployed workers, and rising economic insecurity. A *New York Times* story on Labor Day headlined that "Workers Are Angry and Fearful" due to worrying about "fast-rising health care costs, slower wage growth and fears about job security." Bushonomics was a disaster for working people and all the gains and prosperity of the Clinton years, now appearing as an economic Golden Age, were dissipating and disappearing for many.

As the economic situation worsened, the Bush gang turned up the heat with calls for war on Iraq, obviously needing a big military victory to deflect attention from their political and economic failings and the potentially regime-changing scandals that Bush and Cheney had been involved in. As the warmongers in the Bush administration accelerated their war talk, there was a sustained array of attacks on the Bush war plans. When Cheney had traveled through the Middle East in March, he had found that every Arab regime had vehemently opposed the U.S. plan for a war against Iraq. As the summer progressed, almost every important U.S. ally came out against the proposed U.S. invasion of Iraq, including countries like Canada and Germany that usually went along with all U.S. military interventions. There was a fierce debate in Britain over whether Tony Blair should support Bush's adventure and an indication that Blair might lose support in his own party and possibly the next election if he went along with Bush.

Moreover, major Republican leaders and generals warned about adverse consequences of an Iraq adventure that could destabilize the Middle East, create havoc in Iraq, turn significant portions of the world militantly against the U.S., disrupt oil supplies, interfere with the war on terrorism, and drive down an already tottering economy. Questions were raised concerning how the Bush administration could pay for a war in Iraq and the Terror War at the same time and whether the U.S. military could take on so many adventures. There were worries that a post-Saddam regime in Iraq might bring chaos and involve the U.S. in a hazardous and violent period of stabilization and reconstruction that could go catastrophically wrong.

Significant figures from Bush Senior's administration, including his National Security Advisor Brent Scowcroft, Secretary of State James Baker, and Lawrence Eagleburger, made strong arguments that it would be a disaster for the U.S. to go it alone in Iraq and that the U.S. would be isolated and endangered without significant support from allies and the UN. The head of the U.S. NATO force in the Kosovo war, General Wesley Clarke, wrote a long piece on the follies of the Bush administration Iraq plan; General Norman Schwarzkopf, leader of U.S. forces in the Gulf War, came out against an Iraq invasion; and General Anthony Zinni, who had recently served as Bush's top envoy to the Middle East, warned against war with Iraq, "saying it would stretch U.S. forces too thin and make unwanted enemies in the volatile region." Making a pointed attack against Bush administration officials like Dick Cheney and Paul Wolfowitz, who were lusting for war but had never served in the military, Zinni remarked: "It's pretty interesting that all the generals see it the same way, and all the others who have never fired a shot and are hot to go to war see it another way."[39]

Dick Cheney, however, continued to beat the war drums, making bellicose and saber-rattling speeches for war against Iraq in late August. Cheney said that UN weapons inspectors "would provide no assurance whatsoever" of Iraqi compliance with UN disarmament resolutions and would instead increase the danger by providing "false comfort." Cheney was, in effect, ruling out any political mediation of the Iraq situation at a time when global forces were furiously attempting to get UN weapons inspectors back in Iraq to get a vigorous weapons inspection process underway. Yet in a September 1 interview with the BBC, Colin Powell stated that UN weapon inspectors should be sent back to Iraq as a "first step" to deal with the threats posed by the regime of Saddam Hussein. Commentators noted that the White House had not cleared Cheney's speech and that there was evident "disarray" in the Bush administration over Iraq policy.[40]

At the same time that Cheney called for war against Iraq, reports circulated on the Internet how when Cheney was CEO at Halliburton, his corporation did more business with Iraq than any other U.S. company. A *Washington Post* story was recirculating that Halliburton had signed contracts under Cheney's leadership worth $73 million through two subsidiaries that sold Iraq oil production equipment and spare parts when there were restrictions against U.S. corporations doing business with Iraq.[41] Cheney denied knowledge of these ventures, but an investigation into his Halliburton stewardship could well reveal that he had knowledge about his company's dealings with Iraq (and if he didn't have knowledge, what kind of a CEO was he?). Indeed, the current Halliburton CEO has stated that Cheney "unquestionably" knew about the Iraq dealings, implying that the vice president is simply a liar. Inquiries into Halliburton under Cheney could also unfold how the company set up dummy companies, much like Enron, to cover business losses and to provide fake profits and other questionable activities that had transpired during Cheney's years as CEO. Cheney was being sued on behalf of stockholders for the collapse of the company's stock value under his leadership, and investigation of this explosive issue could put Cheney in the same category and cell as Ken Lay.

Cheney desperately needed a war against Iraq to deflect attention from his misdeeds. When Tony Blair arrived in the U.S. for a war summit on Iraq on the weekend of September 8, the Bush administration released photos of what was presented as new evidence of an Iraqi nuclear facility. Bush waved the picture and a 1998 report that Iraq was six months away from nuclear bomb capacity at the media, as Blair stood beside him, with Bush proclaiming that "I don't know what more evidence you need" [to bomb Iraq]. But as ABC, NBC, and the *Washington Post* quickly reported,[42] these pictures and reports were fraudulent evidence, showing that the Bush-Cheney gang will resort to lies and deception to legitimate their Iraq adventure. Needless to say, Fox TV played these stories all day to beat the war drums. It remains to be seen if this false evidence discredits Bush, if it alienates Tony Blair from joining in Bush's Iraq adventure (there were reports that he was deeply embarrassed to buy into the "new evidence" scam), or if it becomes an issue that the Bushite Jihad Warriors will be confronted with at all, or if, like other of their lies and misdeeds, it will just pass away in silence.

Meanwhile, on September 8, Cheney and the other top warmongers of the Bush administration were all over the Sunday talk shows making their case for war against Iraq. Cheney repeated on *Meet the Press* all of the well-known crimes of Saddam Hussein, insinuated long-discredited ties between Iraq and Al Qaeda, and even tried to pin the anthrax attacks on Iraq, although all evidence pointed to U.S. weapons-grade facilities. Cheney was going to have a war against Iraq no matter what the price, and it appeared that George W. Bush was equally gung-ho and set on war.

As campaigning for the fall 2002 midterm elections in the U.S. heated up and polls indicated growing doubts concerning public support for an Iraq war, the Bush administration suddenly turned to the UN to get support and forced a resolution through Congress that provided official congressional support for military action against Iraq if they did not cooperate with arms inspectors. This helped the Republicans win a surprising number of congressional seats and enough Senate seats to take back control of Congress in the November election. Shortly thereafter, the UN passed a resolution favorable to the Bush administration and the Bush gang prepared for war with Iraq as Saddam Hussein and his clique began a cat-and-mouse game with the UN and the U.S. with high-stakes consequences.

THE BUSH CATASTROPHE

Thus, as I bring my narrative to a close at the end of 2002, the state of the union is not a good one. The economy is startlingly worse than when Bush became president, in one of the most astounding economic reversals in history. In the sphere of foreign policy, the Bush administration has squandered the good will and sympathy toward the U.S. after September 11 and is alienating allies through his "axis of evil" rhetoric, his new doctrine of preemptive strikes, and his threatened war against Iraq and whoever else his administration perceives as an enemy. The danger of this policy is that it could leave the U.S. alone to fight terrorism: a rogue nation against a network of fanatic Islamic scoundrels. Bush's preemptive strike doctrine could also inspire other countries to strike out against their enemies whenever there were perceived dangers or a good opportunity to engage in military action. Bush's doctrine was highly barbaric, taking the global community to a Darwinist battleground where decades of international law and military prudence were put aside in perhaps the most dangerous foreign policy preemptive strike doctrine that had ever appeared in U.S. history. Bush's policy promised an era of endless Terror War in which a new militarism could generate a cycle of unending violence and retribution such as was evident in the Israel and Palestine conflict.

Moreover, the Bush administration and Pentagon war against terrorism had been at best a partial success, with chaos accelerating in Afghanistan. Unrest in the country finally forced the Bush administration in late August to recognize that international security forces are needed throughout Afghanistan, a demand long made by the Afghans and rational observers. Moreover, a September 3 *New York Times* article by James Risen and Eric Schmitt, "Commanders Want Elite Units Freed from [Al] Qaeda Hunt," suggests the failure of U.S.-Afghan policy, which had spent the year in Afghanistan using U.S. military forces to chase bin Laden and Al Qaeda without significant results. Bombings in Kabul and shooting at U.S. and international forces in Afghanistan heated up in September, and it was clear that the U.S. was in for a long and messy guerilla war in the region.

On September 3, ABC News released a report that an Al Qaeda cemetery outside of Kandahar was said to hold mystical powers and that a steady stream of believers were flocking to the site, licking the salt by the graves, and praying. Obviously, the U.S. did not win the hearts or minds of the Afghan people and could expect opposition to attempts at imperialist intervention and occupation in other parts of the world as well, such as Iraq. A *Salon* report by Phillip Robertson from Asadabad (September 6, 2002), in southeast Afghanistan near the Pakistan border reveals why U.S. troops are not perceived in a friendly fashion:

> For the past six months, American soldiers have been conducting house-to-house searches and arrests in a bid to root out Taliban and al-Qaida sympathizers, although critics say that they are being fed bad information by members of rival tribes seeking to gain advantage. In keeping with security practices, the searches are not announced ahead of time, and the permission of the owner is never asked. This, too, grates on the villagers. They are ethnic Pashtuns, and they consider a forced entry to a family's house as a grievous dishonor, one typically corrected in the tribal system by shedding blood. An Afghan family house has two areas, one reserved for guests and another reserved for women and children. According to *pashtunwali*, the ancient and formal system of honor, hospitality and revenge, no one outside the family may enter the inner part of the house without permission. Breaking this taboo often results in the beginning of a blood feud that can last for generations.
>
> Although most people here understand the nature of the American mission, they all voice concern that the heavy-handed tactics are already backfiring, creating sympathy for the same people they are trying to apprehend.

On September 4, there was a Reuters report that the Afghans were releasing Pakistani Taliban fighters to return to Pakistan, with many saying that they were preparing to fight the United States on another day. On September 5, a car bomb in Kabul killed at least fifteen and there was an assassination attempt on President Hamid Karzai. And a detailed New York Times article by James Risen and Dexter Filkins, "Al Qaeda Fighters Are Said to Return to Afghanistan" (September 10, 2002), reported that of the thousands of Al Qaeda and Taliban fighters who fled Afghanistan, many are returning to Afghanistan in small groups, whereas others have scattered in a "terrorist diaspora" that has counter-terrorism officials deeply concerned. Throughout fall 2002, remnants of Al Qaeda and Taliban forces continued to attack U.S. and other allied forces and the Afghan government of Hamid Karzai. Members of Karzai's administration were assassinated, and Karzai himself barely escaped a September 6 attempt to shoot him. There were reports that the Taliban was planning a big comeback, along with continued guerilla war attacks on U.S. and other Western troops. Moreover, General Richard Myers admitted in after-dinner comments at the Brookings Institution on November 4 that the U.S. was losing "momentum" in the Afghan war.[43]

The respected defense analyst Stratfor issued an August 28 report, noting the stories of Al Qaeda and Taliban regrouping for a major offensive and claiming that the U.S. casualties in Afghanistan are much higher than U.S. officials admit. As cited by Bob Weinberg in his *World War 3 Report*, no. 49 (September 1, 2002), Stratfor asserts:

"Sources in the Afghan government said guerrillas, believed to be Pushtun Taliban members, attacked US troops in the Zawar region of Paktia province on the night of Aug. 4, with several US troops and several attackers allegedly killed. The Pentagon report of the same incident confirmed that a patrol came under heavy fire at that time in Paktia province but said that only two attackers were killed. Similarly, Afghan government sources reported that a rocket attack on a US air base at Jalalabad airport Aug. 28 resulted in casualties among US and allied Afghan troops. However, the US military reported there were no casualties. An Afghan government source also reported that more than 110 US troops have gone missing in Afghanistan since October, the majority presumed dead. And a US military source told STRATFOR that US troops are suffering frequent casualties including fatalities that are going largely unreported in the press. STRATFOR's military sources in countries around Afghanistan have repeated similar accounts for some time: that there is more to many of the reported incidents, and still more clashes are not being reported at all. Sources in Russian and Indian intelligence separately estimate the US military has suffered between 300 and 400 killed in Afghanistan, with an unknown number wounded. The Pentagon says substantially fewer than 100 have been killed. Although foreign estimates may be inflated, there is no way to independently confirm US claims either."

[Weinberg writes:] Reached for comment by WW3 REPORT, Cmdr. Frank Merriman of CentCom responded via e-mail, categorically denying STRATFOR's claims: "We have recorded 19 US soldiers who have died from combat wounds and 22 who have died from non-hostile causes. (One is classified as Died from Wounds Received in Action and is not listed as a KIA.) Total: 41 US dead. We have about 100 wounded in action and about 90 injured and classified as non-hostile casualties. Total casualties (all categories): about 230. Also, we have no missing soldiers (0)." Cmdr. Merriman accused STRATFOR of unprofessionalism. "Using cryptic, unnamed (and therefore unspecific) sources makes it easy to allege whatever information one wants to project," he said. "Why not name names?"

Moreover, the situation in Afghanistan was becoming increasingly chaotic as warlords continued to battle, and there were complaints that the U.S. had excessively strengthened local lords and their militia, making it difficult for the central government to control the country. Bob Woodward claimed in *Bush at War* (2002) that the Taliban collapse was precipitated by the U.S.'s purchase of warlord allegiance. But in retrospect, the arms and money lavished on the warlords by the U.S. and continued U.S. work with such forces undermined the central government and blocked the sort of humanitarian reconstruction of the country desired by the civilized world and many of the Afghan people.

During fall 2002 there was also a new cycle of terrorist attacks with the shooting of U.S. troops in Kuwait, the assassination of a U.S. diplomat in Jordan, and a series of bombings and attacks against Westerners in Bali, the Philippines, Yemen, and elsewhere. Moreover, an audiotape of what appeared to be the voice of Osama bin Laden was played on Al Jazeera on November 12 in praise of the Bali, Kuwaiti, and other attacks. The audiotape contained a chilling call to his followers to continue the Jihad, warning the West: "As you kill, you will be killed, and as you bomb, you will be bombed." Bush was obviously playing bin Laden's Jihad game, enabling him to recruit new troops, and the cycle of violence threatened to be a deadly one.

In retrospect, it is clear that the Bush/Pentagon strategy in Afghanistan failed in significant ways and that U.S. ground forces should have been used against the Taliban and Al Qaeda in Tora Bora and Kandahar to capture or eliminate key radical Islamic forces. Relying primarily on U.S. air power and Afghan proxy forces was largely a mistake, and the use of largely U.S. forces to pursue bin Laden, Omar, and the Al Qaeda and Taliban forces after the fall of the Taliban had also failed. To defeat global terrorism, global forces and a multilateralist coalition are necessary, and the Bush administration unilateralist strategy has not succeeded. There should have been global forces at work in Afghanistan and more emphasis on cultivating a multilateralist antiterrorism network that would be more coordinated and effective in using international police, judicial, financial, and military institutions to shut down the Al Qaeda network. Instead, the U.S. unilateralist and militarist approach to terrorism has isolated the U.S. and the failed military strategy of bombing and relying on Afghan proxies to fight on the ground allowed key Al Qaeda and Taliban forces to escape. Hence, the dispersal of Al Qaeda forces will increase the possibility of terror attacks for years to come, while aggressive Bush administration unilateralism and militarism will augment the possibility that the U.S. will become the target of terrorist attacks in the future.

And so I accuse George W. Bush of flawed national security policies that helped create the conditions for the September 11 terror attacks; of carrying out a predominantly unilateralist and militarist response to the September 11 attacks; and of cobbling together an aggressive foreign policy that has squandered goodwill toward the U.S., created enemies, and that is increasingly isolating the U.S. from the rest of the world. The Bush administration has systematically undermined worldwide institutions, international law, human rights, and global movements toward arms control, the environment, democracy, and social justice. His announced policy of using nuclear weapons and preemptive strikes to take out enemies is probably the most reckless and destabilizing foreign policy position since Hitler and the Nazis, and creates the dangers of an era of New Militarism and endless Terror War.

I also accuse George W. Bush of seriously harming the U.S. economy and undermining the global one with his reckless and failed economic and political policies. Bushonomics has systematically enriched his contributors and corporate allies while the Bush administration has squandered the economic surpluses of the Clinton years and produced astounding deficits and deficit forecasts that will weaken the American economy for years to come. The stock market has plunged more under Bush in his first eighteen months than ever before in U.S. modern history, unemployment is rapidly increasing, and investor confidence throughout the world is questioning Bushonomics and pulling investment money out of the U.S. economy. Furthermore, Bush has no real plan to deal either with the corporate corruption, which was enabled by his policies, or economic crisis.

There has never been a U.S. president in modern history less concerned with the environment than George W. Bush, whose administration is unapologetically anti-environment and pro-business. The Bush administration has refused to ratify the Kyoto Treaty, has been dismissive of reports documenting global warming, has allowed industry to run roughshod over existing environmental accords, and continues to pursue aggressive militarist policies that constitute a sustained war on the environment. During an era in which global institutions, governments, groups, and individuals throughout the world are alarmed about environmental devastation, the Bush administration has systematically taken anti-environment and pro-business positions, thus weakening environmental protection and strengthening the very corporate forces and market ideology that have been accused of placing the environment in grave jeopardy. This was evidenced in fall 2002 at the Johannesburg Earth Summit, which Bush declined to visit, but his administration managed to block every attempt at providing non-market-based reforms and additional moneys for the world's poor, for species preservation, and for other urgent issues. The Bush delegation also organized a coalition to prevent renewable energy sources from being recognized as a major political exigency, and managed to get the Summit Congress to add the words "if possible" to many of the already existing agreements that were achieved at the Rio Earth Summit in 1992, thereby making them unenforceable and meaningless for the future.

Bush's administration has carried out the most sustained attack on democracy in recent U.S. history, establishing Orwellian programs like the USA Patriot Act, Operation TIPS, and a repressive Homeland Security agenda. These programs involve unleashing the government to wiretap and spy on suspects, to enlist ordinary citizens in the spy program, to arrest and hold people indefinitely without charges, to try suspected terrorists in secret military courts, to round up suspected terrorists or protestors in government camps, and to erect the foundation of a police state. The Bush gang has also pursued policies of unparalleled secrecy and has done everything possible to weaken the Freedom of Information Act, to hold back government information from public scrutiny, and to seal up presidential archives so that researchers will not be able to track what the government has been up to during the Reagan and Bush eras. Never before has U.S. democracy been under such systematic assault, and never before have a presidency and administration had such contempt for democracy. Thus, the Bush legacy portends perennial Terror War in foreign policy and unparalleled corruption, mendacity, and assaults on democracy as domestic policy.

I accuse Dick Cheney of pursuing a right-wing extremist agenda from his early days in the Ford White House through his years in Congress and his service in two Bush administrations. Cheney had one of the most right-wing records in Congress, and it is disgraceful and dangerous that this thoroughly reactionary and disgraced individual could assume so much power. As CEO of Halliburton, Cheney was an exemplar of the corrupt corporate executive, cutting deals with Iraq that he later denied, setting up dummy branches to his corporation to cover losses and create false profits, and thus engaging in systematically corrupt bookkeeping. Ironically and appropriately, Cheney spoke in a promotion video for the Arthur Andersen firm that did the bookkeeping, carried out a merger with Dresser Industries that almost bankrupted Halliburton, and then, as Vice President, Cheney bolstered it with Terror War–related contracts to keep the failing company afloat.

I accuse Cheney of pursuing a virulent militarist policy while helping to build up a military-police state that will produce an era of war and a frightening future. Indeed, no one will be safe from terror as long as Cheney is in office. This appalling right-wing extremist and militarist is driving the world toward a potentially catastrophic war in Iraq that could destabilize the region for years to come. If Cheney's recent corporate past were exposed, as well as his failure as Bush's head of a task force on terrorism pre–September 11, his willingness to let energy firms like Enron write the administration's energy policy, and his other granting of government favors to his own previous firm and others that supported the Bush administration, Cheney's career in government would likely come to an end. Consequently, Cheney is fanatically pushing the country to war with Iraq and potential catastrophe to cover his butt and fulfill his ideological obsessions. Until there is a regime change in the U.S. that involves Cheney's retirement and many days in court, neither democracy nor life on earth will be safe from destruction.

I accuse Donald Rumsfeld of pursuing a lunatic fantasy of a National Missile Defense program and decentering the dangers of terrorism in the pre–September 11 era that helped make possible terrorist attacks on the U.S. Early on in the Bush administration, Rumsfeld ordered ships off Afghanistan, which were armed with missiles ready to hit bin Laden and which Clinton had ordered to track bin Laden, to stand down, and Rumsfeld took antiterrorist items out of his pre–September 11 military budget. In the Afghan Terror War, I accuse Rumsfeld of carrying out an intervention that was flawed in concept and poorly executed. His use of the same bombing strategy and reliance on air power deployed in Kosovo and the Gulf War and failure to put significant U.S. troops on the ground enabled bin Laden and Al

Qaeda leadership and Mullah Omar and Taliban leadership to escape, dispersing key terrorist cadres to strike at the U.S. in the future.

Regarding the Afghan war, I accuse Rumsfeld of needlessly and heedlessly targeting civilian facilities and villages, using cluster bombs that continue to maim and kill innocents, and arrogantly and brutally denying or brushing aside concerns about civilian casualties. I also accuse Rumsfeld of systematically lying, bullying the press and allies, and providing a belligerent face of American military power. Although Rumsfeld has obtained rock star status in the U.S. from his televised military briefings, he is perceived globally by many as the Ugly American and Dr. Strangelove. He is seen by many as the stereotype of the Ugly American—aggressive, arrogant, hypocritical, and imperialist. Upon learning of the September 11 terror attacks, Rumsfeld reacted in a Strangelovian fashion: According to notes of Rumsfeld's response that were leaked to CBS News (September 4, 2002), the secretary of defense barked out, "Best info fast. Judge whether good enough hit S.H. [Saddam Hussein] at same time. Not only UBL [Osama bin Laden]. Go massive. Sweep it all up. Things related and not." Such an apocalyptically aggressive response marks Rumsfeld as a dangerous militarist fanatically pushing the U.S. toward military intervention in Iraq and throughout the world, and the global village will not be safe until he is out of office.

I accuse U.S. Attorney General John Ashcroft of systematically undermining the U.S. system of democracy and setting up the structure for a totalitarian military and police state. Ashcroft has long been a hard-right extremist, and George W. Bush's selection of this unqualified and scary creature as attorney general shows Bush's contempt for justice and democracy. Ashcroft has carried out one assault after another on basic civil liberties and the U.S. constitutional order and will long reign in the Orwellian Hall of Shame as one of the worst attorneys generals in U.S. history. In a stern rebuke of the Bush-Ashcroft policies, a federal appeals court said that the Bush administration's policies of secret military courts were "undemocratic" and "in complete opposition to the society envisioned by the Framers of our Constitution."[44] And although Ashcroft was eager to push through measures that would radically undermine the basic civil liberties and rights of American citizens, he refused to modify gun laws to make it more difficult for terrorists to purchase guns and to allow criminal authorities to have access to gun owner databases, thus robbing the country of important weapons against terrorism. Already there have been many calls for his resignation, and while he remains in office there are serious reasons to fear for the future of U.S. democracy.

I accuse Condoleezza Rice of failing miserably in her role as national security advisor. A rabid unilateralist and militarist who in the 2000 election stated repeatedly that she was against "nation-building" and all humanitarian interventions, Rice also floated the term "regime change" to signal the possibility of military intervention in Iraq. Upon assuming office, Rice was briefed by Clinton National Security Advisor Sandy Berger of the dangers of terrorism and in particular the Osama bin Laden network. Berger gave Rice a well-developed plan to deal with terrorism, but Rice tabled it and acquiesced to Bush administration cuts of funds to fight terrorism in the FBI, Justice Department, Pentagon, and elsewhere. Memos of her national security priorities failed to mention terrorism. Reportedly, eight months into her office and a couple of days before the September 11 attacks, Rice provided Bush administration national security groups with a plan to fight bin Laden and terrorism that analysts deemed pretty much the same as the Clinton one. But it was way too late and the September 11 attacks revealed the consequences of Rice and the Bush administration failing to take terrorism seriously enough. Thus, Rice failed to protect national security, consequently did not carry out the primary responsibility of her office, and should therefore resign in disgrace.

In short, I accuse the Bush administration of failing the country on the issues of national security, foreign policy, the economy, and domestic policy, while failing to preserve the system of democracy. The Bush legacy now appears to be virulent unilateralism in foreign policy that greatly undermines national security while isolating the U.S. as a rogue state and creating new enemies; a failed economic policy that enriched its supporters and corporate allies while turning economic surpluses into deficits, creating massive unemployment, and wrecking the stock market; and a sustained policy of attacks on democracy, civil liberties, justice, and the U.S. constitutional system of checks and balances.

I have argued throughout this book concerning the dangers of unilateralism and the need for a multilateral approach to global problems. As we have seen, the Bush administration is aggressively unilateralist and there is little hope that they will reform their ways. It is more likely that as economic conditions worsen, as the scandals in the corporate sector and Bush administration expand, and as media scrutiny and public anger increase with the near-catastrophic situation that the Bush administration has produced, there will be calls for its investigation and the likelihood of a resounding defeat in the 2004 election. There may also be court time for many of the administration's major players, including possibly Bush and Cheney. Or, there may be a series of devastating wars in which Orwell's society in *1984* will appear as a utopia and life in the Bush era may be increasingly nasty, brutish, and short.

In the meantime, citizens have the responsibility to become informed about the malfeasance of the Bush administration and their corporate allies and to seek political and philosophical alternatives. Grand Theft 2000 and the disasters of Bushonomics, unilateralism, and military aggression suggest that profound changes need to be carried through in the U.S. economic, political, and cultural system. It is unlikely that mainstream political parties and the media will be overly active and committed to bringing about these changes or exposing and addressing the problems. It is therefore up to engaged individuals, public intellectuals, and oppositional social movements to take on the Bush administration and the problems of a system that would allow the Bush-Cheney gang to seize power and wield it in ways that enrich and empower their favored groups at the expense of everyone else. I conclude, therefore, with some reflections on democracy and social movements, sketching out parameters of a progressive politics for the new millennium.

Conclusion: For Democracy and against Terrorism and Militarism

I n conclusion, I want to argue that in light of the Bush administration attacks on democracy and civil liberties in the United States and elsewhere in the name of a war against terrorism, there should be a strong reaffirmation of the basic values and institutions of democracy, especially as they come under attack by regimes like the Bush administration. Furthermore, there needs to be a global movement *against* terrorism, militarism, and social injustice and *for* democracy, peace, environmentalism, human rights, and social justice. Rather than curtailing democracy in the naming of fighting terrorism, we need to strengthen democracy in the name of its survival (and, indeed, the survival of the planet) against the forces of violence and destruction. Rather than absolve the Bush administration's domestic and foreign policy from criticism in the name of patriotism and national unity, as the administration's supporters demand, we need more than ever a critical dialogue on how to defeat terrorism and how to strengthen democracy at home and throughout the world.

Democracy is, in part, a dialogue that requires dissent and debate as well as consensus. Those who believe in democracy should oppose all attempts to curtail democratic rights, liberties, and a free and open public sphere. Democracy also involves the cultivation of oppositional public spheres and, as in the 1960s on a global scale, there should be a resurrection of the local, national, and global movements for social transformation that emerged as a reaction to war and injustice in the earlier era. This is not to call for a return to the 1960s, but for the rebirth of a global movement for peace and justice that builds on the lessons of the past as it engages the realities of the present and future.

In addition to reaffirming democracy, we should be against terrorism and militarism. This is not to argue for a utopic pacifism, but to argue against militarism in the sense that military action is currently offered as the privileged solution to the problem of terrorism, is significantly expanded, as in the Bush administration's massive military buildup, and is promoted unilaterally. Thus, although I hold that military action against terrorism is legitimate, I oppose U.S. unilateralist militarism outside of the bounds of recognized military conventions and law, and favor more multilateral action in the context of global law and coalitions.

There is little doubt that the bin Laden and Al Qaeda terrorists are highly fanatical and zealous in their ideology and actions, of a sort hard to comprehend by Western categories. In their drive for an apocalyptic Jihad, they believe that their goals will be furthered by creating chaos, especially war between radical Islam and the West. Obviously, dialogue is not possible with such groups, but it is equally certain that an overreactive military response that causes a large number of innocent civilian deaths in Muslim countries could trigger precisely such an apocalyptic explosion of violence as was dreamed of by the fanatic terrorists. It would seem that such a retaliatory response was desired by the bin Laden group that carried out the terrorist attacks on the U.S. Thus, to continue to attack Arab and Islamic countries could be to fall into the bin Laden gang's trap and play their game—with highly dangerous consequences.

Furthermore, we need to reflect on the global economic, social, environmental, and other consequences of promoting militarism and an era of warfare against terrorism, other states, or groups that the government of the moment denominates as "enemies." Evoking and fighting an "axis of evil" called for by the Bush administration is highly dangerous, irrational, and potentially apocalyptic. It is not clear whether the global economy can survive constant disruption through warfare, nor can the environment stand constant bombardment and warfare when ecological survival is already threatened by unrestrained capitalist development (see Kovel 2002 and Wilson 2002). To carry out continued military intervention, whether against an "axis of evil" or any country that is said to support terrorism by the Bush administration, risks apocalypse of the most frightening kind. The large-scale bombing of Iraq, Iran, or any Arab countries could trigger an upheaval in Pakistan or war between Pakistan and India. It could produce considerable turmoil in Saudi Arabia and other Moslem countries. It could also help produce a dangerous escalation of the Israeli-Palestinian conflict, already at a state of white-hot intensity, whose expansion could engulf the Middle East in flames.

Thus, although it is reasonable to deem international terrorism a deadly threat on a global scale and to take resolute action against terrorism, what is required is an intelligent, multifaceted, and multilateral response. This would require a diplomatic consensus that a global campaign against terrorism is necessary that requires the criminalization and arrest of members of terrorist networks; the regulation of financial institutions that allow funds to flow to terrorists; the implementation of national security measures to protect citizens against terrorism; and a worldwide campaign against terrorist networks, which sets international, national, and local institutions against the terrorist threat. Some of these measures have already begun, and the conditions are present to develop an effective and resolute global campaign against terrorism.

There is a danger, however, that excessive unilateral American military action would split a potential coalition, creating uncontrollable chaos that could destroy the global economy and create an era of apocalyptic war and misery such as Orwell evoked in *1984*. We are living in a very dangerous period and must be extremely careful and responsible in appraising responses to the events of September 11 and other terrorist attacks that are bound to happen. This will require the mobilization of publics on a local, national, and global level to oppose both terrorism and militarism and to seek productive multilateral, global solutions to the social problems that generate terrorism.

Consequently, although I support a global campaign against terrorism, I believe that we cannot depend on war or large-scale military action to solve the problem of global terrorism. Terrorists should be criminalized, and international and national institutions should go after terrorist networks and those who support them with the appropriate legal, financial, judicial, and political instruments. Before and during Bush administration military intervention in Afghanistan, an intelligent multilateral campaign was underway that had arrested many participants and supporters of the bin Laden and other terror networks, that had alerted publics throughout the world to the dangers of terrorism, and that had created the conditions of possibility for a global campaign against terror. But we need global movements and institutions to oppose purely militarist attacks on terrorism and to counter attempts to suppress democracy in the name of the war against terrorism.

I also suggest that another lesson of September 11 is that terrorism is a highly dangerous and volatile force in the contemporary world and that one should oppose movements that systematically or willfully target civilians or innocents. There was a time when it was argued that one person's "terrorism" was another person's "national liberation movement" or "freedom fight," and that the term was an ideological concept not to be used by politically and theoretically correct discourse—a position that Reuters purportedly continues to follow. The term "terrorism" is thus highly contextual and, in terms of contemporary epistemological debates, I oppose absolutism and universalism and am for providing a contextual and historical account of terms like terrorism.

There were times in history when terrorism was an arguably defensible tactic used by those engaged in struggles against fascism, such as in World War II, or in national liberation struggles such as in the movements against oppressive European and later U.S. empire and colonialism. In the current situation, however, when terrorism is a clear and present danger to innocent civilians throughout the world, it seems unacceptable to advocate, carry out, or defend terrorism against civilian populations because of the lethality of modern weapons, the immorality of indiscriminate crime, and the explosiveness of the present situation when terror on one side could unleash genocidal, even species-cidal, terror as a retaliatory response.

It is therefore time for neither terrorism nor reckless unilateral military intervention, but for a global campaign against terrorism that deploys all legal, political, and morally defensible means to tear down the network of terrorists responsible for the September 11 events. It is equally important to develop a progressive global movement that is for democracy, the environment, human rights, social justice, and other positive values. Such a global response to terrorism would put terrorist groups on warning that their activity will be strongly opposed and that terrorism will be construed as a moral and political malevolence not to be accepted or defended. But a progressive global campaign should also not accept militarism, the erection of a police-military state, and the undermining of democracy in the name of fighting terrorism.

Thus, although I support developing a global campaign against terrorism, especially the Al Qaeda network, which could include military action under UN or other global auspices, I do not trust U.S. unilateral military action because of U.S. failures in the region and its sustained history of supporting highly reactionary social forces. Indeed, one of the stakes of the current crisis, and of globalization itself, is whether the U.S. empire will come to dominate the world or whether globalization will constitute a more democratic, cosmopolitan, pluralistic, and just world without domination by hegemonic states or corporations. Now more than ever, global institutions and movements are needed to deal with global problems, and those who see positive potential in globalization should renounce all national solutions to the problem of terrorism and seek global ones. Consequently, whereas politicians like Bill Clinton and Colin Powell have deemed terrorism "the dark side of globalization," it can also be seen as an unacceptable response to misguided and destructive imperial national policies that must be transformed if a world without terror is possible.

A progressive oppositional movement for the new millennium must rethink its nature, agenda, and goals. There may well be a "clash of civilizations" occurring today between the globalizing forces of transnational capital and resistance to global capitalism by heterogeneous configurations of individuals, groups, and social movements. But in its first stages, the movement against capitalist globalization tended to be defined more by what it was against than what it was for, hence the common term "antiglobalization movement." An emergent global social movement for the new millennium should therefore define itself by what it is for as well as against. In the wake of September 11, I am suggesting that local, national, and global democratic movements should be for democracy, peace, environmentalism, and social justice and against war, militarism, and terrorism, as well as the multiplicity of injustices that social movements are currently fighting. Now, more than ever, we are living in a global world and need new global movements and politics to address global problems and achieve multilateral solutions.

Notes

ACKNOWLEDGMENTS

1. See Douglas Kellner, "September 11, Terrorism, and Blowback," *Cultural Studies<>* *Critical Methodologies* 2, no. 2 (2002): 27–39; Douglas Kellner, "September 11, the Media, and War Fever," *Television and New Media* 3, no. 2 (May 2002): 143–151; Douglas Kellner, "'The Axis of Evil,' Operation Infinite War, and Bush's Attack on Democracy," *Cultural Studies<>Critical Methodologies* 2, no. 3 (August 2002): 343–347; Douglas Kellner, "11.September, Gesellschaftstheorie und demokratische Politik," *Sozialwissenschaftliche Literatur Rundschau* 44 (January 2002): 87–96; and Douglas Kellner, "September 11, Social Theory and Democratic Politics," *Theory, Culture, and Society* 19, no. 4 (2002): 149–161.

2. For BlogLeft, see www.gseis.ucla.edu/courses/ed253a/blogger.php. I am grateful to a number of bloggers, and especially Ray McInnis, for comments on my text and providing information, ideas, and stimulus for this study.

INTRODUCTION: THE BUSH ADMINISTRATION AND THE SEPTEMBER 11 ATTACKS

1. See Colum Lynch, "War on Al Qaeda Funds Stalled. Network 'Fit and Well,' Ready to Strike, Draft of U.N. Report Says," *Washington Post*, August 29, 2002. The Bush administration claimed its efforts were a success, but critics indicated that conflicts between the Treasury Department, Commerce Department, the FBI, and other government institutions were creating internal problems in stopping terrorist funds and that the Bush administration's growing unilateralism and conflicts with countries throughout the world were creating difficulties with coordinating control of terrorist funds with other countries.

2. There were reports that the Bush administration dragnet that had arrested over 1,200 terrorist suspects in the United States had not apprehended any major terrorist figures or groups or broken up major rings and plots. Thus, as of summer 2002, the United States had not arrested anyone connected to a major terrorist plot or group; see "Details of Sept. 11 Plot Elude U.S. Investigators," *Los Angeles Times*, April 30, 2002, A16; and Eric Boehlert, *Salon*, June 19, 2002, who writes, "The dragnet comes up empty. In the aftermath of September 11, law enforcement agents detained more than 1,000 people, mostly Middle Eastern–born

men. Some were held for weeks without an attorney. Some were virtually convicted in the press. But none have been implicated in terrorism." In the spring, Ashcroft had boasted to Congress that his terrorism investigations had resulted in the conviction of eighty-six people on criminal charges. But as commentators point out, "What he forgot to say was that none of the charges against the 86—virtually all of whom are Arabs and Muslims—was related to terrorism. Most were minor charges that might never have been filed if the individuals hadn't got caught up in the terrorism dragnet." See Jean AbiNader and Kate Martin, "Just the Facts, Mr. Ashcroft," *Washington Post*, July 25, 2002. There have been some arrests in the United States over the summer and fall of 2002 of individuals believed to be terrorists and claims of foiling terrorist plots, but there have been so far no major arrests by the FBI or Justice Department concerning the September 11 terrorist attack.

3. Although the Bush administration propaganda war was immensely successful at home, garnering support for its Afghanistan war from 85–90 percent of those polled, a number of polls taken in the Arab and Muslim worlds revealed a striking lack of support for U.S. policies, and many did not even believe that Osama bin Laden and his Al Qaeda network were responsible for the September 11 terror attacks. Thus, it is clear that the Bush administration failed miserably in its efforts to communicate and improve relations with the Arab and Muslim world. For a variety of polls on Arab attitudes toward the United States pre– and post–September 11, see www.zogby.com/main.cfm. For the 2002 Gallup Poll on the Islamic world, see www.gallup.com/poll/summits/islam.asp. For a PEW poll that cites growing European criticism and distance from Bush administration policies, see the PEW Institute's report "Americans and Europeans Differ Widely on Foreign Policy Issues," which concludes: "The survey revealed considerable European support for taking a more independent course in security and diplomatic affairs. Majorities in France, Germany, and Italy think that Western Europe's partnership with the United States should not be as close as it has been in the past. People in Great Britain are divided on the question. European support for a more independent approach is not especially linked to negative reactions to recent U.S. policies, such as the steel tariffs. Rather, it is more associated with general criticism of President Bush, the feeling that the United States has ignored allied interests in conducting the war on terrorism, and general disapproval of U.S. policies in the Middle East." See people-press.org/reports/display-.php3?ReportID = 153.

An important December 2002 PEW survey, "What the World Thinks in 2002," indicated that extensive polling in 44 countries revealed an intensifying negative attitude toward the United States in both Western allies and Muslim countries (www.people-press.org). The polls showed that favorable views of the U.S. in Britain declined 12 percent in the last two year and 17 percent in Germany, while in Turkey positive views toward the U.S. dropped from 52 to 30 percent, only 30 percent supported the U.S. campaign against terrorism, and 83 percent opposed any use of the nation's bases to attack Iraq. In other Moslem countries, 75 percent of those surveyed in Jordan had an unfavorable opinion of America, as did 69 percent of Egyptians and Pakistanis and 59 percent of Lebanese. Clearly, the Bush administration policies have created new enemies and endangered U.S. security. And a British poll revealed that 70 percent of British Muslims believe that the war on terrorism is a war against Islam, while two out of three polled said that the U.S. was unjustified in blaming Al Qaeda for the September 11 terror acts; see Andrew Grice, "Most British Muslims do not blame al Qaeda for attacks," *The Independent* (December 24, 2002).

4. For sources describing civilian casualties, see Marc C. Herod, www.cursor.org/stories/

civilian_deaths.htm, and the update at pubpages.unh.edu/~mwherold/AfghanDailyCount. pdf; in an August 8, 2002, *Guardian* article, "Counting the Dead," Herod's "most recent figures were that between 3,125 and 3,620 Afghan civilians were killed between October 7 and July 31." See also Carl Conetta's report, "Operation Enduring Freedom: Why a Higher Rate of Civilian Bombing Casualties," Project on Defense Alternatives *Briefing Report,* no. 11, www.comw.org/pda/0201oef.html. The Pentagon has so far refused to make any estimates concerning civilian casualties from U.S. bombing in Afghanistan. Herod's estimates, just noted, number over 4,000 civilian casualties based on newspaper and other reports, whereas various Human Rights organizations estimate between 1,200–2000 civilian casualties and the interim Afghanistan government estimates the total civilian dead at 1,000–2,000. According to a *Los Angeles Times* report on June 2, 2002, by David Zucchino, "'The Americans. . . . They Just Drop Their Bombs and Leave,'" an investigation of 194 incidents of civilian casualties from U.S. bombing from October 7, 2001, to February 28, 2002, the *Times* found at least 1,071–1,201 civilians could be confirmed as killed by U.S. bombs. But in a *Guardian* article on May 20, 2002, "Forgotten Victims," Jonathan Steele writes:

> The direct victims of American bombs and missiles have commanded most political and media attention, though no one is certain how many even of these there were.
>
> A *Guardian* report in February estimated these casualties at between 1,300 and 8,000 deaths. A *Guardian* investigation into the "indirect victims" now confirms the belief of many aid agencies that they exceeded the number who died of direct hits.
>
> As many as 20,000 Afghans may have lost their lives as an indirect consequence of the US intervention. They too belong in any tally of the dead.
>
> The bombing had three main effects on the humanitarian situation. It caused massive dislocation by prompting hundreds of thousands of Afghans to flee from their homes.
>
> It stopped aid supplies to drought victims who depended on emergency relief. It provoked an upsurge in fighting and turned a military stalemate into one of chaotic fluidity, leading yet more people to flee.

5. For the Gore report, see www.fas.org/irp/threat/212fin~1.html; for the Hart-Rudman report, see www.nssg.gov/News/news.htm; and for the Bremer National Commission on Terrorism report, see w3.access.gpo.gov/nct/. See also Associated Press, "1999 Report Warned of Suicide Hijack," May 17, 2001.

6. See Andrew Buncombe, "US Met Taliban in Bid to Secure Handover of bin Laden," *The Independent,* October 30, 2001.

7. See Greg Palast, "FBI and U.S. Spy Agents Say Bush Spiked bin Laden Probes before September 11," *The Guardian,* November 7, 2001; and Greg Palast, "US agents told: Back off bin Ladens," old.smh.com.au/news/0111/07/world/world100.html. Palast's articles are collected on his homepage, which has a lot of other interesting reports on Bush administration activities; see www.gregpalast.com.

8. In "Ashcroft Knew," Bruce Shapiro names Ashcroft "the official responsible for the most dramatic failures of September 11," *Salon,* May 23, 2002. Ashcroft will indeed emerge as one of the villains of this book, in part because of his stunning incompetence and failures to address the dangers of terrorism due to his fanatic obsession to push through a right-wing law-and-order agenda before and after September 11. Ashcroft also carried out the most systematic assault on civil liberties in U.S. history and emerges as a clear and present danger to constitutional democracy. Yet it is the collective responsibility of the Bush administration for

failing to heed warnings of imminent terror attacks and for its systematically carrying out policies that made the strike more likely, an argument I develop in chapter 1 and elsewhere in this book.

9. The Feinstein memo is at www.senate.gov/~feinstein/Releases02/attacks.htm.

10. See CBS News, "New Terror Task Force: Cheney To Lead at Terrorist Threats to U.S.," May 8, 2001. A June 30, 2001, CNN report headlined, "Cheney is point man for administration," noting that Cheney would be in charge of task forces on three major issues: energy, global warming, and domestic terrorism. It is obvious that Cheney concentrated on energy issues to the detriment of paying attention to terrorism, and there should be an inquiry into what he did and did not do as head of the Bush administration antiterrorism task force. On May 11, 2001, www.disasterrelief.org also posted a report that states: "Bush asked Vice President Dick Cheney to lead the task force, which will explore how attacks against U.S. citizens or personnel at home and overseas may be detected and stopped." To prevent future terror attacks on the United States, it would thus be highly important to see exactly what Cheney did or did not do and address the problems revealed. See discussions of Cheney, Enron, and the oil industries in chapters 9 and 11 and elsewhere in this study.

11. The *Frankfurter Allgemine Zeitung* reported on September 14, 2001, that German intelligence sources gathered warnings from the Echelon spy system that Middle Eastern terrorists were "planning to hijack commercial aircraft to use as weapons to attack important symbols of American and Israeli culture" and passed the warnings to the U.S. government. On Israeli intelligence warning the U.S. of terrorist networks sneaking into the U.S. for attacks, see "Officials Told of 'Major Assault' Plans," *Los Angeles Times,* September 20, 2001. Carolyn Kay has assembled scores of material from Russian, Israeli, German, U.S., and other intelligence sources warning that a major domestic terrorist attack was about to unfold against the United States, but Cheney, the Bush administration, and the national security apparatus failed to respond or prepare for the impending attacks. See makethemaccountable.com/what when/index.html.

12. William Safire blames head of the CIA, George Tenet; see William Safire, "The Williams Memo," *New York Times,* May 20, 2002; and Thomas Powers provides an overview of criticism of the agency in "The Trouble with the CIA," *New York Review of Books,* January 17, 2002. Others blamed the FBI; see David Corn, "Robert Mueller, Sept. 11 Fall Guy," *Albion Monitor,* May 2, 2002. In *The Cell: Inside the 9/11 Plot and Why the FBI and CIA Failed to Stop It,* ABC journalist John Miller and criminal investigative reporter Michael Stone show how FBI, CIA, and Bush administration's blundering helped facilitate the September 11 terror attacks; they noted that upon taking office, the Bush administration pulled out two submarines off of Afghanistan, which were poised to launch an attack on bin Laden's camp there. I blame all the U.S. intelligence agencies and the Bush administration for lack of proper information gathering, coordination and intelligence sharing, and inadequate focus on the dangers of domestic terrorism.

13. See, for example, James Risen and David Johnston, "Agent Complaints Lead FBI Director to Ask for Inquiry," *New York Times,* May 24, 2002; and Jim Yardley, "FBI Didn't Pursue Information on Terror Suspect, Papers Show," *New York Times,* May 24, 2002.

14. Douglas Kellner, *Media Spectacle* (London: Routledge, 2003).

15. See Harold Evans, "What We Knew: Warning Given . . . Story Missed. How a Report on Terrorism Flew Under the Radar," *Columbia Journalism Review* (November-December 2001). Evans points out that the Bush administration blocked planned congressional hearings

on the Hart-Rudman report in May 2001, instead "forming its own committee, headed by Dick Cheney, who was expected to report in October." Even former Republican House Majority Leader and conservative ideologue Newt Gingrich concedes, "The [Bush] administration actually slowed down response to Hart-Rudman when momentum was building in the spring."

16. For previous accounts of Bush family conspiracies, see Douglas Kellner, *Television and the Crisis of Democracy* (Boulder, Colo.: Westview Press, 1990); Douglas Kellner, *The Persian Gulf TV War* (Boulder, Colo.: Westview Press, 1992); and Kellner, *Grand Theft 2000.* Major conspiracy sites for September 11 include Michael Rupert's www.fromthewilderness.com, the Emperor's Clothes site at www.tenc.net, and the compendium of conspiracy theories collected at the Global Research site at www.globalresearch.ca. The bestselling French conspiracy book by Thierry Meyssan was reportedly being translated into English as *9–11, The Big Lie,* New York: USA Books, 2002.

17. See the evidence assembled by scientist Barbara Hatch Rosenberg, indicating the likelihood that the anthrax attacks were the work of a U.S. bioweapons establishment insider, at www.ph.ucla.edu/epi/bioter/compilationofanthraxevidence.html. Moreover, DNA sequencing of the anthrax sent through the U.S. mail confirms that the strain originally came from a U.S. military laboratory at Fort Detrick, Maryland; see "Anthrax Attack Bug 'Identical' to Army Strain," *New Scientist,* May 2, 2002, www.newscientist.com. Later reports that the CIA received the Ames anthrax cultures from Fort Detrick create the chilling possibility that groups within the CIA were involved in the anthrax attacks and may have had pre-knowledge of the September 11 attacks; see the well-documented study by Richard Ochs, "Government by Anthrax," at www.freefromterror.net; and Wayne Madsen, "Anthrax and the Agency— Thinking the Unthinkable," *Counterpunch,* April 8–9, 2002, 3, www.counterpunch.org/madsenanthrax.html. Finally, in August 2002, the FBI very publicly interviewed a U.S. anthrax scientist suspected in the case who strongly denied his guilt, raising the question of whether the FBI had collared the culprit or were setting up a patsy. See further discussion of the anthrax mystery, still not solved, in chapter 3.

18. See Human Rights Watch, "Presumption of Guilt: Human Rights Abuses of Post–September 11 Detainees," at www.hrw.org/press/2002/08/usdetainess081502.htm.

19. On the Bush administration's "fuzzy math" and its disastrous economic policies, see Krugman (2001). I will draw on Krugman's later critiques, published in his *New York Times* column on Bushonomics, throughout this study.

20. Not only were foreign investors pulling money out of the U.S. stock market, but they were also backing off from investing in the U.S. economy. See Louis Uchitelle, "Foreign Investors Turning Cautious on Spending in U.S.," *New York Times,* August 4, 2002. In addition, the Saudis, angry at criticisms from the U.S. media and Bush administration, sold billions of U.S. dollars and assets, driving down the value of the dollar. See Roula Khalaf, "Saudis withdraw billions of dollars from U.S.," *Financial Times,* August 20, 2002.

21. Paul Krugman, "Everyone Is Outraged," *New York Times,* July 2, 2002; and Paul Krugman, "The Insider Game," *New York Times,* July 7, 2002.

22. In August 2002, allegations also emerged that Bush evaded income taxes in his shady Harken dealings. See the excellent overview of Bush's Harken activities in Bob Fertik, "Did George W. Bush Evade Income Taxes on His Harken Loans?" at www.democrats.com/display.cfm?id=290. For more on Bush economic and political scandals, see chapters 1 and 11.

23. See Anthony York, "The hypocrite in chief," *Salon,* July 2, 2002; BBC News, "Cheney accused of corporate fraud"; "Sticky Business," *Newsweek,* July 22, 2002; and the collection of material, "Who Is Dick Cheney?" at www.moveon.org.

24. See the sources in note 23; and Jeff Gerth and Dan van Natta, "In Tough Times, a Company Finds Profits in Terror War," *New York Times,* July 13, 2002; and Citizen Watch's report, which indicates that Halliburton under Cheney avoided paying taxes five of the six years in which Cheney was CEO, at www.citizenworks.org/admin/press/halliburton-pr.php.

25. For a discussion of Orwell's prophetic novel, see Douglas Kellner, "From *1984* to *One-Dimensional Man:* Reflections on Orwell and Marcuse," *Current Perspectives in Social Theory:* 223–252. In the light of the Bush administration projected Terror War, however, it could well be Orwell and not Huxley and Marcuse, as I argue in the article cited here, who provide the most prescient templates of the future present.

26. See Jonathan Turley, "Camps for Citizens: Ashcroft's Hellish Vision," *Los Angeles Times,* August 14, 2002. U.S. Attorney General John Ashcroft was awarded the annual "1984 Award" in 2002 for "Worst Government Official" by Privacy International. The watchdog group said the top U.S. law enforcement officer "is responsible for a massive increase in wiretapping of phones and other electronics and for the imprisonment without charge of as many as 1,200 people in the United States after the Sept. 11 attacks on America." See Reuters, April 19, 2002.

27. See Kellner 2001 for documentation and systematic critique of Bushspeak.

28. See also Thomas E. Ricks and Vernon Loeb, "Bush Developing Military Policy of Striking First," *Washington Post,* June 10, 2002, A1. For a sharp critique of Bush's new preemptive strike policy, see "Werther Report: Is Preemption a Nuclear Schlieffen Plan?" at www.d-n-i.net/fcs/comments/c453.htm.

29. For further discussion of the debate over a forthcoming war against Iraq militated for by the Bush administration in summer and fall 2002, see chapter 11.

30. See William Saletan, "Shoot First: Bush's whitewashed national security manifesto," *Slate,* September 20, 2002; Peter Slevin, "Analysts: New Strategy Courts Unseen Dangers, First Strike Could Be Precedent for Other Nations," *Washington Post,* September 22, 2002; and Paul Krugman, "White Man's Burden," *New York Times,* September 24, 2002.

31. William Galston, "Perils of Preemptive War," *The American Prospect* 13, no. 17 (September 23, 2002).

32. An article by Neil Mackay, "Bush planned Iraq 'regime change' before becoming president," *The Sunday Herald,* September 15, 2002, which widely circulated through the Internet, called attention to the sort of lunatic global strategic vision that informed Bush administration policy. The 2000 plan is available at www.newamericancentury.org/Rebuilding AmericasDefenses.pdf. In "Dick Cheney's Song of America," David Armstrong argues that the origins of the Bush administration plan for world domination were in Dick Cheney's Defense Planning Guidance document of 1992 that continued to be refined during the 1990s and was released as official U.S. policy in 2002 (*Harper's Magazine,* October 2002).

33. Tariq Ali captures this dialectic in his book *The Clash of Fundamentalisms: Crusades, Jihads and Modernity* (London: Verso, 2002), whose cover pictures George W. Bush shading into the visage of Osama bin Laden, two fundamentalists whose families had long been linked in shady business practices (see chapter 1) and who personally represented the competing fundamentalisms of the ongoing Terror War.

1 THEORIZING 9/11

1. Francis Fukuyama's book, *The End of History* (New York: Free Press, 1992), was an expansion of a 1989 article published in the conservative journal *The National Interest*. His texts generated a tremendous amount of controversy and were seen by some as a new dominant ideology proclaiming the triumph of Western ideals of capitalism and democracy over all of their opponents. With a quasi-Hegelian gloss, Fukuyama proclaimed the victory of the Ideas of neoliberalism and the "end of history," and his work prompted both skepticism ("It ain't over, till it's over") and impassioned critique. If terrorism and the Bush administration militarism soon pass from the historical scene and a neoliberal globalization driven by market capitalism and democracy returns to become the constitutive force of the new millennium, Fukuyama would end up being vindicated after all. But in the current conflict-filled situation, his views appear off the mark and superseded by the present situation.

2. Ali (2002) also notes on p. 282ff. that after the 9/11 attacks, Huntington modified his "clash of civilization" thesis to describe the post–Cold War era as an "age of 'Muslim wars'," with Muslims fighting each other or their specific enemies; see Huntington's essay in *Newsweek*, Special Davos Edition (December-January, 2001–2002). As Ali maintains, besides being a highly questionable overview of the present age, it contradicts his previous model, reducing Huntington's thought to incoherency. Yet in fairness to Huntington, it is rarely noted in the many criticisms of his work that he suggests in the conclusion of his book that the West is in cultural disorder, showing signs of "moral decline, cultural suicide and political disunity" (1997, 304). For Huntington, the West's great danger is a failure to believe in itself, and it should thus avoid cultural confrontation with the rest of the world and concentrate on strengthening itself. Moreover, Huntington warns the U.S. against unilateralism, urging closer ties with Europe, and proposes three rules of international diplomacy: (1) the abstention rule that core states must "abstain from intervention in conflicts in other civilizations," (2) the joint mediation rule that core states should negotiate with each other, and (3) the commonalties rule that civilizations and nations should search for shared values and not promote conflicts (316–320). Thus Huntington himself does not advocate a "clash of civilizations" in the vein of Bush administration pseudo-warriors who use his work to legitimate aggression; in fact, Huntington wants to mitigate clashes of civilization, an agenda that both the Al Qaeda forces and Bush unilateralist forces are intensifying (see chapter 2).

3. For an astute analysis of the different senses of Jihad and a sharp critique of the Islamic terrorists' distortions of Islam, see Ahmed Rashid, *Jihad: The Rise of Militant Islam in Central Asia* (New Haven, Conn.: Yale University Press, 2002).

4. I provide my own historical and theoretical account of the background to the events of September 11 in this chapter. Put abstractly, such a theory would combine the Hegelian-Marxian perspectives of a globalized world and the vicissitudes of capitalism with concrete historical study of specific events, like the 9/11 terrorist acts, and the lessons for contemporary social theory and democratic politics. It would combine historical, political, economic, and cultural analyses in a multiperspectivist model that eschews reductionistism and simplistic monocausal models. In the light of the importance of the media in the construction of the 9/11 spectacle and subsequent Terror War, I also employ the tools of cultural studies and media critique.

5. Chalmers Johnson, *Blowback: The Costs and Consequences of American Empire* (New York: Henry Holt, 2000). In addition to Johnson, who provides a conceptual overview of the

concept of blowback that I am using to interpret the September 11 terrorist acts, I am also drawing upon a series of studies of U.S. foreign policy and Afghanistan, including Ahmed Rashid, *Taliban: Militant Islam, Oil and Fundamentalism in Central Asia* (New Haven, Conn.: Yale University Press, 2001); Rashid, *Jihad*; John Cooley, *Unholy Wars: Afghanistan, America and International Terrorism* (London: Pluto Press, 2000); Ali, *The Clash of Fundamentalisms*; Mary Ann Weaver, "Blowback," *Atlantic Monthly* (May 1996), www.theatlantic. com/issues/96may/blowback.htm; a collection of articles contextualizing the events at *The Nation* website, especially Dilip Hiro, "The Cost of an Afghan 'Victory,'" www.thenation. com; various articles collected at www.counterpoint.com; and a variety of other books and articles that I will cite as I proceed.

6. See Alexander Cockburn and Jeffrey St. Clair, "The Price: Was it *Really* Worth it, Mrs. Albright?" *Counterpunch*, September 26, 2001. See their archive for useful daily postings on the current crisis at www.counterpunch.org/wtcarchive.html.

7. Brzezinski had the gall to blatantly lie in his 1997 book *The Grand Chessboard* (New York: Basic Books) where he wrote: "The Soviet invasion of Afghanistan precipitated a two-pronged American response: direct U.S. assistance to the native resistance in Afghanistan in order to bog down the Soviet army; and a large-scale buildup of the U.S. military presence in the Gulf War as a deterrent to any further southward projection of Soviet political or military power" (p. 7). As he admitted a year later, he provoked Soviet intervention by supporting Afghan Islamicist rebels. See the 1998 *Le Monde* interview with Brzezinski posted October 8, 2001 at www.counterpunch.org/wtcarchive.html. For a full account of the background of the Brzezinski-Carter decision to intervene in Afghanistan politics and the Soviet response, see Cooley, *Unholy Wars*, 9ff.

8. Gilles Kemper claims that the name "Al Qaeda" emerged around 1986 when bin Laden began making a database of members of the Jihad network, with Al Qaeda signifying "the base," *Jihad: The Trail of Political Islam* (Cambridge, Mass.: Harvard University Press, 2002, p. 152). On the bin Laden network, see also Jean-Charles Brisard and Guillaume Dasquie, *Forbidden Truth* (New York: Thunder's Mouth Press/Nation Books, 2002).

9. According to one account, it was "irrational hatred" of Sudan by the Clinton administration that prevented the West from gaining access to Sudan's detailed files on Al Qaeda, which they were reportedly willing to share with the West but which were repeatedly refused; see David Rose, "Resentful west spurned Sudan's key terror files," *Guardian*, September 30, 2001 and "The Osama Files," *Vanity Fair*, January 2002, 64ff. Rose especially blames Clinton's Secretary of State Madeleine Albright, who reportedly blocked the FBI from gaining the Sudan files on the grounds that Sudan was a "terrorist state." Three days later, the Clinton administration bombed Sudan in retaliation for the Al Qaeda bombings of U.S. embassies in Africa. A Clinton administration member, Gayle Smith, however, claims that the Sudanese were not serious about sharing their intelligence files and did not provide any useful information on the bin Laden group; see *Los Angeles Times*, December 7, 2001, B15. A twisted, tortured tale of failed U.S. policy in the region remains to be told. For an overview of Clinton administration policy toward bin Laden and terrorism, see Barton Gellman, "U.S. Was Foiled Multiple Times in Efforts to Capture Bin Laden or Have Him Killed: Sudan's Offer to Arrest Militant Fell through after Saudis Said No," *Washington Post*, October 3, 2001; and Barton Gellman, "Clinton's War on Terror: The Covert Hunt for bin Laden," *Washington Post*, December 19, 2001.

10. On the background of the Unocal pipeline project, see Rashid, *Taliban*, chapters 12

and 13. In the Southeast Asian press, there have been speculations that the U.S. policy in Afghanistan under Bush II was to stabilize the country under Taliban rule to enable the Unocal corporation to build a gas pipeline across Afghanistan and exploit its potential natural gas and oil resources. See Ranjit Devrag, who writes:

> Where the "great game" in Afghanistan was once about czars and commissars seeking access to the warm water ports of the Persian Gulf, today it is about laying oil and gas pipelines to the untapped petroleum reserves of Central Asia. According to testimony before the U.S. House of Representatives in March 1999 by the conservative think tank Heritage Foundation, Azerbaijan, Kazakhstan, Turkmenistan and Uzbekistan together have 15 billion barrels of proven oil reserves. The same countries also have proven gas deposits totaling not less than nine trillion cubic meters. Another study by the Institute for Afghan Studies placed the total worth of oil and gas reserves in the Central Asian republics at around U.S.$3 trillion at last year's prices.
>
> Not only can Afghanistan play a role in hosting pipelines connecting Central Asia to international markets, but the country itself has significant oil and gas deposits. During the Soviets' decade-long occupation of Afghanistan, Moscow estimated Afghanistan's proven and probable natural gas reserves at around five trillion cubic feet and production reached 275 million cubic feet per day in the mid-1970s. But sabotage by anti-Soviet *mujahideen* (freedom fighters) and by rival groups in the civil war that followed Soviet withdrawal in 1989 virtually closed down gas production and ended deals for the supply of gas to several European countries.
>
> Natural gas production and distribution under Afghanistan's Taliban rulers is the responsibility of the Afghan Gas Enterprise which, in 1999, began repair of a pipeline to Mazar-i-Sharif city. Afghanistan's proven and probable oil and condensate reserves were placed at 95 million barrels by the Soviets. So far, attempts to exploit Afghanistan's petroleum reserves or take advantage of its unique geographical location as a crossroads to markets in Europe and South Asia have been thwarted by the continuing civil strife.
>
> In 1998, the California-based UNOCAL, which held 46.5 percent stakes in Central Asia Gas (CentGas), a consortium that planned an ambitious gas pipeline across Afghanistan, withdrew in frustration after several fruitless years. The pipeline was to stretch 1,271 km from Turkmenistan's Dauletabad fields to Multan in Pakistan at an estimated cost of $1.9 billion. An additional $600 million would have brought the pipeline to energy-hungry India (from *OnLine Asia Times*, October 6, 2001, atimes.com/global-econ/CJ06Dj01.html).

After the collapse of the Enron corporation in fall 2001, it was reported that one of its many projects was a feasibility study of the Unocal oil and gas pipeline across Afghanistan; see the documents assembled in www.bushwatch.com and note 17 below.

11. See Brewton 1992, 221ff; Hatfield 2000, 55–56; and Brisard and Dasquie, *Forbidden Truth*. According to Hatfield (p. 56), after Bath's shady business deals were exposed, Bush denied ever doing business with Bath, with whom he had served in the Texas National Guard and was reportedly good friends. But inspection of later court papers revealed that Bath indeed invested in Bush's Arbusto oil company, representing the bin Laden family. Bush Senior has also had longtime relations with members of the bin Laden family and other Saudis who provided money to the bin Laden network. For Bath's colorful story, including business and bank scandals and illegal support for the contras, and alleged recruitment into the CIA by George Bush, Senior, see Brewton 1992. The BBC reported as well on bin Laden invest-

ment in Bush's oil company on November 7, 2001, and Bush administration orders to U.S. special agents to back off the bin Laden family and Saudi royals after Bush became president; see the summary and detailed reporting in "U.S. agents told: Back off bin Laden," smh.com.au, Nov. 7, 2001.

12. Sally Slate's explosive column is available at www.onlinejournal.com/Commentary/Slate103001/slate103001.html; the PBS *Frontline* commentary is at www.pbs.org/wgbh/pages/frontline/shows/binladen/who/family.html. An editor's note was added to the *Frontline* report, stating: "The above paragraph is inaccurate. Salem bin Laden was piloting a light aircraft, not a BAC 1–11, when he crashed. As for 'secret Paris meetings between U.S. and Iranian emissaries' in October 1980, such meetings have never been confirmed." For sources that claim that such meetings took place and that George H. W. Bush was involved in the negotiations, see the sources in note 13. For the official bin Laden family position that Osama is an outcast, see Michael Moss, "Bin Laden Family Strives to Re-establish Its Reputation," *New York Times*, October 28, 2001. A BBC report, however, indicated that several members of the bin Laden family were connected with groups suspected of supporting and financing terrorist networks; see the summary and detailed reporting in "U.S. agents told: Back off bin Laden," smh.com.au, November 7, 2001.

13. On the October Surprise, see Sick 1990 and the documents assembled by Robert Parry in www.consortiumnews.com.

14. See also the assembled documents from various sources including the *Wall Street Journal* and *New York Times* that document Bush Senior's connection with the Carlyle group at www.bushwatch.com, as well as Oliver Burkeman and Julian Borger, "The Ex-president's Club," *Guardian*, October 31, 2001; Dan Briody, "Carlyle's Way: Making a Mint inside 'the Iron Triangle' of Defense, Government, and Industry," *Red Herring*, January 8, 2002; and Tim Shorrock, "Crony Capitalism Goes Global," *The Nation*, April 1, 2002, 11–16. The bin Laden family sold their Carlyle Fund interests after 9/11, members of the family in the U.S. reportedly fled the country by private jet following the 9/11 terror acts, and the Bush and bin Laden family connections became a source of embarrassment to the Bush family that so far has not been systematically explored by the media.

15. Sally Slate, www.onlinejournal.com/Commentary/Slate103001/slate103001.html; the tape of Saudi clerics visiting bin Laden was found in Afghanistan and released to great fanfare and controversy in December 2001, and documents the strong support for bin Laden in Saudi Arabia, an issue I discuss in chapter 7.

16. See Greg Palast, "FBI and U.S. Spy Agents Say Bush Spiked bin Laden Probes before September 11," *The Guardian*, November 7, 2001; and Greg Palast, "US Agents Told: Back off bin Ladens," at old.smh.com.au/news/0111/07/world/world100.html. Palast's articles are collected on his home page that has a lot of other interesting reports on Bush administration activities; see www.gregpalast.com and his book (Palast 2002).

17. See Wayne Madsen, "Afghanistan, the Taliban, and the Bush Oil Team" who claims that Afghanistan interim president Hamid Karzai was an advisor to the Unocal Corporation interested in the Central Asian Gas pipeline, that Enron did the feasibility study for the project, that Cheney's Halliburton company was set to do the construction work, and that the Bush administration's top representative in Afghanistan today, Zalymay Zhalilzad, had also been a Unocal advisor and member of the Bush administration GOP (Grand Oil Plan); see www.democrats.com, January 2002, and globalresearch.ca/articles/MAD201A.html.

18. Some critics are skeptical that creation of a gas or oil pipeline across Afghanistan is a

major motivation for the Bush administration's Terror War policy. See, for instance, Ken Silverstein, "No War for Oil!" *The American Prospect*, August 12, 2002, 27–30. Although it would be a mistake to reduce Bush administration policy to serving oil industry interests, there is no doubt but that the oil-obsessed Bushites have long been viewing the prospects of controlling Caspian Sea basin oil and natural gas. Moreover, since the Afghanistan invasion, as I note later in this study, U.S. bases have been built throughout the area, deals have been made with the Afghanistan and Pakistan government for oil pipelines to be built that follow the original Unocal/Enron plans, and one imagines that the ultimate insider/realist legitimization for the extent of the U.S. military involvement in the region is to gain access to energy supplies in case Persian Gulf supplies are threatened or become depleted. There have, however, been recent reports that the amount of oil reserves in the Caspian Sea area has been exaggerated and that some oil exploration efforts have failed to yield expected riches. See Dale Allen Pfeiffer, "Much Ado About Nothing—Whither the Caspian Riches?" and "Colin Campbell on Oil," both at www.fromthewilderness.com. For an excellent account of the role of oil "resource" politics and how the drive to control oil supplies has been fueling U.S. post–Cold War policy, see Michael Klare, *Resource Wars: The New Landscape of Global Conflict* (New York: Metropolitan Books, 2001).

19. Brinkley elaborated his position in a forum at Columbia University on October 5, 2001; see www.columbia.edu/cu/news/01/10/historical_reflection_9_11.html.

20. Kemper 2002, 152; on the bin Laden network, see also Brisard and Dasquie, 2002.

21. See Greider 1998 and www.abcnews.com, November 1, 1999.

22. For Virilio, every technology has its accident that accompanies it, so the airplane's accident is the crash, the automobile's a wreck, and a ship's its sinking. For Virilio, the accident the Internet faces is "the accident of accidents," as he calls it: the entire collapse of the global system of communication and information, and thus the global economy. On Virilio, see Kellner 1999.

2   9/11, THE MEDIA, AND WAR FEVER

1. For an account of Election 2000 that raises questions about Bush's legitimacy, see Douglas Kellner, *Grand Theft 2000* (Lanham, Md.: Rowman & Littlefield, 2001).

2. For systematic analysis of media spectacle in the contemporary era, see Douglas Kellner, *Media Spectacle* (London and New York: Routledge, 2003). There has been no official inquiry so far into how it was possible that four hijacked planes could fly unopposed by U.S. military aircraft, especially since there was more than an hour between the first World Trade Center crash and the downing of the plane in Pennsylvania. Nor has there been a sustained inquiry into how it was possible to crash a plane into the Pentagon and why the center of U.S. military power was not protected by missiles or other anti-aircraft weapons. The failure of the Bush administration and Pentagon to provide answers to these questions has generated a wealth of conspiracy theorizing; see the sources in note 4 below.

3. See David E. Sanger and Don Van Natta, Jr., "Four Days That Transformed a President, a Presidency and a Nation, for All Time," *Washington Post*, September 16, 2001; and the mythologizing account in Dan Balz and Bob Woodward, "America's Chaotic Road to War," *Washington Post*, January 27, 2002. Later, White House spokesman Ari Fleischer took a slap at *Politically Incorrect* host Bill Maher, who called U.S. military strikes on faraway tar-

gets "cowardly." Fleischer blasted Maher, claiming it was "a terrible thing to say," and sent a chilling message to the press that criticism of the Bush administration would not be tolerated, noting: "There are reminders to all Americans that they need to watch what they say, watch what they do, and this is not a time for remarks like that; there never is." Eventually, Maher's series was cancelled, although Fleischer's "watch what they say" was not appreciated by the press that criticized his attempt to curtail free speech and opinion.

4. Questions were also raised concerning why, in a press conference on the evening of September 11, Bush's Press Secretary Ari Fleischer began with a detailed run-through of Bush's day and response to the terror attacks that left out Bush's inexplicable failure to respond quicker to the attacks. Equally bizarre, Bush himself misspoke in later town hall meetings in January and February when he claimed that he had seen the planes hitting the World Trade Center towers. In fact, the first hit had not been televised and Bush was sitting with his hands folded and listening to kids reading during the second attack. For websites that contain a wealth of speculation concerning Bush's strange behavior during the attacks, the failure of the U.S. military to send planes to protect the Pentagon, and other theories pointing to U.S. government sins of omission or possible involvement in the 9/11 attacks, see Michael Rupert's www.fromthewilderness.com; the detailed time-line posted at the Center for Cooperative Research, www.cooperativeresearch.org/home.htm; the Emperor's Clothes site at www.tenc.net; the Center for an Informed America site at davesweb.cnchost. com/index.htm; the compendium of material collected at the Global Research site at www. globalresearch.ca; Meyssan 2002; and Bob Fertik, "In the Infamous 9–11 Fundraising Photo, Did Bush Order the Shootdown of the Flight 93 Heroes?" at www.democrats.com/display. cfm?id = 282, which assembles material that suggests that Flight 93 might have been shot down by the U.S.

5. Another unexplained mystery of the September 11 terror spectacle involved reports that just before the attack on the World Trade Center there was an unusual amount of speculation on stocks concerning the airlines industry, insurance companies, corporations with offices in the World Trade Center, and other economic victims of the September 11 attacks. Conjecture first centered on concern that the terrorists themselves had carried out the stock investment strategy, perhaps making hundreds of millions on their speculations. No one, apparently, cashed in their investments from U.S. markets, though conspiracy theorists were intrigued that many of the stock options were purchased through a German bank previously run by a former U.S. CIA official. See the collection of articles in Rupert's www.fromthe wilderness.com. Widespread media coverage of the stock options speculation on American and United Airlines, on stock brokerages located at the World Trade Center, and on insurance companies obviously prevented whoever purchased these put options from cashing them in on the New York Exchange, which was closed for some days after the bombing (although speculators may have benefited on foreign exchanges); see the article by Christian Berthelsen and Scott Winokur, "Profits Sit Uncollected: Airline Investors Seem to Be Lying Low," *San Francisco Chronicle,* September 29, 2001.

6. I attended a three-part symposium telecast live in the Beverly Hills Museum of Radio and Television, which included media executives and broadcasters throughout the world who described how they processed the events of September 11. Representatives from Canada, European countries, China, and elsewhere described how they got footage to broadcast, how the story dominated their respective media outlets, and how the story was truly global in reach. An archive is collecting video and commentary on September 11 broadcasting throughout the world at tvnews3.televisionarchive.org/tvarchive/html/index.html.

7. In this section, I am indebted to students of my UCLA Cultural Studies seminar and to Richard Kahn, who developed a website where the class posted material relating to the September 11 events and Afghan war; the following study draws on this material, which can be found at: www.gseis.ucla.edu/faculty/kellner/ed270/index.html.

8. The Bush-Baker-Carlyle connection was documented in many English newspapers, the *New York Times*, and other sources, collected on www.bushwatch.com and Phil Agre's *Red Rock Eater* at dlis.gseis.ucla.edu/people/pagre/rre.html. See also the assembled documents from various sources including the *Wall Street Journal* and *New York Times* that document Bush Senior's connection with the Carlyle group at www.bushwatch.com, as well as Oliver Burkeman and Julian Borger, "The Ex-president's Club," *Guardian*, October 31, 2001; Dan Briody, "Carlyle's Way: Making a Mint inside 'the Iron Triangle' of Defense, Government, and Industry," *Red Herring*, January 8, 2002; and Tim Shorrock, "Crony Capitalism Goes Global," *The Nation*, April 1, 2002, 11–16.

9. In retrospect, I believe that one of the reasons why the Bush administration did not ever publish its White Paper with evidence against the bin Laden group is that previous intelligence collected on the group indicated the likelihood and imminence of a terror attack on the U.S. and even the possibility that airplane hijacking might be involved. Release of such documentation would pose the questions of why the Bush administration did not do more to protect the country against the attacks, issues vetted when it was announced on May 6, 2002, that Bush had received a CIA briefing on dangers of Al Qaeda attacks. The craven media, in fact, did not initially raise the question of Bush administration responsibility for the attacks, and only much later suggested the need for an investigation of FBI, CIA, and intelligence agencies' failures to anticipate and prevent the attacks. There was no mainstream media investigative reporting into the connections between the Bush family and bin Laden and Al Qaeda, such as I provided in chapter 1; no investigations into how previous Bush administration policies toward the Taliban and terrorism had facilitated the attack; and no criticism whatsoever of Bush administration responsibility for the September 11 attacks until May 2002. As I noted, it was made taboo to dare to criticize Bush or the U.S. government in the hysterical climate following the September 11 attacks. In retrospect, this episode appears as one of the major failures of the U.S. media to do their job of investigative journalism and criticism of government policies.

10. See Greg Palast, "FBI and U.S. Spy Agents Say Bush Spiked bin Laden Probes Before September 11," *The Guardian*, November 7, 2001.

11. Professor Sami Al-Arian had been accused years before of running a now-defunct think tank that supported Palestinian terrorists and had been cleared of the charges; O'Reilly went national with the old accusations, which rapidly circulated through the media, and the professor was fired in a case now being appealed. See Eric Boehlert, "The prime-time smearing of Sami Al-Arian," *Salon*, January 19, 2002.

12. Sources on George W. Bush's life and career include Hatfield 2000; Ivins and Dubose 2001; Begala 2000; and Kellner 2001.

13. For the astonishing story of the Bush gang election theft, see Kellner, *Grand Theft 2000*, which also draws on sources grounding the thumbnail sketch of Bush's life presented here and cited in note 12. All of these stories are well-documented in websites like www.bush watch.com, as well as a series of books cited above, but the mainstream media prefer to neglect the more unsavory aspects of the life and times of George W. Bush, in favor of puff pieces on the rascal.

14. Falwell was quoted from an interview on Pat Robertson's *CBN Club*, cited in *Washington Post*, September 13, 2001. For a summary of the inflammatory remarks made by Jerry Falwell and Pat Robertson, see "Verbal assaults . . . by Fundamentalist Christian leaders," www.religioustolerance.org.

15. In an October 5, 2001, *Wall Street Journal* editorial, Rush Limbaugh wrote: "Mr. Clinton can be held culpable for not doing enough when he was commander in chief to combat the terrorists who wound up attacking the World Trade Center and Pentagon." Shortly thereafter, Limbaugh confessed that he was almost fully deaf and had been feigning dialogue on his radio show all year. On right-wing attempts to blame Clinton for the terrorist attacks, see also John F. Harris, "Conservatives Sound Refrain: It's Clinton's Fault," *The Washington Post*, October 7, 2001, A15.

16. Shortly after this and other outbursts, the frothing Coulter was fired from *National Review* when she reacted violently to efforts to tone down her rhetoric by the editors, helping to provide her with martyr status for the U.S. Talibanites.

17. Gaffney, Bennett, and other right-wingers who populate the Bush administration are old-time Cold Warriors who continued to see Russia, China, Cuba, and North Korea as major threats to the U.S. Jason Vest speculates that it is precisely the obsolete Cold War mentality of so many in the Bush administration that accounts for their inability to see new and harder-to-grasp enemies like terrorist networks. See Jason Vest, "Why Warnings Fell on Deaf Ears: For the Bush Administration the Cold War Never Ended—So Al Qaeda Had to Get in Line behind More Serious Enemies," *The American Prospect*, June 17, 2002. Vest claims that the Gaffney group's website claims that "22 of the center's advisory council members now occupy key national security positions in the Bush administration." Thus, the Cold War continues to haunt the United States as those who share its mentality in the Bush administration fail to understand the challenges of a different world and historical era.

18. See Howard Kurtz, "CNN Chief Orders 'Balance' in War News: Reporters Are Told to Remind Viewers Why U.S. Is Bombing," *Washington Post*, October 31, 2001; and the critical commentary in FAIR, www.fair.org/activism/cnn-casualties.html. Even more striking, Norman Solomon notes, "An October internal memo from the daily in Panama City, Florida, warned its editors: 'DO NOT USE photos on Page 1A showing civilian casualties from the U.S. war on Afghanistan. Our sister paper . . . has done so and received hundreds and hundreds of threatening e-mails. . . . DO NOT USE wire stories which lead with civilian casualties from the U.S. war on Afghanistan. They should be mentioned further down in the story. If the story needs rewriting to play down the civilian casualties, DO IT' "; see www.fair.org/media-beat/011213.html.

19. Lynne Cheney and some right-wing cronies organized a Defense of Civilization Fund, releasing a document, "Defending Civilization: How Our Universities Are Failing America and What Can Be Done About It?" November 2001, accessed at www.goacta.org. For critiques of Cheney's blatant attempt to crush critical dissent from Bush administration policies, see the commentaries collected in *Taboo* 6, no. 1 (Spring-Summer: 2000).

3   OPERATION ENDURING FREEDOM AND THE PROLIFERATION OF TERROR WAR

1. In the following sections, I draw upon daily reading of several major U.S. and British newspapers on the Afghan war and articles collected at www.bushwatch.com, www.buzzflash.com, and Phil Agre's frequent posting of articles on his *Red Rock Eater* list, which have

been collected and archived at dlis.gseis.ucla.edu/people/pagre/rre.html and many other sources including Institute for War and Peace Reporting bulletins and Bill Weinberg's *World War 3 Report*. The first major book on the Afghan war, Bob Woodward's *Bush at War* (New York: Simon & Schuster) mythologizes Bush as a great war leader, leaves out all of the messy effects of the U.S. Afghan intervention, and repeatedly makes the unconvincing claim that the Pentagon had no plans for an Afghan war and improvised on the fly.

2. See "Floridians Stockpile Anthrax Antibiotics" and "Bioterrorism Jitters Close Subway Stop, IRS Center," *Los Angeles Times*, October 10, 2001, A3.

3. "Jitters," *The New Yorker*, October 29, 2001. Rice's suggestion that U.S. television censorship would help fight the bin Laden network is ludicrous, as any interested parties could receive such messages from the Internet or through the broadcasts of Arabic-language and other overseas media. On the other hand, there are good reasons not to broadcast live the bin Laden messages since instant translation is atrocious and the communiqués require context and commentary to make sense to Western audiences. But the Bush administration failed to make sensible arguments to the networks, which cravenly went along with their political masters' instructions and intensified the propagandistic context of their programming for good measure.

4. Paul Krugman, who has written an excellent book on Bush's "fuzzy math" by exposing the fraudulent numbers used by the Bush administration in pushing through its tax giveaway to the rich (2001), continued to argue that Bush administration economic policy was using the war hysteria to push through its economic programs that amounted to corporate bailouts and tax giveaways to the rich. See Paul Krugman, "Another Useful Crisis," *New York Times*, November 11, 2001; and Paul Krugman, "Other People's Money," *New York Times*, November 14, 2001.

5. Relevant documents and analysis are found on www.bushwatch.com; see also Hatfield 2000; and Ivins and Dubose 2000.

6. See William Safire, "Inside the Bunker," *New York Times*, September 13, 2002. This story was soon revealed to be a Karl Rove fabrication. The same fallacious story was fed by Bush administration propagandists to *Washington Post* reporters; see David E. Sanger and Don van Natta Jr., "Four Days That Transformed a President, a Presidency and a Nation, for All Time," September 16, 2001.

7. See Julian Borger, "Pentagon Split over War Plan," *The Guardian*, October 15, 2001; Seymour Hersh, "King's Ransom," *The New Yorker*, October 22, 2001; "Millions at Risk in Afghan Crisis," BBC News, October 14, 2001; and Zeeshan Haider, "Stench of Death in a Flattened Village," *Guardian*, October 15, 2001.

8. See Christopher Kremmer, "Alarm Grows over Scale of Civilian Casualties," *Sydney Morning Herald*, October 15, 2001.

9. See Jason Burke, "US Admits Lethal Blunders," *Guardian*, October 14, 2001; Richard Lloyd Parry, "It Was As if the Rocks Themselves Were on Fire," *Independent*, October 14, 2001; Ian Williams, "He Is Burying His Wife Bit by Bit As He Digs Her Out of the Rubble," *The Times*, October 15, 2001; Kathy Gannon, "Taliban Shows Fresh Graves and a Village Ruined by War," *International Herald Tribune*, October 15, 2001; and Julian Borger, "Rumsfeld Blames Taliban for Civilian Deaths," *Guardian*, October 16, 2001.

10. See Bill Weinberg, *World War 3 Report*, no. 4, October 20, 2001. Weinberg's weekly newsletter contains a multitude of well-documented reports, focusing on topics not covered in the U.S. media, such as civilian casualties of U.S. bombing, refugee problems, the ways

that the U.S. campaign was blocking food and humanitarian aid, and criticism of the U.S. campaign.

11. See Said Aburish, "The Coming Arab Crash," *The Guardian,* October 18, 2001.

12. See Laura Miller's interview with Laurie Garrett, "The First Line of Defense," *Salon,* October 17, 2001, and Carlos Bongioanni, "Expert Picks apart Government's Handling of Anthrax Investigations," *Stars and Stripes,* October 16, 2001. The latter attacks the government's tardiness in investigating the first anthrax attack in Florida and its incompetence in handling the later New York media anthrax exposures.

13. A major Bush administration issue of summer 2001 was putting forth a policy on stem cell research, which was dramatically presented in a live television address by President Bush. The Bush administration policy limited stem cell research to existing stem cell lines, and it turned out that many of the lines that remained open were controlled by the University of Wisconsin Alumni Research Foundation (WARF) and their financial backer, Geron Corporation. Further, Health and Human Services Secretary and former Wisconsin Governor Tommy Thompson had long been connected with WARF, a group that was now privileged by the Bush administration policy on stem cell research. For analysis of the issues of cloning and stem cell research and a critique of Bush administration policy, see the forthcoming article by Steven Best and Douglas Kellner, "Biotechnology, Democracy, and the Politics of Cloning."

14. As noted in the introduction and as I will discuss in more detail, Ashcroft's Jihad against civil liberties helped produce the USA Patriot Act, one the most regressive pieces of legislation in U.S. history. The Bush administration's assault on U.S. democracy was noted throughout the media on October 17 and 18 with critical articles appearing in the *Washington Post, New York Times,* and other major newspapers, who called for clarification of domestic threats from the secretive Bush administration that would justify such draconian legislation and restriction of traditional U.S. civil liberties; see, for example, Todd S. Purdum, "Information, Please," *New York Times,* October 16, 2001. Honorable conservatives and liberals were becoming worried about the Bush administration assault on civil liberties by mid-October and would intensify critical discussion of its assaults on democracy, but these issues were rarely raised in television discussion shows.

15. David Neiwert, "Homegrown Terror," syndicated, October 26, 2001. On possible domestic biochemical government sources of the anthrax used in the attacks, see Barbara Hatch Rosenberg, www.ph.ucla.edu/epi/bioter/compilationofanthraxevidence.html; "Anthrax Attack Bug 'Identical' to Army Strain," *New Scientist,* May 2, 2002, www.newscientist.com; Richard Ochs, "Government by Anthrax," at www.freefromterror.net; and Wayne Madsen, "Anthrax and the Agency—Thinking the Unthinkable," *Counterpunch,* April 8–9, 2002, 3, www.counterpunch.org/madsenanthrax.html.

16. On the Bush administration's "stupid white men," see Michael Moore's book with that title (2002). Moore's publisher attempted to block publication of his polemic after September 11, but a librarian group caught wind of this censorship, publicized the issue, and the book was released without much support from the publisher, although word of mouth and the Internet made it a bestseller.

17. See the news release by the Sunshine Project, "U.S. Armed Forces Push for Offensive Biological Weapons," May 8, 2002, www.sunshine-project.org.

18. Within days of the September 11 attack, there was a shocking report circulating on the Internet that the Justice Department had been warned of an impending attack by Chicago attorney David Schippers, head of the Clinton impeachment team. Schippers asserted on the

Alex Jones radio show that the Justice Department had detailed information on 9/11 weeks before the attack was carried out, claiming that he personally sent information about the impending September 11 attacks to Attorney General Ashcroft asking for an investigation, but Ashcroft had refused to do anything. Schippers alleged that he received his information from FBI agents, who had collected information about the impending attack and the terrorists subsequently involved, but that it was ignored. There were, in fact, many reports from Russian, Israeli, German, U.S., and other intelligence sources warning that a major domestic terrorist attack was about to unfold against the U.S., but the Bush administration and the National (In)security Apparatus failed to respond. See makethemaccountable.com/what when/index.html, which collects the warnings concerning a terror attack ignored by the Bush administration. There was even a report that a Taliban minister warned both U.S. and UN sources about an impending Al Qaeda attack on the U.S.; see Kate Clark, "Revealed: The Taliban Minister, the U.S. Envoy and the Warning of September 11 that Was Ignored," *The Independent*, September 7, 2002.

19. See Eric Lichtblau and Charles Piller, "War on Terrorism Highlights FBI's Computer Woes," *Los Angeles Times*, July 28, 2002.

20. See Richard C. Ochs, "Government by Anthrax," www.freefromterror.net.

21. For two summaries of the anthrax evidence, see the well-documented study by Richard Ochs mentioned in note 20 and Wayne Madsen, "Anthrax and the Agency—Thinking the Unthinkable," April 8–9, 2002, 3, www.counterpunch.org/madsenanthrax.html. Ochs collects several other analyses at his site.

22. In June 2002, Barbara Hatch Rosenberg posted a report that indicated that the probable source of the anthrax attacks was a U.S. scientist working in the biochemical defense industry who was also a CIA liaison; she met with Congress on June 18; see "I'm Ready for My Close-up, Sen. Daschle: A Leading FBI Critic with Her Own Theories about Post–9/11 Anthrax Attacks Makes a Quiet Visit to Capitol Hill," *Salon*, June 21, 2002. See also Nick Peters, "War on Terror: FBI 'Guilty of Cover-up' over Anthrax Suspect," *Scotland on Sunday*, June 16, 2002. In August 2002, the FBI raided the home of a former biochemical scientist, indicating that he "was a person of interest to the Department of Justice," and the media circulated many negative stories about the scientist, Dr. Steven J. Hatfill. Hatfill responded with a vigorous attack on the FBI; see Ron Kampeas, "Hatfill Files Complaint on FBI Probe," Associated Press, August 26, 2002. An article on Hatch Rosenberg by Anthony York, "Biosleuth or Crackpot?" (*Salon*, August 31, 2002) provides background on Rosenberg, her credibility within the scientific community, and the specific criticisms made of her by Hatfill. The episode is one of the more intriguing stories of the Terror War and has already given rise to wildly different interpretations.

23. Later, it came out that a communications breakdown and inefficient coordination of police and fire department efforts caused the needless deaths of many police and firefighters. See the discussion of media neglect of this issue in Eric Boehlert, "Too Hot to Handle," *Salon*, August 20, 2002. For a detailed account of activity at the World Trade Center site after the terror attacks, see Langewiesche 2002.

24. See Langewiesche 2002. His account of the stolen jeans was contested in its details by critics, but Langewiesche sticks by his story and New York journalists who I talked to at a conference on 9/11 at the University of Wisconsin-Milwaukee in October 2002 confirmed that the story had validity and was going to appear on U.S. television, but a network decided not to run a report that would offend some viewers who saw the firemen as heroes. See the

discussion of the story and a defense of Langewiesche in Timothy Noah, "Lay off Langewiesche," *Slate,* October 17, 2002.

4 SPECIAL OPERATIONS, BOMBING, AND PROPAGANDA WAR

1. On postmodern war, see Best and Kellner 2001, chapter 2.

2. Warren P. Strobel and Jonathan S. Landay, "Pentagon Hires Image Firm to Explain Airstrikes to World: U.S. Trying to Reverse Rise in Muslims' Outrage," *San Jose Mercury News,* October 19, 2001. One Pentagon official admitted that "we are clearly losing the 'hearts and minds' issue."

3. "Afghan Survivors Recount Bombings: Civilian Deaths Turn Them against U.S.," *Chicago Tribune,* October 27, 2001.

4. The BBC led off its October 24 newscast with a detailed report of deaths from the unexploded cluster bombs in an Afghan village, but the U.S. TV networks and wire services ignored the story until the *New York Times* published reports the next day, "Errant Cluster Bomb Leaves Danger Behind, U.N. Says" and "U.S. Hits Taliban Stronghold; Cluster Bomb Toll Climbs to 9." Discussing official fact-finding investigations of civilian casualties from U.S. bombing during the Gulf, Kosovo, and Afghanistan wars, Bill Arkin notes that in Iraq, "I don't think it would be an exaggeration to say that more civilians have been killed or injured in Basra by cluster bomb accidents since Desert Storm than were killed by accidental bombings during the war itself." Likewise, in Kosovo, "Cluster bombs again caused a disproportionate number of civilian deaths and injuries in Yugoslavia." Arkin suggests that the U.S. military failed to learn the lessons from these previous use of cluster bombs, implying that their use in Afghanistan was unjustified and unwise. See Bill Arkin, "Not Good Enough, Mr. Rumsfeld," *Washington Post,* February 25, 2002. The use of these highly controversial munitions shows the Bush administration and Pentagon's arrogance and disregard for world public opinion, undermining the need to win hearts and minds for the war against terror and in fact creating more enemies for the U.S. Human Rights Watch published a report in December 2002 indicating that the U.S. violated international law by indiscriminately dropping cluster bombs on populated areas; see Vernon Loeb, "Group Says U.S. Broke Law in Use Of Cluster Bombs in Afghanistan," Washington Post (December 18, 2002: Page A27).

5. See Bill Weinberg, "Is Pentagon Using Depleted Uranium in Afghanistan?" *World War 3 Report,* no. 25 (March 24, 2002). Weinberg reports that the Pentagon has denied that it is using depleted uranium in Afghanistan, but that critics are skeptical. Although there was general media silence on the issue in the U.S., the European Parliament called for an investigation of possible use of depleted uranium in Afghanistan and such an investigation is indeed pressing and important, as the use of radioactive weapons that caused such ongoing suffering in Iraq and Yugoslavia should be found unacceptable; see www.xs4all.nl/~stgvisie/VISIE/europ-parliament-afghanDU.html. For a useful analysis of the "Hazards of Suspected Uranium Weapons," see the report at www.eoslifework.co.uk/u23.htm.

6. See "Pentagon: Afghan Village a 'Legitimate Target,'" November 2, 2001, www.cnn.com.

7. Seamus Milne, "The innocent dead in a coward's war. Estimates suggest that U.S. bombs have killed at least 3,767 civilians," *The Guardian,* December 20, 2001.

8. See Jason Burke, "Desperate call from the valley of death: 'Help us. . . .'" *Guardian*, October 28, 2001. There were also many reports that the CIA had failed to adequately support Haq, that they had "hung him out to dry," and that his death was attributed in part to CIA incompetency. Later speculation suggested that Haq was too independent and could not be controlled by the U.S., and that Hamid Karzai was a preferable choice for president of Afghanistan from the Bush administration perspective. Indeed, Haq had urged the U.S. not to bomb Afghanistan, claiming it would drive Afghans toward the Taliban and bring on more devastation and chaos to an already tortured nation; see Eric Margolis, "Anthrax and Abdul Haq: What Goes Around, Comes Around," syndicated, November 4, 2001, at www.foreign correspondent.com. For a rich portrait of Abdul Haq, see Robert Kaplan, *Soldiers of God: With Islamic Warriors in Afghanistan and Pakistan* (New York: Vintage, 2001).

9. See Thomas E. Ricks and Vernon Loeb, "Quiet Commander in the Hot Seat. Franks Criticized on Pace of War," *Washington Post*, November 9, 2001; and "Splits Open in UK–U.S. Alliance," *Guardian*, November 9, 2001.

10. Dexter Filkins, "Taliban's Foes Say Bombing Is Poorly Aimed and Futile," *New York Times*, November 2, 2001.

11. Sir Michael Howard's speech was published on www.thisislondon.com on October 31 and was widely distributed on the Internet.

12. R. W. Apple, Jr., "Afghanistan as Vietnam," *New York Times*, October 31, 2001; the Perle quote is from Jason Vest, "Bush's War Hawk," *The American Prospect*, November 5, 2001; and on the CIA failure, see "Doubts Grow over U.S. War Strategy," *The (London) Times*, October 27, 2001.

13. As I noted in the introduction, Cheney's former Halliburton company, in serious financial crisis and struggling for survival because of the terrible management when Cheney was CEO, was receiving much-needed government contracts in the Terror War; see introduction, notes 23 and 24 for sources.

14. See David Firestone, "The Leader in Airport Security, and in Lapses," *New York Times*, November 9, 2001.

15. Even liberal commentators were arguing for the justification of torture in the terrorism hysteria of the time; see Jonathan Alter, *Newsweek*, November 5, 2001; and Allan Dershowitz, "The Legal Prohibition against Torture," *Los Angeles Times*, November 8, 2001.

5 VICISSITUDES OF TERROR WAR

1. An article in *Salon*, November 9, 2001, reported that according to a survey by Jupiter Media Metrix, the British *Guardian's* online site was attracting 600,000 American readers a day, while the British *Daily Telegraph* website cited had gained 500,000 visitors since September 11. As I indicate throughout, I learned much more about the Afghan war through my daily scrutiny of British newspapers and TV than by reading U.S. papers (which had many fewer reporters in the field than the Brits) and watching U.S. television (which had degenerated into a propaganda apparatus).

2. See Jessica Hodgson, "U.S. Networks Criticized for 'Jingoistic' Coverage," *The Guardian*, November 14, 2001; "Are Americans Getting the Full Picture?" *Sydney Morning Herald*, November 18, 2001; and Anthony Collins, "The BBC: How to Be Impartial in Wartime," *The Chronicle of Higher Education*, December 21, 2001.

3. See Nina J. Easton, "Blacked Out," *American Journalism Review* (March 2002); Neil Hickey, "Access Denied: The Pentagon's War Reporting Rules are the Toughest Ever," *American Journalism Review* (March 2002); and The Reporter's Committee for Freedom of the Press White Paper, "Homefront Confidential. How the War on Terrorism Affects Access to Information and the Public's Right to Know," www.rcfp.org/news/documents/Homefront_Confidential.pdf.

4. "Don't swap one evil for another: Northern Alliance is not the answer," *The Observer,* November 11, 2001.

5. Totally triumphalist stories on November 11, 2001, include Dexter Filkins, "With One Prize in Hand, Afghan Rebels Press On," *New York Times;* and William Branigan, "Jubilant Afghan Fighters Set Sights on Kabul," *Washington Post.* A November 11 *Los Angeles Times* story, "Taliban Forces Retreat After Rebel Assaults," by contrast, described a bloody fight still going on in Mazar-i-Sharif with more than 1,000 Taliban holdouts fighting on. Yet another story by Doug Struck claimed "Taliban Allies Lost in Strange City," *Washington Post;* according to Struck, trapped Pakistani volunteers were abandoned in Mazar by their Taliban allies who had fled the country. As it turned out, Islamic Jihad volunteers were being arrested or killed, and later accounts described scores of bodies and mass executions. On the Sunday morning talk shows, Bush administration and Pentagon officials were being cautious in describing Northern Alliance progress, although a triumphalist tone began to be heard in Washington and would intensify as the Taliban collapsed.

6. In a revealing story in the *Washington Post,* November 11, 2001, Steven Mufson and Thomas E. Ricks noted that the "New Front Illustrates [an] Evolving Strategy." The article cites U.S. military planners and commentators who admit that the first phase of the U.S. bombing campaign was ineffective and undirected, and that only by getting U.S. Special Forces on the ground did they have adequate intelligence; this eventually evolved into a strategy resulting in success in the taking of Mazar-i-Sharif. A right-wing spin on the story was provided by conservative armchair generals William Kristol and Robert Kagan in "Fighting to Win," *National Standard,* November 12, 2001. "Generals" Kristol and Kagan blamed the slow pace and apparent failure of the first month of the U.S. bombing campaign on Colin Powell's State Department, which supposedly failed to trust the Northern Alliance and was too concerned with Pakistan and world public opinion to unleash a virile enough bombing campaign. Then, the True Men in the Pentagon led by Big Don Rumsfeld took over, bombed the hell out of the Taliban, and the Northern Alliance kicked their ass. Kagan and Kristol's narrative is made more complex, however, by the fact that the Pentagon itself reportedly distrusted the Northern Alliance, admitted to insiders that its bombing targets were flawed because of poor intelligence, and simply needed more time to come up with a coherent plan. Kagan and Kristol's ideological goal was to discredit their increasingly bitter enemy Colin Powell and to urge the unleashing of the Wild Warriors of the Pentagon to wage Jihad forever, until every nation that supports, or has ever supported, terrorism is destroyed. Another armchair warrior, the "realist" Jim Hoagland of the *Washington Post,* urged in a column "Don't Lose Sight of the Quarry," November 16, 2001, that with the apparent rout of the Taliban the U.S. should not forget that its "national interests" are at stake and that it must go after all of the Evil Terrorist Empire, in "plain language, that means Iraq." A similar argument was made by "Generals" Kristol and Kagan, "Getting Serious," *National Standard,* November 19, 2001.

7. Oliver Burkeman, "Simpson of Kabul," *Guardian,* November 14, 2001. John Simp-

son announced, "It was only BBC people who liberated this city. We got in ahead of Northern Alliance troops." An ITN reporter found himself riding into the city on a Northern Alliance tank driven by the tank commander's 11-year-old son and took over control himself according to an ITN spokeswoman; see Jessica Hodgson, " 'BBC liberated Kabul' says Simpson," *Guardian,* November 14, 2001.

8. See Matt Wells, "Al-Jazeera accuses U.S. of bombing its Kabul office," *Guardian,* November 17, 2001. One of the Al Jazeera reporters in Kabul, who had just left the office before the missile hit, tells of how he was beaten by anti-Taliban Afghans and forced to flee for his life; see Reuters, November 15, 2001. The *New York Times Sunday Magazine* contained a long story on Al Jazeera by Fouad Ajami, "What the Muslim World is Watching," November 18, 2001, that stresses its pro-Arab and anti-U.S. biases.

9. On November 13, *The Guardian* reported that "Downed US Jet's Engine 'Unsafe,'" noting that U.S. safety officials had earlier in the year concluded that the Airbus A300, made by General Electric, had an "unsafe condition." The National Transportation Safety Board, in turn, believed that the tail fell off of the airliner, but there were other suspicions. Steve Dunleavy cited in his *New York Post* column (December 2, 2001) a retired firefighter, Tom Lynch, who was jogging on Rockaway Beach Boulevard the day of the crash and claimed that he saw "a small explosion, about half the size of a car. The plane kept on going straight for about two or three seconds . . . then 'vwoof'—the second, big explosion on the right wing. It was only then that the plane fell apart. It was after the explosion and I'm telling you, the tail was there until the second explosion." Lynch insists that he has thirteen people who saw the plane on fire before the breakup.

At the end of 2002, the U.S. government has not yet released a report on what caused the crash, although in a National Transportation Safety Board hearing, the pilot was accused of overly aggressive use of the plane's rudder that caused the tail fin to fail; see Ricardo Alonso-Zaldivar and Eric Malnic, "Copilot's Actions at Heart of Hearings in Flight 587 Crash," *Los Angeles Times,* November 1, 2001, A16.

10. See the story on Robinson's initiative in *Newsday,* October 12, 2001. Mary Robinson herself, however, was pressured by the U.S. to resign her UN position, as she recounts in an interview with *Salon,* July 26, 2002.

11. "War May be Costing $500M–$1B a Month," Associated Press, November 1, 2001; and "U.S. Is Expecting to Spend $1 Billion a Month on War," *New York Times,* November 12, 2001. An earlier AP article "U.S. Will Have Favors to Return," October 9, 2001, notes that in return for the support of Pakistan, the three neighboring "stan" former Soviet Republics (Uzbekistan, Turkmenistan, and Tajikistan), Turkey, and other countries, the U.S. would have to pay out billions in foreign aid grants, as they were indeed promising to do and had done in the Gulf War. The November 12 Associated Press article opens by stating: "A U.S. helicopter lost in Afghanistan a week ago cost up to twice as much as the government spends yearly on scenic byways. Each cruise missile is worth several American homes." How long would such insanity and obscenity continue?

12. Defense of Civilization Fund, "Defending Civilization: How Our Universities are Failing America and What Can Be Done About It?" November 2001, www.goacta.org. Another missive widely distributed at the same time had Senator Joseph Lieberman (D-Conn.) as Cheney's cosigner, an ignoble fall for Al Gore's vice presidential running mate! Lynne Cheney and her right-wing allies had long dreamed of crushing radical voices of dissent in the university and had long waged a cultural war against their academic enemies. The

conservative Jihad was launched during the Reagan era when Cheney was head of the NEH, which she governed like a Taliban, rooting out all politically incorrect policies and personnel and going after progressives in the academic world. There were some speculations that the U.S. left/right culture wars were suspended in favor of national unity against terrorism, but obviously Cheney and her Taliban were not going to miss a chance to go after their longtime adversaries.

13. See Tony Capaccio, "Missile Defense Early Warning Systems in Disarray, Panel Says," *Bloomberg News*, November 7, 2001. A study by the House Appropriations Committee indicated that the cost of a new system of early warning satellites has soared and its heat-seeking sensors that are critical to detecting enemy missile launches do not work. Eventually, Rumsfeld and Bush were able to exploit Terror War hysteria into getting support for the fanciful missile defense system, although it continues to have fierce critics among those who believe that the U.S. cannot afford to pursue every military fantasy desired by the Pentagon. On problems with a missile defense system, see Francis Fitzgerald, *Way Out There in the Blue: Reagan, Star Wars, and the End of the Cold War* (New York: Touchstone Books, 2001), and Steven Weinberg, "Can Missile Defense Work?" *The New York Review of Books* (February 14, 2002).

14. See the discussion in chapter 1 and Brisard and Dasquie, *Forbidden Truth.*

15. On Bush and Noriega, see Leslie Cockburn, *Out of Control* (New York: Atlantic Monthly Press, 1987); and Robert Parry, *Fooling America* (New York: William Morrow, 1992); see also the collection of articles on Parry's website, www.consortiumnews.com/index.html.

16. It was claimed in many Internet sources that some of the "plans" for nuclear and other weapons of mass destruction found in the Al Qaeda headquarters were taken from an Internet spoof site; see James Ridgeway, *The Village Voice*, November 18, 2001; and David Cassel, "Phoney Bomb Humor Fools Taliban?" *Alternet*, November 19, 2001.

17. Richard Sale, "US, SAS's unreported casualties," United Press International, November 18, 2002.

18. For a systematic examination of Bushspeak, see Kellner, *Grand Theft 2000*, chapter 9.

19. An article by Ben Barber, "The Taliban's deadly 'refugees,'" *Salon*, November 22, 2001, presented the refugee camps along the Afghan-Pakistan border as havens for fleeing Taliban guerrillas who were using the camps to recruit new fighters, for medical services, and as a home base.

6   COLLAPSE OF THE TALIBAN

1. A *New York Times* story by Dexter Filkins, "Taliban Foes Say Kunduz Is Theirs," on November 26, 2001, suggested that the Pakistanis had indeed flown in and taken out some of its citizens, although it was not sure why the Pentagon had allowed the Pakistanis to take out their fighters when the U.S. had made it clear that they did not want free passage for radical Islamic fighters to make trouble elsewhere. There were also reports that many Pakistanis had fled Kunduz and escaped across the border back into Pakistan.

2. See also Phillip Robertson, "All Crazy on the Kunduz Front," *Salon*, November 29, 2001, for an account of his efforts to visit the town of Choge Nawabad, where he confirmed

that U.S. bombing raids had accidentally hit a civilian village, killing whole families and at least twelve people.

3. See Pamela Constable, "Report of Mass Afghan Graves Won't be Probed, Envoy Says," *Washington Post*, August 28, 2002; see also Michelle Goldberg, "When Does a Massacre Matter?" *Salon*, August 20, 2002.

4. See Justin Huggler, "Kunduz Falls, and a Bloody Vengeance Is," and Patrick Cockburn, "Alliance Struggles to End Bloody Uprising at Fortress Jail," *Independent*, November 27, 2001; Rory McCarthy and Nicholas Watt, "Alliance Accused of Brutality in Capture of Kunduz," *Guardian*, November 27, 2001; Dexter Filkins, "In Kunduz, a Deathly Peace Settles In," *New York Times*, November 27, 2001; and Paul Richter, Maura Reynolds, and Peter Gosselin's reports in the *Los Angeles Times*, November 27, 2001.

5. Justin Huggler, "Legacy of Civilian Casualties in Ruins of Shattered Town," *The Independent*, November 27, 2001.

6. The transcript of the call between the *Time* reporter on the scene and his editor was widely disseminated on the Internet on November 26 and was later published in *Time*, December 11, 2001. For other accounts, see Oliver August, "CIA Blunder sparked Taleban revolt that became a mass suicide," *The (London) Times*, November 28, 2001; Carlotta Gall, "Alliance Declares Revolt Is Crushed," *New York Times*, November 28, 2001; and overviews of the aftermath of the prison battles in Matthew Campbell, "The Fort of Hell," *The (London) Times*, December 2, 2001. Interesting epistemological issues arise in the unfolding of the story, as wildly different accounts appeared on the origin and reasons for the prison revolt, its unfolding, the killing of the CIA officer, and the quelling of the revolt. Sources included various on-the-scene journalists, Northern Alliance troops, and other on-site observers. Interest in the American Taliban, John Walker Lindh, who emerged from the battle continued with fevered debate over whether he was a traitor or an innocent youth duped by religious fanaticism.

7. Much later, it was revealed that the Baton Rouge Islamist who was allegedly a second American Taliban, Yaser Esam Hamdi, was born in Louisiana but soon afterward moved to Saudi Arabia with his parents. See, "Lindh Lawyers Offer New Account of Captivity," *Los Angeles Times*, May 23, 2002, A28. Hamdi was declared an "enemy combatant" and so far has not been allowed a lawyer or the possibility of a trial. Senior U.S. District Judge Robert G. Doumar has deemed Hamdi's incarceration without charges or access to a lawyer "idiotic" and "mind-boggling," and the Bush administration fiat allowing them to arrest and hold indefinitely U.S. citizens as "enemy combatants" is being challenged in courts and is probably on its way to the Supreme Court. See Richard Leiby, "An American Justice: Free-Spoken Judge Challenges the White House Over 'Combatant' Rights," *Washington Post*, September 6, 2002.

8. The interview, broadcast by CNN, was carried out by Robert Pelton, who was described as an "author of adventure books." In a story on the interview by Cynthia Cotts, "Midnight Confession," *Village Voice*, January 2–8, 2002, Pelton later told CNN that he was staying with notorious Northern Alliance commander Abdul Dostrum when Walker Lindh and other Taliban fighters were captured after the prison uprising. Pelton informed CNN that Walker Lindh was "dazed and confused" and "didn't even know where he was." Initially, Walker Lindh was allegedly hostile to Pelton and refused an interview, but when Pelton arranged medical treatment, including morphine, the young Taliban recruit began talking in a videotaped conversation, which was taken as his "confession." Cotts notes that Walker

Lindh had not consented to the videotaping and its distribution and had resisted an interview until he was administered the drugs. Thus, in Cotts's view, the tape was highly manipulative in setting up Walker Lindh as a traitor, although it would have ambiguous status as a legal document given the circumstances of its production.

9. Larry Chin suggested that Bush Senior's rage might have been induced by the sight of Walker Lindh's lawyer James Brosnahan, who was a former federal prosecutor and member of Lawrence Walsh's Iran-Contra team, which was documenting Bush Senior's misdeeds and came very close to pinning numerous crimes on the former CIA head and vice president; had Bush I not won the election in 1988 and ended the Iran-Contra investigations into his past, Bush Senior might well be in jail or exile and we would have been spared the disasters of Son of Bush, Return of the Monster. See Larry Chin, "Marin Hot Tubbers, Iran-Contra Ghosts, and Other Fears of the Bush Clan," January 27, 2002, www.yellowtimes.org.

10. See Andrew Sullivan, "Parallel Lives: The CIA Man and the Taliban Fighter from California," *Sunday Times*, December 16, 2001. Sullivan's ludicrous dichotomy was undermined by the release of the videotape of Spann interviewing Walker Lindh; on the tape, rather than exhibiting cool professionalism, Spann was completely incompetent in interviewing Walker Lindh, either missing that he was an American and thus a potentially valuable intelligence asset or completely failing to connect with him. Spann snapped his fingers in Walker Lindh's face and barked at him rather than trying to engage the American Taliban in conversation. Spann then was seized by Taliban and Al Qaeda forces, who killed him as they began a prison uprising that caused a rash of deaths and injuries on all sides. On a BBC program on November 28, British reporters on the scene blamed Spann and his CIA colleague "Dave" for inciting the prisoners to riot due in part to their aggressive questioning techniques, leading to Spann's murder. See "U.S. 'Hero' May Have Triggered Mazar Revolt," *Times of India*, December 2, 2001. While such professional failure should not exactly qualify Spann as an all-American hero, he was lionized in a *Parade* cover story, "Love in a Time of War," August 18, 2002, and was favorably presented in an *A&E* August 2002 documentary on his fatal encounter with Lindh.

11. See Anthony York, "The Proud Principal Who Wasn't," *Salon*, January 4, 2001.

12. See *The National Enquirer*, January 7, 2001.

13. Walker Lindh was the first in the Afghan war to be publicly tried and sentenced. After some open court hearings and the beginning of a trial for treason that could have led to his execution, Walker Lindh's lawyer cut a deal with the government for his client to serve a sentence of at least twenty years in prison on lesser charges. See Richard Serrano, "Lindh Pleads Guilty, Agrees to Aid Inquiry," *Los Angeles Times*, July 16, 2002.

14. Rowan Scarborough, "Special Forces Get Free Rein," *The Washington Times*, November 23, 2001; and Michael Evans, "Delta Force 'Has Killed Hundreds,'" *The (London) Times*, November 24, 2001. The latter quoted a U.S. official as saying, "From the reports I have seen, they have killed in the hundreds and there have been no deaths on our side." A UPI report that I cited earlier, however, claimed that Bush administration officials admitted that at least 40–50 U.S. Special Ops forces had been killed in the fighting and that the U.S. had decided not to acknowledge Special Ops deaths; thus it was really impossible to know the true U.S. casualty count.

15. Frank Rich, "Wait until Dark," *New York Times*, November 24, 2001. Rich correctly noted that "this kind of high-handedness and secrecy has been a hallmark of the [Bush] administration beginning Jan. 20, not Sept. 11," citing Cheney's secret meetings with big

energy corporations to help construct energy policy while refusing Congressional requests to clarify his meetings, having a secret commission on Social Security reform, and signing executive orders blocking access to presidential papers. Secrecy and conspiracy have long been trademarks of the Bush family and Cheney. For other criticisms of the United States' antiterror policy, see Anthony Lewis, "Right and Wrong," *New York Times,* November 24, 2001; BBC News, "Criticism of U.S. anti-terror efforts grows," November 20, 2001; and many other commentaries, circulated through www.bushwatch.com, www.buzzflash.com, and Phil Agre's *Red Rock Eater* list. Mainstream television on the whole ignored the dangerous erosion of civil liberties, although the issue was discussed in BBC and Canadian TV. For critiques of the USA Patriot Act, see the Center for Constitutional Rights Report at www.ccr-ny.org/whatsnew/usa_patriot_act.asp and the Electronic Frontier Foundation report at www.eff.org/Privacy/Surveillance/Terrorism_militias/20011031_eff_usa_p atriot_analysis.html.

16. Maureen Dowd, "Uncivil Liberties," *New York Times,* November 25, 2001. Usually Dowd and the liberals could be counted on to provide critique of the worst assaults of the Bush administration against civil liberties and the open society, but in the war hysteria they too surrendered, leaving but a few honorable people to defend civil liberties and rights under assault by the Bush administration.

17. Ashcroft had lost his Senate seat in a hotly contested Missouri election to the wife of a deceased candidate (Governor Mel Carnahan, who was killed in a plane crash three weeks before the 2000 election). Carnahan remained on the ballot and defeated Ashcroft, who had led the impeachment charge against Bill Clinton and who had technically lost the election to a dead man. Bush would later name Ashcroft his designate for attorney general and there would be a very hot confirmation fight, as Ashcroft was one of the most extreme right-wing members of the Senate. Receiving a 100 percent rating from the Christian Coalition, Ashcroft was ranked by the *National Journal* as the most conservative member of Congress. He had received an honorary degree from the right-wing Bob Jones University and had praised an ultra-segregationist pro-Confederacy journal, *Southern Partisan.* Most scandalously, he had blocked the appointment of an African American to a federal judgeship by blatantly lying, claiming that the designee was soft on criminals and would not use the death penalty when the facts were that neither was the case; see Douglas Kellner, *Grand Theft 2000* (Lanham, Md.: Rowman & Littlefield, 2001).

18. See Dick Morris, "On to Baghdad!" *New York Post,* November 20, 2001. The right wing of the Bush administration would also take up the call to take the Terror War to Iraq during 2002; see chapter 11.

19. This hypothesis was suggested in an article by William J. Broad and Judith Miller, "Anthrax Inquiry Looks at U.S. Labs," *New York Times,* December 2, 2001. The piece explores the hypothesis set forth by Barbara Hatch Rosenberg, an expert in biological weapons, who believes that the grade of anthrax produced suggests a "knowledgeable insider," someone who had worked in U.S. biological weapons labs or had access to its high-grade material. Later reports also indicate that the FBI is currently investigating government labs and its contractors. See Barbara Hatch Rosenberg, www.ph.ucla.edu/epi/bioter/compilationofanthraxevidence.html; and "Anthrax Attack Bug 'Identical' to Army Strain," *New Scientist,* May 2, 2002, www.newscientist.com.

20. As of the end of 2002, major U.S. bioscientists and other scientists throughout the world had mysteriously disappeared or died, although there was no sustained discussions in the media; see Lisa Belkin, "The Odds of That," *New York Times,* August 11, 2002. As noted,

in August 2002 there was also intense media focus on one particular American bioscientist as a chief suspect who ferociously fought his accusers, proclaiming his innocence.

21. See "Bible Belt Worships Terror Survivor," *The (London) Times,* November 24, 2001.

22. Later investigations revealed that the "friendly fire" incident that almost killed Karzai was traced to a dead battery on a Global Positioning System device that automatically changed the system's coordinates to their own location after a battery change! See Vernon Loeb, "'Friendly Fire' Deaths Traced to Dead Battery: Taliban Forces Targeted, but U.S. Forces Killed," *Washington Post,* March 24, 2002, A21. There were also reports that many more U.S. and Afghan casualties resulted from the mistaken targeting than were originally reported. See John Hendren and Maura Reynolds, "The U.S. Bomb That Nearly Killed Karzai: Target Finder's Error Cost about 28 Lives to 'Friendly Fire,'" *Los Angeles Times,* March 27, 2002. Yet one article claimed that Karzai's seizure of the provincial capital of Tarin Kot and the subsequent U.S. hi-tech massacre of Taliban forces who tried to retake the town was a turning point that precipitated the rapid and surprising collapse of the Taliban in the south of the country; see Karl Vick, "Rout in Desert Marked Turning Point of War. U.S. Firepower Decimated Taliban at Tarin Kot," *Washington Post* (December 31, 2001). In general, little is known about the collapse of the Taliban in the southern half of the country as there were few journalists in the area and no detailed reports or narratives.

7 THE HUNT FOR BIN LADEN

1. The *Washington Post* headlined its story by Dana Milbank on the Bush power grab, "Bush Exercises Executive Muscle," describing Bush's assault on democracy as if it was a weightlifting routine, December 13, 2001.

2. See Kim Sengupta, "Americans 'Duped' into Attack on Convoy," *Independent,* December 24, 2001.

3. A later article in the *Los Angeles Times,* May 18, 2002, A1, "Officials Reveal bin Laden Attack," indicated that the assassination of Masoud was part of an Al Qaeda offensive that included the September 11 terror attacks. This should have alerted American intelligence that Al Qaeda was on the move and to be taken very seriously.

4. See David Rose, "Bloody Search for DNA to Discover bin Laden's Fate," *The Guardian,* January 13, 2002.

5. See Peter Foster, "U.S. Bombs 'Kill 107 Villagers,'" *(UK) Telegraph,* January 1, 2002; Rory Carroll, "U.S. Accused of Killing over 100 Villagers in Air Strike," *The Guardian,* January 1, 2002; and Rory Carroll, "Blood Evidence of U.S. Blunder," *The Guardian,* January 7, 2002. As FAIR notes in a critique, the *New York Times* failed to cover the story; see "NYT Buries Story of Airstrikes on Afghan Civilians," January 9, 2002.

6. Carroll, "Blood Evidence."

7. See Suzanne Goldenberg, "Day 100: another raid in the bombing war without end," *The Guardian,* January 15, 2002. The story documents the cycle of U.S. bombing of Zhawar during 2002, complaints by the local residents, and claims that villages and civilians had been bombed who had nothing to do with Al Qaeda or the Taliban.

8. See Meagan Stack, "The Afghan Warnings That Went Unheeded at Tora Bora," *Los Angeles Times,* April 25, 2002, A5; and *Newsweek,* "How Al Qaeda Slipped Away. . . . The Inside Story of Al Qaeda's Mass Escape," August 19, 2002. The latter concluded: "What is

not in dispute is that by mid-December, 1,000, or more Al Qaeda operatives, including most of the chief planners and almost certainly Osama bin Laden himself, had managed to escape . . . most of the top echelon and even rank-and-file fighters are still on the loose."

9. See Andy McSmith, David Usborne, and Geoffrey Lean, "Blair Warns of New Threat to Britain from al Qaeda," *The Independent,* November 20, 2002. Former National Security Council members Daniel Benjamin and Steven Simon reach similar conclusions in "Al Qaeda's Dangerous Metamorphosis," *Los Angeles Times,* November 11, 2002, writing, "As it metamorphoses into a virtual network, depriving its enemies of a geographic target, al Qaeda may become a greater threat than it was before its leadership melted away at Tora Bora." The escape of Al Qaeda and Taliban leadership discloses the ludicrousness of George W. Bush's comments to Bob Woodward for his *Bush at War* book that spending millions to buy Afghan support was "one of the best 'bargains' of all time" (2002: 316), since relying on Afghan forces and failure to use U.S. troops to arrest or eliminate Al Qaeda leadership was what resulted in their escape.

8 THE NEW BARBARISM: WORLD IN TURMOIL

1. In a stunning display of pure mendacity, Bush's buffoonish spinmeister Karl Rove told the American Enterprise Institute in a December 2001 talk that Bush was "never a unilateralist." I have documented in *Grand Theft 2000* Bush's succession of unilateralist gestures during his first months in office, ranging from rejection of the Kyoto environmental treaty to renunciation of several major weapons treaties. The Bush administration leaked to the press before the U.S. bombing of Afghanistan why they did not want coalition partners to restrain their military activity, and they seemed determined to go it alone in a continuing war on terror against a large list of designated targets, including Iraq. As I document in this study, Bush has continued an aggressively unilateralist foreign policy that had been increasingly criticized by European and other U.S. allies. From this perspective, one of the more laughable elements of Woodward's *Bush at War* (2002) is his constant stressing that Bush himself insisted on a humanitarian component to the Afghanistan operation, demanding that food be dropped with bombs from the first day. The compliant corporate media spun the line that the Afghan intervention had a serious humanitarian component at the beginning, although it soon became clear that U.S. military intervention blocked humanitarian relief efforts. As I document in this study, the U.S. military blocked major efforts—from November 2001 following the collapse of the Taliban well into the next year—to promote humanitarian and relief efforts that other countries wished to advance.

2. C. J. Chivers, "400 Experts Try to Harvest Afghanistan's Field of Mines," *New York Times,* December 18, 2001. Bush administration official Kenton Keith claimed that although "the coalition did not create this problem, we will step forward to help Afghanistan deal with it." Chivers comments: "Some Afghans took exception to those assertions, noting that the United States sent billions of dollars of arms and military aid through Pakistan into Afghanistan in the 1980s to assist the guerrilla resistance to the Soviets. The aid included mines and explosives training, several former guerrillas said. Mr. Keith also did not acknowledge the problem of unexploded American bombs, which in places are thick." Further, the head of Halo Trust was highly critical of the use of cluster bombs, which were roughly the same color and size of food supplies and were leading to many injuries.

3. See www.cnn.com, "Police Ponder Charges in Airport Grenade Incident," December 18, 2001; and www.cnn.com, "Suspect in Custody in Atlanta Airport Incident," November 16, 2001.

4. Interestingly, it later turned out that one of the barbaric military "commentators" employed by the Fox Network, Joseph Cafasso, had lied about his military record and exploits and was fraudulently presenting himself as an authority!

5. See www.buzzflash.com, "Publisher of *Sacramento Bee* Booed at Graduation Ceremony," December 16, 2002; and Scott Petrak, "Dawg Pounded: Disputed Calls Fuels Fans' Fury," Associated Press Sports, November 13, 2001.

6. By January 6, 2002, over twenty-seven young arsonists, dubbed "Lucifers" by the local press, had been questioned about or charged with arson. There were also reports that Sydney police were in pursuit of a mysterious "phantom," a "sinister backwoodsman," believed to be the source of many of the fires that had now ravaged the Sydney area; see *Sunday Times*, January 6, 2002.

7. See the special section on "State of Emergency," *Theory, Culture, and Society* 19, no. 4 (2002), introduced by John Armitage, pp. 27–38, for contrasts between state of emergency doctrines of Nazi Germany and the Bush and Blair regimes.

8. See Mark Steel, "The Secret Plans of the World's Most Dangerous Rogue State," June 19, 2001, *The Independent*. This section is extracted from a forthcoming article "Postmodern Military and Permanent War" in a book edited by Carl Boggs, whom I thank for many editorial suggestions on the following discussion.

9. On Bush administration military budgets, see articles in *Los Angeles Times* (February 14, 2001: A14); *Washington Post* (June 23, 2001); *Los Angeles Times*, (Sept 18, 2002); and *Washington Post* (October 10, 2001). In a February 2002 testimony to the House Budget Committee, Lawrence J. Korb of the Council on Foreign Relations and Business Leaders for Sensible Priorities noted that the Bush military budget represented a 30 percent increase over the previous year. If approved, U.S. military spending would exceed the total defense outlays "of the next 15 countries in the world combined." Furthermore, the proposed "increase of $48 billion alone is more than the total military budgets of every nation in the world." Lawrence Korb, cited in James Carroll, "Bush's radical shift in military policy," *Boston Globe* (February 19, 2002).

10. See "Missile Shield Analysis Warns of Arms Buildup. U.S. System could lead other nuclear powers to enhance arsenals, spread technology, report says." *Los Angeles Times* (May 19, 2000: A1 and A22) and "Risk of Arms Race Seen in U.S. Design of Missile Defense," *New York Times* (May 27, 2000). For a damning critique of the Star Wars/missile shield programs, see Francis Fitzgerald, *Way Out There in the Blue: Reagan, Star Wars, and the End of the Cold War* (New York: Touchstone Books); and Steven Weinberg, "Can Missile Defense Work?" *The New York Review of Books* (February 14, 2002). On the militarization of space, see Karl Grossman, *Weapons in Space* (New York: Seven Stories Press, 2001). Finally, for critique of excessive Pentagon spending and the "iron triangle" of the defense industry, the military, and Congress which perpetuates this obscenity, see Greider, *Fortress America*.

11. Dr. Robert M. Bowman, "Wounding National Security. Star Wars II Endangers the American People," *The News Insider*, July 23, 2001. Bowman criticizes his own participation in the earlier Star Wars program which he now terms "military lunacy." He argues that the new Star Wars II would seriously harm U.S. national security by increasing the arms race, isolating the U.S., eating up resources, and violating treaties, while presenting no real protec-

tion against nuclear terrorism. Bowman and many other critics also argue convincingly that the Star Wars II shield just cannot work. In addition to Fitzgerald and Weinberg crited in the note above, the Internet is full of critiques of the unworkability of the Star Wars program; see, for example, www.ucsusa.org/security/CM-exec.html.

12. Secretary of Defense Donald Rumsfeld, popularly referred to as "Dr. Strangelove" in light of his obsession with space and missiles, announced on May 8, 2001, a sharply increased interest in outer space in U.S. strategic military planning. See James Dao, "Rumsfeld Plans to Seek a Military Strategy Using Outer Space," *New York Times*, May 8, 2001, and the critique of the proposed militarization of space, "The Risks of a New Space Race," *New York Times*, Op-Ed, May 13, 2001. The post–September 11 Terror Wars temporarily postponed confrontation over the missile defense program that is proceeding apace without serious debate or opposition.

13. See Best and Kellner, *The Postmodern Adventure*.

14. Leader, "Proliferator-in-Chief," *The Guardian*, July 26, 2001.

15. Ibid.

16. There was little detailed analysis of the defunding of the INC in the U.S. press; see, however, "Iraq Exiles Accused of Wasting $2m Aid," *The (London) Times*, January 26, 2002, which describes the group as "Gucci guerillas" whose "members spend more time at its Knightsbridge headquarters than opposing Saddam's forces on the ground."

17. See "Warlords Steal Food Shipments, Hampering Efforts to Relieve Famine," *New York Times*, January 4, 2002; and "Afghan City, Free of Taliban, Returns to the Rule of the Thieves," *New York Times*, January 6, 2002. See also the report from northern Afghanistan by Ravi Newssman, "Afghans eat grass as aid fails to arrive," *Guardian*, January 9, 2002; and Medea Benjamin, "Feeding the Hungry May Be the Prime Task of Peacekeepers," *Milwaukee Journal Sentinel*, December 16, 2001, on the task of feeding the hungry and providing adequate shelter throughout the country.

18. A Gallup Poll of Arab countries revealed shockingly low support for U.S. military action, disbelief that bin Laden and Al Qaeda actually carried out the September 11 terror acts, and other indicators that suggest the U.S. propaganda efforts had failed. (See introduction, note 3.) Although one could question the methodology of the poll, it seemed likely that the Bush administration had failed in its efforts to win hearts and minds in the Arab world.

19. See "Arroyo under Fire for U.S. Special Forces Deployment in Philippines," *Yahoo! News*, January 16, 2002. Chalmers Johnson, who wrote the book *Blowback* that I used in chapter 1, claimed in an interview in *Salon* published on June 8, 2002, that Abu Sayyaf was not a terrorist organization connected to Al Qaeda but "a kidnapping ring that's been kidnapping people for extraordinary ransoms." He also claimed that the intervention was motivated by a desire for U.S. military presence in the area. A similar analysis is found in Raymond Bonner, "Antiterror Fight: Why the Philippines?" *New York Times*, June 10, 2002.

20. See for example, Terry Jones, "Spare our blushes and put a sack on it," *Guardian*, January 6, 2002; Mary Robinson, "Denying captives rights will return to haunt us," *Independent*, January 19, 2002; unsigned editorial, "It Is Shameful for Britain to Support the Degradation of These Terrorist Suspects," *Independent*, January 22, 2001; Donald Macintyre, "Why Mr Blair Must Make an Urgent Call to the President," *Independent*, January 22, 2001; Robert Fiske, "Congratulations, America: You Have Made bin Laden a Happy Man," *Independent*, January 22, 2001; and Terry Waite, "Justice or Revenge?" *Guardian*, January 23, 2002. In a press conference after this volley of criticism, Rumsfeld aggressively defended the

indefensible U.S. policy and mocked its critics, intensifying in turn criticism in the British press of the "Rumsfeld problem."

21. See "Camp X-Ray Row Threatens First British Split with U.S.," *Guardian*, January 22, 2001; "Camp X-Ray Could Split Allies," *The Times*, January 21, 2001 and the editorials cited in note 11. By contrast, U.S. cable television talk shows attacked criticism of the U.S. detainee camp and defended U.S. policy, showing the extent to which sectors of the U.S. public were falling prey to the New Barbarism.

22. Indeed, there were reports that prisoners held in Afghanistan were being incarcerated in extremely brutal and deadly conditions. See Bill Weinberg, "Taliban POWs Face Cattle Cars and Desert Camps," *World War 3 Report*, no. 12 (December 15, 2001); Bill Weinberg, "War Captives Face Brutal Conditions," *World War 3 Report*, no. 16 (January 12, 2002); and Bill Weinberg, "Taliban POWs Face Cattle Cars and Desert Camps," *World War 3 Report*, no. 16 (January 12, 2002).

23. As a curious aside, I might note that the U.S. military regularly refers to Guantanamo Bay as "Gitmo," a racist construction that holds the Spanish language in contempt and in its ordinary language connotations signifies "get more," a perfect formula of imperialism (i.e., get more land, resources, and wealth from them there natives!).

24. See Katty Kay, "U.S. 'Will Send Most Detainees Home,'" *The (London) Times*, January 23, 2001; see Katharine Q. Seelye, "Powell Asks Bush to Reverse Stand on War Captives," *New York Times*, January 27, 2002.

25. See Matthew Engel, "U.S. Is Not the Problem, Rumsfeld Says," *The Guardian*, January 23, 2002; and Richard Norton Taylor, "Rumsfeld Attacked over Cuba Prisoners," *The Guardian*, February 25, 2002.

26. ABC News, November 8, 2002; on the release of aged detainees, see Tim Reid and Dumeetha Luthra, "'Why Arrest Me? I'm Just an Old Man,'" *The Times*, October 30, 2002. See Greg Miller, "Many Held at Guantanamo Not Likely Terrorists" for an excellent piece of investigative reporting that shows that the U.S. military arrested many terrorist suspects in Afghanistan and brought them to the camp in Cuba without adequate evidence, incarcerating scores that were not really hardcore members of Al Qaeda or the Taliban; then the government was not able to release many of those who turned out not to be dangerous because of red tape and bureaucratic inertia (*Los Angeles Times*, December 22, 2002).

9   THE WAR AT HOME: POLITICAL BATTLES AND THE ENRON SCANDAL

1. The close connection between the Bush-Baker clique and Enron has been documented by honorable conservative Kevin Phillips, one of the few Republicans to speak out against Bush gang corruption. See, "The Company Presidency: Enron and the Bush family have boosted each other up the ladder of success, but have their ties created a Teapot Dome?" *Los Angeles Times*, February 10, 2002, M1, 6.

2. For the insider trading allegations, widely circulated in the Texas press during Bush's first run for governor against Ann Richards, see J. H. Hatfield, *Fortunate Son: George W. Bush and the Making of an American President* (New York: Soft Skull Press, 2000); and Molly Ivins and Lou Dubose, *Shrub: The Short but Happy Political Life of George W. Bush* (New York: Random House, 2000). For an update on the story by investigative reporter Knut Royce,

released on the Center for Public Integrity website, see "Bush's Insider Connections Preceded Huge Profit on Stock Deal," www.public-i.org/story_01_040400.htm. As I note in the introduction, the Bush insider trading story became a major focus of the media in May 2002 following a couple of Paul Krugman columns in the *New York Times*.

3. Douglas Kellner, *Grand Theft 2000* (Lanham, Md.: Rowman & Littlefield, 2001).

4. See www.thenation.com/special/2002enron.mhtml, which collects *The Nation* articles that document the impact of the Enron collapse on investors, pension plans, and the national and global economy, with many articles documenting the longtime relation between the Bush family and the Enron crooks. Another site, *The Daily Enron,* published regular commentary on the Enron scandal and other Bush outrages and collected the material at www.thedailyenron.com.

5. The connections between the Cheney-Bush and Enron robber barons were exposed by a June 2001 PBS *Frontline*, "The California Energy Crisis." The program featured interviews with the previous head of FERC, who tells how Ken Lay called to dictate policy; when the head of FERC would not follow Lay's commands, Lay called Cheney, who then replaced him with a Bush crony from Texas who is still the head of FERC.

6. By the end of 2002, Enron had pretty much disappeared from intense public scrutiny and the Bush administration had successfully framed the issue as an economic and not a political scandal. Enron executive Jeff Skilling faced a wide array of federal charges and one of his underlings, Michael J. Kopper, agreed to testify in exchange for lesser charges. But in the 2002 midterm election, the Democrats rarely raised the issue of Enron and corporate corruption and it was no longer an intense media focus. Indeed, the poor Democratic Party showing could be partly due to failure to link the Bush administration with the corporate scandals of the past years, the decline of the economy, and its failures in national security, themes that are a major dimension of this book.

7. See Jason Leopold, "Tom White Played Key Role in Covering up Enron Losses," *Salon*, August 29, 2002. White's office challenged some of the allegations made against the former Enron executive, now secretary of the army, and as of the end of 2002 he remains in office despite frequent predictions of his demise. For a dossier of memos and material that suggest White's direct involvement in crooked accounting schemes at Enron, see "The Thomas E. White Affair—The Documents," www.scoop.co.nz/mason/stories/HL0211/S00018.htm.

8. Kellner, *Grand Theft 2000*.

9. Indeed, Pitts was forced to resign from the SEC when he recommended former FBI and CIA Director William Webster to run the new Public Company Accounting Oversight Board that was supposed to regulate corporate accounting and stock exchange practices. Pitts chose Webster over a reformer who many favored, and Pitts neglected to tell the board voting on the head regulator that Webster had worked for a firm accused of accounting malpractice. A firestorm of controversy followed, leading to Pitts's resignation on election eve. See Floyd Norris, "Help Wanted at the S.E.C.: Help Needed for Reform," *New York Times,* November 13, 2002.

10. Cronyism in the Bush administration is astounding. Not only has Bush surrounded himself with his father's friends and former officials, but the relatives of Dick Cheney, Colin Powell, John Ashcroft, and several lesser figures have been hired for key government positions, as well as relatives of two Supreme Court justices, William Rehnquist and Antonin Scalia, who illicitly awarded Bush the presidency. See Dana Milbank, "In Appointments, Administration Leaves No Family Behind," *Washington Post,* March 12, 2002, A19.

11. Kellner, *Grand Theft 2000.*

12. Bill Moyers *Now!* featured interviews in an August 2002 show with former government officials who had resigned from various environmental agencies in protest against the Bush administration's anti-environment policies.

13. "A Decade of Deficits," *The Economist,* June 20, 2002.

14. A videotape of Mrs. Lay's testimony was available on www.ifilm.com in February 2002, under the rubric "Enron Crocodile Tears."

15. Douglas Kellner, *The Persian Gulf TV War* (Boulder, Colo.: Westview Press, 1992).

16. See www.counterpunch.org, February 5, 2002.

10 THE AFGHAN NIGHTMARE AND THE "AXIS OF EVIL"

1. See Eric Schmitt, "U.S. Says Tribal Leaders Balk at Aiding Search for Taliban," *New York Times,* January 17, 2002.

2. See the detailed summaries of civilian casualties from U.S. bombing in Marc C. Herod, www.cursor.org/stories/civilian_deaths.htm; Marc C. Herod, update, pubpages. unh.edu/~mwherold/AfghanDailyCount.pdf; Marc C. Herod, "Counting the Dead," *Guardian,* August 8, 2002; Carl Conetta, "Operation Enduring Freedom: Why a Higher Rate of Civilian Bombing Casualties," Project on Defense Alternatives *Briefing Report,* no. 11, www.comw.org/pda/0201oef.html; David Zucchino, "'The Americans. . . . They Just Drop Their Bombs and Leave,'" *Los Angeles Times,* June 2, 2002; and Jonathan Steele, "Forgotten Victims," *Guardian,* May 20, 2002.

Although the Pentagon initially claimed that the Hazar Qadam raid was a successful strike on an Al Qaeda compound and later said that the men captured there were Taliban fighters, eventually they released the prisoners and admitted that they were local men who had fought against the regime. As British reporters describe it, "The freed men said they had been punched, kicked and clubbed by U.S. special forces while in detention. Two of the dead men were found with their hands bound behind their backs, fuelling suspicions that they were executed. One man told the *Los Angeles Times* he had seen his cousin being bound with white plastic handcuffs by American soldiers. He later found his cousin dead, still handcuffed, with bullet holes in the neck, chest and stomach. Relatives of the dead said they had been handed up to $2000 per family, which some called 'hush money.' American officials conceded that CIA officers distributed money, but said it was compensation," The *Independent,* March 31, 2002.

3. Throughout 2002, there were agonizing reports of continued deaths by cluster bombs in Afghanistan and it is a crime that these vicious antipersonnel munitions are not banned; see David Edwards and David Cromwell, "Cluster Bombs and 'Calamity Conditions' in Afghanistan," *ZNet,* January 24, 2002; and Robert Fisk, "Return to Afghanistan: Explosives that the US knew would kill innocents continue to take their toll," *Independent,* August 10, 2002.

4. Rumsfeld's quote is available in an October 31 press release available at www. usa.or.th/news/press/2001/nrot113.htm. Discussions throughout this book demonstrate the falsity of this claim.

5. Although British and other foreign media had published articles clarifying the "legali-

ties" of POW detention and the Geneva Convention for weeks, with many experts criticizing U.S. policy, it wasn't until January 29 that the *New York Times* published articles quoting the precise Geneva Convention definitions of prisoners of war in question and offered an op-ed piece criticizing Bush administration policy. See Nicolas Kristof, "Let Them Be P.O.W.s." Kristof argued that it was in U.S. interests to defend international law and the Geneva Convention, and to treat the prisoners according to those norms to help assure protection of U.S. troops or citizens under similar conditions. For a probing analysis of both the Geneva Convention and the Bush administration's handling of "detainees," see Judith Butler, "Guantanamo Limbo," *The Nation*, April 1, 2002.

6. The laughable Hughes embarrassed the Bush administration when she gushed ignorance of Taliban mistreatment of women and banning of motion pictures. This provincial Texan spindoctor had been involved in the failed attempts at "public diplomacy" during the Afghanistan intervention in a botched effort to try to spin the Terror War for an Arab audience. Hughes shocked the world when she announced that she was returning to Texas in May 2002, but in fact her expertise was in crafting daily sound bites for right-wing audiences and no doubt she could continue this craft in her home state. Obviously, she had been way over her head in Washington, but this will probably not prevent corporations from putting her on corporate boards and receiving lucrative lecture contracts.

7. Budget analysts noted that although it was claimed on page 396 of Bush's budget that the 2002 deficit would be $106 billion, on page 417 it is admitted that "the amount of government debt outstanding at the end of this year will rise by fully $367 billion to a new world record of $6.1 trillion." Thomas Oliphant, "Bush Budget's Fuzzy Math," *Boston Globe*, February 12, 2002. When Senator Ernest "Fritz" Hollings confronted Bush administration budget director Mitch Daniels with this discrepancy, Daniels admitted that "we hid it but you found it." According to Oliphant, the Bush administration plans to help cover the gargantuan deficit by raiding Social Security and Medicare. For an earlier critique of Bushian "fuzzy math," see Krugman 2001.

8. See note 6.

9. See Seamus Milne, "Can the U.S. be defeated?" *Guardian*, February 14, 2002.

10. I return to criticism of Bush administration policy and these themes in chapter 11.

11. In addition to daily newspaper and television reports, I have relied on several in-depth retrospective studies on Operation Anaconda, including "Fierce Fight in Afghan Valley Tests U.S. Soldiers and Strategy," *Los Angeles Times*, March 24, 2002; the two-part series by Bradley Graham in the *Washington Post*, May 24–25, 2002; and the critical analysis by Brenden O'Neil, *Spiked*, March 22, 2002, who dissects contradictory reports on the episode and claims as to what actually happened.

12. Alissa J. Rubin, "U.S. Bombers Pound Al Qaeda Mountain Lair," *Los Angeles Times*, March 4, 2002, A1 and A7.

13. Kandea Mosley, "Fresh Memories of War," *The Ithaca Journal*, May 25, 2002.

14. On environmental destruction in the Gulf War, see Douglas Kellner, *The Persian Gulf TV War* (Boulder, Colo.: Westview Press, 1992); on Kosovo, see Ruth Yarrow, "The Continuing War in Yugoslavia: Environmental Effects," www.afsc.org/pwork/0999/0912.htm.

15. Vernon Loeb, "Report Defends U.S. on Afghan Airstrike: Deaths Blamed on Antiaircraft Fire," *Washington Post*, September 7, 2002, A12.

16. The Canadian press claimed that the American pilot who dropped a 500-pound bomb on Canadian troops had been told twice not to deliver his ordnance, but had done so anyway;

see "Pilot Ignored Orders," *National Post,* April 19, 2002. A later story by Glen McGregor, "Fatigue Dogged U.S. Pilots: Crews Urged to Use Amphetamines Days before Canadian Troops Killed," *Vancouver Sun,* June 3, 2002, alleged that the American pilots involved had been exhausted from heavy flight missions, including flying regularly over Iraq, and that pilots claimed they had been "advised to speak to a flight surgeon about so-called 'go/no pills'— amphetamines used to help stay awake on long missions, and sedatives to help sleep." Later, the U.S. troops who bombed the Canadians were charged with contravening orders and faced a trial, although CNN reported on June 28 that there were attempts to develop support groups to pressure the military to drop the charges. On December 20, ABC News and its magazine 20/20 featured reports that indicated that the U.S. military had warned the pilots that they could be found unfit to fly if they did not take amphetamines—drugs that had been found dangerous and addictive and that had been banned by the military after the Gulf War. Moreover, the two U.S. pilots were using the policy of forced speed pills to provide an explanation for their role in the friendly fire incident involving the deaths of the Canadians. See "Need for Speed" at abcnews.go.com (December 20, 2002).

17. See David Talbot, "Axis of Stupidity," *Salon,* February 14, 2002.

18. See "Rumsfeld Backs Plan to Hold Captives Even if Acquitted," *New York Times,* March 29, 2002; "Royal Marines to Treat Afghan War Captives As PoWs," *The Independent,* April 30, 2002; and "Lawyers Take U.S. to Court for Breach of Camp X-Ray Detainees' Rights," *The Guardian,* June 1, 2002.

19. See the interview with Ahmed Rashid—whose book *Taliban* I referred to in earlier chapters—in "Betraying Afghanistan, Again," *Salon,* April 1, 2002. Rashid argues that the major U.S. mistake was failure to work with other countries and groups in reconstruction efforts, that would build up Afghanistan's agriculture and industry, give young people incentive to put down arms and demilitarize, and generally build up the country. Rashid ends his interview with a warning that a U.S. attack on Iraq in the context of highly volatile Mideast conditions would be potentially catastrophic.

20. See Michael Gordon, "U.S. Backs Increase in Peacekeepers for Afghanistan," *Los Angeles Times,* August 30, 2002.

11   THE NEW MILITARISM, LIES AND PROPAGANDA, AND THE HIGH COSTS OF THE BUSH PRESIDENCY

1. Cartoonists, naturally, had fun drawing "axis of evil" images with George W. Bush, Dick Cheney, and Donald Rumsfeld; see also Edward Herman, "Axis of Evil—Washington D.C.," *Znet,* March 16, 2002.

2. See Pratap Chatterjee, "Cheney's Former Company Wins Afghanistan War Contracts," *CorpWatch,* May 2, 2002; and Mac MacArthur, "It Is Time for Dick to Go," *American Politics Journal,* May 29, 2002, www.americanpolitics.com/20020529Cheney.html.

3. See the *Guardian* commentary, "Unmade in China: Bush's Asian Ramblings Fail to Impress," February 22, 2002; Ron Furnier, "Bush Empty-Handed after Jiang Talks," Associated Press, February 21, 2002; and ex-President Jimmy Carter, Associated Press, February 21, 2002, who said that Bush's statements seriously jeopardized progress made with North Korea,

Iran, and Iraq in recent times: "I think it will take years before we can repair the damage done," Carter concluded.

4. See "Beers Asks Congress For Nearly $600M Propaganda Budget," *Washington Post*, May 1, 2002.

5. On the OSI, see James Dao and Eric Schmitt, "Pentagon Readies Efforts to Sway Sentiment Abroad," *New York Times*, February 19, 2002. On the IAO and Poindexter, see John Sutherland, "No More Mr Scrupulous Guy: How One of the Two Brains behind the Iran-Contra Scandal This Week Became One of America's Most Powerful Men," *The Guardian*, February 18, 2002; and John Markoff, "Pentagon Plans a Computer System That Would Peek at Personal Data of Americans," *New York Times*, November 9, 2002.

6. Douglas Kellner, *Grand Theft 2000* (Lanham, Md.: Rowman & Littlefield, 2001).

7. For a typical ripe right-wing account of these stories, see Deroy Murdock, "Scamalot: Waiting in Vain for the Clintons' Final Insult," *National Review Online*, January 31, 2002; www.nationalreview.com/murdock/murdock013101.shtml. Within days, these rumors of the Clinton team trashing of the White House and stealing from Air Force One, presented by the right as news, were deflated as mere disinformation by the Bush propaganda ministry.

8. For a revealing overview of Rove, see Louis Dubose, "Bush's Hit Man," *The Nation*, March 5, 2001, which describes Rove's history of dirty tricks and smear campaigns in Texas politics, his whispering campaign against John McCain in the Republican primaries, his deep-seated conservative beliefs, his key role in the Bush administration, and propensities to spin and lie as techniques of public policy and governance.

9. A report released in June 2002 by the General Accounting Office (GAO) acknowledged that there was White House vandalism, most prominently breaking W's off of a number of computers, but denied the most serious allegations of vandalism by Bush administration officials, whose often petty and ludicrous complaints were appended in a 75-page report that complained about graffiti that proclaimed, "Jail to the Thief" and "See you in four, Al Gore." On the whole, the report was most interesting for depicting "the lengths to which the Bush administration went to try to make the scandal charges stick," and how it was willing to use hundreds of thousands of dollars of taxpayers' money to promote its own ideological agendas. See Kerry Lauerman, "The Real White House Vandal Scandal," *Salon*, June 13, 2002.

10. Interestingly, Bill Gates Senior and a group of 120 mostly Republican and conservative billionaires signed a petition opposing the excesses of Bush's tax cut program. See Joan Walsh, "Plutocrats to the Rescue!" *Salon*, February 15, 2001. Joshua Micah Marshall suggested in an *American Prospect* note, February 12, 2001, titled "Shameless, Brazen and Disgusting" that words applied to Clinton's behavior during his last days in the White House could usefully be applied to Bush's tax cut proposals.

11. The Stockman quote was in a much-discussed interview with William Greider, "The Education of David Stockman" (*The Atlantic*, December 1981), which recorded Reagan's Budget Director's disillusionment with "supply-side economics" and the Reagan administration's compromises with corporate forces. See the discussion in the Walsh article cited in note 10. In an article on Bush's tax "plan," Bob Herbert, "Voodoo Redux," *New York Times*, March 1, 2001, recalls that in Lou Cannon's biography of Reagan, Reagan's Secretary of Treasury James Baker regretted that budget deficits had "gotten away" from the Reagan administration and that he wished that "he had paid more attention to the consequences of the tax cuts." In fact, the Reagan administration doubled the previous national debt, while

Bush senior in his four disgraceful years doubled Reagan's doubling. As Yogi Berra would say, it's déjà-vu all over again.

12. White House press release, February 27, 2002.

13. See Brendan Nyhan, "Losing the 'Trifecta'," *Salon*, June 18, 2002, who documents Bush's use of the "trifecta" example in his recent speeches and claims the story that Bush had previously specified three conditions for deficit spending and raiding Social Security "is blatantly false. No one has found any evidence that Bush made such a statement, and the White House has pointedly failed to provide any."

14. See the systematic expose of Ari Fleischer and "Bush Lies" at www.bushwatch.net/bushlies.htm. As the Bush administration and Bush himself multiplied their daily lies about the economy, the Iraq–Al Qaeda connection, and whatever served their purposes of the moment, a series of articles appeared dissecting the Bush instrumental relation to truth. See Dana Milbank, "For Bush, Facts Are Malleable," *Washington Post*, October 22, 2002; Paul Krugman, "Dead Parrot Society," *New York Times*, October 25, 2002; and Eric Alterman, "Bush Lies, Media Swallows," *The Nation*, November 25, 2002.

15. In terms of Hughes's power, a July *Esquire* story referenced in the next note quoted Bush media advisor Mark McKinnon as stating: "There are a hundred decisions he has to make every day, big decisions, with a lot riding on each one. So he'll give 20 of them to Karen to make. He trusts her completely. He trusts her like he trusts no one." It is frightening to think that the provincial advisor and Bushspeak spinner Hughes would amass so much power. See Ron Suskind, "Mrs. Hughes Takes Her Leave," *Esquire* 138, no. 1 (July 2002). On Hughes's intellectual and political limitations, see James Rideway, "Karen Hughes Finds Her Ruby Slippers," *Village Voice*, April 23, 2002; for a very long list of "Bush Jr.'s Skeleton Closet," see www.realchange.org/bushjr.htm#insider.

16. Christopher Marquis, "Bush Aide Reveals Worry Over Loss of Advisor," *New York Times*, June 6, 2002. According to a July *Esquire* story, White House Chief of Staff Andrew Card was in despair over the more pragmatic conservative Hughes leaving, afraid that the right-wing barbarians would reign unopposed. See Suskind, "Mrs. Hughes Takes Her Leave."

17. See Juliet Eilperin, "On Capital Hill, Enron's Fall Was Felt at the Personal Level," *Washington Post*, June 15, 2002, A5.

18. On the Bush-Rove-Nixonian connection, see also Miller 2001, 43ff. Miller follows Hatfield 2000 in stressing the centrality of George W. Bush in the dirty tricks against Dukakis in the 1988 election, pointing to a mean and vicious streak beneath W's smiling exterior. On the connection between Nixon and the Bush family, see Kellner 2001, especially 136–137.

19. Rove told the American Enterprise Institute in a December 2001 talk that Bush was "never a unilateralist." I have documented in *Grand Theft 2000* Bush's succession of unilateralist policies during his first months in office, ranging from rejection of the Kyoto environmental treaty to renunciation of several major weapons treaties. The Bush administration leaked to the press before the U.S. bombing of Afghanistan why they did not want coalition partners to restrain their military activity, and they seemed determined to go it alone in a continuing war on terror against a large list of designated targets, including Iraq. As I document in this study, Bush has continued an aggressively unilateralist foreign policy that had been increasingly criticized by European and other U.S. allies.

20. Howard Wolfson, "Populist Pitch—Without the Punch. Both Parties Claim Title, but Neither Makes Full-Scale Attack on Moneyed Interests," *Washington Post*, February 6, 2002. Ron Suskind's article "Why Are These Men Laughing" published in the January 2003

Esquire and the John DiIulio letter published on the magazine's website (www.esquire.com) make clear that the Bush administration is bereft of public policy ideas and is merely driven by politics and right-wing ideology, thus making clear the mendacity of Karl Rove's claim that "policy drives politics" in the administration.

21. See David Corn, "What Would Bobby Say? Karl Rove spins RFK to the Right," www .thenation.com, June 6, 2002. Corn presents quotes from Bobby Kennedy, who of course is antithetical politically and personally to the fraudulent George W. Bush. To Rove, we might retort: "Karl, we know all about Bobby Kennedy, and George W. Bush is no Bobby Kennedy." He's not much of anything, in fact. All hat and no cattle.

22. See "Attack on Iraq Is Unavoidable: US Official's Warning," *Dawn,* February 5, 2002. For a telling portrait of Perle, known as the "Prince of Darkness," see Chris Suellentrop, "Richard Perle—Washington's faceful bureaucrat" in www.slate.com, August 23, 2002. Jude Wanniski once described Perle as "the world's No. 1 hawk . . . who has been the chief architect of our policy toward the Arab/Islamic world. There is no single American more responsible for inciting outrage among Muslims globally than Richard, whose maniacal prescriptions led inexorably to last week's cataclysm." See "The Prince of Darkness" at polyconomics.com/ showarticle.asp?articleid = 1634. And Eric Boehlert provides a useful overview that documents how many times Perle has been dead wrong on Iraq and other Middle East issues that he presents himself as an expert on. For Boehlert, Perle can consistently be seen as one of "Israel's strongest, most ardent right-wing allies in Washington," who always pushes Israeli interests.

23. See Jim Lobe, "Bush quickly losing ground with allies," *Albion Monitor,* April 2, 2002; and Bill Kristol and Robert Kagan, "Cheney Trips Up. The vice president's Middle East expedition didn't help the war on terror," *Weekly Standard,* April 1, 2002.

24. Julian Borger, "US paves way for war on Iraq," *The Guardian,* March 27, 2002.

25. See John Donnelly, "Pentagon Finalizing Iraq Plans," *Boston Globe,* April 28, 2002; Thomas E. Ricks, "Military Sees Iraq Invasion Put on Hold. Joint Chiefs Sought Delay, Citing Manpower Needs," *Washington Post,* May 24, 2002, A1; and Robin Wright, "U.S. Finds Concern Over 'Iraq, the Sequel.' Allies' fears about a post-Hussein regime are blocking Bush's campaign," *Los Angeles Times,* June 4, 2002, A5.

26. In a May 19 interview on *Meet the Press,* the mendacious Cheney denied that he had warned Daschle not to investigate the September 11 terror attacks, but the following week on the same show Daschle repeatedly asserted that Cheney had made the demand.

27. Joseph Curl, "Alerts Tied to Memo Flap," *Washington Times,* May 22, 2002; and Geoffrey Gray, "Ari's Faux Pas? White House Flack Pins Official Warnings on 9–11 Memogate," *Village Voice,* May 23, 2002.

28. "Bush Goes Nuclear," *The Nation,* April 1, 2002, 3. *The Nation* editors also note that the report "envisions nuclear weapons not as unthinkable engines of holocaust—their very use a crime against humanity—but as the next logical battlefield step from bunker-busters and daisy-cutters."

29. Gerard Baker, "A Callow Cowbody Stumbles," *Financial Times,* May 31, 2002; and John Lichfield, " 'Friends' act by Bush and Chirac fails to heal rift," *The Independent,* May 27, 2002. Commenting on Bush's continual equation of bin Laden and Hitler and claim in the German Bundestag that the West's enemies hated "justice and democracy," Robert Fiske in *The Independent,* May 27, 2002, commented in "The Coming Firestorm" that "Bush's rhetoric sounds like the crazed videotapes of bin Laden." There continued to be silence, how-

ever, concerning the Bush family's connections to fascism. See Loftus and Aarons (1994) who document how Prescott Bush and Herbert Walker managed the major bank and businesses that supported Hitler's fascism. George Herbert Walker Bush and George Walker Bush are thus part of an infamous family whose scandalous history may yet be their undoing.

30. Bill Sammon, "Weary, Bush Mocks Reporter," *Washington Times,* May 27, 2002; and Dana Milbank, "The Adventures of 'Intercontinental' Man," *Washington Post,* May 28, 2002, A15. See also Mike Allen and Dana Milbank, "On Bush's Trip, Some Discordant Messages. President Draws Mixed Reviews," *Washington Post,* May 30, 2002, A20. The latter story noted that at "the same time Bush's longtime critics back home are beginning to find their voices, world leaders were less deferential of him during his week abroad than they had been as he assembled his antiterror coalition after Sept. 11. The stereotypes of Bush as a bumbler were revived by European opinion makers, an impression Bush fueled by his uneven performance during the trip, which ended Tuesday night. Even as Bush assuaged some European concerns about his policies, analysts said, he aggravated doubts about himself. Bush, who at one point volunteered that he was feeling the effects of jet lag, had a heavy schedule, with events sometimes lasting until midnight. The result reinforced what Philip H. Gordon, director of the Brookings Institution's Center on the United States and France, called 'the perception in Europe that he is unsophisticated.' . . . London's *Independent* said from Rome that Bush 'sometimes seems unsure which European country he is visiting.' An article in London's *Daily Mirror* began by saying, 'Bumbling George Bush Was Lost for Words Last Night.' *The Times* of London carried a preview headlined, 'How the Atlantic Widened under George W. Bush,' then followed up with a dispatch beginning, 'Like certain distinctive wines, President George W. Bush does not travel well.' "

31. Mike Allen, "Bush Stays Quiet amid Mideast Turmoil," *Washington Post,* March 30, 2002, A4.

32. See also Thomas E. Ricks and Vernon Loeb, "Bush Developing Military Policy of Striking First," *Washington Post,* June 10, 2002, A1. For a sharp critique of Bush's new preemptive strike policy, see "Werther Report: Is Preemption a Nuclear Schlieffen Plan?" www.d-n-i.net/fcs/comments/c453.htm.

33. On Michael Powell's disastrous record as FCC chairman, see John B. Judis, "Cable Access. Michael Powell v. The Economy," *The New Republic,* September 2, 2002.

34. In December 2002, New York attorney general Eliot Spitzer, working with the SEC, cut a deal with five of Wall Street's most powerful securities who agreed to pay a $1.4 billion settlement, acknowledging conflicts of interest and wrong-doing in its interactions with the big corporations under fire for corruption and fraud. See Walter Hamilton, "Strategy Shift Kept Deal From Dissolving," *Los Angeles Times* (December 23, 2002).

35. See "Twice as bad as Hoover," July 23, 2002, www.consortiumnews.com.

36. See John Vidal, "EU caves in to U.S. over green pact," *The Guardian,* September 3, 2002; Geoffrey Lean, "Summit agreement is struck, but U.S. blocks deal on clean energy," *The Independent,* September 3, 2002; and "Powell Booed and Jeered at Global environment Meeting," *New York Times,* September 4, 2002.

37. See Jonathan Weisman, "Forecast: Deficits to Last into '05. Tax Receipts Hit a 56-Year Low," *Washington Post,* August 28, 2002; and Paul Krugman's commentary, "Just Trust Us," *New York Times,* August 30, 2002.

38. See Economic Policy Institute, "The State of Working America 2002–2003," www.epinet.org.

39. See Mike Salinero, "Gen. Zinni Says War With Iraq Is Unwise," *Tampa Tribune*, August 24, 2002.

40. Julian Borger, "White House in Disarray over Cheney Speech," *The Guardian*, September 2, 2002; Andrew Gumbel and Marie Woolf, "U.S. in Disarray over Iraq As Powell Backs Call for Weapons Inspectors," *The Independent*, September 2, 2002; and Howard Fineman and Tamara Lipper, "Same as He Ever Was," *Newsweek*, September 9, 2002. The latter contains the claim that Cheney had not cleared all the details of his speech with the Bush administration. There were also rumors floating about Washington that Colin Powell was going to resign before the 2004 election and maybe sooner. Woodward (2002, 346) notes how "Cheney was beyond hell-bent for action against Saddam. It was as if nothing else existed." And despite constant references to Al Qaeda and Iraq connections by Bush, Cheney, and others, there was widespread skepticism concerning their allegations; see Sebastian Totella, "Allies Find No Links between Iraq, al Qaeda," *Los Angeles Times,* November 4, 2002, which states, "Evidence isn't there, officials in Europe say, adding that an attack on Hussein would worsen the threat of terrorism by Islamic radicals."

41. Colum Lynch, "Firm's Iraq Deals Greater than Cheney Has Said; Affiliates Had $73 Million in Contracts," *Washington Post,* June 23, 2001.

42. See Karen DeYoung, "Bush, Blair Decry Hussein," *Washington Post*, September 8, 2002.

43. Thomas E. Ricks and Vernon Loeb, "Afghan War Faltering Military Leader Says Myers Cites Al Qaeda's Ability to Adapt," *Washington Post,* November 8, 2002. The story notes that "Ivo H. Daalder, a senior fellow at the Brookings Institution . . . said he doubted whether Myers or Defense Secretary Donald H. Rumsfeld would commit U.S. forces to 'tackling the fundamental security problem in Afghanistan, which is not al Qaeda, but a byproduct of the way we fought—arming the warlords. What needs to be done is to take away the power of the warlords and give it to the central government, and that requires real military force,' Daalder said. 'Are we prepared to take on the very guys we empowered? I don't see any evidence that is the case.'" Some December 2002 articles note the resurgence of Al Qaeda forces in Afghanistan and elsewhere in the world, suggesting limitations of U.S. Terror War policy; see Robert Fisk, "With runners and whispers, al Qaeda outfoxes U.S. forces," *The Independent* (December 6, 2002); Zahid Hussain, "Al Qaeda arms build-up on Afghan border," *The (London)Times* (December 6, 2002); and Colum Lynch, "Al Qaeda is Reviving, U.N. Report Says. Wave of Volunteers Said to Inflate Terrorist Group's Membership, Capabilities," (*Washington Post*, December 18, 2002).

44. See Charles Lane, "Debate Crystallizes on War, Rights. Courts Struggle over Fighting Terror vs. Defending Liberties," *Washington Post,* September 2, 2002; "For Whom the Liberty Bell Tolls," *The Economist*, August 29, 2002; and Nat Hentoff, "General Ashcroft's Detention Camp. Time to Call for His Resignation," *Village Voice*, September 4, 2002.

References

Ali, Tariq. 2002. *The Clash of Fundamentalisms: Crusades, Jihads and Modernity.* London and New York: Verso.

Barber, Benjamin R. 1996. *Jihad vs. McWorld.* New York: Ballantine Books.

Begala, Paul. 2000. *Is Our Children Learning? The Case against George W. Bush.* New York: Simon and Schuster.

Best, Steven, and Douglas Kellner. 2001. *The Postmodern Adventure: Science Technology, and Cultural Studies at the Third Millennium.* New York and London: Guilford and Routledge, 2001.

———. Forthcoming. "Biotechnology, Democracy, and the Politics of Cloning." In *Democracy and Nature.*

Brewton, Pete. 1992. *The Mafia, CIA, and George Bush.* New York: SPI Books.

Brisard, Jean-Charles, and Guillaume Dasquie. 2002. *Forbidden Truth.* New York: Thunder's Mouth Press/Nation Books.

Chomsky, Noam. 2001. *9–11.* New York: Seven Seals Press.

Cockburn, Leslie. 1987. *Out of Control.* New York: Atlantic Monthly Press.

Cooley, John. 2000. *Unholy Wars: Afghanistan, America and International Terrorism.* London: Pluto Press.

Feenberg, Andrew. 1999. *Questioning Technology.* New York and London: Routledge.

———. 2001. *Critical Theory of Technology.* New York: Oxford University Press.

Fitzgerald, Francis. 2001. *Way Out There in the Blue: Reagan, Star Wars, and the End of the Cold War.* New York: Touchstone Books.

Friedman, Thomas. 1999. *The Lexus and the Olive Tree.* New York: Farrar, Straus, Giroux.

Fukuyama, Francis. 1992. *The End of History.* New York: Free Press.

Greider, William. 1981, December. "The Education of David Stockman." *The Atlantic.*

———. 1998. *Fortress America: The American Military and the Consequences of Peace.* New York: Public Affairs.

Hatfield, J. H. 2000. *Fortunate Son: George W. Bush and the Making of an American President.* New York: Soft Skull Press.

Hersh, Seymour. 1998. *Against All Enemies. Gulf War Syndrome: The War between America's Ailing Veterans and Their Government.* New York: Simon and Schuster.

Horkheimer, Max, and T. W. Adorno. 1972. *Dialectic of Enlightenment.* Boston: Continuum Books.

Huntington, Samuel. 1996. *The Clash of Civilizations and the Remaking of World Order.* New York: Touchstone Books.

Ivins, Molly, and Lou Dubose. 2000. *Shrub: The Short but Happy Political Life of George W. Bush.* New York: Random House.

Johnson, Chalmers. 2000. *Blowback: The Costs and Consequences of American Empire.* New York: Henry Holt.

Kellner, Douglas. 1990a. "From *1984* to *One-Dimensional Man:* Reflections on Orwell and Marcuse." *Current Perspectives in Social Theory:* 223–252.

———. 1990b. *Television and the Crisis of Democracy.* Boulder, Colo.: Westview Press.

———. 1992. *The Persian Gulf TV War.* Boulder, Colo.: Westview Press.

———. 1995. *Media Culture.* London and New York: Routledge.

———. 1999. "Virilio, War, and Technology: Some Critical Reflections." *Theory, Culture, and Society* 16, nos. 5–6: 103–125.

———. 2001. *Grand Theft 2000.* Lanham, Md.: Rowman and Littlefield.

———. 2003. *Media Spectacle.* London and New York: Routledge.

Kepel, Gilles. 2002. *Jihad: The Trail of Political Islam.* Cambridge, Mass.: Harvard University Press.

Klare, Michael. 2001. *Resource Wars: The New Landscape of Global Conflict.* New York: Metropolitan Books.

Kovel, Joel. 2002. *The Enemy of Nature: The End of Capitalism or the End of the World.* London: Zed Books.

Krugman, Paul R. 2001. *Fuzzy Math: The Essential Guide to the Bush Tax Plan.* New York: Norton.

Langewiesche, William. 2002. *American Ground: Unbuilding the World Trade Center.* New York: North Point Press.

Loftus, John, and Mark Aarons. 1994. *The Secret War against the Jews.* New York: Saint Martin's Griffin.

Mann, Michael. 2001. "Globalization and September 11th." *New Left Review* 12: 51–72.

McLuhan, Marshall. 1964. *Understanding Media.* Cambridge, Mass.: MIT Press.

Meyssan, Thierry. 2002. *9/11: The Big Lie.* New York: USA Books.

Miller, Mark Crispin. 2001. *The Bush Dyslexicon.* New York: Norton.

Mitchell, Elizabeth. 2000. *Revenge of the Bush Dynasty.* New York: Hyperion.

Orwell, George. 1961 (1948). *1984.* New York: Signet.

Palast, Greg. 2002. *The Best Money Democracy Can Buy.* London: Pluto Press.

Pizzo, Stephen. 1989. *Inside Job: The Looting of America's Savings and Loans.* New York: McGraw Hill.

Rashid, Ahmed. 2001. *Taliban: Militant Islam, Oil and Fundamentalism in Central Asia.* New Haven, Conn.: Yale University Press.

———. 2002. *Jihad: The Rise of Militant Islam in Central Asia.* New Haven, Conn.: Yale University Press.

Sick, Gary. 1991. *October Surprise: America's Hostages in Iran and the Election of Ronald Reagan.* Collingdale, Pa.: DIANE Publishing Company.

Tarpley, Webster Griffin, and Anton Chaitkin. 1992. *George Bush: The Unauthorized Biography.* Washington, D.C.: Executive Intelligence Review.

Urry, John. 2002. "The Global Complexities of September 11th." *Theory, Culture, and Society* 19, no. 4: 57–70.

Weinberg, Steven. 2002. "Can Missile Defense Work?" *The New York Review of Books,* February 14, 2002.

Woodward, Bob. 2002. *Bush at War.* New York: Simon and Schuster.

Index

ABC, 104, 113, 253; and Afghanistan war, 76; and September 11, 55
Abdullah, Abdullah, 142
Abu Sayyaf, 293n9
Adelphia, 248
Afghanistan: and blowback, 31–33; Bonn negotiations on, 144–45; Bush (I) administration and, 5; chaos in, 121–26, 203–23, 254–55; Cold War and, 119; earthquakes in, 219; rebuilding, 203–4; terrorists in, Bush administration on, 208; warlords in, 122–24, 142, 175–76
Afghanistan war, 91–107; beginning of, 71–90; collapse of Taliban, 127–46; costs of, 77, 118; course of, 109–26; enthusiasm for, 49–70; failure in, 3–4, 222–23, 255; goals of, 58–59; guerilla phase of, 221; lack of end strategy for, 5, 97, 140; oil industry and, 5, 170–71, 272n10, 274n18; skirmishes in, 216–23. *See also* Terror War
Agre, Phil, 25
Ailes, Roger, 60, 66
airplane attacks, intelligence on, 7–8, 11, 238, 268n11
airport security, 99–100, 157–58, 167
al-Assad, Bashar, 98
Albright, Madeleine, 240, 272n9
Albrow, Joe, 82
Aldrich, Gary, 64
al-Haq, Zia, 32
Ali, Tariq, 28–29, 270n33, 271n2
Al Jazeera network, 72, 79–80, 113, 128, 151, 255, 285n8
Allen, Joe B., 187

allies of U.S., 239–40, 302n30; on arms control, 173–74; criticism of U.S. policies, 135, 227, 240, 266n3; on State of the Union address, 211; on treatment of prisoners, 178–79, 181–82; and U.S. unilateralism, 2–3, 20
Al Qaeda, 2; blowback and, 32; Clinton administration and, 10; criminalization of, recommendations for, 140–41; globalization and, 41; and Internet, 43; name, 34, 272n8; at Tora Bora, 153–55; weapons of, 121–22; Zhawar training camp, 160–61, 203
Altman, Robert, 53
Al Wafa, 141
al-Zawahri, Ayman, 72, 160
American Airlines flight 587, crash. *See* jet crash
Amnesty International, 131, 175
Anaconda, battle of, 216–23
Annan, Kofi, 103
anthrax attacks, 14, 42–43, 75, 80–90, 138, 269n17, 281n22
Arab/Muslim world, 79, 293n18; assault on civil liberties and, 101; and axis of evil speech, 214; on bin Laden, 116, 125; and bin Laden video, 151; Bush administration and, 3–4, 63; and civilian casualties, 165–66; FBI and, 87; on U.S., 93–95, 266n3
Arafat, Yasser, 163
Arbusto Energy, 35, 62
Argenbright Security, 100
Argentina, 168

307

About the Author

Douglas Kellner is the George F. Kneller Philosophy of Education Chair at UCLA and author of numerous books including *Television and the Crisis of Democracy*, *The Persian Gulf TV War*, *Grand Theft 2000*, and *Media Spectacle*.